THE
WELSH QUESTION

Nationalism in Welsh Politics

1945–1970

THE
WELSH QUESTION

Nationalism in Welsh Politics

1945—1970

ALAN BUTT PHILIP

CARDIFF
UNIVERSITY OF WALES PRESS
1975

© University of Wales Press, 1975

ISBN 0 7083 0537 7

Printed in Great Britain
at the University Press, Oxford
by Vivian Ridler
Printer to the University

TO
MY MOTHER

'Wales's greatest tragedy is that she is so far from God and so near England.'

Extract from a motion on broadcasting carried unanimously by the annual conference of the North Wales Free Church Council, 22 April 1970

PREFACE

NATIONALISM has been a recurring theme in the history of Wales. For more than a thousand years the Welsh have sought to preserve and defend their land and language, their culture and their religion. Defensive attitudes have contributed materially to the Welsh sense of identity, and to the development and expression of Welsh nationalism. In the past, nationalism has been a transient phenomenon in the Welsh political context. In the 1960s Welsh nationalism was championed by a separate political party, *Plaid Cymru*, without roots in the system of government based in London. In contrast, Lloyd George's nationalist revolt in the 1890s occurred within the ranks of the Liberal Party. Nationalism has thrived in both Scotland and Wales in recent years, but the two movements, though supported by similar short-term grievances, manifested some very different characteristics and operated within different political and cultural frameworks. The growth of the Scottish National Party and of *Plaid Cymru* from 1966 was remarkable more for its dissimilarities than for its similarities.

This research into the political and sociological significance of Welsh Nationalism since 1945 is intended to set the development of *Plaid Cymru* in this period in a wide Welsh political and social background, to analyse the composition of the party, to show the sections and groups which provide the *Blaid* with its base, and to trace the impact of Welsh Nationalism on the general political life of Wales. For this purpose nationalism is defined as the active solidarity of a human collectivity which shares a common culture (or a common fund of significant experiences and interests), which conceives of itself as a nation, and which strives for political unity and self-government.

No discussion of the significance of Welsh nationalism in connection with Welsh literature has been included in this volume. This would be too large a subject to include in a full discussion of the political and sociological aspects of Welsh nationalism. Any student of political science would also have difficulty in doing justice to the strong encouragement Welsh writers have given to the modern nationalist movement in Wales, although the prominent role played in *Plaid Cymru* by certain writers has not been overlooked.

Since this research is concerned with contemporary history, it has been inevitably limited by the absence of access to government or private political records of the period. In compensation, a large number of the principals involved in Welsh politics are still surviving and could be approached in connection with this research. Much information contained in this book was given from personal recollection and interpretation in the course of over 150 private interviews. Where possible, such information has been checked against other sources, particularly newspapers, whose reliability is sometimes open to question, and the printed records and files of various Welsh organizations. In the course of the research, officials and members of Welsh political and cultural bodies made available confidential material, and such information has been used freely.

The extent to which relevant research material was available radically affected the methods of the writer. When the research was originally conceived it was hoped that two approaches could be adopted towards the recent development of *Plaid Cymru* in Wales. One was to trace and evaluate the nature of the expansion of party membership and activity at all levels, and its consequences for the internal organization of the *Blaid*. The other approach was to trace the political effects of the party's expanded support on the *Blaid*'s electoral platform. Attempts have been made, especially in Chapters 7 and 8, to develop these approaches but they are based on incomplete material. The writer was fortunate in being able to consult confidentially a number of papers and records concerned with the development of *Plaid Cymru* since 1925, and he is particularly grateful to those who allowed him access to their private collections of documents.

The writer owes many Welsh people a long apology for the time taken in interview and discussion, and an irredeemable debt to them for their contributions to the research and to his understanding of Wales. Hundreds of individuals—civil servants, politicians, academics, trade unionists, and others—generously gave their time and attention in this way. The Social Science Research Council underwrote almost the whole cost of the research, which involved *inter alia* travel to every county of Wales and subscription to a course in the Welsh language at the University College of Wales, Aberystwyth. The liberal use of the Council's funds contributed materially to the comprehensive approach of the research. The Fellows of St. John's College and of Nuffield College at Oxford kindly afforded the writer every facility and support as an advanced student. Invaluable help was given by the staff of the Bodleian Library, the British Museum, the Gladstone Library in the National Liberal Club, the Bibliothèque Albertine in Brussels, the libraries of all the University Colleges in the University of Wales and, in particular, the National Library of Wales, especially its Keeper of Manuscripts, B. G. Owens. The continuous help and advice over three years of Geraint Thomas and Richard Hughes, both of the Plaid Youth branch in Carmarthen were of great value to the writer. The co-operation and patience and goodwill in the face of insatiable questioning of Elwyn Roberts, Dafydd Williams, and, particularly, Dr. Gareth Morgan Jones were essential to the preparation of the book. The guidance and interest of Maurice Shock and Dr. David Butler were a major source of encouragement, and the constant support and detailed, liberal, and instructive supervision of Dr. Kenneth O. Morgan were of priceless benefit to the conduct and development of the research. However, it must be emphasized that all the opinions expressed in these pages together with any omissions or errors of fact are entirely the responsibility of the writer.

ALAN BUTT PHILIP

Oxford 1973

POSTSCRIPT: 1970–1974

SINCE this book was written, two further general elections have taken place and events in Wales have moved swiftly in furthering political nationalism. The Nationalists' disappointment with the result of the 1970 election masked the solid gain in support they had achieved to poll 175,000 votes in an election fought on 'British' issues. *Plaid Cymru* was a much better organized political movement and its base had been considerably broadened, in South Wales especially. Perhaps as a reflection of this, the party's conferences of 1970 and 1971 showed a new concern with urban and industrial problems, and a leftward switch against the EEC and in favour of industrial democracy. But though the *Blaid* was in good shape at grass-roots level it was unable to sustain the challenge and momentum that had been founded on the run of sensational by-elections in Wales and Scotland between 1966 and 1968. In local government elections the *Blaid*'s performance continued to be patchy, if not poor, although substantial progress was made in the Aberdare, Merthyr, and Caerphilly districts. Between 1970 and 1974 there proved to be only one by-election in a Welsh seat. This was held in April 1972 in the Merthyr Tydfil constituency as a result of the death of S. O. Davies, who had so sensationally captured the seat as an Independent in 1970. The nominations for both Labour and the *Blaid* produced surprises with the former Cardiff M.P., Ted Rowlands, displacing leading local politician Tal Lloyd as Labour's choice, and Emrys Roberts making a sudden reappearance to carry the torch for the *Blaid*. The result was another dramatic fourfold increase in the Nationalist vote, even though Labour was no longer saddled with the unpopularity of being in government as in the late sixties. The figures were a mirror image of the Caerphilly by-election result in 1968 with Tory and Liberal opponents crushed at the foot of the poll. What Merthyr showed in 1972 was that Welsh Nationalism was not just the creature of socialist disillusion with Labour but a permanent feature of the political landscape; this view was confirmed by the strong showing of Nationalists in Scotland in by-elections held during the life of the Heath government. But without this by-election in Merthyr the *Blaid* would have made almost no impact at all during the period of the Heath administration; as it was, the massive Liberal revival starting in the autumn of 1972 began soon afterwards to eat away at the *Blaid*'s chances in most of Wales. The initiative in matters of Welsh concern was largely ceded either to the Welsh Language Society or to other political parties.

In view of the absence of a parliamentary dimension to the *Blaid*'s campaigns the need for a party chairman as well as a president was probably less after the 1970 election than for some years. Dr. Phil Williams was elected to this post by the party conference in 1970 and retained it at subsequent elections. Meanwhile, the face of the party organization was changing elsewhere. Elwyn Roberts retired from the general secretaryship in 1971 and was succeeded by Dafydd Williams, who had been assisting Dr. Gareth Morgan Jones in the Cardiff office. Dr. Morgan Jones left the service of the *Blaid* late in 1970 and took no further part in its leadership. The only new personality to emerge in the Nationalist ranks between 1970 and 1974 was that of Glyn Owen, an energetic Aberdare councillor and the *Blaid*'s organizer in Glamorgan. At *Plaid*'s annual conference in 1973, however, Gwynfor Evans announced after his re-election as president that he proposed not to stand for the post in 1975 when the presidency again came up for election. On completing thirty years as the *Blaid*'s president and leader he said he would consider it time to make way for another person. But it was by no means obvious upon whom that mantle would fall, and events in 1974 threw the *Blaid*'s leadership question wide open.

Meanwhile, the cause of nationalism in Wales was proceeding in other directions than the strictly political. The Welsh Language Society began casting its net wider than road signs and paid increasing attention to the issue of broadcasting. A wave of militancy flowed through the movement and hundreds of prosecutions were brought against its members arising out of sit-ins, demonstrations, and acts against public property. Dafydd Iwan relinquished his hold on the Society and even stood as a *Plaid Cymru* candidate in Anglesey in the two general elections in 1974; his place was taken by a more collective and less charismatic leadership among whom Fred Ffransis and his wife-to-be Meinir Evans, Gwynfor's daughter, were prominent. A campaign against second-home ownership in Wales was launched by the Society and met with great sympathy in political circles. Welsh-only housing associations such as *Adfer* thrived, albeit in a small way, and there was a move in many nationalists' thinking towards concentrating on the need to protect the social and cultural integrity of the traditional Welsh-speaking areas of Wales. The issue of the Welsh language remained central to Welsh life and the 1971 Census results published in 1973 showed that Welsh was only spoken by just under 21 per cent of the population aged three and over. Although the most Welsh areas showed some of the biggest declines in Welsh-speaking there were signs in the Census results to show that the expansion of Welsh teaching in schools was beginning to have a lasting effect. The *Urdd* decided to initiate a conference in 1973 to discuss the official institutions needed to protect the Welsh tongue but found it was pre-empted by the decision of Peter Thomas, the Secretary of State for Wales, to set up a permanent Welsh Language Council to advise the Welsh Office on linguistic problems. While most observers considered this a move in the right direction there were few who could see any real benefit deriving from one more non-elected, non-executive Welsh committee. The National Eisteddfod nevertheless continued to enjoy a sizeable following and success although it began to run into serious financial problems.

The period of Conservative government between 1970 and 1974 did not help the Conservatives to improve their standing in Welsh eyes. Peter Thomas remained Secretary of State for Wales throughout this period while representing the London suburban seat of Hendon South in the House of Commons. There were no dramatic initiatives from the Welsh Office during this time but equally there were no embarrassing outbursts either. The Conservative M.P.s for Welsh constituencies entrenched their local standing and everyone survived the two general elections of 1974. Indeed their numbers increased to eight as a result of a redistribution of seats in the Cardiff area and the striking success of Sir Raymond Gower in holding on to his truncated seat at Barry. At the same time Tory support in Wales over all fell below a quarter of the total votes cast.

The Labour Party in Wales continued to be led by George Thomas but its M.P.s became more sympathetic to devolution. Younger spirits sprang to prominence such as Ted Rowlands, Elystan Morgan, and the new M.P. for Wrexham, Tom Ellis, who took a very sympathetic interest in language issues. The Labour reaction to the Kilbrandon Report was to insist that it would implement its main recommendation for an elected Welsh assembly. As the signatories of the Report were divided as to the extent that devolution should be pursued there remained plenty of political leeway. The Welsh Labour M.P.s caused occasional upsets to the Conservatives by using their majority in the Welsh Grand Committee against the government. Labour's opposition to the proposals of the British Steel Corporation to close down the East Moors and half of the Shotton works together with its espousal of the miners' cause during the industrial troubles of 1973 and early 1974 helped to reassert its leadership of the working class. Even so at both the 1974 elections Labour failed to gain half the votes cast in Wales, for the first time in forty years. With the new Wilson government there were many important developments affecting Welsh Labour circles. George Thomas was elected Deputy Speaker of the Commons and so made way for John Morris as Secretary of State for Wales. Michael Foot became Secretary of State for Employment and James Callaghan Secretary of State for Foreign Affairs, both of them South Wales M.P.s. Ted Rowlands became Morris's deputy at the Welsh Office, but Elystan Morgan was not re-elected and Cledwyn Hughes was excluded from the Cabinet. Hughes was, however, elected Chairman of the Parliamentary Labour Party in November 1974, ousting the Left-wing incumbent, Ian Mikardo.

The Liberal Party started the 1970s with the shock of its defeat in the 1970 election although in organizational terms it was stronger in Wales than it had been for twenty years. Local elections provided little comfort for the Liberals until 1973 when the party in Wales benefited almost everywhere from the Liberal revival, particularly in Cardiganshire and in anglicized parts of Wales. Morale was much revived in February 1974 when Liberal candidates fought 31 out of the 36 Welsh seats and a second Liberal M.P. from Wales, Geraint Howells from Cardigan, was elected to sit with Emlyn Hooson. In the October 1974 election, the Liberals fought every Welsh seat and captured about 16 per cent of the total vote, well ahead of *Plaid Cymru*'s static 10·8 per cent share of the poll.

The 1974 elections also showed that *Plaid Cymru* was maintaining its hold over parts of Welsh-speaking rural Wales while generally losing ground in the industrial south of the country. In both elections, as in 1970, twenty-six out of thirty-six *Plaid* candidates lost their deposits. Real progress was made only in five seats and three of these were won by the *Blaid* in October 1974. Dafydd Wigley won Caernarfon and Dafydd Elis Thomas won Merioneth in February 1974, both being victories over sitting but vulnerable Labour M.P.s. Gwynfor Evans failed by a mere three votes to retake Carmarthen in the February election, but was elected comfortably the following

October as were *Plaid*'s two other M.P.s. Thus *Plaid Cymru* established a small group in the House of Commons to press the case for Welsh self-government and the leadership of the party passed into the hands of the parliamentarians. *Plaid*'s role was made all the more significant by the election in October of eleven Nationalist M.P.s from Scotland, where the S.N.P. vote rose to over 30 per cent of those cast and the Conservatives were relegated to third position. The new parliament met amid the general belief that a measure of devolution to Scotland and Wales would be enacted during its life. The official Labour proposals for devolution were more far-reaching for Scotland than for Wales although they envisaged the creation of a directly elected Welsh assembly without real legislative powers.

A. B. P.

December 1974

CONTENTS

1

THE NATIONALIST LEGACY

SOME people today look back to the Wales of the two Llewelyns in the thirteenth century as the golden age when Wales was last independent. When Edward I defeated the forces of Llewelyn ap Gruffydd in 1282, the concepts of 'nation' and 'nationality' were scarcely precise or commonly understood. Nevertheless the Welsh felt themselves to be distinct from the English. The revolt of Owain Glyn Dŵr in 1400 revived Welshmen's memories of past greatness and pointed to the failure of the Edwardian settlement to pacify Wales, let alone to integrate it into a united kingdom. But it was the Tudors who first seriously attempted to bring the Welsh into the English ambit by devising a political framework which would make the Reformation in Wales succeed.[1] This was the main reason for the Acts of Union of 1536 and 1542, which gave the Welsh representation in the English Parliament and some autonomy but which, in extending English administration and law to Wales, prohibited the use of the Welsh language in official and legal business.

The Reformation in Wales was in fact imposed from above without active support or opposition from within Wales. There was little in Tudor Wales to suggest that puritanism and nonconformity might one day dominate its worship. The Tudors did, however, help to ensure the survival of the Welsh language by ordering the translation of the Bible and the Prayer Book into Welsh and their use in Welsh parish churches.[2] This translation of the Bible also ensured the continuance of uncorrupted Welsh and maintained the living proof of separate Welsh identity, the Welsh language.[3]

In the seventeenth century Wales was a Royalist stronghold during the civil war, and Dissent was so weak that Cromwell was forced to put through special legislation to strengthen its position.[4] It was only

[1] David Williams, *Modern Wales* (London, 1950), pp. 34 and 46, and Ch. 3 *passim*.
[2] An Act of Parliament was passed accordingly in 1563, but it was not until 1588 that Bishop Morgan's translation was approved by the Privy Council. See David Williams, op. cit., pp. 62–78. [3] Ibid., p. 78.
[4] Especially the 1650 Act for the Propagation of the Gospel in Wales. See David Williams, op. cit., p. 115.

in the eighteenth century that religious and educational movements began to have a real and simultaneous impact. The famous Griffith Jones circulating schools, staffed by itinerant teachers, taught 158,000 pupils in their Welsh bible-reading classes between 1737 and 1761.[1] Methodism was also beginning to gain ground under the leadership of Howell Harris, Daniel Rowland, and, later, Thomas Charles. In the cultural sphere, the Morris brothers founded the Cymmrodorion Society in London; branches were set up in Wales, and local *eisteddfodau* were revived.

The nineteenth century produced a massive industrial exploitation of Wales, considerable political changes, and the ascendancy of nonconformity. For Wales it was an age of industry, of oratory, and of emotional religion. The Methodists broke with the established Church in 1811 and developed specifically Welsh forms of nonconformity. Methodism thus counteracted anglicization, and changed the national, social, and moral consciousness of the people. Two notable religious revivals swept through Wales in 1859 and 1904, by which time nonconformists outnumbered Anglicans by five to two.[2] Religion and education in Wales were both attacked in the Report of the Commissioners inquiring into Welsh education, published in 1847. This report exposed the inadequacy of the schools system as it existed; it also deplored the survival of the Welsh language and even questioned the chastity of Welsh women, especially during nonconformist services.[3] These comments provoked furious controversy and played a great part in stimulating national consciousness in Wales. The report has been described ever since as the treachery of the Blue Books.

By the middle of the nineteenth century Wales was already well marked by the pattern of industrial development which was to be the mainspring of her prosperity until the 1920s. The iron industry had recovered by the 1850s. Railways rapidly unfolded across Wales. Coal was increasingly mined for sale, and especially for export. The manufacture of tinplate had become virtually a Welsh monopoly. Simultaneously there were great shifts of population. Rural depopula-

[1] See W. Rees, *Historical Atlas of Wales* (London, 1959) and David Williams, op. cit., pp. 145 et seq.

[2] See Report of the Royal Commission on the Church and other religious bodies in Wales, vol. V, quoted in Kenneth O. Morgan, *Wales in British Politics 1868–1922* (Cardiff, 1963), Appendix B.

[3] David Williams points out that the three commissioners were all very junior barristers and had no prior knowledge of Wales, education, or the working class (op. cit., pp. 255–6).

tion was first noticed in the Census of 1851. At least the drift to the valleys of Glamorgan and Monmouthshire from rural Wales prevented an exodus of Irish proportions, although it was English people as much as Welsh people who were attracted to South Wales.[1] Between 1815 and 1914 the population of Wales rose fourfold, more so in Glamorgan and Monmouthshire which together contained by 1914 over 60 per cent of the entire population of Wales.

Nineteenth-century Nationalism in Wales 1868–1914

The Victorian era was, therefore, one of industrialization in Wales, and one which saw the emergence of Welsh radicalism, increasingly nationalist in outlook.[2] The year 1868 was a watershed in Welsh politics; from then onwards Tory interests have always been on the defensive and radicalism has dominated the thinking of Welsh leaders and voters.

The change to radicalism and to the Liberal Party from 1868 is understandable. The extension of the franchise in 1867, and again in 1884, brought into the polling booths radical voters who had previously been excluded. These political radicals comprised nonconformists seeking to be freed from legal disabilities, small tenants of large Tory or Whig landowners, and workers in the mines and foundries protesting against poor social and working conditions.[3] In rural areas, the evictions that followed the 1868 election confirmed the small tenant farmers in their support for the Liberals.[4] The economic uncertainty that periodically cloaked the farming, metal, and coal industries until the First World War and thereafter strengthened this radicalism, as did the continuing process of industrialization, which involved large movements of population and the growth of monopoly capitalism. For the most part, the social cleavages of land, religion, and class matched and reinforced one another throughout Wales.

It is not enough, however, to assume that the natural radicalism of late nineteenth-century Wales would inevitably be nationalist in character simply because the newly enfranchised Welsh workers and farmers had inherited a different cultural tradition. In an obvious

---

[1] Brinley Thomas (ed.), *The Welsh Economy* (Cardiff, 1962).
[2] Much of this section is based on Kenneth O. Morgan, *Wales in British Politics* (Cardiff, 1963).
[3] S. M. Lipset, in *Political Man* (London, 1960), suggests that left-wing voting behaviour is to be explained in terms of insecurity of income, the lack of satisfying work, and the need for status. All these were acutely felt in late nineteenth-century Wales and in early twentieth-century Wales.
[4] Kenneth O. Morgan, op. cit., pp. 25–7.

sense the British pattern of politics did impose itself on Wales in that the Liberal Party and later the Labour Party were the chosen instruments of Welsh radical demands. Yet often the terms of political debate in Wales differed from England—the battles for separate legislative treatment and for national institutions, the temperance issue, the payment of tithes to the Church, the early demands for secondary education and for a University of Wales, the self-government movement known as *Cymru Fydd*[1] and, most important, the whole campaign for Welsh disestablishment. Liberal politicians at Westminster increasingly accepted after 1868 that these issues were specifically Welsh issues, or at least should be treated as such. Here lies the key to the question. The Welsh demands were demands that were not only heard in Wales. Education, temperance, land reform, and disestablishment were issues debated all over Britain and were essential food for every Liberal's digestion. In many cases the problem in Wales was virtually identical with that in England. But one key difference was the proportion of nonconformists in the population. Whereas only 5 per cent of the population of the United Kingdom as a whole could be claimed as nonconformists at the beginning of this century, the proportion in Wales was 25 per cent; conversely the established Church could claim only 10 per cent of the Welsh as adherents.[2] Furthermore, all the leading issues which were claimed by Welsh nationalists in the 1880s and 1890s as specifically Welsh had a special interest for nonconformists. Denominational religious instruction in schools had long been a bone of contention with them; so had the payment of tithes on land to the Church, licensing, and temperance, and the extent of Church endowments.[3] In each of these fields, Wales would normally have to expect to wait on a change of policy in Anglican Britain. Naturally this was bitterly resented by nonconformists when they outnumbered Anglicans in Wales so heavily.[4] The position was exacerbated by the evident revival of the Anglican Church as the century drew to a close.[5]

---

[1] *Cymru Fydd*, best translated as 'Young Wales', was a movement which flourished within the Liberal Party between 1886 and 1896. Its object was to secure self-government for Wales, and its leaders included, at various times, Tom Ellis, M.P., David Lloyd George, M.P., and D. A. Thomas, M.P.

[2] See the Report of the Royal Commission on the Church and other religious bodies in Wales, vol. V (1910).

[3] See Kenneth O. Morgan, 'Freedom or Sacrilege' (Church in Wales, 1966) for a history of the disestablishment campaign.

[4] Nonconformists totalled 550,280 communicants in 1905, and Anglicans 193,081. (Report of the Royal Commission on the Church and other religious bodies in Wales, 1910.)   [5] Morgan, op. cit., p. 21.

It was therefore convenient for nonconformists in Wales to demand separate Welsh legislation and even self-government. It was a device by which nonconformist demands could be met sooner in one part of the United Kingdom than in the remainder.

However, there were other significant factors in addition to nonconformity working for greater Welsh consciousness at the time. The Welsh language, for example, was strong throughout Wales. In 1891 there were still over half a million people in Wales who spoke no English, a quarter of the population.[1] When so much politics and business was needed to be conducted in so different a language from English, it is difficult not to conclude that, as the franchise was extended, the difference in language made for more nationalist political attitudes among Welsh-speakers, particularly as the language barrier supplemented other lines of social cleavage. The Welsh-speaking community was also beginning to realize the threat posed to the Welsh language by the process of industrialization, the huge English immigration that accompanied it, the improvement in communications, and, above all, the 1870 Education Act. This Act, passed by a Liberal government, completely overlooked the teaching of Welsh in schools. The language of all the elementary schools it set up was English, and English only.[2] In many such schools in Wales teachers would punish children who used the Welsh language in or out of class.[3] The Welsh language had gained a considerable boost from the Welsh press. Five years after the abolition of paper duties in 1861, it was estimated that there were five quarterlies, twenty-five monthlies, and eight weeklies in the Welsh language with a combined circulation of 120,000; 70,000 Welsh Bibles alone were sold in 1867.[4] One authority has concluded that 'the growth of the Welsh press and its early association with the outlook of nonconformists was a fundamental factor in shaping the outlook and sensibilities of people throughout Wales. . . . The press became a vehicle for every effective popular leader from Gwilym Hiraethog to David Lloyd George, and a powerful medium for invigorating and extending the Welsh language.'[5]

[1] Census of England, Wales, 1891.
[2] This was a continuance of the policy formalized by Robert Lowe's Revised Code of 1861, which is discussed in *Welsh in Education and Life* (H.M.S.O., 1927), the report of the Departmental Committee on Welsh in the educational system of Wales.
[3] This situation led to the founding of the Society for Utilizing the Welsh Language in 1885, which had the ear of Henry Richard, the celebrated M.P. for Merthyr, and which began to achieve results with the passage of the 1889 Intermediate Education Act (Wales).
[4] Henry Richard, *Letters on the Social and Political Condition of Wales* (London, 1867), pp. 36 and 37.   [5] Kenneth O. Morgan, *Wales in British Politics*, p. 9.

The attitudes of the intellectuals and leaders of Wales were under-going major changes in the mid nineteenth century, the product partly of the spread of European nationalist ideology. Mazzini, Kossuth, and Garibaldi were much admired, as to a lesser extent were Irishmen such as Thomas Davis. In Wales there were nationalist thinkers too. 'Emrys ap Iwan' (Robert Ambrose Jones) was the first Welsh political nationalist who was not concerned with noncon-formist issues; most important was Michael D. Jones, the founder of the Welsh colony in Patagonia. The views and theories of such thinkers were widely diffused and discussed by intellectuals and publicists such as Thomas Gee, 'S. R.' and Gwilym Hiraethog.[1] But the rise of political nationalism among the leaders of Wales must be seen in the context of a more gradual but more secure change of attitudes towards the Welsh cultural and literary tradition. The origins of this change lie in the eighteenth century and in the romantic revival throughout Europe. The growth of interest was cumulative. It was helped by the isolation and dispersal of most Welsh townships and communities, and by the religious revival of 1859. The Blue Books controversy stimulated interest in education and led to the successful campaigns for improved secondary education and a University of Wales. Romanticism, literary research, and patriotism gave birth to a remarkable literary renaissance at the end of the century.

The distinctive social structure of Wales and its relevance to the land question was another significant factor in stimulating Welsh national consciousness in the late nineteenth century. Tom Ellis in his election campaign of 1886 synthesized the two when he fought for both Welsh land law reform and disestablishment. He sought a 'Jacob's ladder' which would allow 'equality of opportunity for every boy and girl in Wales'.[2] The division in Welsh agrarian communities between landlord and tenants-at-will (i.e. tenants without security of tenure) was virtually the same as that between Anglican and non-conformist, and was aggravated by the evictions of the 1850s and

---

[1] The influence of Michael Daniel Jones appears to have been considerable in the case of David Lloyd George, M.P. for Caernarfon Boroughs from 1890. Tom Ellis, M.P. for Merioneth, chose Mazzini as his mentor.

[2] Tom Ellis was born in 1859 the son of a Llandderfel, Merioneth, tenant farmer and Methodist deacon. Educated at Bala grammar school, University College, Aberyst-wyth, and Jesus College, Oxford; M.P. for Merioneth from 1886 until his death in 1899; was Junior Whip in Gladstone's last government, and Chief Whip in Lord Rosebery's administration. He was one of the early leaders of the *Cymru Fydd* move-ment, and a leader of the Welsh nationalists in the House of Commons until 1893. See N. Masterman, *The Forerunner* (Cardiff, 1972).

1860s and by the economic depressions of the period; 'from this clash of two societies, modern Wales was to be forged'.[1] Ellis's concern with the improvement in social status of individuals paralleled demands for status and recognition for Wales on a national level. The issue focused on the nonconformists because the rights of nonconformists in particular were curtailed in education, in the payment of tithes, and in licensing. In many ways, the Welsh national movement was a bid for equality for Wales and for national recognition rather than the work of separatist forces. If the intention and the effect of the Welsh national movement was to achieve essentially nonconformist ends, however limited relative to the declared objectives of the movement, then it is possible to explain the fading of the movement in terms of its own success. The movement succeeded in persuading the political leaders at Westminster that Wales had the right to be legislated for separately from England. Gladstone was won over to the principle between 1870 and 1881;[2] Lord Salisbury agreed it in 1889. Thus came about a Welsh Sunday Closing Act in 1881, a Welsh Intermediate Education Act in 1889, and the granting of a charter to the federal University of Wales in 1893. A number of reports were commissioned; one on education in 1880, one on land in 1893, and one on the Welsh Church in 1906.[3] During the Liberal government of 1905–15, with Lloyd George in the Cabinet, a Welsh Department of the Board of Education was set up (1907), as was the National Library of Wales, the National Museum of Wales, a Welsh Insurance Commission, a National Council of Wales for agriculture, and two Welsh commissioners, for smallholdings and development respectively.[4] The greatest achievement of the national movement was undoubtedly the secure position it gained for Welsh disestablishment in the Liberal platform, second on the list of the Newcastle programme of 1891.[5] However, it was not until 1920 that

[1] Morgan, op. cit., p. 10.
[2] In 1870 Gladstone rejected the demands of a Commons motion for Welsh disestablishment on the grounds that the issue was really that of English disestablishment. In a speech to the National *Eisteddfod* at Mold in 1873 he uttered a paean of praise for Welsh nationalism.
[3] The Departmental Committee under Lord Aberdare was set up by Gladstone to report on Welsh education and it paved the way for action on higher education in Wales in 1889 and 1893. The commissions on land and the Welsh Churches were both Royal Commissions.
[4] List given to E. T. John introducing his Government of Wales Bill to the House of Commons in March 1914.
[5] A taste of the Liberal commitment is given in the report to the annual assembly of the National Liberal Federation in January 1893. Commenting on the recent general election results of 1892 it says: 'It is pleasing to turn to the spectacle of the results

the consequent Welsh Church Act—postponed by the First World War—finally became law.

In terms of individual needs for status many new avenues for social advancement, especially for nonconformists, had been opened up. Upward social mobility through the educational system was encouraged by the Acts of 1870, 1889, and 1902, while, most significantly, the leadership of the Welsh counties and the new local government powers under the Local Government Act of 1888, which set up elected county councils, and the Parish Councils Act of 1894 added new career opportunities for nonconformists. Overnight a massive blow was struck at the local ascendancy of the Welsh gentry as local magistrates and leaders. In the first county council elections in Wales held in January 1889, the Liberals took control of every county in Wales except Breconshire. 'The very effectiveness of this transfer of power on a local basis eventually blunted the appeal of the wider objective of Welsh Home Rule.'[1] Home Rule had more meaning for the Welsh at a county than at a national level, county administration absorbing the energies of active local Liberals. In the 1890s Ellis and Lloyd George were to find it hard to get the county councils to act in common through a national joint (advisory) council. The *Cymru Fydd* movement for self-government, founded in 1886, showed signs of disintegration from 1891 and was finally impaled in 1896 on the rivalries between North and South Wales, between Lloyd George and D. A. Thomas.[2]

The demise of *Cymru Fydd* is indicative of the other main cause of the vanishing interest in the national movement in Wales. Not only did it die out because it was too successful, but also because the interest of the Welsh in their nationality and the national community was overtaken by a concern for economic problems and by the steady evolution of a class structure in the economic relationships between employers and workers, principally in populous South Wales. The figures for representation in the House of Commons tell their own tale (see Table 1.1). The decline of the Liberals and the rise

achieved by Wales. . . . This overwhelming majority has clearly justified the action of the Federation in putting Disestablishment for Wales to the forefront of the Liberal programme and constitutes an unanswerable argument in favour of attention to the question at the earliest possible moment.' Asquith in a speech to the assembly similarly said: 'Wales . . . has claims which it would be both disloyal and ungrateful on our part to postpone or to refuse to satisfy.' (National Liberal Federation, *Annual Report*, 1893.)

[1] Morgan, op. cit., p. 107.
[2] Morgan, op. cit., especially pp. 160–5 and William George, *Cymru Fydd: Hanes y Mudiad Genedlaethol Gyntaf* (Liverpool, 1945).

TABLE 1.1

Representation in the House of Commons 1885–1970

General Election	North and West Wales*				Glamorgan and Monmouthshire			
Years	Lib.†	Lab.	Con.‡	Plaid	Lib.	Lab.	Con.	Ind.
1885	17	..	3	..	13	..	1	..
1900	17	..	3	..	10	1	3	..
1910								
Jan.	18	..	2	..	9	5	..	..
1924	9	1	3	..	1	15	6	..
1929	9	4	..	..	..	21	1	..
1935	6	3	4	..	..	15	7	..
1945	6	4	3	..	..	21	1	..
1955	3	8	3	..	..	19	3	..
1968	1	10	2	1	..	21	1	..
1970	1	9	4	..	..	18	3	1

In 1868 Wales returned 23 Liberals and 10 Conservatives to Parliament.

  * Excludes the University of Wales seat which existed between 1918 and 1950 and which was won by the Liberals at every election except that of 1923.

  † The Liberal total includes Independent Liberals (Lloyd George family) who sat in the Commons between 1931 and 1945.

  ‡ The Conservative total includes M.P.s describing themselves as Liberal National after 1931.

of Labour in South Wales was rapid and complete; in North and West Wales it was very gradual and far from total. In South Wales the electors were not satisfied with limited equality of opportunity provided by an improved educational system and a system of government that was in the hands of the nonconformist middle classes at county level and the property-owning classes in London. The nonconformists, who were almost synonymous with the Liberals because of the disestablishment issue, brought disaster upon the Liberal Party by refusing to cater for the claims of an increasingly articulate and organized working class. Although about half the population of Wales in this period was not affiliated to any religious organization, nonconformity was in fact dominant in Welsh society at the turn of the century. Its tradition had a far greater acceptance than figures for chapel attendance would suggest. The nonconformist leaders, with four exceptions, refused to take up social issues in the depressed coal and tinplate industries. Obsessed by the issue of disestablishment and stressing the homogeneity of interests between man and man in any community, they could not recognize or support the claims of organized labour against its employers. Nonconformity was generally hostile to trade unionism, and to socialism and its principal agent in South Wales, the Independent Labour Party. It associated them with atheism and often responded to demands to fight against social injustice by expelling from the chapels those that uttered them. Similarly when rugby, soccer, and the music hall began to attract large numbers of followers the nonconformists reacted to the threat these entertainments posed to their leadership in the community by declaring them sinful.[1] The nonconformists therefore proved incapable of adjusting to the changes and the new demands of urban Wales. When the issue of disestablishment was settled in 1920, most Welsh people had long since past caring about the outcome of the dispute. As the hegemony of the nonconformists declined and as organized labour began to take over their role in society, so attention for the 'national' question diminished. As 1914 approached, the discussion of Welsh Nationalism was increasingly tinged with racialism, and mainly exercised intellectuals and nonconformists. The prose of their arguments was still biblical in allusion and stamped with chapel oratory. There was little interest, for example, in E.T. John's Government of Wales Bill presented to the House of Commons in 1914. The prophesy of Beriah Gwynfe Evans that 'a measure of autonomy for Wales . . . will be introduced before Mr. Asquith again appeals to the country' was forlorn.[2] The onset of the First World War dealt a crushing blow to the last lingering hopes of the nineteenth-century Welsh nationalists.

Nationalism in Eclipse: 1914–1945

The period in which Lloyd George dominated British politics was also a period in which Welsh Nationalist claims were increasingly less canvassed. The Welsh over-identified themselves with their leader and treated the fact that Lloyd George was Prime Minister for six years (1916–22) as sufficient evidence that Wales was getting maximum benefit from British government. During the First World War Lloyd George used his Welsh connections to the full, and recruitment to the forces in Wales and Welsh casualties in the war were noticeably above the British average.[3] The experience of the

---

[1] For a full discussion of these points see C. R. Williams, 'The Welsh Religious Revival', *British Journal of Sociology*, 1952.

[2] Beriah Gwynfe Evans, 'Cymru Fydd: II', *Wales*, Oct. 1913.

[3] Morgan in *Wales in British Politics*, p. 274, cites figures to the effect that 13·82 per cent of the Welsh population were in the forces, compared with 13·3 per cent for

war probably changed the attitudes of Welsh people generally more than it changed those of Lloyd George. Thousands set foot outside Wales for the first time in their lives, and lost their parochial outlook in the trenches of Flanders and France. Lloyd George was portrayed as the new St. David, and many intellectuals and nonconformist leaders, succumbing to a wave of patriotism, became able recruiting sergeants for the armed forces.[1]

The First World War delayed the implementation of disestablishment and obscured the issue of Welsh home rule. The interwar years were dominated by massive unemployment (rarely lower than 20 per cent of the workforce and reaching a peak of 38 per cent in 1932) and by the world economic crisis. The labour force in the mines in 1939 was only half what it had been in 1920.[2] Inevitably there was industrial unrest, especially in the mines. The list of mining strikes in Wales speaks for itself; major strikes occurred in 1915, 1918, 1919, 1920, 1921, 1926 (the year of the General Strike), 1931, and 1944. The 1926 mining strike involved the loss of 145 million working days. Emigration from Wales was for many the only alternative to unemployment. Net migration from Wales between 1921 and 1939 amounted to a staggering 450,000 persons.[3] Interest in nationalism evaporated during the crisis and confirmed the South Walians in their belief in a socialist solution. Syndicalism took root for a while in parts of the coalfield, in the tradition of Noah Ablett and the famous *Miners' Next Step* published in 1912. Meanwhile the young Aneurin Bevan, M.P. for Ebbw Vale from 1929, was rising to challenge Lloyd George and to speak for the conscience of Wales. Lloyd George himself was much discredited by his handling of the coal industry's problems while in office, and in particular for refusing to nationalize the mines or the mineowners' royalties following the Sankey Commission of 1919. Not a single Liberal M.P. sat for a Glamorgan or Monmouthshire seat after the 1924–9 Parliament, despite Lloyd George's plans to conquer unemployment announced before the famous 1929 election. In any event, the Liberals in Wales were busy tearing themselves

England and 13·02 per cent for Scotland. Lloyd George began the war effort with his famous 'little nations' speech at the Queen's Hall in London which included the remark that 'God has chosen little nations as the vessels by which he carries the choicest wines to the lips of humanity'.

[1] Cf. *Wales*, 1911–15, *passim*.

[2] See W. E. Minchinton in G. Manners (ed.), *South Wales in the Sixties* (London, 1964). In 1920 there were 272,000 workers in the coal industry; in 1939 there were only 136,000. Production of coal in 1913 had been 56·8 million tons. In 1939 it was down to 35·3 million tons.

[3] Brinley Thomas (ed.), *The Welsh Economy* (Cardiff, 1962).

apart, as in the rest of Britain, though Lloyd George had retained the loyalty throughout of nearly every Liberal Association in Wales.[1] The Liberals had neither the inclination nor the opportunity to do much about home rule. Many of Lloyd George's followers in the early twenties were proud to call themselves Welsh Nationalists, but in the political arena they did not attempt any sustained campaigns.[2]

At parliamentary level, the Speaker's conference which was set up in 1919 to 'consider and report upon a scheme of Legislative and Administrative Devolution within the United Kingdom' could not agree on the composition or the method of election of the local legislatures it wished to set up. Nothing came of the conference and it had never raised many hopes. As Labour came to dominate South Wales and Liberalism remained entrenched in the rest of Wales, the desire of Welsh M.P.s to act in common diminished and their interests diverged. Questions were asked in 1928 and 1930 by individual M.P.s about the possibility of a Secretary of State for Wales and they aroused no enthusiasm.[3] There was some discussion about Nationalist demands in 1936 and two Liberal M.P.s, Clement Davies and Ernest Evans, sponsored a Secretary of State for Wales Bill in 1937 which achieved little. Some concessions to devolutionary feeling were made during the war. A Welsh Reconstruction Advisory Council was established to help plan the post-war reconstruction programme in 1942. Legislation was passed in the same year to allow greater use of Welsh in the courts, and in 1944 (October) the first ever Commons debate exclusively concerned with Welsh affairs took place.

The fortunes of Welsh political nationalism were at a low ebb between 1914 and 1945, its only significant manifestation being the foundation of the Welsh National(-ist) Party, *Plaid Genedlaethol Cymru*, in 1925. However, important developments did occur in the cultural sphere in Wales. The founding of *Urdd Gobaith Cymru* and of *Undeb Cymru Fydd* and the development of Welsh broadcasting against considerable odds began to show results after 1945.

---

[1] The Merioneth and Montgomery Liberal Associations were the two exceptions. Cardiganshire Liberal Association was also hostile for a time. See M. Kinnear, *The British Voter* (London, 1968) and Kenneth O. Morgan, 'Cardiganshire Politics: The Liberal Ascendancy, 1885–1923', *Ceredigion V*, No. 4 (1967), pp. 331–7.

[2] Lloyd George himself was described in *Dod's Parliamentary Companion* as a Radical and a Welsh Nationalist from 1890 to 1922. In 1923 that description was replaced by the term Liberal, the first time that description was used in Dod for Lloyd George.

[3] Sir Reginald Coupland, *Welsh and Scottish Nationalism: A Study* (London, 1954), p. 368.

The early Welsh Nationalist Party 1925–1945

The formation of the Welsh Nationalist Party in 1925 occurred with the merger of three different nationalist groups, based mainly in the University of Wales, and it was the product of many factors.[1] There was the disillusion with the performance of the Liberal Party and the promises of the Labour Party. The Liberal Party in the twenties was certainly losing interest in the home rule issue, as was Wales generally. The Labour Party had been committed since 1918 to Federal Home Rule, but by 1929 this had been modified in tone.[2] The growth of a separate party pledged to a Wales with independent political institutions was the logical development from the failure of the *Cymru Fydd* movement, in the Nationalist view. The battle for parliamentary devolution had been waged within the Liberal Party in the 1880s and 1890s; now it had to be taken outside the traditional party structure. The lesson for Welsh Nationalists of the abortive attempts to achieve Home Rule all round was that they should cut off their links with the all-embracing British parties and try again. They did not believe that there had been too little support for home rule from within Wales for it to be achieved. In founding a separate party the Nationalists were undoubtedly spurred on by the post-war developments in Ireland.[3] Not only was the creation of the Irish Free State in 1922 an example for every Welsh Nationalist to admire: the removal of the Irish Nationalists from the Westminster Parliament also ended the previous home rule deadlock which had allowed talk of Scottish and Welsh home rule to flourish, and removed the need for the main parties either to dress up their concessions or to meet Scottish and Welsh devolutionary pressures under the banner of home rule all round.

It is not easy to assess the personal motives of those who gathered to found the Welsh Nationalist Party in 1925—in a Temperance hotel during the National *Eisteddfod* in Pwllheli. In their desire to set up a separate party to win self-government for Wales they seem to have been most influenced by two considerations. Gwynfor Evans, the President of *Plaid Cymru* since 1945, wrote: 'the present

[1] See Gwynfor Evans, 'The Twentieth Century and *Plaid Cymru*', in A. W. Wade-Evans, *et al.*, *The Historical Basis of Welsh Nationalism* (Cardiff, 1950) and J. E. Jones, *Cychwyn Plaid Cymru 1925–1955* (Cardiff, 1955).
[2] The Labour manifesto for 1929 said that Labour 'would support the creation of separate assemblies in Scotland, Wales and England, with autonomous powers in matters of local concern'.
[3] See J. E. Jones, *Tros Gymru* (Swansea, 1970), p. 30.

national movement is largely the creation of ex-servicemen who saw, during the last war, the incongruity of fighting for the freedom of nations abroad while their own was still in bondage.'[1] The Nationalist survivors of the First World War found that it was Lloyd George who signed the Treaty of Versailles for Britain in 1919, a treaty whose guiding principle in the redistribution of three European empires had been the observance of nationality in the making of new European states.

More significant than the events of the First World War in moving nationalists to found a Welsh Party was their desire to build up defences for the Welsh culture. Welsh self-government would allow Welsh nationalism the fullest form of political expression; self-government was not conceived by them as an end in itself but as a means of strengthening and preserving the Welsh identity. Indeed, it was not until 1932 that self-government became part of the official Welsh Nationalist platform. The three aims of the *Blaid* in 1925 were all connected with the Welsh language.[2] The early Nationalists saw a Welsh government acting as a national focus and as the best means of harnessing the national will, and embodying the Welsh traditions of democracy and co-operation. Material considerations were notably absent from the thinking of the Nationalists. As one Nationalist later described the purpose of the party:

> Our main task is a spiritual one. It is to restore a sense of Welsh nationhood, a feeling of pride in our own people, a pride in the greatness of our heritage, a pride in the qualities and potentialities of our people, and a sorrow for their afflictions that stings as does a hurt to the members of one's own family.[3]

These emotional attitudes towards the life of Wales and the Welsh nation, and also the belief of many Nationalists in co-operative democracy, were outlined in Saunders Lewis's lecture to the first annual *Plaid* summer school held in Machynlleth in 1926.[4] The Welsh Nationalists stood then, as many have done in the post-war period,

[1] *The Welsh Nationalist*, Jan. 1945.
[2] See J. E. Jones, op. cit., pp. 72–4, and Alan Butt Philip, 'Life and Times', in *Planet* 2 (1970). The initial aim of *Plaid Genedlaethol Cymru* was 'to keep Wales Welsh-speaking. That is, to include (*a*) making the Welsh language the only official language of Wales and thus a language required for all local authority transactions and mandatory for every official and servant of every local authority in Wales, (*b*) making the Welsh language a medium of education in Wales from the elementary school through to the university.' (Author's translation from H. R. Jones's manuscript in the possession of *Plaid Cymru*.)
[3] D. Myrddin Lloyd, *Plaid Cymru and its Message* (Cardiff, 1949).
[4] Saunders Lewis, *Egwyddorion Cenedlaetholdeb* (Caernarfon, 1926).

for specific values and a specific way of life, religious, co-operative, highly individualist, and opposed to the consequences of urbanization and industrialization. They stood for the community life of the small towns and villages of Wales where the Welsh language and folk-culture still flourished and where *Cymru Fydd* had once taken hold. Much though the *Blaid* owed to the work of Dr. D. J. Davies for its economic programme—which had no immediate cure for unemployment and whose central point was the setting up of agricultural and industrial co-operatives—the Welsh Nationalists started in politics for cultural reasons. Professor J. E. Daniel, Lewis's successor as President of the *Blaid*, wrote in 1937 that culture and social well-being were two sides of the same coin.

It is in the poetry of Taliesin and Dafydd Nanmor, in the ruling conceptions of the ancient laws of Wales, far more than in the Special Areas Acts or Five Year programmes that the salvation of Wales is to be found.[1]

Another well-known Nationalist writing in the Independents' journal, *Y Tyst*, during the Second World War felt:

Welsh society is fast being shattered, remembering that it is a Christian society. The new order which is being thrust upon us and slavishly accepted by our local authorities, is a Godless civilisation. Do our churches realise that when Welsh civilisation disappears, they too will disappear?[2]

Saunders Lewis himself was willing to admit that

It was the realisation of the fundamental connection between the literature and the traditional social life of Wales which drew me from doing literary work only to take up public activities and to found the Welsh Nationalist Party.[3]

It is clear that the Welsh Nationalist Party was at the outset essentially intellectual and moral in outlook, and socially conservative. Its principal concerns were the Welsh language, the Welsh identity, and Christianity in Wales. Saunders Lewis, the foremost Nationalist thinker in the twentieth century, was much affected by the papal encyclicals on co-operation in society.[4] These strands of thought influenced the *Blaid*'s economic policy as much as any other field:

In industry, no less than in agriculture, the ideal form of ownership and management is no doubt the co-operative one, since this is the form which

---

[1] J. E. Daniel, *Welsh Nationalism—What It Stands For* (London, 1937), p. 40.
[2] Reverend Dyfnallt Owen, *Y Tyst*, 28 Aug. 1941.
[3] Saunders Lewis, *Paham y Llosgasom yr Ysgol Fomio* (Caernarfon, 1937).
[4] Saunders Lewis, *The Party for Wales* (Caernarfon, 1942). The encyclicals he mentions are 'Rerum Novarum' and Quadrigesimo Anno'.

permits of the fullest human development of the worker and encourages individual initiative together with the sense of responsibility and solidarity; and this is the ideal at which a Welsh National Government should aim.[1]

Co-operation is not just a piece of economic machinery which can be imposed from above by the State; it is the product of the voluntary social action of individuals and demands a readiness to sacrifice and a spirit of service to the community. That spirit cannot be engendered merely by the force of economic interests, to which the Labour Party constantly appeals . . .

. . . Co-operation is a system which, without violent revolution and without injuring anybody, can grow within the capitalist system and gradually undermine it and transform it from within, and which experience has shown to be practically immune from capitalist attacks.[2]

The inter-war years were not a period of great activity for the Welsh Nationalists, but they were years in which the ideology of the party was moulded. The peak of activity in the Nationalists' calendar was usually the annual summer school, which included the party conference, the *cynhadledd*, at which many of the leading Welsh-speaking intellectuals were present. Since 1932 all *Plaid* members have had to agree to three objectives; self-government, the preservation of the Welsh language and culture, and Welsh representation at the League of Nations (later the United Nations Organization). The three essential objectives were never extended to cover acceptance of the co-operative principle, though the *cynhadledd* agreed to support it. But it is interesting that the *Plaid* never restricted its sights and official goals solely to the foundation of a Welsh nation-state. The devotion of these early Nationalists was first to the Welsh language although in theory the language is an issue extraneous to nationalism. A Welsh nation-state is conceivable without a Welsh language, but Saunders Lewis and his sympathizers were Nationalists because they believed the survival of the Welsh language was inconceivable without a Welsh nation-state—the only means of securing for the language a continued and worthwhile use.

If they (the Welsh people) decide that the literary revival shall not broaden out into political and economic life and into the whole of Welsh life, then inevitably Welsh literature in our generation will cease to be living and valuable. I do not think that the Welsh language will disappear rapidly even if that should happen. But it will cease to be a language worth

[1] D. J. Davies, *The Economics of Welsh Self-Government* (Caernarfon, 1931).
[2] D. J. Davies, *The Welsh Nationalist*, May 1932.

cultivating. .... Believe me, there is something worse and more tedious than the death of a language, and that is its functionless survival.

You cannot artificially encourage the language and literature and arts of a people and at the same time refuse them any economic and political recognition.[1]

TABLE 1.2

Plaid Genedlaethol Cymru 1925–1945: Membership, Branch Organization, and Finance

Membership

1925	6
1930	500
1939	2,000
1945	2,500

(*Sources*: *The Welsh Nation, The Welsh Nationalist*, and private information.)

Number of branches (as at the annual summer school)

1933	52
1934	64
1935	67
1936	72
1937	94
1938	111
1944	137

(*Sources*: *Plaid Cymru* annual reports and *Ysgol Haf* registers.)

Finance

Subscriptions to the St. David's Day Fund 1934–44.

1934	£250	1938	£770	1942	£1,400
1935	£500	1939	£880	1943	£1,500
1936	£700*	1940	£1,000	1944	£1,750
1937	£700*	1941	£1,200		

* These figures exclude amounts raised for the party in other funds. The election fund raised £150 in 1936. The Defence fund for the three who burnt the bombing school raised £1,000 in 1937.

The public activity of the *Blaid* was small in scope, and its leaders were not politicians by inclination or background; most of them were involved in the Welsh literary and academic scene and in nonconformity. At the outbreak of the Second World War the party had grown until it could claim a membership of 2,000 in 111 branches (see Table 1.2). By the close of the war membership was 2,500, and the party was able to contest eight seats in the general election of 1945—a remarkable feat in view of the hostile attitude the party had taken towards the war and the consequent social, legal, and political pressures inhibiting party activity. The party ran two newspapers monthly for most of the period. *Y Ddraig Goch* (The Red Dragon)

[1] Saunders Lewis, *The Banned Wireless Talk* (Caernarfon, 1930).

was founded in 1926 and had Ambrose Bebb as its first editor. Its English-language counterpart, *The Welsh Nationalist*, was first published in January 1932. *Y Ddraig Goch* had an average monthly circulation of 4,000 in the mid thirties, rising to 7,000 in the first six months of 1938; the *Welsh Nationalist* usually sold less than 2,000 copies per edition.[1] From 1926 until 1939 Saunders Lewis was President of the party. He was succeeded in 1939 by Professor Jack Daniel, Professor of Christian Doctrine at Bala–Bangor College, who had clearly emerged as heir-apparent. Lewis had been considering retirement from office for some time, and was particularly worried at the embarrassment that his known Catholicism had caused the party in Wales.[2]

The *Blaid* decided at an early stage to fight elections, though it seems to have had difficulty in fielding candidates with the party label at both local and national level. Only four out of the thirty-six parliamentary constituencies in Wales were contested prior to the 1945 election. The *Blaid*'s first contest occurred in 1929 in Caernarfonshire where the Revd. Lewis Valentine, a young Baptist minister and the *Blaid*'s President from 1925 to 1926, was their candidate. The Nationalists decided after this that they would have done better not to imitate *Sinn Fein* in refusing to take any seat in Parliament that they won. At the 1930 *cynhadledd* this policy was dramatically reversed, and the Nationalist vote in Caernarfonshire improved at the elections of 1931 and 1935 (Table 1.3), though their candidate lost his deposit each time. Saunders Lewis stood twice for Parliament, in each case fighting the University of Wales seat—in 1931 and in 1943. It was in this seat that the *Blaid*'s best results were achieved, although the seat remained safely Liberal until it was abolished in the redistribution of 1950.

The Welsh Nationalist Party first sprang into prominence in Wales over the burning in 1936 of the R.A.F. bombing school at Penyberth, in the Llŷn peninsula. This was the concerted work of three leading *Plaid* members, Saunders Lewis, D. J. Williams, and the Revd. Lewis Valentine, which they undertook only in their individual capacities. Entreaties from hundreds of churches and institutions in Wales had failed to persuade the government to reverse the plans to build the school and practice range. The story of the ensuing trials of the three leaders, first in Caernarfon, where the jury failed to agree, and then

[1] *Plaid Cymru*, Report for 1938.
[2] *Plaid Cymru*, Minutes of the Executive Committee for 1938.

TABLE 1.3

Plaid Genedlaethol Cymru: Performance in Parliamentary Elections 1925–1945

Year of election	Type of election	Seat fought	Total vote	% of electorate voting for *Plaid*	No. of candidates contesting seat	Plaid candidate	M.P. elected and Party
1929	g.e.	Caernarfonshire	609	1·1	4	Revd. L. E. Valentine	G. Owen (Lib.)
1931	g.e.	Caernarfonshire	1,136	2·2	4	Prof. J. E. Daniel	G. Owen (Ind. Lib.)
		Univ. of Wales	914	17·9	2	S. Lewis	E. Evans (Lib.)
1935	g.e.	Caernarfonshire	2,534	5·7	3	Prof. J. E. Daniel	Sir G. Owen (Ind. Lib.)
1943 (Jan.)	by.	Univ. of Wales	1,330	n.a.	5	S. Lewis	Prof. W. Gruffydd (Lib.)
1945 (Apr.)	by.	Caernarfon Boroughs	6,844	n.a.	2	Prof. J. E. Daniel	Seaborne Davies (Lib.)
1945 (May)	by.	Neath	6,290	n.a.	3	Wynne Samuel	D. J. Williams (Lab.)
1945	g.e.	Caernarfon Boroughs	1,560	3·2	4	Prof. J. E. Daniel	D. Pryce-White (Con.)
		Caernarfonshire	2,152	4·1	3	Ambrose Bebb	G. O. Roberts (Lab.)
		Neath	3,659	5·3	3	Wynne Samuel	D. J. Williams (Lab.)
		Univ. of Wales	1,696	14·4	2	Dr. Gwenan Jones	Prof. W. Gruffydd (Lib.)

Note. Results for the 1945 general election are not complete. The information concerning the four contests mentioned is for the purpose of comparison.

Abbreviations. g.e.—general election; by.—by-election; n.a.—not available; Lib.—Liberal; Lab.—Labour; Ind.—Independent; Con.—Conservative.

at the Old Bailey, their imprisonment in Wormwood Scrubs, followed by their triumphal return to Wales is one of the most moving episodes in the history of British political protest in the twentieth century and roused many Welshmen, including Lloyd George.[1] The *Blaid* had earned its first martyrs. There was an unmistakable growth in the party at all levels. Membership nearly doubled; the number of branches rose from 72 to 111 in two years; £1,000 was raised to pay for the defence costs in the trials, and the circulation of the *Ddraig Goch* rose by 2,000. One of the participants argued subsequently that the good work done for the party by the burning of Penyberth was all undone by the *Blaid*'s uncompromising condemnation of the Coronation late in 1937.[2] There is at present little objective evidence to support this view. The Penyberth incident was probably responsible for two other changes in the *Blaid*. One was an influx of nonconformists in the pacifist tradition into the *Blaid*. The other was the approval by the 1938 *cynhadledd* of a resolution opposing the use of force in the pursuit of politics and advocating non-violent direct action in suitable cases; this was proposed by the young Gwynfor Evans.

The outbreak of the Second World War put an immediate damper on Nationalist activities. The party adopted a neutral standpoint towards the hostilities and encouraged conscientious objection to war service. Inevitably restrictions were imposed on some party members, especially those who objected to war service on nationalist grounds only, and the *Blaid*'s organizing secretary, J. E. Jones, was fined on several occasions for refusing to do work which would help the war effort. Many party members served in the armed forces, however, and as the war continued so the *Blaid* found its ranks swollen with new members joining from the Services. The *Blaid* in this period was frequently described as being Fascist, a charge often made in the thirties. The *Gwerin* (folk) movement, founded in 1935 in the University College of North Wales at Bangor by Goronwy Roberts (later M.P. for Caernarfon), refused to associate with the *Blaid* because it detected Fascist leanings amongst its leaders.[3] The *Gwerin*

[1] See Saunders Lewis, *Paham y Llosgasom yr Ysgol Fomio* (Caernarfon, 1937). Lloyd George wrote angrily to his daughter, Megan, about the government's decision to move the trial to London. 'I hope the Welsh Members will make a scene, and an effective one, in the House. . . . To take it out of Wales altogether and, above all, to the Old Bailey is an outrage which makes my blood boil.' D. Lloyd George to M. Lloyd George, 1 Dec. 1936 (written from Jamaica), N.L.W. 20,475 C, 3151.
[2] See Table 1.2 and D. J. Williams, *Codi'r Faner* (Cardiff, 1968).
[3] See *Omnibus*, the magazine of the University College of North Wales, 1934–6.

movement was a new attempt to marry socialism and nationalism in Wales—exactly what many *Plaid* activists imagined they were trying to do. These accusations of Fascism were brought to a head in 1942 by a speech of Dr. Thomas Jones, the deputy secretary to the Cabinet, and by an article written by the Revd. Gwilym Davies, secretary of the Welsh League of Nations Union.[1] Soon afterwards the University of Wales seat in the House of Commons fell vacant: Saunders Lewis was quickly nominated as Nationalist candidate and circulated an impressive list of nominators.[2] There was no obvious Liberal to fill the breach so that when Professor W. J. Gruffydd, the University's Professor of Celtic since 1918, accepted the Liberal nomination, the Welsh Nationalists were bitter and astounded. Professor Daniel, writing the foreword of Lewis's election address, suggested that the Liberals had searched for

. . . the candidate most likely to keep Mr. Lewis out. Their choice has fallen on Professor W. J. Gruffydd of Cardiff, who has postponed any serious interest in politics to this, the penultimate stage of his career, and whose intermittent excursions into politics were connected with the Welsh Nationalist Party, of which he claims to have been a member 'before Mr. Saunders Lewis', i.e. before 1925, and from which he has never formally resigned. . . .[3]

Certainly Professor Gruffydd's nomination was extraordinary. He had been a known *Plaid* member in the 1930s, and had been nominated on at least three occasions to serve on the Executive Council of the party, and once, in 1938, for the post of Vice-President of the *Blaid*.[4] Gruffydd's action caused a rift between certain prominent Nationalists which still coloured Welsh politics a quarter of a century later.[5] When Lewis was defeated by Gruffydd in the election, he decided to leave active politics for good, believing that he had been badly served by Wales and victimized for his Catholicism.

The principal concerns of the *Blaid* during the war were with

---

[1] Dr. Thomas Jones, C.H., *The Native Never Returns* (Aberystwyth, 1946) and Revd. G. Davies, 'Cymru Gyfan a'r Blaid Genedlaethol', *Y Traethodydd*, July 1942. Replies to the latter by Saunders Lewis and Professor J. E. Daniel were printed in *The Party for Wales* (Caernarfon, 1942).

[2] The list of 73 nominators which accompanied the election address included the names of 31 lecturers and teachers, and 22 clergymen.

[3] J. E. Daniel, *Wales Make or Break* (1943). A similar attack was made in a profile of W. J. Gruffydd published in *The Welsh Review*, Mar. 1946.

[4] See the *Plaid Cymru* conference agendas for 1934, 1936, and 1938.

[5] Gruffydd did not appear to take a very serious view of his Liberal allegiance. He wrote: 'I was elected to the House as a Liberal, which means, as things are at present, that I can be eclectic in my politics.' W. J. Gruffydd, 'Wales in Parliament', in *The Welsh Anvil*, Apr. 1949.

conscription, the anglicizing effect of the English evacuee children in Wales, and the government's powers to direct labour out of Wales. As a result of strong pressure from *Undeb Cymru Fydd* and Welsh M.P.s a Welsh Courts Act was passed in 1942 which for the first time allowed evidence given in Welsh in court to be translated into English without charge. With the setting up of the Welsh Reconstruction Advisory Council, the *Blaid* realized that it would have a battle to persuade the government to treat Wales as a single unit after the war. It fought for separate treatment of Wales as a planning unit, and later for similar treatment whenever decentralization occurred in the gas and electricity supply industries, and in the management of the railways. When the *Blaid* contested two Welsh by-elections early in 1945, it formally suspended its declared objectives of self-government for Wales and the preservation of the Welsh language and culture, and fought its campaigns on the limited issue of the future planning of Wales.[1] Professor Daniel in his election address in the by-election in Caernarfon Boroughs entirely omitted mention of Welsh language issues. The ease with which the *Blaid* adapted its platform to meet the situation was indicative of future developments in the party, and seems to have passed almost without comment at the time. The *Blaid* had failed to make itself a significant political force in its first twenty years of existence, yet it had survived as a political entity. The prospects for the party as the war ended seemed as uncertain as the prospects for social and economic life in Wales as a whole.

[1] *North Wales Pioneer*, 12 Apr. 1945. Report of speech by J. E. Daniel made in St. Mary's Church Hall, Bangor, on 7 Apr.

2

SOCIO-ECONOMIC CHANGE
IN WELSH SOCIETY SINCE 1945

Introduction

IN many respects, Wales and England have social structures that are similar and that have been subject to the same social changes experienced throughout Western Europe since the end of the Second World War. However, Welsh society is distinct from English society. Wales's industrial structure, its forms of agriculture, its geography, language, cultural institutions, and values ensure this. Welsh society is far from being a special case of the wider British society.

Wales does not cohere very well as a single social unit. Apart from the familiar boundary problem of where one country ends and another begins, there is the outstanding fact that Wales has polarized into urban-industrial and rural-farming sections, with ports and tourist resorts scattered along the coasts. The urban-industrial concentrations are mainly confined, in South Wales, to East Carmarthenshire, Glamorgan, and the western mining valleys of Monmouthshire, and, in North Wales, to the Wrexham, East Flintshire, and Dee-side complex. In 1961 the density of the population of Wales was found to be 329 per square mile, the comparable figure for England being 863 per square mile. Yet 70 per cent of the people of Wales live in only three of its thirteen counties, Glamorgan, Monmouthshire, and Flintshire. This is only one indicator of the different nature of the urban and the rural environment in Wales which makes it so difficult to talk about one Wales with similar interests. We shall find increasingly that the rural and industrial cultures of Wales deserve separate consideration.

Welsh Social and Demographic Change: An Overview

In the fifty years before 1939 the three pillars of the Welsh economy were the coal, steel, and farming industries. The war years 1939–45 saw a considerable restructuring of Welsh industry and encouraged diversification into other forms of manufacture. The trend of the post-war years was clearly set during the war. The hegemony of coal, steel, and agriculture has been steadily whittled away ever since. Other manufacturing industries, especially in engineering, as well as service industries have offered alternative sources of income and employment. This trend has been constant and unmistakable.[1] Economic changes of this order have had important social and cultural effects on the communities of Wales.

The patterns of rural and urban settlement have very largely determined the way of life and the social conventions of the Welsh people. The 'Welsh' way of life is an imprecise concept usually associated with a scattered rural and farming society punctuated with small market and service centres. It is a striking fact that outside the two industrial complexes of Wales (defined above) there is not a single town of over 30,000 inhabitants; the largest town is Colwyn Bay, a North Wales holiday resort with an estimated population in 1969 of 25,060. Outside Glamorgan and Monmouthshire, Wrexham, whose estimated population in 1969 was 37,620, is the largest town in Wales.

The farming areas of Wales have suffered a population decline dating from the middle of the nineteenth century. Agricultural holdings have become larger, mechanization and productivity have increased at the expense of the small-holding and its farming family. Farmers, and more especially their children, have had to leave home to find work, and more often than not have had to leave Wales altogether.[2] Depopulation has not been uniform in its effects or its causes. Poor employment opportunities have always been one cause of depopulation in the rural parts of Wales, and this was the experience also of many South Wales valleys in the 1960s. In rural Wales the standard of education and qualifications attained by generations of young people has never been matched by commensurate employment prospects. Higher education has thus reinforced an already apparent trend. Symptomatic of this is the fact that the teacher-training colleges of Wales are believed to be exporting onet housand newly graduated schoolteachers to the rest of the United Kingdom every year.[3] Nevertheless, the principal cause of depopulation in Wales is the absence of sufficient jobs to meet the

[1] See Brinley Thomas (ed.), *The Welsh Economy* (Cardiff, 1962) and Gerald Manners (ed.), *South Wales in the Sixties* (Oxford, 1964).
[2] H. R. Jones, 'Rural Migration in Central Wales', in *Transactions of the Institute of British Geographers*, No. 37 (Dec. 1965), p. 31.
[3] *Primary Education in Wales* (H.M.S.O., 1968), (a report of the Central Advisory Council for Education (Wales) under the chairmanship of Professor C. E. Gittins), pp. 483 and 506–7, and *Digest of Welsh Statistics*, No. 16 (1969), p. 34.

natural increase of the labour force at the same time as the claims upon labour of the coal, steel, and farming industries are diminishing. The Gittins Report of 1968 pointed out how serious and widespread are the effects of rural depopulation on the social structure of Wales.[1] Rural areas usually have a higher proportion of elderly people than the rest of Wales and the sex-ratios differ significantly from those in urban areas, with fewer women than men.

For those who stay in Wales employment and income opportunities are restricted. Wealth may be more evenly distributed in Wales than elsewhere in the United Kingdom, but average earnings and average income per head in Wales are still below the United Kingdom average.[2] Social class is none the less an important factor in Welsh society, although its significance in colouring socio-political attitudes varies considerably as between rural and urban Wales.

The Gittins Report found that parental attitude surveys in England *and* Wales revealed 'a high degree of consistency in the expected associations between parental occupation and aspirations for and attitudes towards the education of the children'.[3]

Population and Demographic Change

The total population of Wales has changed little over the last fifty years, varying between 2,500,000 and 2,750,000 (see Table 2.1). Net migration out of Wales since 1931 has mostly cancelled out the expected rise in the population of the country from the natural excess of births over deaths. Many parts of Wales have yet to make up in numbers for the depletion of their population arising from the depression in the inter-war years. The rise in the total population of Wales has accelerated gradually since 1951.

TABLE 2.1

Total Population of Wales 1921–1970

(Rounded off to the nearest thousand)

1921	2,658*	1951	2,584*	1968	2,720‡
1931	2,590*	1961	2,644*	1969	2,725‡
1939	2,567†	1967	2,710‡	1970	2,734‡

* Census figures.   † Mid-year estimate.   ‡ Registrar-General's estimate.

[1] *Primary Education in Wales*, pp. 11–13 and 106–33 *passim*.
[2] J. Parry Lewis, 'Income and Consumers' Expenditure', in B. Thomas (ed.), *The Welsh Economy*. See also the *Digest of Welsh Statistics*, No. 16 (1969), Table 56.
[3] *Primary Education in Wales*, p. 14, para. 3.3.

Within the figure for the total population of Wales there have been important changes, many of them socially significant. The birth rate is lower than that in England, although, when allowance is made for the different age-structure of their populations, the Welsh birth rate is found to be 5 per cent higher than the English rate. The variations in age-structure referred to are caused by shifts of population, mainly in the form of high emigration from rural and old industrial Wales to places outside Wales, and to a lesser extent to the North and South Welsh coastal belts. This takes place soon after the education of the young is over when jobs with good career prospects are sought (see Table 2.2).

TABLE 2.2

Depletion of Young Age-Groups 1931–1951
Wales compared with England and Wales

	% of population aged	
	5–19 in 1931	25–39 in 1951
Wales	27·3	21·7
England and Wales	24·9	22·1

Source: J. Parry Lewis, 'Population' in B. Thomas (ed.), *The Welsh Economy*, p. 179.

	% of population aged	
	10–19 in 1951	20–9 in 1961
Wales	13·2	11·9
England and Wales	12·6	12·4

Source: 1951 and 1961 Censuses of England and Wales.

	Numbers in the population aged		% change
	10–19 in 1951	20–9 in 1961	
All Wales	344,493	312,752	−9·2
Wales (excl. Glam. and Mon.)	126,644	109,607	−13·5
England and Wales	5,516,408	5,724,450	+3·8

Source: 1951 and 1961 Censuses of England and Wales

Migration out of Wales between 1961 and 1966 occurred at the rate of about 22,000 people a year; a similar number of people migrated into Wales during this period.[1] Net emigration from Wales

[1] 776 HC Deb. Fifth Series, c. 356 (Written Answers), 29 Jan. 1969.

in the late 1960s reached a rate of 3,000 people a year, according to government estimates.[1] Migration out of Wales leaves its mark in the form of large gaps in the generations, and a larger-than-average proportion of old people in the population of rural Wales. Migration into Wales also makes its mark. Marriage to a Welsh spouse is one reason for it. In rural Wales it is also older or retired people, from the north-west of England in particular, who come to make their last homes or to find a weekend or a holiday cottage near the noted beauty spots. Thus more than a quarter of the population of Caernarfonshire is not Welsh-born. In industrial Wales, it is the skilled and the technically qualified workers and managers who come into Wales,

TABLE 2.3

Birthplace of the Welsh Population

(A) Proportions of the Welsh population born in Wales or in England in 1961: regional analysis

	% Welsh-born	% English-born
All Wales	82·8	13·9
South-east Wales	85·9	10·9
Rest of Wales (9 counties)	74·9	21·5

Source: the 1961 Census of England and Wales.

(B) Percentage of the Welsh population born in Wales in 1951, 1961, and 1966: county analysis

	1951	1961	1966
Anglesey	81·5	78·8	75·1
Caernarfonshire	77·4	75·1	73·5
Merioneth	77·2	77·4	79·4
Cardiganshire	85·2	82·1	81·2
Carmarthenshire	91·4	91·3	90·1
Pembrokeshire	82·8	79·8	77·9
Denbighshire	75·1	74·8	74·0
Flintshire	64·8	65·4	66·4
Montgomeryshire	81·8	81·5	80·7
Radnor	73·7	73·8	74·3
Breconshire	84·9	84·4	86·6
Monmouthshire	83·2	82·7	85·0
Glamorgan	85·5	86·4	86·6

Source: the 1951, 1961, and 1966 Censuses of England and Wales.

[1] 780 HC Deb. Fifth Series, cc. 116–17 (Written Answers), 19 Mar. 1969.

some for a period of only a few years at an outlying branch of an English-based company. Over all, however, it is the northern and mostly rural counties of Wales that have the highest proportions of people not born in Wales (see Table 2.3). In recent years, many people, especially nationalists, have become alarmed at the rate at which houses in rural Wales have been bought up for holiday or retirement purposes. They have argued that the partial use of these homes stunts the life of local communities by denying use of such houses to local people who would live in them permanently, and play a full part in town or village life. It is probably more correct to say that the conversion of houses in rural Wales into holiday homes is most often a way of using houses which would otherwise remain empty, and serves to conceal the extent of rural depopulation.

Wales is becoming more urbanized even if its absolute population is almost unchanged. The drift from the country to the towns continues unabated. But population change in the urban districts and boroughs has been far from uniform. The decline of the population of the Rhondda has been very marked, for example; the Rhondda lost 11,000 inhabitants between 1951 and 1961. Since 1921 the Rhondda population has fallen by nearly 70,000 to 94,300. Most of the townships in the valleys of Glamorgan and Monmouthshire have seen their populations remain static or decline. In partial compensation, however, the coastal belts of Glamorgan and Monmouthshire have seen sizeable rises in population, as has the north-east Wales industrial complex. The population of Flintshire has risen by 65 per cent to 160,000 since 1921.

The exact extent of urbanization in Wales is not known. The 1951 census published figures showing that of the population at that time living in Wales 24 per cent lived in towns with over 100,000 inhabitants, 14 per cent in towns with between 25,000 and 100,000 inhabitants, and 10 per cent in towns with populations of between 10,000 and 25,000. In recent years, Swansea, Cardiff, and Newport have all seen their populations grow. The largest cities and the larger market towns and service centres have been gaining at the expense of the medium-sized valley towns and the rural areas (see Table 2.4). The trend has also been towards more settlement on the north and south coasts of Wales. Since 1931 the boroughs and urban districts situated on the coasts of Denbighshire, Flintshire, Glamorgan, and Monmouthshire have witnessed an increase of population of more than 21 per cent. The population of the rest of Wales is still one per cent below the comparable figure for 1931 (see Table 2.5). In social and political terms these trends are highly significant. The characteristic Welsh way of life is enjoyed by and known to a declining proportion

TABLE 2.4

Extent of Urbanization in Wales

Percentage of the population living in towns, 1951.

Over 100,000 inhabs.	23·6
25,000 to 100,000 inhabs.	14·2
10,000 to 25,000 ,,	10·5
5,000 to 10,000 ,,	4·2
Less than 5,000 ,,	46·5

Source: the 1951 Census of England and Wales.

TABLE 2.5

Extent of Coastal Settlement in Wales

Increase/decrease in population in percentages, 1931–68.

	1951/1931	1961/1951	1968/1961	1968/1931
All Wales	−0·2	+2·3	+2·9	+5·0
Glamorgan and Monmouth (coastal boroughs and urban districts)	+5·0	+5·0	+6·7	+17·6
Flints.–Denbs. (coastal boroughs and urban districts)	+28·5	+7·9	+11·9	+55·2
Combined rise (Glam., Mon., Flt., Denbs., coastal boroughs and urban districts)	+5·9	+6·7	+7·4	+21·3
Rest of Wales	−2·6	+0·5	+0·9	−1·2

Calculated from data provided by the 1951 and 1961 Censuses, and by the Registrar-General's estimate of the population of England and Wales for 1968 (published February 1969).

of the Welsh people. Life on the coast is noticeably different from life in the valleys. The sense of community is absent, and the economic and cultural life of the north and south coastal areas has increasingly been integrated into the standard British pattern.

The Welsh Economy

Political debate surrounding the erratic performance of the Welsh economy since 1945 has tended to conceal the major changes affecting its industrial base. The shift out of coal, iron and steel, and farming into service industries and other manufacturing industries has been continuous and dramatic. The social stresses involved in such a change have not produced the industrial conflict that could have been anticipated. Historians will undoubtedly see this smooth changeover in the Welsh economy as the major achievement of its first twenty-five years after the end of the Second World War. Beside this achievement, the perennial complaints about the rate of unemployment in Wales will look small.

In political terms, however, it was the economic recessions and the rate of unemployment which caused most concern and comment until the 1960s, rather than the change in the industrial structure of Wales. Total unemployment figures for Wales have not been high since the late 1940s, and have never compared with the record rates of unemployment which undermined the Welsh nation in the inter-war years 1919–39. Nevertheless, the average rates of unemployment in Wales have been relatively high when compared with those of England, especially the south-east, and the unemployment rate has been much higher than even the Welsh average at localized points in Wales (see Tables 2.6, 2.7, and 2.8). It should also be remembered that migration out of Wales has served to keep levels of unemployment in Wales down.

TABLE 2.6

Unemployment in Wales 1948–1969

(Percentage rates for June and December)

1948(J)	4·4	1955(D)	1·7	1963(J)	3·0
1948(D)	4·3	1956(J)	1·9	1963(D)	2·9
1949(J)	3·6	1956(D)	2·3	1964(J)	2·1
1949(D)	4·1	1957(J)	2·1	1964(D)	2·7
1950(J)	3·5	1957(D)	3·0	1965(J)	2·2
1950(D)	3·4	1958(J)	3·7	1965(D)	2·9
1951(J)	2·3	1958(D)	4·1	1966(J)	2·2
1951(D)	2·8	1959(J)	3·4	1966(D)	3·9
1952(J)	2·7	1959(D)	3·3	1967(J)	3·6
1952(D)	3·0	1960(J)	2·3	1967(D)	4·2
1953(J)	2·8	1960(D)	2·8	1968(J)	3·6
1953(D)	2·7	1961(J)	2·1	1968(D)	4·0
1954(J)	2·1	1961(D)	2·8	1969(J)	3·6
1954(D)	2·3	1962(J)	2·6	1969(D)	4·1
1955(J)	1·6	1962(D)	3·8		

Sources: the *Ministry of Labour Gazette*, the *Digest of Welsh Statistics*, and the *Department of Employment and Productivity Gazette*.

TABLE 2.7

Unemployment in Great Britain, Scotland, and Wales 1948–1970

(Percentage rates for June)

	Wales	Scotland	Gt. Britain
1948	4·5	3·0	2·0
1955	1·6	2·2	1·0
1958	3·7	3·5	2·0
1961	2·1	2·8	1·2
1965	2·2	2·6	1·2
1968	3·6	3·6	2·2
1970	3·4	3·9	2·4

Sources: the *Ministry of Labour Gazette* and the *Department of Employment and Productivity Gazette*.

TABLE 2.8

Area Unemployment in Wales 1960–1970

(Persons registered at employment exchanges as unemployed expressed as a percentage of the estimated number of employees)

District:	Anglesey	Caernarfon	Llanelli	Milford	Rhondda	Ammanford
Date:						
1960(J)	7·5	4·3	2·5	2·2	n.a.	n.a.
1960(D)	9·2	6·7	5·7	11·5	n.a.	n.a.
1961(J)	5·8	3·7	5·5	6·4	n.a.	n.a.
1961(D)	9·1	5·6	n.a.	10·0	n.a.	n.a.
1962(J)	7·3	3·9	5·0	9·8	n.a.	n.a.
1962(D)	9·7	6·4	5·8	13·5	6·7	4·7
1963(J)	7·6	3·6	4·2	7·9	6·3	4·3
1963(D)	8·9	5·1	3·3	7·0	4·8	3·9
1964(J)	5·9	3·1	2·6	4·4	1·6	3·9
1964(D)	7·0	5·1	2·9	11·9	4·7	4·7

District:	Anglesey	Caernarfon	Llanelli	Milford	Rhondda	Ammanford
Date:						
1965(J)	4·8	3·8	2·6	12·6	4·2	4·5
1965(D)	6·1	4·9	3·2	14·9	5·0	5·3
1966(J)	3·7	3·3	2·8	9·9	3·5	5·6

District:	Wrexham	Bargoed	Llanelli	Rhondda	Ebbw Vale
Date:					
1966(D)	3·6	5·6	5·8	7·6	4·3
1967(J)	3·5	6·9	3·8	8·0	4·9
1967(D)	3·9	7·4	4·0	7·5	5·3
1968(J)	4·7	6·6	3·1	6·4	4·5

TABLE 2.8 (*cont.*)

District:	Wrexham	Bargoed	Llanelli	Rhondda/ Pontypridd	Ebbw Vale
Date:					
1968(D)	4·8	6·5	3·0	4·6	4·8
1969(J)	4·7	6·7	2·3	4·7	3·8
1969(D)	5·6	6·8	2·4	5·4	4·1
1970(J)	4·9	6·5	2·0	4·6	3·9

Source: the *Ministry of Labour Gazette* and the *Department of Employment and Productivity Gazette*.

(J) = June   (D) = December   n.a. = not available

Note. No complete series of statistics is available for the period. The boundaries of each area have been changed several times, so that the figures are not comparable between different sections.

Most of the short-term recessions in the post-war period occurred in the textile, clothing, and electrical goods industries which, as durable goods industries, have been prominent amongst those farmed out to the 'developing areas'.[1] While recessions in these industries in the Midlands and the south-east of England simply took the heat out of the economy and clipped excess demand, in Wales these recessions bore the marks of a trade cycle. Even so, the recessions never led to severe widespread unemployment.

If the record of unemployment in Wales has been unsatisfactory at about twice the rate for the United Kingdom, the increase of output and in productivity in Wales compares well with that in England (see Table 2.9). Investment in Wales since 1945 has been high, but serious lags in the improvement of the Welsh infrastructure, particularly transport facilities, have been allowed to obstruct industrial development. The main beneficiaries of new investment in Wales have been the coal and steel industries, and manufacturing industry which in 1960 employed 23 per cent of the Welsh labour force compared with only 11 per cent before the Second World War. About 40 per cent of the new manufacturing industry set up in non-industrial Wales between 1948 and 1958 was engineering industry.[2] The difficulties in handling the Welsh economy since 1945 can be viewed as 'the growing pains associated with technical progress'.[3] Wales has a strong industrial sector in its economy, with a high proportion of science-based and expanding industry; but as yet no government has proved capable

[1] B. Thomas, 'Conclusion', in B. Thomas (ed.), *The Welsh Economy*, p. 192.
[2] B. Thomas, 'Post-War Expansion', ibid., p. 50.
[3] B. Thomas, 'Conclusion', ibid., p. 197.

of generating sufficient jobs for the people of Wales to change the pattern of emigration from the country. The new natural resource of Wales is water rather than coal. The new earners of foreign currency will be the tourist and the manufacturing industries, not coal or slate.

TABLE 2.9

Index of Production in Wales and the U.K.

	Wales	U.K.
	Index of GDP, 1954 = 100	
1951	87	93
1954	100	100
1958	105	107
1960	115	118
	Index of Industrial Production, 1963 = 100	
1964	111	108
1966	115	113
1967	117	114
1968	$125\frac{1}{2}$	120
1969	123	123
1970	$124\frac{1}{2}$	124

Sources: G. McCrone, 'Is a Separate Scotland Viable?' in *New Outlook*, No. 75 (Dec. 1968), *Digest of Welsh Statistics*, No. 18 (1971), *Board of Trade Journal*, 27 May 1970, and *Trade and Industry*, 25 May 1972.

Farming in Wales employs a larger share of the work force than in England (see Table 2.10). Welsh farms, however, are generally smaller than their English counterparts and the land is poorer. Only 6 per cent of Welsh farms were over 150 acres in 1958 while $13\frac{1}{2}$ per

TABLE 2.10

Proportion of Workforce Engaged in Agriculture: Cross-national Comparisons 1951 (Rounded off)

Ulster	Wales (excl. Glam. and Mon.)	Scotland	All Wales	England
17%	16%	10%	$7\frac{1}{2}$%	5%

Source: Anne Martin, 'Agriculture', in B. Thomas (ed.), *The Welsh Economy*, p. 72.

cent of England's farms were over 150 acres (see Table 2.11). Recent censuses have found that more than 40 per cent of employed persons in Montgomeryshire in 1951 were engaged in agriculture, forestry, and fishing (32 per cent in 1961). The comparable figure for Glamorgan was 2 per cent in 1951 (1 per cent in 1961). From the early 1950s the proportion of Welsh people engaged in farming has declined noticeably. In 1951 8·3 per cent of the Welsh labour force was employed in agriculture, forestry, and fishing: this had declined to 5·9 per cent in 1961 (see Table 2.12).

TABLE 2.11

Wales: Changes in the Size Distribution of Agricultural Holdings, 1939–1969

Size of Holdings (acres)	1939 %	1958 %	1969 %
1–20	45·3	40·1	36·4
30–50	24·0	24·5	23·2
50–100	19·0	20·8	22·4
100–50	6·3	8·7	9·8
150 and over	5·5	6·0	8·2

Source: Anne Martin, 'Agriculture', in B. Thomas (ed.), *The Welsh Economy*, Table 36, p. 78, and *Digest of Welsh Statistics*, No. 16 (1969).

TABLE 2.12

Distribution of Occupied Persons by Industry Order—Wales 1921–1961

	1921 %	1951 %	1961 %
Agriculture	9·0	8·3	5·9
Mining and Quarrying	26·4	12·7	9·7
Manufacturing	17·0	27·9	28·1
Construction	2·5	6·6	7·8
Services	45·1	47·3	48·5

Source: 1921, 1951, and 1961 Censuses of England and Wales.

In recent years the major declining sector of the Welsh economy, both in terms of output and in terms of manpower, has been the coal industry. The main factors in the run-down of the industry have been competition from the oil industry, reducing demand for coal fuel, and the increasing age of the collieries being worked and the men working them. These trends were greatly accelerated by government policy in the 1960s (see Tables 2.13 and 2.14). Manpower in the mines

TABLE 2.13

Average Number of Wage-earners
on Colliery Books (Wales) in thousands

1948	115	1966	63
1954	110	1967	59
1960	91	1968	52
1962	85	1969	46
1964	78	1971	41

Sources: The Digest of Welsh Statistics,
and the Ministry of Power.

TABLE 2.14

Coal Production and Production Units (Wales)

Annual Coal Production (million tons)		Number of N.C.B. mines producing coal in Wales	
1948	25.66	1950	171
1954	27.39	1959	137
1960	22.38	1962	116
1962	22.29	1964	103
1964	23.64	1966	81
1966	20.62	1968	66
1967	19.82	1970	54
1969	16.09		
1970	14.49		

Sources: The Digest of Welsh Statistics, and the
Ministry of Power.

at less than 50,000 is now about 40 per cent of what it was in the late 1940s. Production is running at about 60 per cent of what it was in 1945. Cuts in both manpower and production, causing serious dislocation to individuals and communities almost wholly dependent on mining, are planned throughout the 1970s.

The effect of the phased run-down of the coal industry in South Wales has been dramatic in the life of the mining valleys. Not only has the typical occupation of the inhabitants changed; so have the links between them, their expectations, and their way of life. The young Rhondda school-leaver no longer works in the pit (see

Table 2.15). The old miner remains part of an ageing community, increasingly unable to sustain its traditional culture. The male-voice choirs, the working-men's institutes, and the chapels are all in decline. Economic insecurity and cultural decline of this intensity can

TABLE 2.15

Employment of Young Persons
(*Boys including Apprentices*) *in Wales 1962–1968*

Wales

	1962 %	1963 %	1966 %	1967 %	1968 %
Agriculture	9	9	8	7	6½
Engineering and Manufacturing	29	29	31	32	35
Mining and Quarrying	9	9	6	6	3½
Construction	13	13	14	15	14
Distribution	19	19	17	17	17
Other Services	20	22	23	23	24
	100	100	100	100	100
Total N =	16,682	16,358	14,127	13,082	13,655

Sources: the *Ministry of Labour Gazette*, and the *Digest of Welsh Statistics*.

Rhondda

	1962/3 %	1963/4 %	1964/5 %	1965/6 %	1966/7 %
Coalmining	30	5	5	1	3
Engineering	8	8	13	6	12
Manufacturing	23	40	44	59	40
Building	9	12	7	7	10
Distribution	9	16	9	12	23
Clerical	..	..	..	..	12

Source: T. J. Farmer, 'A Study of Redundancy, Re-Deployment and Re-Training of Personnel Resulting from Colliery Closures in South Wales' (an unpublished report to the Welsh Office, 1967).

have politically explosive consequences as by-elections in the Rhondda and Rhymney valleys revealed in 1967 and 1968. The third pillar of the Welsh economy—the steel and metal manufacturing industry has also reduced its manpower since 1945. Productivity and output have both risen and major new developments in steel plant have been initiated at Trostre (near Llanelli), Margam (Port Talbot), Ebbw

Vale and Llanwern (near Newport) (see Table 2.16).[1] The new integrated steel plants, each employing thousands of men, have since the end of the Second World War replaced the old small hand-mills that used to be scattered throughout South Wales. The increased

TABLE 2.16

The Welsh Steel Industry:
Production, Manpower, and Productivity

(A) Finished Steel Production (thousand tons)

1951	3,462
1956	4,588
1961	5,152
1965	7,118
1966	6,806
1967	6,527
1969	7,258

(B) Steel and Iron Employees (thousands)—No. 311 in S.I.C. (1958)

1959	67.1
1964	75.6
1967	73.4
1969	74.6

(C) Steel Productivity: South Wales. Annual output per open-hearth furnace, 1938–59 (thousand tons)

1938	29.1
1946	29.2
1955	51.5
1959	70.4

Sources: *The Digest of Welsh Statistics*, 1954–69, and J. Driscoll, 'Steel' in B. Thomas (ed.), *The Welsh Economy*.

reliance of the industry on imports of iron ore has shifted its centre of gravity to deep-water ports on the south coast, with obviously debilitating consequences for the valley communities, especially in the Amman and Dulais valleys. Nationalization in 1967 and the world steel glut in the mid 1960s forced further rationalization on the steel industry, and thousands of jobs were placed in jeopardy even in the new plants.[2]

[1] E. T. Nevin, *et. al.*, *The Structure of the Welsh Economy* (Cardiff, 1966), p. 6, notes that the Welsh steel industry's output rose by 167 per cent between 1948 and 1964, three times as fast as in Britain generally.

[2] For example, the British Steel Corporation's plans reported in the *Western Mail*, 24 Jan. 1969. When its plans for Ebbw Vale were announced in 1970, the B.S.C. promised new investment amounting to £46 m. at the same time as an expected run-down at the plant of 1,300 jobs within five years—viz. *Financial Times*, 25 Mar. 1970. A further cutback in employment in the Welsh steel industry was announced late in 1972.

The uncertain picture of the major industries of Wales is considerably mitigated by the changing fortunes of Welsh manufacturing industry other than steel. The growth of engineering, vehicle-building, oil, and chemical industries in Wales was foreshadowed during the Second World War when the numbers employed in these industries leapt from 22,000 to 147,000. Since then, all these industries have grown considerably—in Wales as in the rest of Europe, and the effect has been to strengthen and to diversify the base of the Welsh economy. The total number of employees in employment in the Welsh economy rose by 3 per cent over the period 1961–6 (+8 per cent in the manufacturing sector, −24 per cent in the extractive sector).[1]

In passing, it may be observed that the change in the type of industry dominant in South Wales has had major political consequences. The balance of power inside the predominant Labour Party in Wales has been altered with the growth and added power of the engineering and white-collar unions at the expense, principally, of the National Union of Mineworkers. A simple index of this is the reduction of the number of miners' M.P.s sitting for Welsh constituencies in the House of Commons. In 1959 there were ten miners' M.P.s elected for Welsh seats; in 1970 there remained only three. At the same time, I.C.I., Courtauld's, Metal Box, Hoover, British Leyland, and Pilkington's factories exemplify the growing integration of the Welsh economy with the larger British economy. These firms are now as much a feature of the industrial landscape of Wales as elsewhere.

Growth has also occurred in the service sector of the Welsh economy, partly as the standard concomitant of an ever more complicated industrial structure, and partly through the expansion of the tourist industry. The over-all percentage of the population of Wales occupied in this group of industries has risen from 45·1 per cent in 1921 to 48·5 per cent in 1961, and this growth continues (see Tables 2.17 and 2.18).

Conclusion

Despite increased government attempts to develop regional economic policies, the Welsh economy in the late 1960s was still not an expanding economy, and was still undergoing major structural changes. There is, however, a danger that in concentrating upon the

[1] *Wales: The Way Ahead*, Cmnd. 3334 (H.M.S.O., 1967), Table 6.

TABLE 2.17

Percentage of Occupied Persons in Wales
Employed in Service Industries 1921–1961

1921	45·1% of occupied persons
1951	47·3% „ „
1961	48·5% „ „
1961	46·9% of employees in service industries
1966	48·8% of employees in service industries

Sources: the 1921, 1951, and 1961 Censuses, and *Wales: The Way Ahead*, Cmnd. 3334 (H.M.S.O., 1967).

TABLE 2.18

Numbers employed in selected
Service Industries 1948–1966 (in thousands)

(A) 1948–58 (occupied persons)

	1948	1953	1958	% increase 1948–58
Building and Contracting	66.0	62.9	62.0	−6
Transport and Communications	91.4	86.2	85.1	−7
Distribution	82.7	83.7	93.3	+13
Professional services, etc.	58.4	67.9	76.3	+31
Miscellaneous services	73.5	65.4	66.8	−9

(B) 1959–66 (employees in service industries)

	1959	1963	1966	% increase 1959–66
Building and Contracting	70.7	77.2	84.7	+20
Transport and Communications	83.2	76.0	70.9	−15
Distribution	100.6	111.1	106.6	+6
Professional services, etc.	88.1	100.1	118.2	+34
Miscellaneous services	75.5	77.8	86.0	+14

Source: Tables compiled on same basis as Table 2.17.

changing factors in Welsh social and economic life, the constant factors will be overlooked. The balance of the Welsh economy has certainly shifted in the last twenty years, but it is still similar now to what it was in 1951, as Table 2.15 shows. Coal, steel, and agriculture are still major focal points in the Welsh scene. Socio-economic change in the last twenty years in Wales has not been as great and has not been as disturbing a process as the socio-economic upheaval of the preceding twenty years. Economic changes in the war years 1939–45 appear now to have been crucial in setting the Welsh economy on the path to modernization and rationalization, but social changes consequent upon economic change appear to have been slower in working themselves out. Attitudes fixed and scarred by the experience of the misery of the 1920s and 1930s have not moved in step with the changed industrial pattern of modern Wales. It has been left to the succeeding generation in Wales to see the situation more clearly as it is, to rid itself of fears based mainly on past, not on present experience, and to look to the future. If the economic renaissance of Wales was the outstanding phenomenon of the 1940s, the cultural renaissance of Wales was the outstanding phenomenon of the 1960s in Wales. But this cultural development was dependent upon the renewal of Welsh life brought about by the economic changes. There seems no alternative explanation for the change from the stagnant Welsh society of the 1950s to the confident Wales of the 1960s, and it is the cultural changes underpinning this reversal which must now be considered.

3

THE WELSH CULTURE

'THE WELSH CULTURE', a phrase that is often used but rarely defined, is a combination of customs and social institutions, principally expressed in the spheres of literature and religion and frequently articulated through the medium of the Welsh language. This chapter is an attempt to analyse the strength of the components of this culture. It could be argued that there is nothing specially Welsh about the features that distinguish Wales from England, and that these features are characteristic of many rural societies in the European world. However, it is in relation to English culture that the distinctiveness of Welsh culture needs to be judged, for it is this contrast with the English culture that gives the Welsh and their culture their dynamism. This arises from an awareness of its separate identity and of the need to buttress it in the face of strong, all-pervading competition from England, in particular, and the English-speaking world.

It is this awareness of the threat that exists to the Welsh culture that has inspired the foundation of most nationalistic organizations in Welsh life today. It is an awareness that has grown amongst the people of Wales as the question has continued to be discussed, and as fewer and fewer areas remain immune to the expanded activities of the communications network that centres on London, the Midlands, and Merseyside. Welsh nationalism is in many ways a reaction against the forces of industrialization, modernization, and centralization that have swept through Europe. The nationalists are trying to defend the *status quo*, even if they cannot put the clock back.

The forces which challenge the hold of the Welsh culture on Wales do so mostly by accident. It is, however, their effects rather than their origins which the people have to live with. These forces are commonly known as forces of 'anglicization', and it is this term which will be used below, even though it is not fully descriptive of the processes at work.

The Forces of Anglicization

The anglicization of Wales dates at least from the conquest of Wales by Edward I in 1282–4. Some Welshmen today regard the terms of the Act of Union of 1536, which *inter alia* outlawed the use of the Welsh language in official business, as the most important manifestation of the anglicizing trend in Wales. The instructions of the Act of Union directly affected only a small proportion of the population of Wales, those who held or sought property or position, but it established an opinion which became a social norm—that the Welsh language was an inferior form of speech and that it deserved to carry a social stigma. The tragedy, from the point of view of the Welsh language, was that this view became widespread in Wales itself and that it still exists today. But the Welsh people must bear as much responsibility for this as Henry VIII. The Tudor Acts of Union were equally crucial to the centralizing of the administration of Wales under the Crown.[1]

The most important period of anglicization in Wales was the late nineteenth century which brought about the vast industrial expansion of South Wales and the accompanying immigration into Wales of thousands of English people.[2] This period also saw the beginning of compulsory education in Wales, one which did not have a place for the Welsh language. The consequences of the industrial revolution at this time are still working themselves out today. Integration with the English economy has been strengthened, and the early boom in coal has been followed by a swift decline in the years since 1945.

Economic integration has been the most important single anglicizing force in Wales. The language of industry, commerce, and administration has been almost exclusively English. A knowledge of the Welsh language has until recently yielded no economic rewards except in the field of education. The result has been that a large majority of the Welsh people have come to believe that their own language serves no useful purpose other than communication within their own country where English is just as, if not more, efficacious. This has had the effect over time of stunting the development of the Welsh language. Whole areas of human experience and knowledge have eluded the language, so that it is very difficult to think about these subjects in the Welsh language. Most of the biological and

---

[1] G. R. Elton, *England Under The Tudors* (London, 1955).
[2] B. Thomas, 'Wales and the Atlantic Economy', in B. Thomas (ed.), *The Welsh Economy*.

natural sciences, the law, mathematics and applied sciences, and social science are all areas where little development in the language has occurred in the last five centuries, except in the last decade. Welsh words for use in public administration, now that the era of bilingual forms has been inaugurated, have had to be specially invented in many cases, and come strangely even to Welsh-speakers.[1]

The natural language of administration throughout Wales is still English. The English language also has its attractions from the cultural point of view, and few of the Welsh would wish to be without it. English offers them the key to an international corpus of knowledge and culture in which hundreds of millions of people in the world share. The Welsh language which, according to the 1961 Census, is understood by about 650,000 people and read by many fewer than that, cannot begin to compete. But the cultural domination of the English language in Wales over the last century was substantially the result of Welsh parents wishing to see their children fluent in the English language as a means of economic and social improvement. This largely explains how the advent of compulsory education after 1870 found no place for instruction in the native language of Wales. Few people at the turn of the century foresaw the erosion of the language and its supporting agencies.

Such a situation would never have arisen but for the proximity of England and Wales, and it is this fact of geography which many Welsh nationalists find difficult to accept. The proximity of England has brought the Welsh language very near to death, and has enabled substantial emigration from Wales to England to take place. England is at most but a few hours away at the end of a road or a railway line. Equally the nearness of Wales to most of England, and the long border which these two countries share, has encouraged major transfers of both capital and labour between the two countries. This is now a regular feature of Welsh life. An index of the extent of English permeation of Wales is given by the figures in recent censuses of the number of people living in Wales who were born in England. One in five of the population of Wales in 1966 was born outside Wales: one in seven was born in England. The proportion of English-born people in North and mid-Wales is well over one in five of the population. Not all of these people come to Wales to retire or to marry. A large number come to Wales to work for a period with an

---

[1] The University of Wales has published booklets which provide Welsh equivalents for English specialist and technical terms, particularly in the sciences.

English-based company with branch-factories in Wales. Similarly, Welsh employees employed by the same firms leave Wales to work in English factories and offices. This is often where the road to promotion within British-based firms leads.

This is even more marked in the professions. Senior positions in teaching, the law, medicine, or the civil service are most commonly found on the London–Liverpool axis. The advantage to talented people in Wales of attachment to a career structure whose apex is in London rather than Cardiff is that they can expect a wider choice of challenging jobs and a better salary. If this is a tempting prospect, or if a Welshman cannot find in Wales a job for which he is qualified, then he becomes part of a British-oriented organization, be it private industry, the professions, or a government department. In most cases, a loyalty to these British-oriented bodies is confirmed and a taste for the English way of life is developed. The élite of Wales, in politics, industry, or the professions, looks to London, even if it does not live there. That is inevitable while London remains the administrative and commercial capital of England and Wales.

Alongside the economic development of Britain, and of Wales in particular, has occurred the increasing urbanization of the population. In Wales, rural depopulation has taxed the community since the middle of the nineteenth century. As the land has become unable to support a growing population, the sons and daughters of farmers have been and still are forced to seek work in the growing conurbations of England and Wales. This process has meant an increasing struggle for survival among the scattered settlements of rural Wales where the community has been deprived of the activity of the young and the highly educated in its affairs. The Welsh migrants to the cities in Wales (mainly Swansea and Cardiff) have found there a largely non Welsh-speaking population with much less attachment to the religious and cultural interests of inner Wales. In the course of their work and new social life these migrants to the towns have found it ever more difficult to sustain the *eisteddfodau* and the Welsh-speaking chapels that were the hallmarks of the communities they once belonged to. Social and economic pressures have tended to make them adopt a more English style of life. The larger the towns grew, the more anglicized they became. Historically, the towns of Wales have always been the centre of anglicizing forces, for reasons of trade and administration.[1] With their

[1] H. Carter and J. G. Thomas, 'Population and Language', in E. G. Bowen (ed.), *Wales* (London, 1957).

rapid expansion in the nineteenth century, this reputation was doubly confirmed by a vast influx of English people, as well as Welsh, in search of work. Table 3.1b shows how the growth of the population of certain Welsh towns has been accompanied by a more than average decline in the number of people in them able to speak Welsh. Where Welsh and English have mixed together in large numbers, as in Merthyr, the Welsh language has been the loser. It is difficult to say how far this fact has been the result of the supposed inability of the language to adapt to industrial circumstances. No such difficulty was found in the mining valleys of south-west Wales, but here the structure of society was similar to the rural communities of Wales, and the influx of population with the expansion of the coal industry was mainly Welsh-speaking. This suggests that urbanization or industrialization as such should not be regarded as an anglicizing force. Rather it is immigration, the growth of certain types of industry and trade employing a mixed labour force, and social pressures which were the anglicizing forces.

Since the middle of the nineteenth century there have been other anglicizing influences at work in Wales. One such is the great improvement in the means of communication between different parts of Britain. The nineteenth century saw the advent of the railway; the twentieth century the motorway. Both have greatly facilitated travel between England and Wales, and recently also within Wales. Not only does this mean that emigration and immigration to and from Wales, as well as tourism, has been encouraged. It also means that Welsh people have had a greater opportunity to explore their own country and to meet their fellow-countrymen as well as English outsiders. This has probably helped to strengthen their loyalty to Wales as an entity as distinct from their local community pride. Not only can distance be covered more quickly, but Welsh people now have the money for such travel.

Nor can the impact of service in the armed forces during two world wars be overlooked. Two generations of young Welshmen have been conscripted and sent abroad in company with other British troops: in the Second World War, Welsh women were frequently directed to work in England. The effect on the attitudes of the Welsh was two-edged; those that liked the world outside Wales often stayed outside Wales when the war ended, and tended to lose their Welsh identity or to sentimentalize it: some of those who did not like the world outside or the English with whom they fought became more nationalist on their return to Wales. Many young servicemen joined *Plaid Cymru* while still in the ranks during the war, even though the *Blaid*'s policy towards the war was one of neutrality. Thus the advantage taken of improved communications in and out of Wales worked for and against anglicization, but more often for than against.

The impact of English culture has also to be faced. The increasing literacy of the people, and their extended education, coupled with the development of the film, radio, television, and the paperback book have offered the Welsh all the riches to be found in English-language arts and culture. These are now in everyday competition with the artistic achievements of Wales in either language, given modern communications and tastes. It is not a situation in which the Welsh or the Welsh-speakers can seriously compete, simply because of the paucity of resources and talent in relation to their English cultural challengers. Welsh-language publishers have great difficulty in selling books in Welsh, despite the younger generation's enthusiasm for the language. Moreover, popular entertainments such as football or the cinema have since the beginning of the twentieth century diverted attention in Wales away from *eisteddfodau* and the activities of the chapels.

The consequences of the introduction of compulsory education in Wales from 1870 without any place being found for the Welsh language have already been referred to. In the early days of state education in Wales, Welsh parents sent their children to school primarily to learn the English language, and thought little of the omission of Welsh from the school curriculum when their children used it so freely at home. A thorough knowledge of English opened up much larger career opportunities for Welsh children. Even the most patriotic Welsh schoolmasters banned the use of Welsh on school premises and punished those who broke this rule, the so-called 'Welsh not'.[1] The position was unchanged when secondary education developed in Wales following the passing of the Intermediate Education Act in 1889. Thus Welsh grammar school pupils did not learn about the Welsh language or literature in their schools, but only about the English language and literature. Similarly, they did not learn about Welsh history in school, only English history. Battles concerning these issues are still fought out in present-day Wales. The impact of such a restricted education can only have been to further the anglicizing trend in Wales by extending Welsh pupils' knowledge

[1] See, for example, James Griffiths, *Pages from Memory* (London, 1969) and Glyn Jones, *The Dragon Has Two Tongues* (London, 1968).

of the world in an English direction and from a largely English viewpoint. The rule of the 'Welsh not' must have greatly buttressed the social stigma attached to use of the Welsh language inaugurated in the Acts of Union. It may also have been the reason why Welsh was not used when government activity and administration was expanded throughout Wales and Britain. The view that the Welsh language is inferior to the English language persists to a degree even in modern Wales, and many Welsh people find it convenient to lose even their accent as they rise in the world.

Countervailing Welsh Forces

Against the anglicizing forces at work in Wales over the last century must be set the forces which have served to preserve or strengthen Welsh identity. These have usually been cultural forces, although they are typically associated with a particular form of organization of society—the scattered rural farming and urban communities of Wales. The major supports of the Welsh culture in the face of anglicization continue to be the Welsh language, organized religion, the Welsh press, and elements in the educational system. New sources of support have developed in the Welsh worlds of education and broadcasting, and in the emergence of particular organizations which set out to foster Welsh consciousness.

TABLE 3.1.a

Welsh-Speaking Population: Percentage of Population aged 3 and over at censuses of 1901, 1931, 1951, and 1961

	Welsh Monoglots (%)				All Welsh Speakers (%)			
	1901	1931	1951	1961	1901	1931	1951	1961
Anglesey	48	24	10	6	92	87	80	76
Brecknock	9	2	1	1	46	37	30	28
Caernarfon	48	21	9	5	90	79	72	68
Cardigan	50	20	7	5	93	87	80	75
Carmarthen	36	9	4	3	90	82	77	75
Denbigh	18	5	2	1	62	49	39	35
Flint	8	1	—	—	49	32	21	19
Glamorgan	7	1	—	—	44	32	20	17
Merioneth	51	22	9	6	94	86	75	76
Monmouth	1	—	—	—	13	6	4	3
Montgomery	16	7	3	1	48	41	35	32
Pembroke	12	4	2	1	34	31	27	24
Radnor	—	—	—	—	6	5	5	5
All Wales	15	4	2	1	50	37	29	26

Sources: Censuses of England and Wales, 1951 and 1961.

Table 3.1.b

*Changes in the Numbers of Welsh Speakers 1901–1961
compared with changes in the total population aged over 3*

		1901	1961
Newport	Total pop.	62,281	102,608
	Welsh sp.	2,270	2,221
	% Welsh sp.	3·6	2·1
Cardiff	Total pop.	151,924	243,246
	Welsh sp.	12,395	11,545
	% Welsh sp.	8·2	4·7
Merthyr	Total pop.	63,681	56,244
	Welsh sp.	36,393	11,169
	% Welsh sp.	57·2	19·9
Rhondda	Total pop.	103,748	95,846
	Welsh sp.	66,744	23,233
	% Welsh sp.	63·4	24·2
Swansea	Total pop.	87,885	159,344
	Welsh sp.	28,428	27,947
	% Welsh sp.	32·4	17·5
Pontardawe R.D.C.	Total pop.	19,206	29,491
	Welsh sp.	17,794	22,483
	% Welsh sp.	93·5	76·2

Sources: Censuses of England and Wales, 1901 and 1961.

The first and most important of these supports is the Welsh language. Welsh has survived as a medium of communication in Wales against heavy odds. Whereas Welsh was the language of many parts of England a thousand years ago, today the language line has retreated into rural and upland Wales. Yet there are still large areas of Wales where the Welsh language is the first and natural language of speech. The 1961 Census found that between 68 per cent and 76 per cent of the population over three years old in the counties of Anglesey, Caernarfon, Merioneth, Cardigan, and Carmarthen were Welsh-speaking. Even Glamorgan revealed 198,960 Welsh-speakers in its population (17·2 per cent of the total).[1] The fact that knowledge of the Welsh language is widespread does not prove that it makes those who use it feel distinctive from non Welsh-speakers or English people. But the language carries with it unique idioms, concepts, and thought-processes as well as the entrée to a cultural tradition and to many social organizations where Welsh-speaking is the norm, not least of which are the chapels.

[1] Census of England and Wales, 1961.

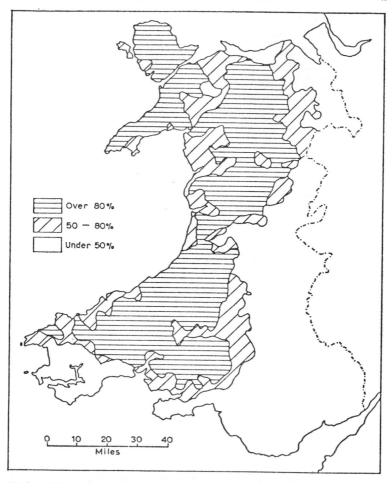

Wales 1961: Percentage of population able to speak Welsh generalized from
Parish data

Reproduced from H. Carter and J. G. Thomas, 'The Referendum on the Sunday
Opening of Licensed Premises in Wales as a criterion of a Culture Region', *Regional
Studies*, vol. 3 (1969).

The survival of the language in the remoter areas of Wales has
depended on many factors—the policy of the schools in the area, the
extent of migration of Welsh-speakers out of, and of non Welsh-
speakers into the community, the language of the principal available
mass media, and the state of the local chapels. However, the most
important single factor which has saved the language is the desire of

Welsh-speaking parents to bring up their own children with a knowledge of Welsh. This requires the use of Welsh in the home, as well as general support from Welsh-speaking communities for a policy of Welsh instruction in the schools. The W.J.E.C. Language Survey 1961 found that there is still considerable 'leakage' where Welsh-speaking parents were concerned.[1] A large minority of children with two Welsh-speaking parents have grown up without learning the language. Where only one parent is Welsh-speaking a large majority of the children do not learn the language, especially if the mother does not speak Welsh. At the same time there was a considerable desire amongst non Welsh-speaking parents throughout Wales that their children should learn the Welsh language through the schools (Table 3.2). This indicates that a sizeable proportion of the Welsh population regard the Welsh language as a thing of value, regardless of whether they can speak it themselves. If such an attitude persists in the community, then there is plenty of scope for local initiatives to try to restore the position of the language in parts of Wales. Success will depend upon the patience and enthusiasm of individual families and of their communities. However, educational research suggests that much of the backing given by Welsh-speaking parents to the Welsh language has to do with the convenience to their children of being able to communicate with the family and the community in the language. The Gittins Report of 1968 found that only 18 per cent of the Welsh-speaking parents in their survey gave participation in literary–cultural activities as a reason for their view that it was an advantage to know the Welsh language.[2] This raises the question of how far an active policy of Welsh instruction in the schools can achieve the perpetuation of the language. Where active policies for a bilingual system of education, especially in the secondary sector, have been proposed they have often met with hostility from sections of the community. There is a reluctance to see Welsh as a compulsory part of the curriculum, even amongst those who wish the language well.[3] Most efforts since the war have concentrated on the policy of the schools towards Welsh, and the policy of Government towards the Welsh language in the administration. This has been encouraged by the passing of the Education Act 1944 and by the Welsh Language Act 1967. But uncertainty as to the efficacy of

---

[1] Welsh Joint Education Committee, *Language Survey* (1961).
[2] *Primary Education in Wales*, p. 236, para. 11.10.10.
[3] Ibid., p. 238, para. 11.10.12–13. Hostility has arisen in the cases of Cardiganshire, Flintshire, Wrexham, and Cardiff parents.

TABLE 3.2

Intergenerational Loss of the Welsh Language, and Parental Support for their Children Learning Welsh

(A) Intergenerational loss of the Welsh language

	Percentage of pupils whose first language is Welsh from homes where		
	Father and Mother speak Welsh	Father alone speaks Welsh	Mother alone speaks Welsh
Wales (1953)	70 (N = 46,406)	6 (N = 1,528)	11 (N = 2,263)
Wales (1961)	73 (N = 39,172)	7 (N = 1,849)	12 (N = 2,730)
Merioneth (1953)	96	19	43
Caernarfon (1953)	91	20	39
Glamorgan (1953)	42	4	7

Sources: The Place of Welsh and English in the Schools of Wales (H.M.S.O., 1953). Welsh Joint Education Committee, *Language Survey 1961*.

(B) Advantages or disadvantages seen by parents in the child learning Welsh, related to the linguistic status of the home

	Mother cannot speak Welsh %	Only Mother speaks Welsh %	Both parents speak Welsh %
Yes, parents saw advantages	46	74	85
No, saw no advantages	52	23	14
Did not know	2	3	1
	N = 913	N = 65	N = 159

Source: Primary Education in Wales, Table 11.10.9b.

(C) Opinions on the teaching of Welsh held by parents of children taught Welsh as a subject in English-medium schools.

Parents saw:	Welsh Wales	Mid Wales	Glam.*	Four County Boroughs*	All
Advantages (%)	67	60	49	45	52
Disadvantages (%)	22	10	7	14	11
	N = 63	N = 100	N = 282	N = 92	N = 537

Source: Primary Education in Wales, Table 11.10.11.

    * The figures for Glamorgan exclude the three County Boroughs of Cardiff, Swansea, and Merthyr. The four County Boroughs referred to in the table comprise the three Glamorgan County Boroughs together with the borough of Newport.

these means in entrenching and extending the language has encouraged official delay and vacillation, particularly when public opinion to specific proposals is divided. The Gittins Report concluded that 'The school is more likely to succeed in teaching Welsh if it is backed by Welsh-speaking in the home and the community, and is unlikely to succeed without this support'.[1]

TABLE 3.3

Denominational Strengths in Wales

	1962–3	1967–8
Church in Wales	170,000	160,000
Presbyterian (Calvinistic Methodists)	137,000	113,000
Independents	111,000	93,000
Baptists	90,000	79,000
Methodists (Wesleyans)	53,000	36,000

Sources: *Baptist Handbook, Congregational Yearbook, Y Blwyddiadur* (Presbyterian Church of Wales), *Methodist Church Yearbook*, the *Western Mail*, The Church in Wales.

The second factor which has helped to preserve the position of the Welsh language in Wales is organized religion. The significance of the translation of the Bible into Welsh in the late sixteenth century has already been underlined. After the Methodists split with the Anglican Church in 1811, Wales developed a quasi-national church, the Calvinistic Methodist (now Presbyterian) Church of Wales. Nonconformity became the dominant Christian persuasion in Wales by the middle of the nineteenth century, even though it was divided. The three main sects were, and still are, the Presbyterians, the Independents (Congregationalists), and the Baptists. After the implementation of the Welsh Church Act in 1920, the disestablished Anglican Church, the Church in Wales, saw its membership rise by a quarter to 260,000 in 1938. The disestablishment controversy proved to be the stimulus to renewal and reform in the Church, which has become distinctly more Welsh in appearance and attitude. However, the ancient antipathies between chapel and church are still real, even if largely traditional phenomena in Wales; the same is true of sectarianism within Welsh nonconformity.

[1] *Primary Education in Wales*, p. 239, para. 11.10.14.

The churches throughout Wales have lost much of their power to lead their communities because of the contraction in public support for them, and the quality of the remaining members' allegiance to the denominations appears to have changed for the worse. Once the individual nonconformist was a member of the priesthood of believers in search of God; his denominational allegiance was a deliberate act of choice founded upon religious conviction. Now the family has taken over as 'the controlling factor in deciding religious affiliation. . . . Sectarianism deteriorated into a matter of belonging to a hereditary in-group with no apparent *raison d'être*'.[1]

The number of members, church buildings, and ministers of all the large nonconformist denominations has fallen since the end of the Second World War. With them has declined the hold on the Welsh population of two traditional standards of social behaviour which were associated with nonconformity—teetotalism and sabbatarianism. Churchmen believe this has been particularly marked since the mid 1950s.[2] The best available index of these attitudes are the results of the two referenda on the question of whether public houses should open on Sundays in Wales, held in the winters of 1961 and of 1968. The proportion of those voting for a 'dry' Sunday fell between 1961 and 1968 in every county and county borough where a vote was taken, and by an average 12 per cent of those voting in each voting area: turnout for the poll dropped on average by 13 per cent in each voting area. Yet the numbers of those voting 'wet' rose in ten of the sixteen areas voting in 1968, and in every county that voted 'dry' in 1961. The variation in the voting patterns of the counties and county boroughs correlates strongly with the relative hold of the nonconformist churches and the Welsh language on the population. It was in these areas that turnout was also highest in the poll, excepting Radnorshire (see Table 3.4).[3]

The hold of the churches and chapels over the Welsh people is nevertheless still considerable. A majority for the closing of pubs on Sundays was still found in five counties (Anglesey, Caernarfon, Merioneth, Cardigan, and Carmarthen) in November 1968. A survey by the Gallup Poll in January 1968 found that 55 per cent of their

[1] T. M. Owen, 'Chapel and Community in Glan-llyn, Merioneth', in E. Davies and A. D. Rees (eds.), *Welsh Rural Communities* (Cardiff, 1960), pp. 200–1.

[2] Private interviews with Revd. T. Ll. Evans, Revd. Dr. R. T. Jones, Revd. D. Evans, and Professor I. Foster.

[3] H. Carter and J. O. Thomas, 'The Referendum on the Sunday Opening of Licensed Premises in Wales as a Criterion of a Culture Region', in *Regional Studies*, vol. 3, pp. 61–71.

interviewees claimed to go to church or chapel once a month or more,[1] while another survey taken in September 1968 found more than 90 per cent of respondents answering to Christian faith.[2] Even if these findings over-estimate the strength of Christianity in Wales they show that an impressive amount of goodwill exists towards the churches. It has been suggested that more than half the adult Welsh-speaking population are regular members of churches or chapels.[3]

TABLE 3.4

Sunday Closing of Public Houses: Referenda of 1961 and 1968

County or County Borough	Percentage of electorate voting for Sunday closing		% of population of 15 yrs. and over, Welsh speaking (1961)	
	1961	1968		
Merioneth	50	40	76	
Cardigan	46	35	75	
Anglesey	43	28	77	
Caernarfon	42	31	68	
Carmarthen	40	27	78	1968 Dry Frontier
Montgomery	33	21	34	
Denbigh	28	19	37	
Pembroke	27	20	26	1961 Dry Frontier
Brecknock	25	12	30	
Radnor	23	12	5	
Flintshire	18	7	21	
Swansea CB	17	6	20	
Merthyr CB	17	5½	23	
Glamorgan	17	6	25	
Newport CB	13	*	2	
Monmouthshire	12	3½	5	
Cardiff	10	4	6	

* No vote was taken in Newport in 1968.

The individualistic outlook of Welsh nonconformity, and its ideals of religious and political equality and liberty, mean that liberalism is still the dominant social and political philosophy where non-conformity's hold is still substantial. This may help to explain why the Conservative Party has found it so difficult to establish itself in rural Wales, and why the Labour Party in rural Wales has mirrored

[1] Gallup Poll CS 8433.
[2] Opinion Research Centre, Poll No. 228.
[3] Council for Wales and Monmouthshire, *The Welsh Language Today* (H.M.S.O., 1963). Cmnd. 2198, and Pennar Davies *et al.*, *The Christian Value of the Welsh Language* (Swansea, undated, 1960s).

the style and pattern of leadership exercised by the Liberals when they dominated these areas. There is a large overlap in industrial and rural Wales between those who are active in religious life and those who are leaders in other associational life in their communities, including the political.[1] It is still the tradition in many parts of Wales for the minister and the schoolmaster, often the only highly educated persons in small depopulated communities, to give a lead in the social activities of those communities. This is especially true and natural where social life still revolves to some extent around the chapels.[2]

In general, however, theological differences and religious observance in Wales have declined, much more than the figures for membership of the churches would suggest. The Church in Wales is least strong in west Wales. The Welsh Baptists are strongest in Pembrokeshire, Carmarthen, and Glamorgan. The Presbyterians draw their main strength from the counties of Anglesey, Caernarfon, Merioneth, Montgomery, and Cardigan. Support for the Independents is more widely distributed but strongest in Carmarthenshire. These differences are largely historical, and the theological implications of such divisions, in terms of differing social attitudes, do not appear to have much force outside the leadership of these churches. In a limited way, however, churches have tried to use their influence on such issues as the use of the Welsh language in schools, depopulation, home rule, and pre-eminently over the question of Sunday closing. The Independents and the Baptists were most well-disposed to home rule in the 1960s.

The decline of organized religion is universal throughout the Western world: the demand for a personal relationship between God and individuals in the world is much less pronounced than a hundred years ago, and the Christian ethic and church organizations are being challenged. In this respect Wales displays a normal tendency. However, other factors affecting Wales need also to be considered. One is the impact of the growth of specialist voluntary organizations in rural as well as industrial Wales. It is argued that the advent of bodies such as the Women's Institute and youth associations such as the Young Farmers' Clubs and *Urdd Gobaith Cymru* have cut across the traditional forms of organized community activity, the family group and the chapel congregation. The specialist interests of these new

[1] See, for example, T. Brennan, E. W. Cooney, and H. Pollins, *Social Change in South-West Wales* (London, 1954), pp. 111–45.
[2] T. M. Owen, op. cit., pp. 183–248.

organizations have also been secular 'in contrast to the formal activities which have hitherto been mostly centred on the chapel'.[1] Thus the churches have not been able to check or to respond to the increasingly secular orientation of their congregations, and interests within the congregations have diverged.

The churches are more ready to accept the criticism that they have not been willing, in general, to grasp social issues and make them their own. Yet in Wales the churches have always been strongly identified with Sunday closing, an image prolonged by the Licensing Act 1961 which provided for septennial referenda on this question. The 1968 referendum saw the churches very much divided on the issue, and only the Presbyterians gave a clear recommendation to safeguard the remaining 'dry' areas. The principal reason advanced for Sunday closing was still the Sabbatarian argument, the need to set apart Sunday from the rest of the week as the day for paying respect to God. As such, the argument has had a declining appeal. But Sabbatarianism remains a strongly held form of social behaviour even among those who do not profess Christian beliefs. In the 1960s sabbatarianism had come to be accepted by some who are nationalistically-minded as a way of emphasizing the difference between Wales and England. *Plaid Cymru* has not, however, given a firm lead on the issue, although its President, Gwynfor Evans, is a total abstainer and campaigned to keep the pubs closed on Sundays in Carmarthenshire both in 1961 and 1968.

Sabbatarianism characterizes another impression of the churches in Wales, that of the preservers of traditional patterns of behaviour and of the old way of life. Increasingly, the chapels seem to regard changes in the environment of the community they serve as direct threats to their own existence. Thus ministers often adopt a nationalist position, failing to find ways of extending their influence beyond a traditional and declining form of society. The danger is that their appeal will be to an increasingly small section of society in Wales—the Welsh-speakers who are not yet living in large conurbations.

In their attempts to reclaim the sector of the Welsh population lost to Christian influence, the churches have almost without exception become more political and politicized but often only at a national and area level. This reflects a division between the leadership, especially the ministers, and the rank-and-file membership of the

[1] T. M. Owen, op. cit., pp. 206–18.

churches. Two aspects of politics in which they have shown special interest are education through the medium of the Welsh language, and nationalism. Many church leaders seem to see these issues as ones which give them an opening into the minds of young people, so helping to re-establish the position of the Church in the community. These are, however, important issues which have severely divided the community. The churches may therefore feel justified in trying to relate these issues to the Christian message. Individual ministers, however, reach widely differing conclusions about the nature of the lead they should give. A feature of Investiture year in Wales was the way in which ministers were called to account by their congregations for their nationalist views, and for bringing politics into the pulpit.[1]

In showing their interest in the development of Welsh-medium nursery, primary, and secondary schools in anglicized and in largely Welsh-speaking areas, Welsh ministers and clergy have been anxious to arrest a decline in moral, religious, and cultural standards in their communities. When so many of the churches still conduct their services through the medium of the Welsh language, the steep decline in the number of children able to speak or understand that language is naturally a cause of immediate concern. The thinking behind the churches' support for the language and its extended use in the schools of Wales is that it is a part of the Welsh culture that deserves to be protected for its own intrinsic value, and that it is the key to a unique kind of religious experience transmitted through the medium of the Welsh language. A large number of the chapels in Wales, perhaps even a majority, still use Welsh as the principal medium of communication, even though only a quarter of the entire population claimed ability to speak Welsh in the 1961 Census. Church leaders in the late 1960s commented on the fact that an expansion in the knowledge of Welsh amongst the young in their congregations had boosted morale in the chapels and attendance at church services and Sunday schools.[2]

The other area of politics in which the churches seem to take a special interest is nationalism. It is a natural development in that the nationalist issue has been widely discussed in Wales, and it cuts across class ties in the community. In this sense the churches have felt

---

[1] One example from Bridgend was reported in the *Western Mail*, 6 Sept. 1969. Other examples have been cited to me from Caernarfonshire, Carmarthenshire, and Montgomery.

[2] This was claimed, for example, by Professor Stephen J. Williams, *Western Mail*, 12 June 1969.

sufficiently united to try to give the public a lead on this question. Two specific issues within this interest in nationalism have been subject to the attention of the church leaders—the issue of a Parliament for Wales (and the related debate about devolution), and the attitude of the churches towards the Investiture of the Prince of Wales in 1969.

The Investiture posed a specific problem to all major churches in Wales, because each one was invited to be represented at the ceremony in Caernarfon. The churches had to make a decision to send representatives, and thus questions of principle involving the legitimacy of the event and of the Prince of Wales were sometimes raised. The Union of Welsh Independents decided as a body not to send representatives to the Investiture. The Presbyterian Church decided by only a small majority to send representatives. All the other major churches were represented at the ceremony. This is an interesting gauge of the degree to which church leaders in Wales have been subject to nationalist thinking. At a more local level this hostility towards the Investiture was reflected in the refusal of certain ministers or area councils to co-operate in the organization of events for *Croeso* 69 year, which promoted tourism and the Investiture in Wales.[1]

Nonconformist churches have a long record of support for Welsh home rule, although the issue had not been widely discussed after 1945 until the late 1960s. The Parliament for Wales Campaign, in the first half of the 1950s, had found the churches favourable, but until the late 1960s the churches inclined not to address themselves to political issues. More recently the Presbyterian Church and the Independents have become more willing to pronounce on political issues. In 1968 the Union of Welsh Independents, the Welsh Baptist Union, and the North Wales Presbyterians all carried motions supporting home rule for Wales. The attitude of the Church in Wales was even more forthright in the latter half of the 1960s. The Bishops of Bangor and of St. Davids both declared support for Welsh home rule, and the Archbishop of Wales made three major interventions in the political debate between September 1968 and June 1969. On the question of the language, the Archbishop, Dr. Glyn Simon, supported the extension of bilingualism at official levels, and warned

---

[1] See, for example, *Liverpool Daily Post*, 25 Jan. 1968, which reported that the Arfon Presbytery had voted not to send delegates to the committee drawing up a programme of Investiture celebrations at Caernarfon.

of the dangers of a kind of apartheid developing in Wales based not on race, but on language. He was also moved to comment in a letter to the *Western Mail* on the heavy fining of Welshmen for disfiguring English monolingual road-signs. 'It would be a pity if unreasonable and stupid official attitudes to reasonable demands should seem to encourage the violence we all deplore', he noted. On the more general question of the rise of nationalism in Wales, Dr. Simon enthusiastically supported a nationalism that was 'sanctified, disciplined, and purified' and he urged the City of Cardiff always to support 'an enlightened Welsh nationalism, a nationalism that sincerely believes that Wales has a part to play in the Councils of the world, and in the destinies of these islands, and that she will not play this part as she ought without the preservation of the spiritual and cultural values enshrined in an ancient language, which is proving itself more and more capable of a lasting vitality in a new and threateningly monochrome world'.[1] The spirit of such remarks is not confined to the leaders of the Church in Wales only, but is reflected in the debate inside the Church at lower levels. As such it shows how far the Church has moved from its position at the start of the twentieth century when it was generally regarded as the 'alien church'—an image that still persists in modern Wales.

The educational system is increasingly becoming a force in Wales for buttressing the position of the Welsh language and culture. This has always been the intention of the Welsh Department of the Ministry of Education set up in 1907: but it is an intention that has proved slow and difficult to realize through the schools and local authorities. The position has improved considerably since the 1944 Education Act and since the decision of Glamorgan and Flintshire, two of the largest education authorities in predominantly anglicized areas, to operate a policy at primary school level under which children in primary schools would normally be taught Welsh. The Gittins Report in 1968 disclosed that 'only three local education authorities have no bilingual policy and these are in anglicized areas where the decline of Welsh has been most marked. . . . About half the education authorities have introduced, or are beginning to introduce, the teaching of Welsh as a second language at the age of 5.'[2] This policy is not common in the secondary schools, and where it is possible to continue with Welsh and Welsh-language instruction

[1] Glyn Simon, *A Citizen of No Mean City* (Llandybie, 1969), p. 12.
[2] *Primary Education in Wales*, p. 214, para. 11.4.1.

right through the school system, as in Flintshire, there is a high fall-off rate in the numbers wishing to study through the language at secondary school level.[1] The Gittins Report itself found that 66 per cent of Welsh-speaking parents and 90 per cent of English-monoglot parents did not wish their children to be taught through the medium of Welsh at the secondary stage.[2]

The effectiveness of all the attention given by Welsh local education authorities to the use of Welsh in the schools is not as great as might at first appear. The growth of the Welsh Schools movement points to the failure of the mainstream maintained schools to fulfil their promise. The Gittins Report noted that 'practice in the schools has not always followed precept and . . . official policy itself has not always been unequivocal or given precise, practical guidance about the approaches to be adopted in furthering a bilingual education, nor have education authorities always been whole-hearted about accepting such developments as the Welsh School'.[3]

TABLE 3.5

The Growth of Ysgolion Cymraeg *in Wales*

	No. of Ysg. Cym.	No. of pupils
1951*	15	996
1965†	39	3,000
1968‡	57	6,478

* *The Place of Welsh and English in the Schools of Wales*, H.M.S.O. (1953), p. 35.
† *Primary Education in Wales*, H.M.S.O. (1968), p. 221.
‡ Figures supplied by Undeb Cenedlaethol Athrawon Cymru in 1968, including *adrannau* (departments) in English schools.

A more detailed treatment of the Welsh Schools movement will be given in Chapter 9. In twenty years it has succeeded in establishing nearly sixty schools, mainly in anglicized parts of Wales, and has attempted to provide an education for the pupils of these schools that does full justice to the Welsh language and culture. It has operated at primary, and pre-primary level sometimes with the help of the local education authorities. Even so in 1968 only 6,478 pupils were estimated to be attending *Ysgolion Cymraeg* out

[1] Figures supplied by the Director of Education for Flintshire suggest that at the last count there were 4,124 pupils in the first and second years at county secondary schools taking second language Welsh courses, as compared with 813 in the third year. For many pupils Welsh is a compulsory subject for the first two years of secondary education.
[2] *Primary Education in Wales*, p. 238, para. 11.10.12.
[3] Ibid., p. 210, para. 11.1.

of a total primary school population in Wales of over 250,000.[1] The Welsh Schools affect a small section of the new generation in Wales, and they are fighting against generations of prejudice and neglect in this field. Few secondary schools carry on their work after the primary stage; in 1970 there were six such Welsh secondary schools (all bilingual) at Rhyl, Mold, Wrexham, Pontypridd, Ystalyfera, and Llanelli.[2]

The provision of further education in Wales on a national basis was one of the first developments following the intervention of the state into education in 1870. The University of Wales received its charter in 1893 as a result of nationalist as well as educational pressures, and has retained a strong sense of responsibility for the needs of Wales. Certain departments in the Welsh University Colleges have a nationalist outlook, particularly some Welsh and Education departments. The Constitution of the University of Wales allows political pressures from the community which the University serves to influence the policy of the University.[3] It was the Court of the University that gave the final rebuff to those inside the University who wished to defederalize the constituent colleges of the University. It was through the Court of Governors of the University College at Aberystwyth that the initiative was made to extend instruction in the University through the medium of the Welsh language in 1968–9, and which necessitated further appointments in the University reserved for Welsh-speakers. There is a potent pressure group of nationalists, many of them prominent members of *Plaid Cymru*, in the Court of the University which has had to be reckoned with. There is also a lobby within the University that regards special treatment for the Welsh language in the instruction and syllabuses of the University Colleges as a threat to the academic standards and the international standing of the University as a whole. This conflict of perspective in the University arises mainly from the fact that the University recruits a high proportion of its staff from outside Wales, who stay a few years at a Welsh college, do not think in terms of a career inside the one University, and may not be sensitive to the history and tradition of the institutions to which they belong.

[1] No account has been taken in these figures for schools in Welsh-speaking areas which teach Welsh as the first language, since no figures or estimates are available.

[2] Letter from Miss O. Arnold (2 July 1970), Department of Education and Science, Education Office for Wales, Cardiff.

[3] The composition of the Court of the University, for example, includes a majority of representatives of local authorities.

The anglicization of the University of Wales has not gone unnoticed amongst staff, students, or nationalists, and has become an
occasional issue that has cut across, and sometimes obscured, more
general staff–student conflicts of opinion and interest. The decision
of the Council of the University College of Wales at Aberystwyth
to set up a hostel reserved for Welsh students in 1968 was a recent
and telling example of this cleavage along nationalist lines. But if the
staff of the University of Wales has become anglicized, so have the
students. In the session 1968–9 no constituent college of the University of Wales had half of its students coming from Wales. The over-all
figure for 1968 for the University was about 40 per cent coming from
Wales. This reflects the fact that a majority of students from Wales
prefer to study outside Wales when it comes to choosing a university, while many students from the rest of Britain and overseas are
willing to come to Wales to study. As the University of Wales has
expanded, so the proportion of students of Welsh origin in the
University has declined, as has the number of Welsh-speakers and the
proportion, often relatively *and* in absolute numbers, willing to study
the Welsh language (see Table 3.6). As far as individual colleges are
concerned, the traditionally Welsh colleges at Bangor and Aberystwyth have both been subject to this trend. Whereas more than 90 per

TABLE 3.6

The Anglicization of the University of Wales: the Proportion of
Full-time Students from Welsh homes at the University of Wales
1938–1968 (%)

College	1938–9	1948–9	1958–9	1963–4	1968–9
Aberystwyth	93	82	72	55	44
Bangor	91	69	49	34	24
Swansea	100	91	74	57	42
Cardiff	96	83	76	54	40
Whole Univ. of Wales	95	80	71	50	39
Total number of full-time students	N = 2,606	N = 4,575	N = 5,681	N = 8,094	N = 12,184

Sources: Report of the sub-committee of the College Council of the University
College of North Wales, Bangor, 26 Mar. 1965, Appendix B. *Liverpool Daily
Post*, 23 Dec. 1969, *Yr Haul a'r Gangell, Rhif* XLIV, *Gaeaf* 1970.

Note. The proportion of full-time students from Welsh homes attending courses
at the University of Wales was stated to have risen to 44 per cent in the academic
year 1970–1.

cent of Bangor's intake before the First World War was from Wales, Welsh students now account for less than 20 per cent and Welsh speakers for less than 10 per cent of the intake. At Aberystwyth, the University College recruited 90 per cent of its students from Wales in the late 1930s; in 1970 only 41 per cent of its new students came from Wales, 10 per cent being Welsh-speaking.[1]

Another feature of higher education in Wales is the surplus of trained teachers emerging from Welsh training colleges. This is no new social phenomenon in Wales. In 1927 the Departmental Committee on Welsh in the Educational System of Wales revealed that 175 of the students leaving Bangor Normal College in the years 1923–5 had found employment in England, while 168 had taken up appointments in Wales over the same period.[2] In 1968, 106 of the new graduates from the same college took up posts in England, compared with 86 who found vacancies at Welsh schools. One quarter of those who were trained in the medium of Welsh left college to take positions in England. The Gittins Report estimate that 'between one third and one half of the students leaving Welsh secondary schools go to colleges of education in England for their teacher training. We have no evidence to suggest that these teachers are likely to return to posts in Wales, but it does appear that slightly more than half the students trained in Wales in any given year take up posts in England, so that Wales produces many more teachers than it can absorb in any given year.' These calculations suggest that Wales exports to England 1,000 newly trained teachers every year.[3] The Gittins Report found that 40 per cent of their sample of Welsh teacher trainees did not apply at all for a post in Wales. As for the Welsh-speakers in this sample, only 52 per cent found first posts in Wales compared with the 77 per cent who wanted such a post. The anxiety surrounding the quest for teaching appointments was probably a contributory factor to the success of nationalism in the teacher-training colleges in the 1960s.[4] The fact that the Department of Education's quota system forced a certain number of trained teachers out of Wales deliberately every year could be blamed on the London government. The disposition to enter the teaching profession is a strongly Welsh characteristic, and

[1] *Western Mail*, 30 Nov. 1970.
[2] *Welsh in Education and Life*, p. 119.
[3] *Primary Education in Wales*, p. 483, para. 27.3.1.
[4] See I. Carter, 'An Analysis of Support for *Plaid Cymru* as a Test of Class Theories of Voting Behaviour in Great Britain' (unpublished M.A. Thesis, University of Essex, 1968).

can be traced partly to a desire amongst the academically accomplished in the remoter areas of Wales to acquire status and to escape from their closed communities. This is reflected in the heavy representation of Welsh-speakers in the teacher-training colleges—about 40 per cent of students coming from Wales, and among teachers in Wales.[1]

The three major education reports, published in 1927, 1953, and 1968 (The Gittins Report), have each been remarkable documents which have influenced informed opinion. Each has tried to advance the position of the Welsh language and the Welsh cultural heritage in the schools, and each has been accepted by the government of the day. The Gittins Report was accepted very quickly by all four major political parties in Wales, and has only met with criticism from some of the teaching profession and the Welsh area of the National Union of Students. This is a considerable achievement in view of the radical nature of the Report's proposals for a strictly bilingual primary education for every Welsh child, and in view of its criticisms of Welsh teaching practice in the schools. It remains to be seen how successfully the government can persuade local authorities in Wales to change their policies.[2]

The quality and quantity of the Welsh-medium mass communications system has also been an important determinant in the development of modern Welsh culture. The recent history of the expansion of Welsh-language broadcasting has been offset by the decline of the Welsh-language press and the stagnation of the market for Welsh-language books. In none of these areas, however, does the Welsh communications network compete with the range or quantity or penetration of the cultural products of the English market and communications networks. Nevertheless, there have been significant developments on the Welsh side which merit a brief review.

About three-quarters of the Welsh-speaking population in Wales do not read a Welsh-language newspaper or periodical regularly.[3] The remaining quarter of the Welsh-language publications market finds a selection of reading material in Welsh that falls into four categories—newspapers, religious journals, literary journals, and children's publications. There were seven Welsh-language newspapers being published in Wales in 1969, all of them weekly, and none of

---

[1] One recent estimate was that as many as 70 per cent of the teaching profession in Wales was Welsh-speaking. (*The Times*, 23 Nov. 1970.)

[2] Department of Education and Science Circular, 2/69.

[3] *Western Mail*—O.R.C. survey published in Sept. 1968.

them with a circulation of more than 10,000. Of these only *Y Faner* and *Y Cymro* attempt a general distribution throughout Wales. The market seems able to stand fewer newspapers. Four weeklies have closed since 1945, the most recent closure being that of *Y Clorianydd* in May 1969 when it still claimed a circulation of between 4,000 and 5,000. The total circulations of the remaining weeklies amount to less than 35,000 copies in all, but each of these papers claimed that circulation was rising in 1969.[1] In addition, a new political and literary journal named *Barn* started monthly publication in 1962 and within seven years has become part of the established world of Welsh letters, with a claimed circulation of 3,500 in 1969. In political standpoint, these Welsh-language newspapers are not uniform. *Y Faner* and *Barn* have been consistently nationalist in recent years, *Y Cymro* remains independent, and *Yr Herald* liberal in attitude. All the papers have given considerable coverage to the issues raised by Welsh nationalism, and only *Yr Herald* has been consistently critical of *Plaid Cymru*.

TABLE 3.7

*Circulations of Principal Welsh-Language
Current Affairs Journals in 1969*

(A) Weeklies: copies per issue sold

Y Cymro (Oswestry)	10,000
Y Faner (Denbigh)	7,000
Yr Herald Gymraeg \\ *Yr Herald Mon* } (Caernarfon)	9,000 to 10,000
Y Seren \\ *Y Cyfnod* } (Bala)	6,000
Y Dydd (Dolgellau)	2,000
Y Clorianydd (Anglesey—Closed May 1969)	4,000 to 5,000

(B) Monthlies: copies per issue sold

Barn	3,500
Y Ddraig Goch	4,000

Sources: The Western Mail, 21 Aug. 1969. Plaid Cymru.

The other sections of the Welsh press are more influential, but reach a much smaller section of Welsh-speaking opinion. There are the literary journals such as *Y Llenor* and *Y Genhinen*, and denominational papers such as *Y Llan* (Anglican), *Y Tyst* (Independent), *Y Goleuad* (Presbyterian), *Seren Cymru* (Baptist), and *Yr Ymofynydd* (Unitarian). All of these do carry occasional articles on social and

[1] *Western Mail*, 21 Aug. 1969.

nationalist issues. In addition there is the field of the children's market which is almost entirely covered by publications of *Urdd Gobaith Cymru*. Since the mid 1960s their five publications have had a combined circulation of between forty and forty-five thousand, a figure that has not varied substantially in the last twenty years but which has been rising recently.[1] Politics is only occasionally mentioned in a general, and often historical and nationalist, context, in some of these magazines. Most of these publications are distributed through the schools, and the monthly *Bore Da* sells 18,000 copies per issue largely because of L.E.A. subscriptions. This makes *Bore Da* the most widely read Welsh-language periodical, a telling commentary on the state of the Welsh-language press in modern Wales.

Apart from these categories, there are two other Welsh-language publications that deserve attention. One is *Y Ddraig Goch*, the Welsh-language organ of *Plaid Cymru*, which has a monthly print order of four thousand; this circulation has remained strangely unchanged for thirty years.[2] The other is a Welsh pop magazine, *Asbri*, which was founded in May 1969 and appears monthly; this parallels the growth of the market in Welsh-language 'pop' records since 1966.

The Welsh-language press forms, however, a very small part of the newspaper and periodical market in Wales. Most of the local press in Wales is printed in English, as is the only daily paper with a national Welsh coverage. The *Western Mail* is published in Cardiff and had a virtually unchanged circulation of 100,000 and readership of over 400,000 in the 1960s. It has remained a newspaper with a Conservative bias, although it gave greater attention and more sympathetic treatment to nationalist questions in the 1960s. Nevertheless many Welshmen feel that the *Western Mail* is an inadequate spokesman for Welsh opinion, which is normally more radical. This may help to explain why the *Western Mail* sells half its circulation to the upper third of Welsh society. The London dailies dominate the Welsh market with a combined readership of approximately 2,300,000; the *Western Mail* and the Welsh edition of the *Liverpool Daily Post* muster an estimated daily readership of 550,000. The importance of this pattern of readership lies in the extent to which Welsh people in general and sections of Welsh society in particular are exposed to information about Wales and Welsh life. Before the

[1] Annual Reports of *Urdd Gobaith Cymru*, 1945–69. Interview with J. Cyril Hughes, 29 Sept. 1969.

[2] The circulation of *Y Ddraig Goch* seems to have been smaller in the period 1966–70 than it was in 1938.

TABLE 3.8

Percentage of Adult Population Reading Morning Newspapers in Wales in 1961

	All Wales	Social Grade				Age		
		AB	C1	C2	DE	16/24	25/44	45/64
Regional Mornings								
Western Mail	21	38	30	17	13	19	20	23
Liverpool D. Post	7	8	10	7	5	5	8	7
National Mornings								
Daily Mirror	38	13	27	45	44	47	44	34
Daily Express	28	34	32	27	23	28	28	30
Daily Herald	18	4	9	21	24	18	17	21
Daily Mail	15	28	22	12	11	15	14	16
Daily Sketch	8	6	6	10	8	12	7	8
Daily Telegraph	4	20	8	1	1	2	4	5
The Times	1	6	3	..	..	2	1	1
The Guardian	1	5	2	..	..	1	2	1
Financial Times	1	6	2	..	..	1	2	1

Source: *Readership Survey of Wales*, Thomson Newspapers (1961).

large extension of television coverage of Wales in 1963–4 with its consequent expansion of news reporting and documentaries from Wales, forty per cent of the Welsh bourgeoisie and intelligentsia had regular access to detailed Welsh reporting, but only twenty per cent of the working-class sections of society were so exposed. This suggests that television has made national awareness in Wales again a common perspective for the non Welsh-speaking majority, and this may be one of the underlying factors that has allowed nationalism and *Plaid Cymru* a relative success in the latter part of the 1960s. It certainly helps to explain why nationalism tended to be an ideology in Wales that was confined to an intellectual élite. There used to be no mass communications medium that was able to develop nationalism from a non-intellectual perspective in Wales.

The Welsh books market might conceivably have provided a counterweight to the enormous dominance of English cultural products in the Welsh market for publications. There are a score of organizations in the Welsh books field, with three firms based on Llandybie, Llandysul, and Denbigh dominating the market. In 1967 one hundred and fifty-seven titles were the product of the industry, with children's books, religious subjects, and poetry accounting for more than half of these. The total value of sales in this market trebled between 1966 and 1968, but was still only £60,000 in the latter year.[1] There are very few large outlets for these books, and it is with difficulty that 2,000 copies of any book are sold. The main source of support for the Welsh book trade comes from the Welsh Arts Council which provides a grant of £20,000 to the industry. The Government gives £7,500 annually to the University of Wales Press Board, and the Welsh Books Council provides grants to authors.[2] Independent television in Wales has given grants to both the newspaper and book trade in Wales, but Harlech Television were forced to withdraw grants to the value of £7,500 for books and papers in Welsh in August 1969, as an economy measure. This placed the newspaper *Y Faner* and the periodical *Barn* in immediate difficulties, and may have had a more gradual restricting effect on the book publishers. It is pertinent to note that these changes are relatively tiny when contrasted with the progress of the market in English-language and English-produced books. The Welsh market is small and specialized, and almost no market has yet been found for paperbacks. Few books for the general reader are ever published. It is hard not to conclude that the Welsh book trade in its present structure is too confined in appeal to exercise any general positive cultural effect or to be the instrument of general cultural change in Wales. It is run by and for the intelligent Welsh-oriented bourgeoisie.

The more artistic elements in Welsh culture have flourished by any standards in recent years. Welsh singers dominated the British operatic scene in the 1960s, and also made an important contribution to the world 'pop' scene. Musical composition has also been prolific from Wales. The Llangollen International *Eisteddfod* (founded in 1947) has become an important and regular event in Wales. On the literary side, there has been a strange paradox in recent developments. The amount of new work of lasting value has been small, especially in view of the evident renewal of interest in the Welsh language in the 1960s. There are too few writers and poets of quality in the Welsh language under the age of sixty. Meanwhile there has been a steady interest in *eisteddfodau*, local literary and musical festivals, which have for two centuries been an essential part of the Welsh way of life. The National *Eisteddfod*, an annual event held in the first week of August, enjoyed increasing success and interest in the 1960s,

---

[1] *Western Mail*, 29 Oct. 1968.
[2] The Government subsidy increased in 1970 to £12,500.

even though it has resisted pressures to allow the use of the English language in its proceedings. The total attendance at the 1969 National *Eisteddfod* was a record 170,000, remarkable for such a relatively anglicized part of Wales as Flintshire.[1] Television publicity has helped the *Eisteddfod* become a truly 'National' event.

The main stimulus for the Welsh culture in recent years has come from the broadcasting services, especially the British Broadcasting Corporation in Cardiff. When broadcasting began after the First World War, the only regular broadcasts in Welsh emanated from Radio Eireann, and the policy of the B.B.C. was described by the Departmental Committee on Welsh in the Educational System of Wales in 1927 as one of the most serious menaces to the life of the Welsh language.[2] But, after consistent pressure in the early 1930s, the B.B.C. decided in 1935 to allocate a separate wavelength for Wales and to improve the service to Welsh listeners. North Wales received Welsh coverage for the first time, and the number of hours of Welsh language broadcasting was raised to an average of $5\frac{1}{2}$ hours a week. In 1966–7 the average time allocated to Welsh-language broadcasting on the radio was 4·52 hours per week (excluding sports commentaries), but the total output of broadcasting from the Welsh Region of the B.B.C. Home Service was 1,288 hours in 1966–7, representing an average of 25 hours a week. But the position changed dramatically in 1969–70, when the average time allocated to Welsh-language broadcasting on this service rose to 13·1 hours per week, more than half the Welsh Region's broadcasting output.[3]

The advent of television did not manifest itself in a Welsh context until 1952 when the B.B.C. established a regional outpost in Cardiff. Even so Welsh-language broadcasts were minimal in number, because they had to be transmitted from three English transmitters to reach the full Welsh-language audience. It was not until the 1964 Television Act, which followed the Pilkington Report on broadcasting services, that B.B.C. Wales was inaugurated, with responsibility for initiating twelve hours of programmes each week, about half of these being in the Welsh language.

Independent commercial television began to beam its programmes to Wales in 1955. Television Wales and West (T.W.W.) began providing a service for Wales and the South West of England in January

---

[1] Attendance at the National *Eisteddfod* in Ammanford reached 200,000, *Western Mail*, 10 Aug. 1970.

[2] *Welsh in Education and Life*, p. 174.

[3] *Annual Report and Accounts* of the B.B.C., 1969–70 (H.M.S.O., 1970).

1958. Another licence was issued by the Independent Television Authority in 1961 to Wales (West and North) Television Ltd. which was allocated North and West Wales. This company had a small but largely Welsh-speaking clientele, but it was taken over by T.W.W. in 1963 after ten months of broadcasting. T.W.W. then undertook to produce twelve hours of Welsh-initiated programmes each week, with an average of five and a half hours of Welsh language broadcasting each week. The T.W.W. company lost its contract with the I.T.A. in 1967, because the I.T.A. was greatly impressed by the Harlech Consortium's application in all its aspects including its roots in the area and its programme potential.[1] This has been widely supposed to be an implied criticism of the programme content and attention to Welsh needs of the ousted company.

No research has yet been undertaken to discover the effect of regional television on the attitudes of the British people. It can be argued that the increase in regional programmes, especially news and current affairs programmes, has served to promote regional and national loyalties within the United Kingdom by adding a perspective to British news that did not previously exist in broadcasting, and by supplying the public with new and more information about events and developments in their own regions. As far as Wales is concerned, there exist no figures of audience measurement for radio or television for the 1960s by which one could begin to assess the importance of such a judgement. By 1969, 73 per cent of the population of Wales could receive B.B.C. Wales television transmissions, but this does not reveal how many watch them, nor how often they do so. Because of Wales's peculiar geographical qualities for broadcasting purposes, radio and television transmissions from outside Wales overlap with Welsh broadcasts all along the North Wales coast, in eastern Wales, and along the southern coastal fringe of Glamorgan. The same is broadly true of Independent Television transmissions. An index of the extent of the coverage of B.B.C. Wales and the Welsh Home Service amongst the Welsh audience is given by the figures for the sale of the *Radio Times* in Wales. For 1969 the B.B.C. revealed that only 70,000 copies of the B.B.C. Wales edition of the *Radio Times* are sold in Wales compared to 96,000 copies of other regional editions of the *Radio Times*: a ratio of 41 to 59.[2] The B.B.C. believes that its

---

[1] Speech by Lord Hill, when chairman of the I.T.A., delivered on 11 June 1967 and quoted in *ITV 1968: A Guide to Independent Television* (London, 1968).
[2] Letter from T. Rowland Lucas, Information Officer of B.B.C. Wales, 21 Oct. 1969.

Welsh news programmes in the English language hold the largest share of the Welsh audience. The morning news programme, 'Good Morning Wales', was heard daily by between a quarter and a half a million people in Wales in 1969.[1] This indicates that the B.B.C.'s maximum coverage in Wales for its Welsh services is rather low. The same is true of Independent Television where there is considerable overlap between Harlech (Wales) and Harlech (West of England) transmissions in Glamorgan and Monmouthshire; where Harlech is unable to transmit its programmes in large parts of North Wales, viewers are instead served by Granada Television (Manchester).

Nevertheless, the evidence does not fully contradict the thesis that the extension of regional services in broadcasting, and in television especially, has served to heighten Welsh consciousness in Wales. The facts that are known about the Welsh audience merely diminish the universal validity of the argument, but do not rule out the possibility of this influence on large numbers of Welsh people. The view of the B.B.C. and of the political parties in Wales is that this is in fact what has happened in Wales. For the first time, a medium in television has been devised which makes available to the majority of people in Wales regular news information of an all-Welsh character. These broadcasts extend to Welsh people a greater knowledge of the different parts of Wales, and help to break down the isolation of different parts of Wales from each other which arises from geographical factors, economics, and tradition. Thus Wales may have been given a greater sense of cohesion and self-awareness as a result of the development of its separate broadcasting services. There is evidence to suggest that this is very much the desire of the broadcasters themselves.

Conclusion

While the overwhelming direction of Welsh social and economic life has been towards greater integration with the English way of life, since 1945 there have developed several countervailing forces in Wales which have served to strengthen Welsh identity, especially in broadcasting and in education. There is a renewed interest in the Welsh language, but not in its traditional cultural forms. Nonconformity and nonconformist values are strong but declining

[1] Letter from T. Rowland Lucas to the writer, 25 Nov. 1969.

'Welsh' factors in society. These combinations of forces have served to regenerate confidence in Wales's future and interest in its development as a nation; but they have also fostered a form of nationalism that is a reaction to the increased penetration inside Wales of English tourists and residents, English values and media, and English capital. The nationalist position is a mixture of a desire for change and a fear of its consequences for the Welsh way of life. It is one that became acceptable in Welsh life during the 1960s, as the ideological content of the previous politics in Wales seeped away. In general, the Welsh have come to accept their links with Britain for reasons of necessity, inertia, and preference: but they still wish to remain distinct from the general run of English people, and seek recognition of this fact as well as recognition of their social and economic problems. Yet the stronger the sense of Welshness in the people of Wales, the more divided between Wales and Britain their loyalties will be. In politics the role of *Plaid Cymru* in fostering Welsh nationalism and Welsh causes has been crucial in determining the interplay of these loyalties and the extent of the political cleavage they span.

4

PLAID CYMRU 1945–1959: BROADENING THE BASE

PLAID CYMRU emerged from the Second World War stronger than it had been in 1939.[1] Activities had been stepped up since 1944, membership had increased to 2,500, and there were nearly 140 local branches of the party, although most of them were very small.[2] The end of the war also witnessed a change in the party's leader. Saunders Lewis and his successor, Professor J. E. (Jack) Daniel, both found their tenure of the Presidency of the *Blaid* impaled on a religious issue, their connections with the Roman Catholic Church.[3] Daniel withdrew from office after four years, in 1943.[4] Daniel's background was more orthodox than that of his predecessor. He was a prominent nonconformist, was Vice-Principal of Bala-Bangor College, the theological college for Welsh Independents, and he held the professorship of Christian Doctrine at the University College of North Wales, Bangor. Daniel was succeeded by Abi Williams as President of *Plaid Cymru* at the same time as Gwynfor Evans was elected Vice-President.[5] Gwynfor Evans took over from Williams as prospective candidate for Merioneth at the beginning of 1945. He was elected President of the *Blaid* at the party's annual summer school at Llangollen in August of the same year.[6] Evans's election as President at the age of

[1] The name of *Plaid Genedlaethol Cymru* was changed to *Plaid Cymru* shortly after the end of the Second World War, but both names remained operative within the party for some years afterwards.

[2] *Cyflog Gwaseidd-Dra* (The Wages of Servitude) (Annual Report of *Plaid Cymru* for 1944), p. 14.   [3] See Ch. 1.

[4] J. E. Daniel (1902–62) was prominent in Welsh nationalist circles until the end of the Second World War. In 1945 he became an Inspector of Schools in Wales and withdrew from active politics. His wife's conversion to Catholicism had, in part, forced him to resign from Bala-Bangor.

[5] Abi Williams (d. 1963) was not a well-known figure in *Plaid Genedlaethol Cymru* and seems to have been elected President of the party to bridge the gap between J. E. Daniel's and Gwynfor Evans's tenure of this office. He joined the *Blaid* in 1936, having left the Labour Party. As surveyor of roads in Flintshire 'he was cruelly victimised by his enemies and dismissed. His name was cleared in the end and he received substantial compensation' (*Welsh Nation*, Apr. 1963). Briefly prospective candidate for Merioneth, he was forced to resign this responsibility owing to pressure from party workers in 1944 (private information).

[6] Ibid., Oct. 1945.

thirty-two was not unexpected. He had been active in the *Blaid* since his Oxford days in the mid 1930s, both as a speaker and as a publicist.[1] He had learned Welsh as a second language and, although qualified as a solicitor, had spent the war as a market gardener. Like Daniel, Evans was an Independent by denomination, and was also a lay preacher and a teetotaller. Under him *Plaid Cymru* began to move away from the influence of Saunders Lewis.

It was a considerable feat that despite the difficulties *Plaid Cymru* had laboured under in wartime, the party fought eight seats in the general election in July 1945 and collected 16,447 votes; but only Dr. Gwenan Jones, contesting the University of Wales seat under the *Blaid* banner, saved her deposit, polling nearly a quarter of the votes cast. The party leadership was not satisfied with the election results, especially in those seats which *Plaid Cymru* had contested at previous elections, but it remained determined to carry the party's message into as many areas of Wales as possible.[2] Elections, local and national, were to be fought on as wide a front as party finances and workers would permit.

The Labour Party, which was returned at the 1945 election with an over-all majority in the United Kingdom of 156 seats, winning twenty-five out of the thirty-six seats in Wales, did not implement the promises made by some of its candidates in Wales with regard to Welsh devolution.[3] The Welsh parliamentary party, which was dominated by Labour M.P.s, pressed the Prime Minister, Clement Attlee, to see that Welsh interests were fully represented in the Government, demanding in particular that a Secretary of State for Wales be appointed.[4] After months of argument, the Government

---

[1] Gwnfor Evans (b. 1912) President of *Plaid Cymru* since 1945, was formerly Vice-President from 1943–5. Educated in Barry, at the University College of Wales, Aberystwyth, and at St. John's College, Oxford, he was the son of a businessman in Barry who had migrated from Carmarthenshire. Evans joined *Plaid Cymru* in 1934 before going to Oxford. He became Chairman of the Union of Welsh Independents in 1954; he was a founder member of *Undeb Cymru Fydd*. He was first elected to Carmarthenshire County Council in 1949, and has been an Alderman since the mid 1950s. He fought four parliamentary elections in Merioneth between 1945 and 1959, as well as fighting a by-election in Aberdare in 1954. He fought the Carmarthen constituency in 1964 and 1966, before being elected M.P. in the by-election in July 1966.

[2] Viz., J. E. Jones, *Etholiadu 1945 a'r Dyfodol* (The 1945 elections and the future) in *Y Triban*, Sept. 1945.   [3] See Ch. 11.

[4] *The Times*, 15 Oct. 1946. The Welsh parliamentary party originated after the 1886 election when certain Welsh Liberal M.P.s wanted to organize themselves as a separate parliamentary group. The role of the 'party' was summarized in 1943 in the following terms: 'The Welsh Parliamentary Party represents all the Members of Parliament for the Principality and we meet to discuss all matters affecting Wales and to further, by joint efforts, its interests' (Letter to Winston Churchill from Arthur Evans, *et al.*, 7 July 1943, printed in J. Griffiths, *Pages from Memory*, p. 160 [London, 1969]).

set aside in October 1946 one day of Parliamentary time for the discussion of Welsh affairs in the light of a report on the Government's activities in Wales which had been published in advance. These were to become annual events, but from the outset most Welsh M.P.s regarded such concessions as being much too small. In Wales itself two by-elections took place in 1946 which showed that the M.P.s were not alone in their dissatisfaction. A by-election at Ogmore early in June of that year saw the Labour majority tumble from 25,003 to 7,947, with *Plaid Cymru*'s candidate claiming nearly 30 per cent of the votes cast.[1] Admittedly, there was no Conservative candidate in the by-election fight, the turnout of voters was very low, and the Labour candidate, a seventy-one-year-old Glamorgan County Alderman, felt sufficiently vulnerable to protest that whatever his age he was physically fit and mentally alert![2] But an even more impressive Nationalist vote was recorded at the by-election held in Aberdare in December 1946. In a three-cornered fight the *Plaid Cymru* candidate, Wynne Samuel, collected 7,090 votes, 20 per cent of the total vote, leaving the Conservative candidate, a future Lord Mayor of Cardiff, with a lost deposit at the foot of the poll.[3] The *Plaid*'s campaign was fought almost exclusively on the issue of unemployment, and their candidate urged the electors that 'a vote for the Welsh Nationalist Party, as a protest against the present misrule of Wales by an English Party, will be more effective that hundreds of deputations to London'.[4]

These by-elections were significant in themselves and as a pointer to the future development of *Plaid Cymru*. They revealed *Plaid Cymru*'s potential political clientele, because the electors of Ogmore and Aberdare were not choosing a party to govern them but an M.P to represent their interests at Westminster. They showed that large numbers of one-time Labour supporters were prepared to abstain, or defect from the Labour ranks—even in a mining stronghold such as Aberdare, which once returned Keir Hardie to Parliament—if

[1] The result in Ogmore in the 1945 election had been: E. J. Williams (Labour) 32,715; O. E. Davies (National) 7,712; T. Morgan (*Plaid Cymru*) 2,379. At the by-election held on 4 June 1946, the result was: J. Evans (Labour) 13,632; T. Morgan (*Plaid Cymru*) 5,685.

[2] *The Bridgend Advertiser*, 14 June 1946.

[3] The voting in Aberdare at the 1945 election had been: G. Hall (Labour) 34,398; C. G. Clover (Conservative) 6,429. At the by-election held on 7 Dec. 1946, the result was: D. E. Thomas (Labour) 24,215; W. Samuel (*Plaid Cymru*) 7,090; A. Lincoln Hallinan (Conservative) 4,140.

[4] *The Aberdare Leader*, 16 Nov. 1946. Unemployment reached a rate of over eight per cent of the insured population in Wales in 1948.

they were dissatisfied with Labour's performance in office. These two by-elections also showed *Plaid Cymru* to be politically nimble in its ability to stress the issues relevant to any given constituency and to play upon the discontents of local people; they also gave to *Plaid Cymru* the promise of future electoral progress and strength, thus reinforcing the party's electoral aspirations. In clear contrast to the situation following the Carmarthen by-election in 1966, *Plaid Cymru* was strangely unable to capitalize on these relative successes at Ogmore and Aberdare, either locally or throughout Wales. Unfortunately for *Plaid Cymru* there were no further by-elections held in Wales during the 1945-50 Parliament, so that the party was hard pressed to keep up the momentum it had derived from these results. It was meanwhile being troubled by the activities of some of its younger members who called themselves the Welsh Republicans. In 1948, the Labour Government set up the Council for Wales and Monmouthshire, an advisory body to represent Welsh interests to ministers in Whitehall. Although it was certainly a gesture in a nationalist direction, the plan was not well received by *Plaid Cymru* or by a number of Welsh M.P.s, especially the Liberals.[1]

When a general election was held in February 1950, *Plaid Cymru* was only able to field seven candidates who together polled 17,580 votes. In Aberdare, Wynne Samuel polled less than half the number of votes he had collected in 1946; in Ogmore, no official *Plaid* candidate even contested the election; elsewhere *Plaid* candidates improved their position slightly. Moves had already been made before this indifferent election result to broaden the nationalist attack in Wales by means of a general campaign in Wales for a domestic Parliament for Wales. In conjunction with the Liberals, some Labour leaders, and the Communist Party, *Plaid Cymru* joined in organizing a campaign to launch a petition to Parliament for a Parliament for Wales, under the auspices of the non-partisan *Undeb Cymru Fydd* (The New Wales Union). The campaign lasted from 1950 to 1956, but ended in relative failure, with the Welsh Council of Labour and the Welsh Liberal leadership less sympathetic to the idea of a domestic Parliament for Wales than when the campaign was begun.[2] Much of the energies of *Plaid* party workers were devoted to this campaign in this period, but this does not fully account for their

---

[1] Debate in the House of Commons, 24 Nov. 1948, 458 HC Deb. Fifth Series, c. 1262 et seq. Clement Davies, Professor Gruffydd, and Lady Megan Lloyd George all made critical speeches.
[2] See Chs. 10 and 11.

reluctance to fight the 1951 election as widely as the previous election. The fact is that the party was also very short of money, and could not afford to fight an election before it had paid off the debts incurred in 1950. The *Blaid* gave as its reasons for not opposing Goronwy Roberts, Labour M.P. for Caernarfon, and Emrys Roberts, the Liberal M.P. for Merioneth, the fact that they were both leading supporters of the Parliament for Wales campaign. *Plaid Cymru*'s withdrawal from the contest in Merioneth was also calculated to cost the Liberals the seat, which in fact was what happened. The Labour candidate was also a Home Ruler, and it was thought that a Liberal demise would greatly help the *Blaid*'s prospects in the county later on.[1] The party only contested four seats in the 1951 election, but thereafter its political activities expanded and its electoral fortunes gradually improved. Party organizers came to believe that fighting elections on a broad front improved the chances of each candidate individually. When Gwynfor Evans contested the Aberdare by-election in 1954, he secured 5,671 votes, 16 per cent of the votes cast. In the general election of May 1955, *Plaid Cymru* fielded eleven candidates, fighting nearly a third of the Welsh seats, and was supported by 45,119 votes. Notable advances were made in the constituencies of West Rhondda, Llanelli, Merioneth, and Wrexham. But the *Blaid* was at this time becoming increasingly concerned with Liverpool's plans for making a water reservoir out of the Tryweryn valley in Merioneth. This anxiety was shared by the majority of Welsh M.P.s and by Welsh opinion generally, but despite the calling of two national conferences on this question in Cardiff and Welsh opposition at Westminster, the Conservative Government persuaded the House of Commons to approve the scheme, which was contained in a private bill sponsored by Liverpool City Council. By obtaining authority for its plans in this way, Liverpool did not have to secure the consent of the Welsh local authorities affected by the scheme, and it was this that so incensed the Welsh public.[2] The inability of the almost unanimous Welsh M.P.s to prevent the passage of Liverpool's bill has long proved a valuable argument in the Nationalist debating armoury; but *Plaid Cymru* benefited little from

---

[1] Private information. This was borne out in practice. At the 1950 election, the voting in Merioneth was: E. Roberts (Liberal) 9,647, (Labour) 8,577, (Conservative) 3,846, (*Plaid Cymru*) 2,754. The 1951 election result was: (Labour) 10,505, (Liberal) 9,457, (Conservative) 4,505.

[2] Viz., H. T. Edwards, *Hewn from the Rock* (Cardiff, 1967); G. R. Evans, *We Learn from Tryweryn* (Cardiff, 1957).

these events in terms of added political support, not even in Merioneth.[1] More significant in the development of Welsh politics was the report of the Council for Wales and Monmouthshire published in January 1957 which recommended that Wales should have a Secretary of State and a Welsh Office.[2] When the general election was held in October 1959, the party was already beginning to experience doubts within the rank and file as to the universal validity of constitutional and parliamentary methods for securing its objectives. The Tryweryn affair showed how Welsh M.P.s of any party could be overruled at Westminster, and by the same token cast doubt on *Plaid Cymru*'s desire to be represented there with its own M.P.s. The party, however, received a welcome lift to its morale when at the 1959 National *Eisteddfod*, Dr. Huw T. Edwards, one of the most prominent Labour and trade union leaders in Wales, suddenly announced that he was joining *Plaid Cymru*.[3] In the October election, the party fielded twenty candidates and collected 77,571 votes—the largest number of votes it had ever received at a general election. *Plaid Cymru* contested every seat in Dyfed and Gwynedd, made advances in some seats, and polled over a fifth of the votes in Caernarfon and Merioneth. But the level of support for the party was still small in Wales as a whole. In the constituencies contested by *Plaid Cymru*, its candidates averaged only 10·34 per cent of the votes cast (compared with 10·36 per cent in 1955)[4] in an election held at a favourable time for the party. *Plaid*'s pacifism and opposition to nuclear weapons could be counted an electoral asset; disillusion with the Labour Party was rife; memories of the Tryweryn affair were live; and Dr. H. T. Edwards had just joined the party. This result probably represented

[1] The *Plaid Cymru* share of the vote in the 1955 and 1959 elections in Merioneth was almost identical—22·1 per cent in 1955, 23 per cent in 1959. The candidate in both elections was Gwynfor Evans.

[2] Council for Wales and Monmouthshire, Third Memorandum, Cmnd. 53 (H.M.S.O., 1957). Reply of the Prime Minister, Cmnd. 334 (H.M.S.O., 1957). Council for Wales and Monmouthshire, Fourth Memorandum, Cmnd. 631 (H.M.S.O., 1959).

[3] Dr. Huw T. Edwards was brought up in Caernarvonshire, and began work in the slate quarries after leaving school, later moving to work in the coal mines of the Rhondda valley. After the First World War he was active in the Transport and General Workers' Union, becoming a full-time official in North Wales in 1932. He became active in union, national, and local politics. He was an Alderman of Flintshire County Council 1939–59 and first Chairman of the Council for Wales and Monmouthshire from 1949 to 1958, when he resigned over a disagreement with the Prime Minister. He joined *Plaid Cymru* in 1959 and stayed a member until 1965. He was at various times a director of Television Wales and the West Ltd. and *Y Faner*, and Chairman of the Welsh Tourist Board.

[4] In constituencies contested by *Plaid Cymru* in both the 1955 and 1959 elections, the average share of the poll acquired by *Plaid* candidates rose from 11·0 per cent to 13·2 per cent.

the maximum amount of support that the *Blaid* could expect from a predominantly cultural, nonconformist, and rural-oriented appeal. It was not good enough for many of the *Blaid*'s activists[1] and the critics from the summer school in August began to make new moves and demands.

A review of *Plaid Cymru*'s activities in the fifteen years following the end of the war in 1945 must lead to a consideration of the efficacy of its strategy. The main area of its efforts lay in the fighting of elections. In between general elections the party tried to raise money to service its organization which was preparing for the next general election. By-elections would be fought if it was convenient, and some local elections might be contested,[2] with some financial support from party headquarters. Occasionally, a quick succession of elections could embarrass the party, as when in 1951 a general election was called within twenty months of the 1950 election, because the party was still paying off debts incurred during the previous election. Between 1945 and 1959 *Plaid Cymru* spent nearly £24,000 on fielding candidates at general elections,[3] not including the costs of the central party machine during and in between elections. This total sum represents about a quarter of the total income of the party at all levels in the same fifteen-year period.[4] *Plaid Cymru* also contested most parliamentary by-elections in this period, for during a by-election the party could concentrate its limited organizational and financial resources, and gain valuable local and national publicity. Occasional sallies into the local elections in South Wales were also made, with candidates standing under the official party label, although with very little success. *Plaid Cymru* claimed numerous councillors on local authorities throughout Wales were party members, but almost all of them were elected as Independents.[5]

In addition, *Plaid Cymru* published regularly two monthly newspapers, *The Welsh Nation*[6] and *Y Ddraig Goch* (The Red Dragon),

---

[1] Viz., *Welsh Nation*, Nov. 1959, especially the editorial.
[2] Of the nine by-elections held in Wales between July 1945 and October 1959, *Plaid Cymru* contested all but those held in Pontypool (July 1946) and Abertillery (Nov. 1950).
[3] This figure comprises £17,926 in terms of candidates' expenses and £5,850, the cost of thirty-nine lost deposits.
[4] Based on collections for the St. David's Day Fund and Election Funds (approximately £70,000), and an estimate of £30,000 raised locally over the same period.
[5] *Plaid Cymru* claimed in 1958 that over 200 party members were local councillors: *Welsh Nation*, June 1958.
[6] Until January 1948 this was published as *The Welsh Nationalist*. For six months, from July to December 1956, *Welsh Nation* appeared weekly.

with a combined circulation of between five and seven thousand per issue. The party also published a number of pamphlets, and sometimes books as well. The publishing side of the party required a considerable subsidy.[1]

The other activities to which *Plaid Cymru* devoted time and money were the organizing of rallies and conferences, and of protests involving direct action or passive resistance. *Plaid Cymru* in the 1950s held an annual rally, sometimes with a specific theme—such as the Gwynedd rally in September 1957 which highlighted local unemployment; hundreds of party workers and supporters from all over Wales would take part. The annual summer school (*Ysgol Haf*) and conference, which were held jointly, and had continued in an unbroken sequence since 1926, were usually timed to precede in time and place the National *Eisteddfod*. The summer school would normally attract about two hundred people, although attendances of between three and four hundred were noted in the late 1940s in *The Welsh Nation*. The *ysgol haf* was the policy-making body of the party, although most time in its programme would normally be given to lectures of cultural, historical, or political interest. The proceedings would occasionally be briefly reported in some London newspapers. At local levels *Plaid* branches most commonly met monthly, with considerable prominence given to cultural pursuits. Welsh lessons, history lectures, and *nosweithiau llawen* were all popular activities. But the Nationalists also considered less parliamentary methods of drawing attention to their views. Following the burning down of the Penyberth bombing school in 1936 by three *Plaid Cymru* leaders, a motion was passed at the *Blaid*'s *ysgol haf* in 1938 urging the party to use non-violent methods to further its aims; the proposer of the motion was Gwynfor Evans. This was a course of action which the *Blaid* was slow to adopt in practice. The first official instance occurred in September 1951 when a group of Nationalists led by Gwynfor Evans sat down in front of an army camp at Trawsfynydd, in Merioneth, in protest against the proposed extension of lands held by the War Office. But this action was not repeated by *Plaid Cymru* when the issue of the Tryweryn water reservoir was raised in the mid 1950s; a long debate on the subject within the party did not result in any action of this kind being taken. No other direct action was undertaken in the period 1945–59 in *Plaid Cymru*'s name, although certain

---

[1] At various times in this period, the subsidy to party newspapers was of the order of £1,000 per annum.

individuals made their protest as conscientious objectors on nationalist grounds when required to do their national service.[1] It is strange
that direct action as a means of protest was not used more frequently
by *Plaid Cymru* for stimulating discussion concerning the issues it
chose to take up, such as conscription and the requisitioning of land
in Wales for defence purposes, afforestation, or for use as reservoirs.
It was thirteen years before the resolution of 1938 was acted upon
by the party leadership. One reason suggested for this delay is that
it was hard to convince many of the leaders of the party that it was
fitting for respectable and intelligent citizens to practise techniques
of non-violent resistance.

An isolated instance of a different method of direct action was the
slogan-painting which occurred in North Wales early in 1952. An
individual party member organized parties of supporters to paint
slogans for Welsh freedom along several roads. He informed party
headquarters of his actions and was thanked for his activities.[2] In
the 1960s many such slogans were to appear on Welsh roads and
bridges, but *Plaid Cymru*'s official attitude to them was hostile.[3]

A more orthodox device for advancing its views used by *Plaid
Cymru* in these years was formal and informal co-operation with
other political bodies to advance objectives held in common. This
was either the product of political circumstances, as in the case of
the Parliament for Wales campaign,[4] or of deliberate initiatives on
the part of *Plaid Cymru*, and, in particular, its general secretary,
J. E. Jones.[5] The Parliament for Wales campaign which Liberals,
Nationalists, and Communists in Wales, as well as individual

---

[1] Notably Emrys P. Roberts in 1953, later general secretary of the *Blaid*, and
E. Christopher Rees in 1955, later Vice-President of the *Blaid*.

[2] Private information.

[3] Elwyn Roberts, general secretary of the Party, even stated that slogan-painting
had never received the blessing of the party (*Welsh Nation*, Aug. 1967). Two other
attempts at direct action which received party support were:

(i) The foundation of the *Listeners of Wales Association* early in 1955 which en-
couraged Welsh people to pay their licence fees to the Association rather than to the
Postmaster-General. This was in protest against the poor reception and quality of
Welsh broadcasting services.

(ii) The invention of *Radio Wales*, a private mobile radio transmitter, operated by
Nationalists and used for several years to publicize their views on television wave-
lengths late at night, often during election periods.

[4] See Ch. 10.

[5] J. E. Jones (1905–70) was born in Melin-y-Wig on the Denbigh–Merioneth border,
went to school in Bala and on to the University College of North Wales in Bangor.
For a short while he was a schoolmaster in London before returning to Wales and
becoming general secretary of the *Blaid* from 1930 to 1962. See J. E. Jones, *Tros
Gymru* (Swansea, 1970).

prominent Labour Party leaders, supported, was an imitation of the movement for a Scottish Covenant 1949–50 which had received widespread support in Scotland. The Welsh campaign was conceived in 1949, independently by Liberals and Nationalists, launched in 1950, and wound up in 1956. It thus engaged the active attention of *Plaid* party workers over a long period and allowed them the opportunity to influence those disposed to self-government but who were not Nationalists. The campaign itself subscribed to many of the arguments put forward by Nationalists for Welsh self-government, although it proposed a constitutional position for Wales which made it ultimately subordinate to the United Kingdom Parliament. *Plaid Cymru* for its part was quite prepared to sacrifice some of its own prospects in the short term to further the campaign. In May 1951, *Plaid Cymru* issued a statement on self-government in which it declared it would not oppose candidates or M.P.s of other parties who supported Welsh home rule.[1] And in July 1951, J. E. Jones, the party's secretary, was writing that the *Blaid* should make a sacrifice in two or three constituencies to foster inter-party co-operation. His view of the campaign at that time was that if it failed it would delay the work of the *Blaid* for up to twelve years.

Plaid Cymru had other less permanent contacts with bodies outside Wales such as the Independent Labour, Commonwealth, and the Scottish National Parties. Here contacts would involve occasional meetings between representatives of each group, and exchange of delegates at annual conferences of these bodies, or a joint protest on a matter of mutual interest—such as the Home Rule rally held over Easter in 1956,[2] or deputations concerning the refusal to allocate broadcasting time to the small minority parties.

Another movement in which *Plaid Cymru* became involved was the Campaign for Nuclear Disarmament. A resolution at the annual conference in 1957 prompted the party executive the following Christmas to ask its assistant secretary, Emrys Roberts, to begin setting up a Welsh nuclear disarmament campaign. There was, however, some dispute as to whether this should be the job of a paid official of the party.[3] Roberts was in fact secretary of the Welsh

---

[1] *Welsh Nation*, May 1951.
[2] The Three Nations Rally was held in Trafalgar Square on Easter Saturday 1956, and was jointly sponsored by *Plaid Cymru*, the Scottish National Party, the Independent Labour Party and Commonwealth. It followed the publication of the pamphlet, *Our Three Nations*, earlier in the year.
[3] Private information.

National Council of the Campaign for Nuclear Disarmament for the first few months of its existence, but this was not a very onerous responsibility. A number of *Plaid* members supported the campaign, more in the Welsh-speaking areas with a nonconformist tradition than in South-East Wales. But, as with the Parliament for Wales campaign, so with the Welsh branch of the Campaign for Nuclear Disarmament there is no evidence that many joined *Plaid Cymru* as a result of its involvement in the campaign. At best, those who supported the campaign took the party more seriously as a result of its activities, and the campaign may have also proved an outlet for some of those who were urging *Plaid Cymru* to adopt tactics of direct action in other spheres of political interest.

Towards the end of the 1950s there was a distinct shift in the concentration of activity inside the *Blaid,* with the more anglicized parts of Wales taking the lead. The number of party activists at this time was very small, and of the two hundred and fifty branches recognized by the party, perhaps as few as six were really active.[1] A new generation of Nationalists was emerging in South-East Wales which was to prove deeply significant for the party in the years leading up to 1966.[2] The attention of the party's leadership was turned once more to making headway in the industrial areas of South Wales. The activities of an individualist such as Glyn James in the Rhondda appeared to be bringing results in terms of votes. Efforts were made to attract industrial workers, miners, and trade unionists to the party, without much success. The party made a conscious effort to throw off its exclusively Welsh-speaking image and borrowed arguments from the reviving Liberal Party in England about the need for a radical-socialist alternative to replace Labour.[3] This contrast of approach was reflected at the party's headquarters in Cardiff in the persons of the veteran J. E. Jones and his young assistant, Emrys Roberts. A decade previously, starting in 1948, the Welsh Republicans had tried to concentrate *Plaid Cymru*'s attention on capturing the support of the industrial areas of Glamorgan and Monmouthshire. Initially they had operated inside *Plaid Cymru,* but they were forced to leave the party in 1949 and continued to agitate from outside until the mid

[1] Private information.

[2] Including Mike Tucker, Ted Merriman, Glyn James, Emrys Roberts, Ted Spanswick, Trefor Morgan, Raymond Edwards, Harri Webb, Ken Thomas, Alf Williams, and, later, Dr. Phil Williams.

[3] It has long been recognized by *Plaid Cymru*'s leaders that their main enemy was the Labour Party. What was new was this public alignment of the party with radical-socialism.

fifties.[1] Where the Republicans had been unable to make an impact, the new recruits to *Plaid Cymru* in South-East Wales and some of the former Republicans were more successful, possibly because the party at large was in a weaker position to resist. *Plaid Cymru's* attitude to the language had been modified in the fifties towards an acceptance of an ultimately bilingual Wales, rather than an entirely Welsh-speaking Wales as its long-term objective. As the number of Welsh-speakers was declining as a proportion of the population and as the Labour Party in Welsh-speaking Wales strengthened its position throughout the fifties, so industrial Wales was once more looked upon as potentially fertile ground for the party. In the 1959 election *Plaid Cymru* put up nine candidates in the twenty-two Glamorgan and Monmouthshire seats, as compared with four candidates in the previous election (see Table 4.1). Even so when the Executive Committee of *Plaid Cymru* came to prepare advice to candidates concerning the election campaign, the economic case for self-government was given only third priority, behind the need to 'awaken the natural Welshness of people' and the moral case for self-government.

TABLE 4.1

Wales: Votes cast at General Elections 1945–1959

	1945	1950	1951	1955	1959
Labour	779,184	888,674	926,118	825,690	841,447
%	58·5	58·4	60·5	57·6	56·5
Conservative	301,978	418,706	471,269	428,866	486,335
%	22·6	27·4	30·8	29·9	32·6
Liberal	198,553	193,090	116,826	104,095	78,951
%	14·9	12·6	7·6	7·3	5·3
Plaid Cymru	14,751	17,580	10,920	45,119	77,571
%	1·1	1·2	0·8	3·2	5·2
Communist	15,761	9,120	2,948	4,544	6,542
%	1·2	0·6	0·2	0·3	0·4
Others	20,444	2,142	1,643	25,410	408
%	1·6	0·1	0·1	1·8	0·0
Total electorate	1,756,885	1,802,182	1,812,712	1,801,217	1,805,684
% of electors (Wales) voting	75·7	84·9	84·4	79·6	82·6
% of electors (U.K.) voting	73·3	84·0	82·5	76·8	78·7

[1] See Ch. 10.

5

PLAID CYMRU 1959–1966: DRIFT AND FRAGMENTATION

THE disappointment shared by many *Plaid* members at the party's performance in the general election held in October 1959 heralded nearly seven years of drift and questioning inside *Plaid Cymru*. The party certainly made small but significant progress in South Wales in the years 1960 and 1961, when the Labour Party was itself publicly doubting its own ideological foundations and its ability even to win a general election. But the turmoil in the Labour Party did not submerge the doubts which the younger members of *Plaid Cymru* had raised in the summer prior to the 1959 general election concerning the *Blaid*'s commitment to a parliamentary strategy. A willing ally in these doubts was Dr. Huw T. Edwards, the party's distinguished new recruit.

After the 1959 election *Plaid Cymru* leaders frankly admitted their dissatisfaction with the election results, even though new members were enrolled and new branches were formed during the campaign. There was particular regret that Gwynfor Evans had made little progress in Merioneth, which many Nationalists had considered a winnable constituency. Gwynfor Evans himself was disappointed and decided not to contest the seat again.[1] A commission was set up by the *Blaid* to inquire into the party's condition, with Tom Jones (Llanuwchllyn) acting as chairman. This commission blamed a lack of money and poor organization for the party's poor election performance, and suggested, in addition, a redistribution of the functions of some of the party's officials. J. E. Jones, the general secretary, tried to put a gloss on the position in a speech in Montgomeryshire when he said that 'the extensive reorganisation, which is now taking place in *Plaid Cymru*, was made necessary more by the growth of the party than by unsatisfactory results in the General Election'.[2]

---

[1] Gwynfor Evans refused the Merioneth district committee of *Plaid Cymru*'s invitation to stand again as candidate in the autumn of 1961, and later accepted the invitation from the Carmarthen district committee to stand as their candidate: *Welsh Nation*, Nov. 1961.

[2] J. E. Jones, speech to Montgomeryshire County Committee at Llanfair Caereinion, 30 Jan. 1960.

At the beginning of 1960 the problems concerning the future of the *Blaid* were overshadowed by the internal strife in the Labour Party. Labour membership had declined by one-sixth in Wales since the peak of 1957, falling away very rapidly in such marginal seats as Merioneth, South East Cardiff, Newport, and Monmouth.[1] The *Welsh Nation* published the names of prominent Labour officials who had recently joined *Plaid Cymru*,[2] and a large attack of the Labour Party in South Wales was mounted in the local elections in May of 1960. New area committees were reported to have been founded in such anglicized areas of Wales as East Flintshire and mid Glamorgan.[2] The results of these efforts were desultory, except in Dowlais, and in Ferndale (Rhondda) where Glyn James captured a seat on the borough council from Labour with a majority of over 500 votes. The organizing secretary of *Plaid Cymru* concluded that the local election results had been 'excellent in some places, and better than expected in most'.[3] When the annual conference met at the end of July 1960 there was little criticism on the surface, and it was reported that the conference was 'better attended than any previous conference'.[4]

The party's new concern for the problems of industrial South Wales was strengthened when in November a by-election was held in Ebbw Vale following the sudden death of Aneurin Bevan. *Plaid Cymru* organized a strong campaign around Emrys Roberts, a candidate who was widely commended. *Plaid Cymru* leaders were still very interested in problems of a cultural nature at this period, though it was also in 1960 that Gwynfor Evans published his plans for a British Common Market.[5] In connection with the Pilkington Committee's review of broadcasting in Britain, *Plaid Cymru* was active in Wales in forming Welsh opinion, urging the need to have more Welsh language programmes, on television especially, and to have a Welsh broadcasting service. Many prominent Nationalists were in the consortium which was awarded in 1961 the licence by the Independent Television Authority to transmit programmes to West Wales.[6] That same year saw the foundation, in August, of the Celtic

---

[1] Information from Annual Reports of the Welsh Regional Council of Labour, 1950–60.　　　　　　　　　　　　　　　　　[2] *Welsh Nation*, Apr. 1960.

[3] J. E. Jones, circular letter to *Pwyllgor* Rhanbarth secretaries, 13 May 1960.

[4] *Welsh Nation*, Sept. 1960.

[5] G. R. Evans, *Self Government for Wales and a Common Market for the Nations of Britain* (Cardiff, 1960).

[6] The consortium included known Nationalists such as Gwynfor Evans, Moses Gruffydd, and Dr. Thomas Parry. See Ch. 10 for a discussion of Welsh broadcasting.

League, an organization set up to foster Celtic awareness and co-operation, and Gwynfor Evans became its first President. At the end of the year, the *Blaid* was caused much heartsearching by the referendum on Sunday opening of public houses in Wales, which was occasioned by the new Licensing Act of 1961. The party had no official policy on the licensing question, but many *Plaid* leaders campaigned actively to keep the pubs closed—Gwynfor Evans in particular. Some complained that by organizing the voting by county and county borough constituencies the Government was trying to divide Wales. Other people active in the *Blaid* were less enthusiastic about their leaders taking up the licensing issue.[1] After the voting was over, an editorial in the *Welsh Nation* commented acidly: 'From a nationalist point of view, it was somewhat of a shock to discover that in many parts of the country, public opinion generally was more nationalistic than the *Blaid*. . . . The *Blaid*, despite the lead given by its President and some of the local officials, was content to play a game of fence-sitting—usually maintaining in a loud voice that the whole hubbub was much ado about nothing.'[2]

The beginning of 1962 saw the movement towards *Plaid Cymru* and to the Liberals, in South Wales continuing, but when local elections were held in May the tide had begun to turn against the *Blaid*. One of the party's three councillors in Merthyr lost his seat, and the *Blaid* vote was reduced in the Rhondda and in Cardiff; but in Ogmore one gain was made, while another *Plaid* councillor held his seat there with an enlarged majority. With the by-election in Montgomeryshire held late in May 1962, following the death of Clement Davies, the former Liberal leader, the *Blaid* thought it would be able to demonstrate its new electoral strength. Its hopes were dashed when the result showed that the *Plaid* candidate, the writer Islwyn Ffowc Elis, had lost his deposit and that the Liberal revival had reached as far from Orpington as Llanbrynmair and Llanidloes.[3] A period of internal troubles and violent action in some nationalist circles confirmed this adverse tide of fortune for the *Blaid*. The West Wales independent television company, *Teledu*

---

[1] Viz., *Welsh Nation*, Jan. 1962. There had been a division in the *Blaid* as to whether it should, as a political party, take a stand on the licensing issue at the 1953 annual conference: *The Times*, 4 Aug. 1953.

[2] *Welsh Nation*, Dec. 1961.

[3] The result in Montgomeryshire in the 1962 by-election was H. Emlyn Hooson (Liberal)13,181; Robert H. Dawson (Conservative) 5,632; Tudor Davies (Labour) 5,299; Revd. I. Ff. Elis (*Plaid*) 1,594. The 1959 election result had been: Clement Davies (Liberal) 10,970; F. L. Morgan (Conservative) 8,176; D. C. Jones (Labour) 6,950.

Cymru, which Nationalists and others had tried so long to set up, failed and was taken over by its South Wales counterpart, Television Wales and West Ltd.[1] The appeal made inside the *Blaid* for funds with which to frustrate the building of the Clywedog reservoir raised more than twice what was raised to fight the by-election at Swansea East in March 1963.[2] The local elections in 1963 saw the *Blaid* lose ground heavily in all those areas in which it had been most active since 1960—partly because of the impact of militant nationalist activities in the previous year. These losses were repeated in 1964.

Throughout the early sixties all was far from calm within the *Blaid.* Dissension seems to have spread soon after the 1959 election despite some electoral advances in the spring of 1960, followed by the good annual conference. A correspondent to the *Welsh Nation* criticized the conference for glossing over the failure of 1959 and for steam-rollering motions through the delegates. He noted that delegates from the Rhondda and some of the young delegates were more realistic about the state of the party.[3] It was the Rhondda that had seen at the end of 1959 the formation of a new branch of the party, with an all English language rule, the secretary being H. W. J. Edwards—a highly individual figure. In the autumn of 1960, a group of party members including several party workers in South Wales met at the Belle Vue Hotel in Aberystwyth to discuss constitutional and unconstitutional means of furthering nationalist objectives. The Belle Vue Group whose membership overlapped that of *Cymru Ein Gwlad* (Wales Our Country) determined to act as a ginger group inside the party and to press for the use of direct action in selected circumstances as an official part of the work of *Plaid Cymru.*[4] The upshot of these criticisms was a resolution to the annual conference held at Llangollen in August 1961. A motion was proposed on behalf of the group, *Cymru Ein Gwlad,* urging *Plaid Cymru* to meet 'acts of aggression in future with direct action'; Mrs. Catrin Daniel, wife of a former President of the *Blaid,* and Haydn Jones proposed the motion, which was opposed by Elystan Morgan and other members of the party's establishment.[5] This motion was clearly defeated by the delegates present, for even some

---

[1] See Ch. 10.
[2] Annual Report of *Plaid Cymru* 1963–4. By-election funds raised £702 for Montgomeryshire, £325 for Swansea East. The Clywedog appeal raised £802.
[3] Gerald Morgan, *Welsh Nation,* Sept. 1960.
[4] Private information.
[5] *Welsh Nation,* Sept. 1961.

of the party's strongest critics were unable to support the motion's unqualified tone.[1] Another challenge to the leadership came with the elections for officers of the party which coincided with the conference. The Belle Vue Group nominated Trefor Morgan for the Vice-Presidency; the outgoing Vice-President, Dr. Tudor Jones, was prevailed upon by party leaders not to retire in order to beat off the challenge.[2] Dr. Jones was re-elected as Vice-President, and no challenge was made to Gwynfor Evans's position as President. In this way the opponents of the party establishment revealed their essential weakness, their inability to provide an alternative leader comparable in stature and ability to Gwynfor Evans.

But the battle inside the party continued, and the feelings of frustration concerning the *Blaid*'s lack of progress grew and were fanned by a lecture of Periclean proportions delivered by Saunders Lewis, the former President of *Plaid Cymru*, on the B.B.C.'s Welsh Home Service in February 1962. Lewis had retired from Welsh politics nearly twenty years previously. Now he came forward to give the restless nationalists in Wales a lead. He advised them to use the language issue in Wales as a political weapon regardless of whether it brought self-government in its wake.

Welsh can be saved, Welsh-speaking Wales is still an extensive area of the country, and the minority is not wholly unimportant. . . . It should be made immediately impossible for the business of local and central government to continue without using Welsh. Tax forms in Welsh or in English and Welsh must be demanded. The Postmaster-General must be warned that annual licences will not be paid unless they are obtainable in Welsh. This is not a policy for individuals, here and there. It would demand organizing and moving step by step, giving warnings and allowing time for changes. It is a policy for a movement, a movement in the areas where Welsh is in daily use. Every election form and every official form to do with elections must be in Welsh. Welsh must be the chief administrative matter in the district and the county.

Perhaps you will say that this can never be done, that not enough Welshmen could be found to agree and to arrange it as a campaign of importance and strength. Perhaps you are right. All I maintain is that this is the only political matter which it is worth a Welshman's while to trouble himself about today. I know the difficulties. There would be storms from every direction. It would be argued that such a campaign would kill our chances of attracting English factories to the Welsh-speaking rural areas,

---

[1] Opinions vary as to whether the margin of defeat was two to one or six to four. About forty people supported the motion, but Emrys Roberts was not among them.

[2] Private information.

and this would surely be the case. It is easy to promise that the scorn and sneers of the English gutter journalists would be a daily burden. The wrath of local authority and county council officials would be like the blustering of those in the Llanelli Rural District. Fines in the courts would be heavy, and to refuse to pay them would bring expensive consequences, though no more expensive than fighting purposeless parliamentary elections. I do not deny that there would be a period of hatred, persecution and controversy in place of the brotherly love which is so obvious in Welsh politics today. It will be nothing less than a revolution to restore the Welsh language in Wales today. Success is only possible through revolutionary methods. Perhaps the language would bring self-government in its wake— I don't know. The language is more important than self-government. In my opinion, if any kind of self-government for Wales were obtained before Welsh is admitted and used as an official language in local and national administration in the Welsh-speaking areas of our country, then the language will never achieve official status at all, and its death would be quicker than it will be under the rule of England.[1]

Lewis's lecture had an electrifying effect on the *Blaid*'s rank and file and it led directly to the formation of *Cymdeithas yr Iaith Gymraeg* (The Welsh Language Society) at the party's annual summer school and conference, held in Pontardulais in August 1962.[2] Its members were young *Plaid Cymru* members, and Lewis later agreed to become its President.[3] The *Blaid* leadership, however, did not act upon Lewis's instructions, which received critical treatment in the *Welsh Nation*.[4] When the annual conference met in 1962 there were a number of hostile resolutions to be debated. The West Glamorgan District Committee of *Plaid Cymru* unsuccessfully sponsored a motion condemning 'the Party's failure to take practical action in accordance with its own resolutions'.[5] Trefor Morgan again stood as a candidate in the Vice-Presidential election, but so did Wynne Samuel and Elystan Morgan.[6] Samuel, who combined impatience with the leadership together with long service to the party, won the election.

It was in this year that *Plaid Cymru* won an important legal battle when in May a *Plaid Cymru* candidate for the Carmarthenshire

[1] Lecture entitled *Tynged yr Iaith* (The Fate of the Language) delivered 13 Feb. 1962, published as *BBC Welsh Annual Radio Lecture* 1962—quoted in translation in G. Morgan, *The Dragon's Tongue* (Cardiff, 1966).

[2] *The Welsh Language Society* (Cardiff, 1966).

[3] *Y Cyfamodwr* (Cardiff, 1966).

[4] Dr. Bobi Jones of the University College of Wales, Aberystwyth, challenged Lewis's approach.

[5] *Plaid Cymru* Annual Summer School and Conference Agenda and Reports, Cardiff, 1962. The motion was defeated.

[6] Wynne Samuel had been a Belle Vue Group nominee for the Executive elections in 1961.

County Council successfully contested the Ammanford Returning Officer's decision in March 1961 not to accept as valid nomination papers written in Welsh rather than in the usual English form. The judges in the High Court ruled in favour of Welsh because it was a standard language in the local circumstances of Ammanford. With the court awarding costs against the defendants, this was clearly a victory for extra-parliamentary action. But whereas the plaintiffs in the Ammanford case had used the process of law to secure redress and recognition for the Welsh language, with eminently constitutional legal advisers such as Dewi Watkin Powell and Elystan Morgan, a more direct form of action was used at the site of the Tryweryn reservoir by two *Plaid Cymru* members from South-East Wales, David Walters and David Pritchard. They attempted to sabotage the power supply at the site of the Tryweryn dam on 22 September 1962, and were each fined £50 by Bala magistrates for spoiling a thousand gallons of oil there, Elystan Morgan acting as defence solicitor. Both Pritchard and Walters were members of the *Plaid Cymru* executive at the time.[1] Further attempts to disrupt the work of building the Tryweryn reservoir were made the following year. On 10 February 1963 a transformer on the Tryweryn site was sabotaged and a post-graduate student of the University College of Wales, Aberystwyth, Emyr Llewelyn Jones, son of the well-known bard T. Llew Jones, was convicted of the offence and sentenced to a year's imprisonment on 29 March. His two companions were never identified or prosecuted. Another attempt on the power supply to Tryweryn was made on 1 April when an explosion occurred at a near-by pylon at Gelli Lydan. Two young men from Caernarvonshire were convicted for this action, and one of them, Owen Williams, who was chairman of the Pwllheli *Plaid Cymru* youth branch, was sent to prison.[2] Early in 1963 *Cymdeithas yr Iaith Gymraeg* (The Welsh Language Society) made its first major appearance in Welsh political life with a demonstration in Aberystwyth urging equal status for the Welsh and English languages; this was followed by a sit-down on the road at Trefechan bridge when the police declined to arrest any of the sixty demonstrators who were putting posters on official

---

[1] *Western Mail*, 4 Oct. 1962. Pritchard was a twenty-five-year-old electrical planning engineer from New Tredegar. Walters was a twenty-two-year-old underground colliery worker from Bargoed who had married the niece of Morgan Phillips, the former secretary of the Labour Party. Neither of these men were Welsh-speakers.

[2] Owen Williams was later expelled from *Plaid Cymru* in 1967 for his views on violent means in politics, and was prominent in the National Patriotic Front—see Ch. 10.

buildings in the town. The demonstration was led by Edward Millward, a lecturer in Welsh at the University College of Wales, Aberystwyth (who was later to become tutor in Welsh to the Prince of Wales, in 1969).[1] Also in 1963 there appeared the first manifestations of the 'Free Wales Army' which was believed to be a para-military organization trying to secure an independent Wales.[2] The same year, *Y Faner* was to carry an appeal by Dr. Huw T. Edwards, now President of the Welsh Language Society, who urged *Plaid Cymru* to organize the setting up of a breakaway parliament in Wales without the consent of Westminster.[3] However, Dr. Edwards was soon to bring 'the four and a half unhappiest years' of his political life to a close by rejoining the Labour Party in 1965, confirmed in an earlier view that 'the *Blaid* was not the answer for a Socialist'.[4]

The leaders of *Plaid Cymru* in the early sixties faced a difficult time politically in Wales with, first, the Liberal revival which received regular castigation in the *Welsh Nation*, and then the resuscitation of the Labour Party, cutting the ground from their feet. Politics was in a state of flux in Wales, as in Britain at large, for the first time for many years, but the flux did not have a nationalist bent, except temporarily in isolated areas. Lack of electoral progress certainly allowed more fundamental doubts about the party's strategy to be raised and to take a significant hold among party activists. The leadership was under challenge from within—from the youth section, from *Cymru Ein Gwlad* and the Belle Vue Group (somewhat, synonymous alignments), from certain district committees in South Wales, and from respected individuals such as Dr. Huw T. Edwards.

The reactions of Gwynfor Evans and his advisers were only partly accommodating to the views of the discontented rank and file. Constitutional methods were still regarded as the only acceptable means of furthering the party's objectives, and the favourable vote for the leadership on the motion urging direct action discussed at the 1961 annual conference was to encourage the leadership to rule out all direct action as legitimate party activities.[5] Increasingly party members—whether as individuals or in organized groups—felt the need to do something positive rather than rely on fighting elections.

---

[1] The Hughes-Parry committee was set up to investigate the status of the Welsh language later in the year, after two years of pressure from Welsh M.P.s on the Government. An account of the development of *Cymdeithas yr Iaith Gymraeg* is given in Ch. 9.
[2] *The Times*, 26 Nov. 1963.   [3] *Y Faner*, 20 June 1963.
[4] H. T. Edwards, *Hewn from the Rock* (Cardiff, 1967), p. 236.
[5] Private information.

The years 1962 and 1963 were bleak ones in the electoral field, the party losing all its bridgeheads in the Rhondda, Merthyr, and Ogmore, at local government level. By the spring of 1964 the party had only eight councillors elected to local authorities with the *Plaid* label, and only one of these councillors was on a county council or a county borough council; that was Gwynfor Evans himself, in Carmarthenshire.[1] The number of new recruits to the party in 1963–4 was down to two-thirds of the number in 1959–60.[2] The Tryweryn affair had placed *Plaid Cymru* in a quandary. The failure of the party's constitutional strategy was constantly exposed by the steady progress in building the reservoir in the Tryweryn valley. Welsh opinion and Welsh M.P.s had been disregarded, yet *Plaid Cymru* had been unable and unwilling to capitalize on this situation. In the period 1960–5 *Plaid Cymru* had to make the choice while the reservoir was being built of sponsoring direct action at the site (and risking great unpopularity) or of doing nothing (and losing face with its own supporters).

The party leaders were losing control of those members that remained active in the party. In order to retain some authority they were forced from the time of the 1962 summer school to revise their attitudes towards those individuals who were members of the party and who engaged in direct action. Apart from organizing the purchase and sale of multiple plots of land which were to form part of the site of the Clywedog reservoir, during 1962 and 1963, the party leadership was not disposed to initiate any unorthodox action in support of the causes espoused by some of their more militant supporters. The *Blaid*, however, sympathized with what its members were doing of their own accord. Thus after the case against Pritchard and Walters at Bala in October 1962, Gwynfor Evans was to describe their actions at Tryweryn as 'understandable'. He reaffirmed that direct action was contrary to party policy (in itself not an exact interpretation of the party's position) but went on to say:

> Nevertheless we have obviously, as Welshmen, complete sympathy with these men in their action. They are driven to do this by circumstance. . . . It is the English authorities who should be in the dock and not these two Welshmen.[3]

Gwynfor Evans was to issue a similar statement when Emyr Llewelyn

---

[1] *Welsh Nation*, June 1964.
[2] Annual Reports of *Plaid Cymru* for 1960 and 1964.
[3] *Liverpool Daily Post*, 4 Oct. 1962 and subsequently reprinted in *Welsh Nation*, Oct. 1962.

Jones was tried and convicted on a charge of sabotaging a Tryweryn transformer.[1] Equally, Gwynfor Evans congratulated the Welsh Language Society's demonstration at Aberystwyth in February 1963, when he was at that time a member of the Society. All its members were at this time pledged to fight for equal status for Welsh and English, if necessary by personally using the tactics of civil disobedience. But the most substantial publicly-stated concession to the militants inside *Plaid Cymru* was made in December 1963 when the party's general secretary, Emrys Roberts, tried to clarify the party's declared policy on direct action. He told one meeting of party workers that 'we criticise the activists for their lack of political judgment, but we cannot condemn them for action we considered taking ourselves'.[2] He went on to say that

any widespread campaign of violent action in Wales today would be morally justifiable and politically foolish. It would alienate rather than win support. We in *Plaid Cymru* would have nothing to do with it.[2]

However, he also said that:

Violent action cannot be justified if it is a case of a minority trying to force its views on the majority in Wales. But when, as in the case of Tryweryn, it is undertaken in an attempt to force the Government to respect the wishes of the people of Wales, it has ample justification.[3]

Roberts also stated that if the party supported violent action it should be undertaken by major figures in the party who would then give themselves up—the purpose being to gain publicity for their case through the courts. Not only did this resemble closely what had actually happened in 1936 when well-known Nationalists had set fire to the R.A.F. bombing school in Penyberth,[4] but it also revealed that the party leadership had debated the issue of violent action as far back as 1959. In fact the executive committee of *Plaid Cymru* had in that year set up a working party to discuss the methods available.[5] *Plaid Cymru*'s official position with regard to violent as well as non-violent direct action was thus somewhat equivocal at the end of 1963, and can best be summarized as at that time being to tolerate direct action if it was inspired by nationalist motives, and to support it if it was generally popular. In all this period from 1960 to 1965, only

[1] *Western Mail*, 14 Mar. 1963.   [2] Ibid., 12 Dec. 1963.
[2] Ibid. Also recorded in *The Annual Register* (1963), p. 57.
[3] See Ch. 1.
[4] *Western Mail*, 12 Dec. 1963.

one member of the party was expelled for his criticism of the leadership, and he was not known to be implicated in activities using violent direct action.[1] David Pritchard and David Walters, who were executive members of *Plaid Cymru* were never publicly reprimanded for what they did at Tryweryn, and were not at all repentant.[2]

Not unexpectedly, the press paid considerable attention to the activities of the militant Nationalists, especially inside Wales—which must have been especially galling to *Plaid* leaders who had to fight for every inch of publicity for their conventional political activities. The *Western Mail* in the summer of 1963 went so far as to carry seven successive feature articles discussing the tensions inside *Plaid Cymru*.[3] But it was increasingly evident to the leaders of *Plaid Cymru*, if not to the militants themselves, that direct action, particularly when it involved violent methods, was making the cause of nationalism as well as its political voice, *Plaid Cymru*, less popular than ever. The party, however, was much too weak in terms of active workers to take a strong line against members who, in their individual capacities other than in the party's name, went beyond the limits of approved party policy. Some of the militant elements of the party dropped out of its activities of their own accord, when they failed to evoke a practical response from the bulk of its members. In some cases this led to the formation of independent organizations for furthering a particular nationalist objective with its membership overlapping very largely with that of *Plaid Cymru*.

In spite of all this doubt and self-questioning, and the widely-fought but largely fruitless local elections in the Welsh counties and districts in 1964, the annual conference, held that year at Fishguard, was not the occasion for mutual recrimination. *Plaid* leaders knew that they had a hard task ahead with an imminent general election at which they could not 'expect another spectacular advance' in their votes.[4] But one major surprise at the conference occurred in the election for Vice-President. The contest was between Elystan Morgan, widely regarded as Gwynfor Evans's *dauphin*, and Chris Rees, who held more radical views but who was comparatively unknown inside the party. When Rees was declared the victor of the election, there was suspicion that the election had not been conducted in an entirely straightforward manner. It was a personal rebuff to Elystan Morgan,

---

[1] This was Neil Jenkins who had strongly attacked *Plaid* leaders in the press.
[2] D. Walters and D. Pritchard, *The Nationalist*, vol. 1, No. 1 (1963), pp. 38–9.
[3] P. Kane in *Western Mail*, 2, 3, 4, 5, 8, 9, 10 July 1963.
[4] Annual Report of *Plaid Cymru*, 1964.

who announced his decision to leave *Plaid Cymru* the following year.

At the general election of October 1964 *Plaid Cymru* fought in twenty-three out of the thirty-six Welsh constituencies. All the seats outside Glamorgan and Monmouthshire were contested, except the highly marginal seat of East Flintshire, but for the first time since 1951 no Monmouthshire constituency was fought by the *Plaid*. Even though fielding three more candidates than in 1959, the *Blaid*'s total vote was reduced by eight thousand in this election to 69,507 votes. *Plaid* suffered severe setbacks in Anglesey, Merioneth, Llanelli, and West Rhondda, the only noticeable improvements occurring in the Caerphilly and Carmarthen constituencies.[1] The average share of the poll obtained by each *Plaid* candidate in this election was 8·4 per cent, compared with 10·3 per cent in 1959; in the nineteen constituencies fought by the *Blaid* both in 1959 and again in 1964 the average share of the poll obtained by the *Blaid* candidate dropped from 10·6 per cent to 8·6 per cent in 1964. The poor results in 1964 were not unexpected in *Plaid* official circles, and even the *Welsh Nation* for October 1964 carried reports predicting poor results for the party, an unusual way of trying to attract votes and support! Unlike the 1959 election, the *Blaid* did not blame its electoral failure on poor organization. Rather it claimed that its election machinery in 1964 was in a much better state of preparation than it had been in 1959.[2] The party blamed its failure in the election on the mass media, and on its own inability to get its message across to the electorate.

. . . no more than a small proportion of the population of Wales really heard the *Blaid*'s message. The reason was that the channels of communication were under the all but exclusive control of people who were intent on ignoring us and our message. And in modern mass communication it is far more deadly to be ignored than to be attacked. . . . The wonder of it is that 70,000 people were able to withstand all this concentration of power and support *Plaid Cymru*.[2]

The *Blaid* made great play, in particular, of not being allowed any time for party political broadcasts in Wales. Their claims for broadcasting time had long received quite wide support in Wales, and had been endorsed by local authorities, the Welsh Broadcasting Council,

---

[1] In Caerphilly, with Dr. Philip Williams as candidate, the *Blaid*'s share of the poll rose from 8·9 per cent to 11·0 per cent, and in Carmarthen, where Gwynfor Evans was candidate, the *Blaid*'s share rose from 5·2 per cent to 11·6 per cent of the poll.

[2] Annual Report of *Plaid Cymru*, 1965.

and, early in 1964, by Harold Wilson, then Leader of the Opposition. After the advent of a Labour Government, following the 1964 election, the parties' attitude to minority parties having a share of political broadcasting time was relaxed a little, and the *Blaid* made its first political broadcast on 25 September 1965. It lasted for five minutes. *Plaid Cymru* later claimed that this broadcast had directly brought into the party one thousand new members and one thousand pounds in funds.[1]

The outcome of the election and the party's reactions to the new political situation in Wales following the appointment of a Secretary of State for Wales and the setting-up of a fully-fledged Welsh Office, were complicated by controversy caused by the political and personal activities of Emrys Roberts, the *Blaid*'s general secretary.[2] Roberts was suddenly suspended from his post in November 1964 and was later replaced by Elwyn Roberts, who had previously been financial director of the party.[3] But apart from the scandal aroused in the press concerning this dispute inside the party, there was very little of the recrimination that might have been expected after the *Blaid*'s poor showing in the election. Perhaps those who were not interested in constitutional methods had mostly dropped out of the party. But the main reason for the lack of trouble seems to have been that party members had not set their sights very high, as they had done in 1959. In addition, another election was judged to be imminent as the Labour Party's victory in 1964 had been a very narrow one, and this left no time for introspection. The general secretary reported to the party conference in 1965 that:

Without doubt its [the party's] spirit was much better after the 1964 election than after that of 1959. There were individuals who withdrew from the movement—and some of them had made substantial contributions to the party in the past—but there was hardly any of the acrimony which all but overwhelmed the party five years ago.[4]

Even so there was still talk of whether the party should divert its resources into some other activities rather than concentrate on the

[1] Annual Report of *Plaid Cymru*, 1966.
[2] Roberts was involved in divorce proceedings also concerning other party members.
[3] Elwyn Roberts was once a bank official who had been organizer of the National *Eisteddfod* in North Wales and then was seconded to organize the Parliament for Wales campaign between 1953 and 1956. He became director of finance of *Plaid Cymru* in 1960 and was general secretary of the party from 1964 to 1971.
[4] Annual Report of *Plaid Cymru*, 1965.

electoral field.[1] And it was not until it organized a final demonstration against the Tryweryn reservoir, on the occasion of its opening, that the *Blaid* finally found its feet again—late in October 1965.[2] *Plaid* leaders were surprised that more than a thousand people came to such an inaccessible place at an inconvenient time to demonstrate against the opening of the reservoir, and they were delighted by the very considerable publicity that the demonstration attracted.[3] Even though the demonstration marked the failure of the *Blaid* to prevent the reservoir ever being built, it gave the party a fillip just at a time when it was most in need of encouragement. Another general election appeared inevitable soon; Elystan Morgan had just left the *Blaid* to join the Labour Party, and critics of the party leadership were beginning to organize themselves into a new group, the New Nation Group,[4] which was extremely critical of the gap between the party's goals and its actual achievements. One event which the *Blaid* welcomed was the publication of the Hughes-Parry committee's report on the Welsh language in October 1965. This committee, which had been set up by the Conservative Government in 1963, recommended that Welsh should be given the status of equal validity with English in law and public administration.[5]

Early in 1966 it was clear that the *Blaid* would have to strain every resource to fight the next general election on a broad front comparable to previous elections. Apathy and doubt gave way again to the need to organize for the election campaign. In the event, *Plaid Cymru* put forward twenty candidates to contest Welsh seats in the March 1966 election, as many as had fought in 1959, but three fewer than had fought in 1964. Once again the North and West Wales constituencies were fully covered by *Plaid* candidates; once again no candidate ventured into the elections in Monmouthshire. *Plaid Cymru* succeeded in holding most of its vote in this election: the party's share of the poll rose in ten constituencies and fell in nine. Many of the gains were small and occurred in South Wales; this was despite a considerable reduction in spending by the party during the election campaign.[6]

[1] K. O. Morgan, 'Four Constituency Campaigns: Swansea West', D. E. Butler and A. King, *The British General Election of 1964* (London, 1965), pp. 269–70.
[2] The opening took place on Thursday morning, 21 Oct. 1965.
[3] Annual Report of *Plaid Cymru*, 1966.
[4] Leaders of the group were: Emrys Roberts, John Legonna, Harri Webb, and Raymond Edwards.
[5] *Legal Status of the Welsh Language*, Cmnd. 2785 (H.M.S.O., 1965).
[6] Campaign and candidates' expenses, excluding the losses of £150 deposits, totalled £4,398 in 1966, shared between twenty candidates, compared with expenses of £7,647, shared between twenty-three candidates, in the 1964 election.

The great difference, however, between the quick succession of elections between 1964 and 1966, when compared with those held in 1950 and 1951, was that *Plaid Cymru* was able to field twenty candidates in the sixties, given such an unfavourable situation, whereas it had only been able to fight four seats in 1951, in a similar situation. Ironically, the constituency where most was spent in the 1966 election campaign, East Flintshire, produced the worst result, 902 votes, at a cost of thirteen shillings and ninepence a vote![1] Every constituency that raised the *Plaid* share of the poll in 1966 spent less money on its campaign than it had done in 1964.

TABLE 5.1

Wales: Votes Cast at General Elections 1959–1970

	1959	1964	1966	1970
Labour	841,447	837,022	863,692	781,941
%	56·5	57·8	60·7	51·6
Conservative	486,335	425,022	396,795	419,884
%	32·6	29·4	27·8	27·7
Liberal	78,951	106,114	89,108	103,747
%	5·3	7·3	6·3	6·9
Plaid Cymru	77,571	69,507	61,071	175,016
%	5·2	4·8	4·3	11·5
Communist	6,542	9,377	12,769	6,459
%	0·4	0·7	0·9	0·4
Others	408	..	..	29,507
%	0·0			1·9
Total electorate	1,805,684	1,805,454	1,801,872	1,960,521
% of electors voting (Wales)	82·6	80·1	79·0	77·3
% of electors voting (U.K.)	78·7	77·0	75·8	72·0

The causes of the introspection, the disagreements and the loss of confidence which 'all but devoured *Plaid Cymru*' in this period lie in the first instance in the apparent failure of the leaders' constitutional strategy to bring results, and the consequent search for alternative strategies. The party leaders felt that constitutional methods of pressing the nationalist case in Wales were the only methods which were likely to arouse public sympathy for their cause. Elections were fought with the idea of spreading information about the views and

[1] The campaign in East Flintshire cost *Plaid Cymru* £470, plus £150 for a loss of deposit.

intentions of *Plaid Cymru* as much as for bringing pressure on the other competing parties in Wales, or for securing, by some remote chance, the election of M.P.s or councillors. The *Blaid*'s activities in the first forty years of its life yielded no success whatever in parliamentary elections, and only very occasional victories in the local government field when candidates used the party label. Sometimes doubts would be raised as to what the value of any *Plaid Cymru* M.P. would be to the party,[1] and what the *Blaid* had to offer at local government level was often less than clear to its own members, although issues involving Welsh education and the language would evidently occur at local level. One suggestion on local government reorganization made in 1960 was that:

it would be a great day for Wales if a Welsh Parliament could model the administrative divisions of Wales on the basis of the *cantrefi* and *cymydau*.[2]

The *Blaid* thus fought local elections on national as well as local issues, and hoped that its local organizations could be sustained and improved as a result.

Since the party executive was not prepared officially to endorse any of the non-constitutional strategies suggested by party members, although it sympathized with the motives that inspired such suggested action, individual members of *Plaid Cymru* were left free and felt free to experiment with different strategies to further the party's three aims.[3] A series of new moves resulted. One group founded the Triskel Press to publish material of Welsh origin or interest. Some South Wales Nationalists migrated to south Cardiganshire to set up a co-operative farm on traditional Welsh lines. Trefor Morgan organized successfully the foundation of the *Undeb* insurance company with the objective of investing Welsh capital in Welsh industry. Morgan also organized the establishment of the Glyn Dŵr Trust, a private trust to sponsor education through the medium of the Welsh language. Many *Plaid* members were individually pressing their local authorities to set up *Ysgolion Cymraeg* (Welsh schools).[4] Other *Plaid* members gave much time to the Welsh Language Society; one or two preferred to set up the so-called 'Free Wales Army'[5] or engage in acts of sabotage—despite party policy. Groups such as *Cymru Ein Gwlad*

---

[1] e.g., Wynne Samuel, *Welsh Nation*, Jan. 1964.   [2] *Welsh Nation*, Mar. 1960.
[3] The party's three aims appear on every member's membership card. They are: first, to secure self-government for Wales; second, to safeguard the Welsh language and culture; third, to secure for Wales a seat at the United Nations.
[4] See Ch. 9.
[5] Initially known as the 'Welsh Freedom Army'.

and the Cilmeri Group issued their bitter, ephemeral magazines. The annual conference became a forum for proposing militant motions and drastic constitutional changes. At least while *Plaid* members were prepared to work within the party structure they could be disciplined and guided by the leadership. But the formation of separate groups such as the Welsh Language Society and the 'Free Wales Army', which had adopted strategies that differed greatly from the *Blaid*'s declared policy, meant that the party gradually fragmented, relinquishing its control over those individuals whose demands it would not accommodate. Initially there was little difference of principle between *Plaid Cymru* and the Welsh Language Society, but the approach of their leaders increasingly diverged. While the activities of the Society and of *Plaid Cymru* continued to react upon the fortunes of each other to a considerable extent, it proved in retrospect a political mistake for *Plaid Cymru* to lose control of the young Nationalists in the Society. The latter has tended since its foundation in 1963 to become steadily more militant and extreme in its actions.

The initial spur to *Plaid* supporters to act independently of the party was the electoral failure of the party and the refusal of the party leaders to support or suggest political activities other than electioneering. While the *Blaid* leaders may have trimmed their words to suit the militant mood of some of their members, they scarcely altered the nature of their own political activities. They were forced on to the defensive by some of their members, even interviewed by the police about the activities of individual members, but in the main they stood their political ground. However, their position was generally more hostile to direct action and civil disobedience during the 1960s than it had been, for example, in 1951 when the party organized the sit-down at Trawsfynydd; possibly leaders found this an acceptable course of action because at Trawsfynydd the issue involved a protest against war. *Plaid* leaders could not attempt, however, to control the activities of those who observed party policy on direct action and remained loyal at the same time to the party leaders. In effect there was an issue for everyone, and everyone had his issue. A poet in Pembrokeshire, Waldo Williams, refused to pay income tax as a protest against conscription.[1] A housewife in Llangennech, Carmarthenshire, refused to pay her rates until the rate demand was sent in the Welsh language; she eventually succeeded in getting this.[2]

[1] *Welsh Nation*, Oct. 1960.   [2] Ibid,, Apr. 1960.

Individuals would paint slogans for a free Wales as the fancy took them,[1] and the *Welsh Nation* was happy that this form of activity should continue. 'But whoever is responsible for the slogans and the symbols, good luck to them!' it commented. 'They are serving the valuable purpose of keeping the Nationalist ideals before the eyes of our people. . . .'[2]

The party organization, with Emrys Roberts in full command from 1962, tried to spearhead the growth of the *Blaid* in the industrial areas of South Wales. A conscious effort was made to produce more propaganda concerned with economic and industrial problems. The organization now became very frank about the state of the party. Precise membership figures were produced for the first time in years, and it was rumoured that the largest branch of members in the *Blaid*, according to the party's records, had until recently been the branch of those *wedi marw*, who were now party members in heaven, having once been members on earth.[3] Some members of the *Blaid* remained concerned with the Campaign for Nuclear Disarmament, or the question of Sunday opening, thus fully exercising their non-conformist consciences. Even the *Welsh Nation* thundered against a tourist development in Merioneth because it would cause a local housing shortage:

> The so-called 'tourist industry' is an aggravation of the already serious housing situation in rural Wales. But Maentwrog has escaped the full blast of this pestilence. Its houses will be the home of Welsh families, not conveniences for dirty weekends for Birmingham businessmen.[4]

Other members were most concerned with the Welsh language, following the example of Saunders Lewis. The *Welsh Nation* complained that Welshmen had refused to take a political attitude towards the language. 'English Governments of all complexions have always taken a firmly political attitude to the Welsh language. Its deletion has always been considered a political necessity.'[5] Other *Plaid* members warned that if the party wanted to make headway in south-east Wales it ought not to force the Welsh language down people's throats.[6] This epitomized a fundamental conflict of view

---

[1] One of the most publicized was that of Councillor Bill Williams and Meic Stephens, both of Merthyr, who were caught painting slogans on Cyfarthfa Castle in Dec. 1963.

[2] *Welsh Nation*, July 1963. *Plaid* attitudes had changed by 1967. Cf. Ch. 4.

[3] Private information.

[4] *Welsh Nation*, Oct. 1963.   [5] Ibid., Apr. 1962.

[6] e.g., Alf Williams, ibid., Dec. 1961. See also Royston L. Parker, ibid., July 1964.

within *Plaid Cymru*, whether to give first loyalty to Welsh linguistic interests or to the physical territory of Wales.

One way in which dissatisfaction with the style and leadership of the *Blaid* was channelled, was in demands for organizational changes. An inquiry launched in 1963 came to the conclusion that the party organizers should not try to organize the party so much as try to raise money for it.[1] Previously there had been moves by some sections of the *Blaid* to establish the office of party chairman; this was discussed at the annual conference in the summer of 1963. The idea itself was reasonable in that it aimed to separate organizational responsibility for the party from the responsibility of political leadership, the President of the *Blaid* having at the time to bear both responsibilities. However, those who argued for the new post of chairman were not the political friends of the incumbent President of the *Blaid*, Gwynfor Evans, and this made the rejection of the proposal for a chairman almost inevitable. Some constitutional changes were nevertheless achieved. The Vice-Presidency of the *Blaid*, for example, became a two-yearly office, instead of an annually elected one, in 1962.[2] But the executive committee's proposals for constitutional changes were referred back by the annual conference in 1963, and were not remodelled in time for the 1964 conference.[3] Some changes concerning the reduction in the size of the executive by two-thirds and the division of responsibilities between party officers were also introduced early in 1966.[4] A new constitution was finally adopted by the party conference in the summer of 1966, although a note of realism was recorded by the Director of Organization when he stated that information received from party branches indicated that the previous constitution had been 'largely ignored'.[5]

Plaid Cymru in the early 1960s also tried to continue its policy of co-operating with other bodies to further aims held in common. Many *Plaid* supporters were active in the national television conferences held in Cardiff at the turn of the decade to press for an improved television service for Wales; others were better known inside C.N.D. Official party policy opposed all nuclear armaments, and party organs encouraged the boycott of South African goods. The party's annual conference accepted a resolution in 1962 which urged all political parties in Wales to get together when they were in

[1] Private information.
[2] *Welsh Nation*, Sept. 1962.
[3] Annual Report of *Plaid Cymru*, 1964.
[4] *Western Mail*, 3 Jan. 1966.
[5] Annual Report of *Plaid Cymru*, 1966.

broad agreement to press jointly their agreed aims.[1] But some voices were raised in the party against this diversification of effort,[2] and a writer in the party's youth magazine in 1963 complained that:

For 37 years [*Plaid Cymru*] has been boiling with the images and claims of Congoism, Sabbatarianism, CNDism, Pacifism, Roman Catholicism, the lot,—fancies quite irrelevant to the fight for the freeing of Wales. Fancies that strengthen England not Wales in the struggle England versus Wales. . . . What a macabre twist it would be were we to see the Welsh People turn from her new freedom back to a regime of subjugation, and that because of the clattering cacophony of our host of ideals on the rampage.[3]

Events in 1966, however, changed this atmosphere of drift and fragmentation, and rallied the party and its supporters once again to work for its central aim of self-government.

[1] *Welsh Nation*, Sept. 1962.
[2] Ibid., Feb. and Nov. 1960.
[3] J. Legonna, 'From the Crest of the Hill' in *The Nationalist*, vol. 1, No. 1 (June, 1963).

6

PLAID CYMRU 1966–1970: BREAKTHROUGH
OR FALSE DAWN?

THE internal morale of *Plaid Cymru* and the party's status within Wales were transformed within four months of the 1966 general election. A party which had wrestled with constant failure, ridicule, and political isolation, and which had even flirted with unconstitutional activity in its despair, suddenly found itself at the centre of the Welsh political arena, the talking-point of the Welsh nation and the world. This change was brought about by the voting in the Carmarthen by-election on 14 July 1966. In what was the most significant parliamentary election result in a single Welsh constituency for many decades, Gwynfor Evans, the President of *Plaid Cymru*, more than doubled his share of the poll in the constituency, and raised his vote by nearly nine thousand to make a total of over sixteen thousand votes.

Voting in Carmarthen Parliamentary Constituency: 1964–1966

Year	Turn-out	*Plaid vote*	%	Labour vote	%	Liberal vote	%	Con-serva-tive vote	%
GE1964	84·5%	5,495	11·6	21,424	45·5	15,210	32·3	4,996	10·6
GE1966	82·6%	7,416	16·1	21,221	46·2	11,988	26·1	5,338	11·6
By1966	74·6%	16,179	39·0	14,743	33·0	8,650	21·0	2,934	7·0

GE = General Election; By = By-election

This was enough for Gwynfor Evans to capture the seat from Labour; thus he became the first member of *Plaid Cymru* to sit in the House of Commons. The recognition which was accorded to the party as a result of its by-election victory had an immediate effect on *Plaid Cymru*. Confidence and energy replaced apathy and disillusion among the rank and file. Former stalwarts rejoined the party, and new recruits were won over from other parties. The *Blaid* moved away from being a closed order and became much more an open party with widened horizons. Above all, the authority of the party leadership was strengthened, and discontent with its gradualist and constitutional approach to politics evaporated.

It had been an open secret for several months that a by-election was to be expected in the Carmarthen constituency, owing to the ill health of Lady Megan Lloyd George, the sitting M.P. Indeed it was a surprise that she allowed her name to go forward as Labour candidate in the March general election, and her campaign had had to be fought largely by politicians from outside the constituency, with Gwilym Prys Davies acting as her understudy. When Lady Megan died at the end of May, therefore, *Plaid Cymru* was geared for a by-election, and Gwilym Prys Davies was chosen as the Labour candidate, despite his having been both a Welsh Republican and a member of *Plaid Cymru*.[1] From the opening of the campaign the *Blaid* was confident of a good result and an improved vote. In the March election, Gwynfor Evans had raised his vote by two thousand, to poll the largest number of votes ever won by a *Plaid* candidate. The enthusiasm of party activists was thus kindled by their candidate's recent good showing, and by the lift given to the *Blaid*'s morale by the Tryweryn demonstration the previous autumn and by the gift at the beginning of 1966 of two thousand pounds from a founder-member of *Plaid Cymru*, Dr. D. J. Williams.[2] The *Blaid* entered the Carmarthen by-election with the feeling that the contest was an open one, and that theirs was the most impressive candidate of the four in the fight. They mounted an expensive campaign and drafted more than a thousand workers into the constituency from outside.[3] The Labour candidate was unable to rouse the local Labour voters, and as the campaign drew to a close it was clear even to him that he had lost the election. What was not so clear was who would win the election. The Liberals fought a hard campaign stressing the harm likely to come to Carmarthenshire from the newly-introduced Selective Employment Tax which penalized the service industries. But their social base in the county had been declining for some years, and their candidate, Hywel Davies, was not a match for Gwynfor

---

[1] Gwilym Prys Davies was active in *Plaid Cymru* in the mid 1940s, notably in Cardiganshire, but in 1948 he helped found the Welsh Republicans (see Ch. 10) and broke with the *Blaid* in 1949. He joined the Labour Party in 1954. Author of *A Central Council for Wales* (Aberystwyth, 1963), and later Chairman of the Welsh Hospital Board.

[2] This unexpected gift was the sum realized from the sale of Dr. D. J. Williams's home at Rhydcymerau immortalized in his book, *Hên Dŷ Ffarm* (The Old Farmhouse) (Aberystwyth, 1953).

[3] Various reports of the Carmarthen campaign—probably exaggerated.

Evans, the only local man of the four candidates and a man who commanded respect in many parts of Wales. Even the Conservative-inclined *Western Mail* came to describe him as 'the personality of the election'.[1] Similarly, Elwyn Roberts, the *Blaid*'s general secretary, was to describe Gwynfor Evans's victory in Carmarthen as 'a personal triumph . . . due in a large measure to his personality, ability, and sincerity; his vision, his tireless service, his courageous leadership, his undaunted perseverance, over long years, both in his home county and throughout Wales'.[2]

The news of the result of the Carmarthen by-election came as a bolt from the blue for the rest of Wales. It became a much discussed question as to why the voters in Carmarthen had made such a drastic change of political allegiance. Clearly the personality of the candidates in the election was a large factor, and it was true that recent Carmarthen M.P.s had been outstanding in this respect. Sir Rhys Hopkin Morris, who was Liberal M.P. for the constituency from 1945 to 1956, wrested the seat from the sitting Labour member in an election which elsewhere saw a Labour landslide. Morris had been an Asquithian Liberal in Lloyd George's own country, and even so had survived politically. He was an individualist in an individualistic party, and he held his constituency by virtue of his towering personality rather than because of the effectiveness of his political organization.[3] Hopkin Morris died in 1956 and the political vacuum in Carmarthenshire was filled at a by-election in 1957 by Lady Megan Lloyd George. She was the daughter of David Lloyd George and a major figure in Welsh politics in her own right, who had recently left the ranks of the Liberals to join the Labour Party. In 1966, it was the turn of Gwynfor Evans to stamp his mark on the constituency.

But more important than the interplay of personalities in the election was the timing of the by-election. Many politicians had expected the by-election to occur before Harold Wilson called a new general election in 1966. If this had happened, the campaign in Carmarthen and the result of the election would have been crucial to the survival of the Labour Government; a defeat for Labour would have left the Government with a majority of one in the House of Commons. In these circumstances it would have been almost certain that Carmarthen would have returned a Labour M.P. However, these were not the conditions in which the Carmarthen by-election actually took

[1] *Western Mail*, 12 July 1966 (also 1 July 1966).
[2] Annual Report of *Plaid Cymru*, 1966.
[3] T. J. Evans, *Rhys Hopkin Morris: the man and his character* (Llandyssul, 1957).

place. The conditions obtaining were those of a Labour Government recently elected and comfortably in control of the House of Commons with a majority of ninety-seven, and which had just introduced a particularly adverse budget from the West Wales point of view. These conditions were ideal for a thoroughly introspective election in Carmarthen in which personality and local issues would be the decisive factors. The Carmarthen by-election proved to be a massive exercise in *brogarwch*.[1] The Labour Government in Britain as a whole had not yet lost the confidence of the voters, according to the opinion polls (see Table 6.1).

TABLE 6.1

Gallup Polls 1966–1970: Surveys of Voting Intention Summarized

Year		% Con. lead on Labour	% voting 'Other'	Year		% Con. lead on Labour	% voting 'Other'
1966	Mar.	−9½	½	1968	Apr.	24½	3
	May	−15½	1		May	28	5
	Jne	−11	1		Jne	23½	6½
	Jly	−6½	1		Jly	20	7
	Aug.	½	1		Aug.	15	4½
	Sep.	−2	1		Sep.	10	4½
	Oct.	−1	1		Oct.	7½	5
	Nov.	2½	1		Nov.	18½	3½
	Dec.	3	1½		Dec.	25½	4½
1967	Jan.	−2½	1	1969	Jan.	21	4½
	Feb.	−11	1		Feb.	22½	2½
	Mar.	−½	2½		Mar.	18½	3½
	Apr.	6	2		Apr.	20½	5½
	May	6½	1		May	21½	4
	Jne	5	1½		Jne	..	..
	Jly	½	1½		Jly	23½	2½
	Aug.	3½	2		Aug.	12½	3
	Sep.	3	2		Sep.	9½	3½
	Oct.	5	2½		Oct.	2	2
	Nov.	6	4		Nov.	3½	3½
	Dec.	16	5		Dec.	10½	1½
1968	Jan.	15½	4½	1970	Jan.	7½	3½
	Feb.	22½	5		Feb.	7	2
	Mar.	19	4		Mar.	5½	3

Sources: D. E. Butler and J. Freeman, *British Political Facts 1900–1967* (London, 1967). *Daily Telegraph.*

Note. The figures given for 1966 and 1967 are inclusive of those answering 'Don't Know'; figures given for 1968–70 are exclusive of 'Don't Knows'.

[1] Trans. 'affection for locality'.

The impact of the Carmarthen result was not confined to that county. It was regarded throughout Wales as a national event, a portent for the future. Welshmen collectively took pride in their achievement, and many people of all parties were glad that at last Gwynfor Evans had personally received success and recognition in the political field. However, this was not the end of the affair. The *Blaid* victory became the symbol of a nationalistic political perspective that had been growing in Wales for many years. In a day, the political complexion of Wales was radically altered, its new face revealed. *Plaid Cymru* had established its credibility as an alternative party, and all the other political parties began to assess seriously its challenge and its objectives. Historical 'ifs' have a seductive fascination for students of history, politics, or science, that altogether outweighs their value as an aid to human understanding of events. Nevertheless it is important to ask whether a victory for *Plaid Cymru* in Carmarthen as little as a decade before it in fact occurred would have had comparable repercussions in the rest of Wales, or whether what was regarded in 1966 as a serious political event would have been brushed aside in 1956 as an eccentric piece of Welsh political behaviour. It seems that the latter would have been the case, but that the period 1956 to 1966 witnessed considerable changes in the make-up of Wales to allow for such a radical change in its political atmosphere. Some politicians have suggested that world historical trends affected the political outlook of the Welsh people, making them more conscious of their own separate identity, and yet increasingly powerless to choose their own destiny. Inside Wales, there had developed a new consciousness of the unity of Wales, in particular fostered by the advent of regional television from 1958 and the setting up of the Welsh Office under a Secretary of State in 1964. It is very likely that if any Nationalist had won the Carmarthen by-election before these developments had been seen to occur, the event would have been almost ignored. In 1966, however, mass media did exist to make all Wales fully aware of *Plaid*'s achievement in Carmarthen, *and* the media were sufficiently interested in the nationalist upsurge to give it full prominence. The people in the Rhondda heard the news of Carmarthen, and showed that they had done so when they came to vote in the West Rhondda by-election less than nine months later. If there was any doubt that the Carmarthen result was significant for the whole of Wales, the election result in Rhondda West removed it completely in March 1967.

Voting in the Rhondda West Constituency: 1964–1967

Year	Turn-out	Plaid vote	%	Labour vote	%	Conservative vote	%	Communist vote	%
GE 1964	80·7%	2,668	10·2	20,713	79·3	2,754	10·5	..	..
GE 1966	80·3%	2,172	8·7	19,060	76·1	1,955	7·8	1,853	7·4
By 1967	82·2%	10,067	39·9	12,353	49·0	1,075	4·3	1,723	6·8

The Labour Party was humbled in the very heartland of British socialism, and it was humbled again in July 1968 when, a few valleys to the east of the Rhondda Fawr, the electors of the Caerphilly constituency cast their votes at a by-election. The moral for the Labour Party in Wales was made clear. Labour hegemony in the Welsh valleys had ceased to be automatic. Commitments to socialism

Voting in the Caerphilly Constituency: 1964–1968

Year	Turn-out	Plaid vote	%	Labour vote	%	Conservative vote	%	Liberal vote	%
GE 1964	78·4%	3,956	11·0	26,011	72·1	6,086	16·9	..	..
GE 1966	76·7%	3,949	11·1	26,330	74·2	5,182	14·6	..	..
By 1968	75·9%	14,274	40·4	16,148	45·7	3,687	10·4	1,257	3·5

had become blurred in the face of the continuation of pit closures, economic insecurity, and of relatively high rates of unemployment under a Labour Government. *Plaid Cymru* appeared to offer a socialist alternative, a modern and a Welsh alternative too, to the valley people. One journalist who followed the progress of the Caerphilly by-election campaign was moved to conclude that:

In the Midlands, the slump in the Labour vote looked merely like the collapse of a habit: in South Wales, it looks like the death of a religion.[1]

The simulated revivalist atmosphere of the *Blaid*'s whirlwind campaign in the Rhymney valley was equally unmistakable. However, the quality of the *Blaid*'s new support was immediately questioned. Many claimed it was a protest vote; in England the voters had turned to the Conservatives, in Scotland and Wales to the Nationalists. Success had taken the Nationalists by surprise. The *Blaid*'s victory at Carmarthen in 1966 was paralleled in Scotland with the election at

[1] D. McKie, *Guardian*, 20 July 1968.

the Hamilton by-election in November 1967 of Mrs. Winifred Ewing, the Scottish National Party's candidate. Yet a Gallup poll conducted in the Rhondda after the by-election there suggested that the *Blaid*'s improved vote was a temporary phenomenon (see Table 6.2).

TABLE 6.2

Gallup Poll Survey of Nationalist Voters in Glasgow-Pollock and Rhondda West (1967)

Question: 'How would you vote if the contest were a general election and not a by-election?'

Answer:

Nationalist voters only	West Rhondda %	Glasgow-Pollok %
Still vote Nationalist	10	23
Vote Labour	69	30
Vote Conservative	8	23
Undecided	13	24
	N = c. 130	N = c. 100
Total sample size	N = 400	N = 400

Source: *Daily Telegraph*, 9 and 11 Mar. 1967.

The Labour Government's victories had certainly given the S.N.P. and the *Blaid* a tactical opening, but it was not until the general election of 1970 that their progress was admitted to have any depth. Economic discontent was certainly a major factor in the rise of the Nationalists in both Scotland and Wales after 1965, but cultural influences of a lasting nature also contributed largely to the progress of the *Blaid* at this time.[1] The *Blaid*'s victory in Carmarthen presented the party with immediate problems of organization and direction. It may have been 'the crowning event' in the history of *Plaid Cymru*, but the problem now was to consolidate the party's newly-found support and to capitalize on this by-election triumph.[2] Public attention focused immediately on the party. Demands for information and publicity material flowed into the party offices in Cardiff and Bangor, as well as offers of money; these were quickly followed by an army of journalists and research students. The Carmarthen election, claimed party spokesmen, brought *Plaid Cymru* a thousand new

[1] See Chs. 7, 8, and 9.
[2] Annual Report of *Plaid Cymru*, 1966.

members,[1] including three or four hundred in the constituency itself,[2] and quickly raised for the party a thousand pounds. But it also placed heavy organizational demands on the party's staff. At the annual conference in 1966, more constitutional and organizational changes were enacted,[3] the outcome of moves pre-dating the Carmarthen election; Edward Millward, a prominent member of the Welsh Language Society was elected Vice-President for the next two years. The Vice-Presidency was an office that increased in prestige as the prestige of *Plaid Cymru* rose in Wales, and also as the time of the President was further taxed by his constituency and parliamentary duties. One clear lesson drawn from the party conference was the need to fill in the gaps of policy and information in the *Blaid*'s platform, and to rethink some of the party's old policies, some substantially unchanged since before the Second World War, in response to the new political situation in Wales and the new interest in *Plaid Cymru*.[4] With this in mind, it was decided in November 1966 to set up a party Research Group, initially based in London.[5] The founders of this group were very much the young lions of the party;[6] their first priority was the collection of sufficient information and advice to think through again the party's economic policy.[7] In fact *Plaid Cymru* tended to accept without question the findings of this Research Group and to rely on it as its only source of thinking inside the party. Thus it became a powerful instrument of party policy-making. However, the relative isolation of its members from the rest of the party began, two years later, to cause friction within the *Blaid* at the level of its national council.[8] The Research Group reduced its activities in 1969 because it had fulfilled its immediate objective of remedying the dearth of factual evidence and policy which it had discovered in 1966. In its first three years it had largely written the party's economic and constitutional policies.

---

[1] Annual Report of *Plaid Cymru*, 1966.   [2] *Western Mail*, 19 July 1966.
[3] Annual Report of *Plaid Cymru*, 1967.
[4] Viz., the issue of workers' control and economic planning.
[5] *Western Mail*, 21 Nov. 1966.
[6] They were Dafydd Wigley, Dr. Phil Williams, and Dr. Gareth Morgan Jones. Wigley became prospective candidate in Merioneth in 1968, and economic spokesman in 1969. Williams became prospective candidate in Caerphilly in 1968 and Vice-President of the party. Morgan Jones took up the post of assistant general secretary of *Plaid Cymru* and South Wales organizer at the beginning of 1968, and held it until late in 1970. He contested Aberdare at the 1970 general election.
[7] Dr. Phil Williams, private interview, 9 July 1969, and Dafydd Wigley, private interview, 2 Apr. 1970.
[8] e.g., National Council meeting at Newtown early in 1969 debate on growth centres.

The *Blaid*'s performance in local elections is an important gauge of how successful it was in different areas in the years following the Carmarthen by-election. Local elections where *Plaid* members used the party label were almost all fought in South Wales;[1] the party's officials seemed to give up all hope of this happening in North and mid Wales.[2] Its success in local elections is, however, difficult to judge, since the vast majority of those *Plaid* members standing for election did so without using the party label. *Plaid Cymru* claimed in 1967 that it had seven hundred councillors throughout Wales, including parish councillors, and that four hundred of these council seats had been won and gained in 1967 alone[3]—the year of the triennial county and district elections, and the first year in which local elections were held in Wales after the Carmarthen by-election. If, however, one relies entirely on the success of *Plaid Cymru* candidates in local elections who used the party label, a more reliable guide to the party's political standing in South Wales, where most of these candidates stood, can be arrived at.

Table of Plaid *Councillors Elected and Unsuccessful Candidatures using the Party Label at Local Elections 1967–1970*

Year	Cllrs. with *Plaid* party label	No. of *Plaid* cllrs. elected at spring elections	Total no. of candidates at spring elections
1967	36	23	102
1968	41	7	60
1969	51	7	85
1970	48	25	202

Sources: Western Mail, Liverpool Daily Post, Welsh Nation, and confidential reports on local elections circulated within *Plaid Cymru* in 1967, 1968, and 1969.

Note. Candidatures and successes are swelled in the years when triennial county and district elections are held, i.e. 1967 and 1970. Successes at local council by-elections account for the disparity in the numbers of elected councillors shown.

[1] Only 12 of *Plaid*'s 51 councillors in 1969 sat for North Wales seats; in 1969, only 5 out of the 85 *Plaid* candidates contested council seats in North Wales.

[2] The pessimism of party officials on this point is shown in *Forward*, May–Aug. 1969, p. 11.

[3] Annual Report of *Plaid Cymru*, 1967. A number of prominent local figures who were *Plaid* members always contested local elections as Independents, e.g. Tom Jones (Merioneth), Heulyn Roberts (Cardiganshire), and W. R. P. George (Caernarvonshire).

But this general picture of expansion should not obscure the fact that *Plaid Cymru* was able to put forward candidates for a very small proportion of the seats on local councils which fell vacant each year, and few of these candidates were successful. In 1969 the party had secured the election of only two councillors (one in Cardiff, and one in Merthyr) in any of the four county boroughs in Wales which had a combined complement of nearly one hundred and thirty councillors. At the end of 1969 the largest number of councillors the *Blaid* had succeeded in electing to a single local authority was four; these groups of four were sitting on the Carmarthenshire County Council and the Ammanford Urban District Council, in Carmarthenshire. Thus *Plaid Cymru* was still far from challenging the position achieved by the Liberal Party on Welsh local authorities. One reason for this relative failure in local elections was *Plaid Cymru*'s inability to recruit openly to its ranks community leaders of standing and influence, especially in South Wales. These leaders preferred to remain independent of party or to be active in the Labour Party, although *Plaid* officials noted that the party was making better headway in this quarter at the end of 1969 than it had done in the previous three years. Another reason for this lack of success in local elections was that other groups such as Ratepayers' organizations or the Liberal Party had already taken up the role of opposition to the local Labour establishment controlling South Wales local councils, a role which *Plaid Cymru* tried to adopt once it entered local politics. In almost every local contest where comparisons are possible, Ratepayer and Liberal candidates tended to collect a larger share of the poll than *Plaid Cymru* candidates in straight fights with Labour candidates.[1] Where Ratepayers fought against *Plaid Cymru* and Labour candidates in local elections they had generally beaten *Plaid Cymru* challengers in the poll.[2]

The *Blaid* also found itself hampered by extraneous factors when trying to secure the anti-Labour votes which it expected to acquire after the Carmarthen and Rhondda by-election results. First, there was the equivocal stand taken by members of *Plaid Cymru* towards the Investiture of the Prince of Wales in Caernarfon in July 1969. Then there were the explosions that rocked various Welsh dams and

---

[1] See Ch. 7.

[2] In May 1969, in the twenty-one local election contests where *Plaid* and Ratepayer candidates fought each other, Ratepayers won five seats and beat *Plaid* candidates in another seven. *Plaid* candidates beat Ratepayers in nine seats, but won none of those.

public buildings from 1966 to 1969, and which were commonly attributed to Welsh nationalists.[1] Finally there were the activities of the Welsh Language Society, especially its campaign to paint out road-signs which it launched in 1969 and which cast doubts on the *Plaid*'s own attitudes to the Welsh language issue and to protest politics.[2]

The Investiture of the Prince of Wales confronted *Plaid Cymru* with a dilemma which only the conclusion of that event could resolve. The dilemma was whether the *Blaid* should approve of the Investiture because it envisaged the Royal House of Windsor as being the royal house of a self-governing Wales,[3] or whether it should oppose the ceremony on the grounds that the Investiture commemorated Wales's greatest defeat, the conquest of Wales by Edward I following the death of Llewelyn the Last in 1282. Gwynfor Evans declared in May of 1967 that:

. . . I cannot help thinking of the original purpose of giving the male heir to the English Crown the title of Prince of Wales . . . it was taken by Edward I and given to his eldest son in order to weaken Welsh resistance and to pave the way for integrating the Welsh nation with the English state. Not unnaturally I am unenthusiastic about it.[4]

But this was not enough for many activists and members. Carwyn James, the party's parliamentary candidate for Llanelli, was speaking for many party members when he told the *Plaid* Youth conference in April 1968 that 'very few of us hold any brief for the Royal Family whatsoever',[5] but that any outright hostility to the Investiture of the Prince of Wales would lose the party votes which they could ill afford to shed. The chairman of the *Plaid*'s Youth committee wrote in its magazine:

If the prince is non-political in English politics, in Welsh politics an English prince is as much a supporter of one side as Cledwyn Hughes himself. He is as biased politically as if his mother were a paid-up member of the Labour party.[6]

Inevitably the matter was raised again at the party's annual conference in Aberystwyth in September 1968. A resolution submitted by the Bridgend branch of the *Blaid* called upon the party to 'disassociate itself from all functions, meetings, etc., concerning the

---

[1] See Ch. 10.   [2] See Ch. 9.
[3] *Plaid Cymru*'s constitutional plans approved on 7 and 8 March 1970 envisaged the Queen as head of State.
[4] *Liverpool Daily Post*, 18 May 1967.
[5] Carwyn James, speech to *Plaid* Youth Conference, 18 Apr. 1968.
[6] D. Elis Thomas, *I'r Gad*, Spring 1968.

Investiture as Prince of Wales of Charles, the eldest son of the Queen of England'.[1] Despite a moderating amendment from the party's executive committee, the conference finally decided to leave the resolution on the table, after pleas by Wynne Samuel and Dr. D. J. Williams,[2] in an attempt to cover the party against attacks from its political opponents. Meanwhile, the Vice-President of *Plaid Cymru*, Edward Millward, had agreed to act as tutor in Welsh to Prince Charles during his term's studies at the University College of Wales, Aberystwyth, in 1969. The early apathy in Wales for the Investiture and the widespread public reluctance to accept the cost of the pageantry was converted in the early summer of 1969 into considerable enthusiasm for the event. When exposed to the mass media, the full personality of the Prince evoked a great response from the Welsh people, particularly after the incidents during his speech in Welsh to the *Urdd* in May.[3] With several community leaders in the rural areas, in particular ministers of religion and schoolteachers, taking the nationalist view of the Investiture, many villages and communities were split and some turned against their traditional leaders.[4] *Plaid Cymru* received a severe setback because of the divisions and tensions caused by the Investiture for which *Plaid* leaders blamed the Prime Minister and the Secretary of State for Wales. However, a good attendance at the party's annual conference held in Aberystwyth in September 1969 convinced party workers finally that all was far from lost, and that much of the ground that the party had lost the previous summer was recoverable.

The Investiture was not the only cause of *Plaid Cymru*'s unpopularity and embarrassment in the summer of 1969. Another cause was the trial of some members of the so-called 'Free Wales Army' which lasted over four months and which was concluded at Swansea on 1 July, the day of the Investiture. There were also the explosions in North and South Wales which accompanied the approach of the Investiture. *Plaid Cymru* had long before disassociated itself from groups that used violent means to further Welsh nationalism, and at its 1967 conference in Dolgellau the party had voted for the expulsion of 'anyone who is connected in any way with these organizations (the Free Wales Army and the Patriotic

---

[1] *Plaid Cymru* Conference Programme, 1968 p. 7.
[2] Dr. D. J. Williams made a special plea that the party should not repeat the mistakes of 1936 and 1937 (see Ch. 1) in which he had taken part.
[3] See Ch. 9.
[4] Viz., A. A. S. Butt Philip, *Socialist Commentary* (Oct. 1969).

Front) and their activities which are harmful to the best interests of Wales and to the growth of the party';[1] only a handful of delegates opposed this move.[2] However, the party was unable to avoid being tarred with the same brush as those alleged nationalists who were responsible for the explosions in Wales from 1966. The slow advance of the *Blaid* in the 1969 local elections was directly blamed by the party's general secretary, Elwyn Roberts, on the explosions.[3] Repeated repudiations of violence and denials of complicity in the explosions by the party's spokesmen seemed to be only partially effective in allaying public doubts about the *Blaid*'s involvement in these activities; these doubts were never entirely removed.[4] In the event only two members of the party, one of them Owen Williams, were expelled from the party after the 1967 Dolgellau resolution: others were never asked to renew their subscriptions.[5]

Another cause of anxiety in the public mind concerning the *Blaid*'s programme was the party's attitude towards the Welsh language. It is not exactly clear when *Plaid Cymru* changed its view on the language from demanding the return to an all Welsh-speaking Wales, with Welsh as the first language,[6] to the demand for a bilingual Wales. Long after party spokesmen were saying that bilingualism was the *Blaid*'s language policy, there was still no official decision of the party conference on the question. It was not until 1959 that the party began to redefine officially its attitude. A resolution approved at the 1961 conference spelled out in detail the *Blaid*'s language policy which harked back to the *Blaid*'s original ideal of a Welsh-speaking Wales more than to the ideal of a bilingual nation. It was not until the 1969 conference that *Plaid Cymru* specifically mentioned a bilingual nation as its objective, and it remained unclear even then whether this was the *Blaid*'s final objective. Even so, bilingualism was an extremely radical policy for the party to adopt, when three-quarters of the population of Wales in 1969 were not Welsh-speaking. It was a policy that the Hughes-Parry committee on the legal status of the

[1] *Plaid Cymru* Conference Programme, 1967. The motion was passed on 5 Aug. 1967.

[2] One newspaper reported the voting as 8 against, 12 abstentions, and about 250 delegates in favour. *Liverpool Daily Post*, 7 Aug. 1967. Some delegates apparently voted in favour of the motion rather reluctantly, under pressure from party leaders.

[3] *Liverpool Daily Post*, 10 May 1969.

[4] One contributory factor was Saunders Lewis's statement in October 1969 (see below).

[5] Private information.

[6] J. E. Daniel, *Welsh Nationalism. What it Stands For* (London, 1937).

Welsh language had refused to accept in 1965 because of its 'apparently overwhelming difficulties' and because of 'the smallness of the number of those who supported the application of the principle of bilingualism'.[1]

This summary of the development of *Plaid Cymru*'s policy on the language question explains why doubts did arise in the late 1960s as to the exact nature of the party's intentions. There has long been a division in nationalist circles in Wales as to what their ultimate linguistic objective should be.[2] The *Blaid* avoided conflict on this issue by refusing to state its complete position, but by taking this line of action it succeeded in creating in most sections of the party the doubts it tried to remove. Outside party circles, English monoglots, especially in South Wales, have constantly expressed their fears about the expanded use of the Welsh language, in particular as it relates to job appointments and to education policy—fears about a return to an all-Welsh Wales which newer *Plaid Cymru* branches in south-east Wales seemed to share. But for the activities of the Welsh Language Society in the period since 1966,[3] the language question as a central feature of the *Blaid*'s platform might well have receded into the background. But concern within the party was further inflamed by the Caerphilly by-election campaign which all but ignored the language issue.[4] As events turned out, however, the issues of self-government and the Welsh language have remained confused, as they have usually been since the foundation of *Plaid Cymru*.[5]

If others tried to raise delicate issues such as the Investiture or the language with which to attack *Plaid Cymru* politically, the party itself made the economic situation in Wales the main focus of its political attack from 1966 onwards. The publication of the long-awaited Government economic plan for Wales in July 1967 induced scepticism as to whether the Government was really planning anything at all, and the forecasts of the gap between the number of jobs available in Wales in the early 1970s and the number of persons in Wales available to fill them were hotly disputed.[6] The *Blaid* aimed to show that a self-governing Wales could be economically self-

---

[1] *Legal Status of the Welsh Language*, p. 39, para. 170.
[2] See Ch. 8.   [3] See Ch. 9.
[4] Viz., the correspondence in the *Liverpool Daily Post*, 30 July, 9, 13, and 16 Aug. 1968.
[5] See Ch. 1.
[6] *Wales The Way Ahead*, Cmnd. 3334 (H.M.S.O., 1967). A notable disputant was Professor E. T. Nevin who resigned from the Welsh Economic Council on this issue.

supporting, and it was argued that the management of the Welsh economy was bound to be improved if the responsibility was transferred from London to Cardiff. The party's own economic policy for Wales relied on the creation of several growth centres throughout Wales, although it was not immediately clear what the basis of this growth was to be. As the general election approached, the party added another plank to its economic platform—hostility to Wales's entry to the European Economic Community, specifically if Wales was not directly represented at the talks preceding possible entry, and if the E.E.C. was not very much enlarged. The party conference at Aberystwyth in September 1969 revealed rising opposition to the European ideal, and set the tone in this respect of the *Blaid*'s election platform in 1970. The conference was also the scene of a lengthy discussion, for the second conference in succession, of the *Blaid*'s economic plans for Wales. These plans showed that the party leaders had given considerable attention to this aspect of policy, but that the party workers were far from well informed on the subject. The conference virtually shipwrecked the budget it had approved for Wales by subsequently agreeing to the abolition of the Selective Employment Tax, without suggesting any alternative means of raising revenue. Other resolutions had called for the nationalization of the slate industry in Wales 'to be run on a co-operative basis on the level of the individual quarry',[1] while, on local government reorganization, the conference rejected all proposals for concentrating authorities and their powers and decided instead on the policy that:

the present Councils should be given more authority and responsibility, particularly in financial matters, so that the principle of local government can be strengthened and not diminished.[2]

These conference decisions reveal that the *Blaid* had not reached full maturity as a political party, a feeling that was reflected in constant appeals for professionalism in the party's organization made at party conferences in the late 1960s. General questions for political debate in Wales at this time were inevitably regarded in *Plaid Cymru* as secondary to the distinctive and single issue with which the party was concerned, the issue of self-government. This detailed policy, though recognized as important for the image and immediate relevance of the party's appeal, was unlikely to hold great attractions for

---

[1] *Plaid Cymru* Conference Programme, 1969, p. 13.
[2] Ibid., p. 21.

the average party worker. This must in a large measure account for the hegemony of the party's Research Group in the policy field.[1]

In the post-Carmarthen situation *Plaid Cymru*'s undoubted appeal to young age-groups in Wales contrasted oddly with the party's failure to establish an effective national youth movement in Wales. The Youth committee of *Plaid Cymru* had been reconstituted at least twice within twelve years in the period prior to the Carmarthen by-election, but it rarely seemed able to co-ordinate activities on a Wales-wide basis.[2] Even after the Carmarthen by-election, it still suffered from this defect. Individual youth sections were formed at local branch level, although the numbers of these were small when compared to the numbers of and the growth in senior party branches; but these sections found it very difficult to lose their exclusively local orientation. The annual conference of the *Plaid* Youth had difficulty in attracting as many as fifty delegates from Wales and beyond both in 1968 and 1969. One problem was that the senior party tried to control the decisions taken by its youth members on sensitive issues such as the Investiture and the Welsh language. Rather than be subject to reprimand from the party, a number of leaders of the *Blaid*'s Youth committee at national level seem to have moved their efforts out of the *Blaid*, and concentrated on work for the Welsh Language Society. Activities in the Society certainly deprived the *Blaid* of the benefit of the continued work of many of the ablest young Nationalists. To some extent allegiance to the Welsh Language Society clashed with their support for *Plaid Cymru*, the former adopting more militant attitudes towards the defence of the Language than the latter. The *Plaid* branches at the University Colleges of Aberystwyth and Bangor were severely split on this issue in 1969.[3] The *Blaid* was accused of compromising on the language issue and of being ineffective, charges which had first been raised by Professor J. R. Jones in a spirited lecture to the Society at the National *Eisteddfod* in Barry in 1968.[4] One area of dispute in former years which did not trouble the *Blaid* generally after its success in the Carmarthen by-election was the question of the party's strategy, in particular as it concerned co-operation with other organizations, and the use of direct action. The strong need once felt inside the *Blaid* to join with like-minded organizations to further common objectives

---

[1] See this Chapter, p. 112 and pp. 180–183.
[2] Reconstitutions of the Youth committee were effected in 1954 and 1961.
[3] Private information.   [4] *Western Mail*, 9 Aug. 1968.

was much diminished by the party's success in the electoral field. Some members of long standing inside the party continued to take an active interest in the Celtic League. Co-operation with the Scottish National Party, especially at parliamentary level, and on such matters as broadcasting time to be given to the Nationalist parties, was intensified. The only other important area of potential co-operation was with the Liberal Party. Individual Liberals inside and outside Wales did suggest that there was much common ground between Liberals and Nationalists in Scotland and Wales, Mr. Jo Grimond, the former Liberal leader being the foremost among them.[1] These ideas, which were launched unofficially, were finally rejected by official spokesmen of all parties concerned in 1968.[2] Yet there were people inside *Plaid Cymru*, some of them parliamentary candidates, who betrayed some sympathy for these ideas, notably Dr. Phil Williams, who was elected Vice-President of the *Blaid* in the summer of 1968 following his very effective campaign in the Caerphilly by-election. He wrote to the editor of the Liberal magazine, *New Outlook*, at the beginning of 1969 that:

there is a very substantial degree of agreement between the Liberal Party and the National Parties—sufficient certainly for constructive debate. It is a pity that too often party-political considerations obstruct this debate.[3]

These political kites came to nothing, and party loyalties intensified as the general election approached and as Liberals and Nationalists came to realize that they were often competing for the same votes in elections. Yet they did highlight questions that were occasionally raised as to how the *Blaid* hoped to achieve self-government by electing members to a Parliament in London dominated by Englishmen. The result of the Carmarthen by-election resolved for the following four years, at least, the acrimonious conflicts that had once continued inside *Plaid Cymru*'s executive committee over the question of how far the party should depart from constitutional methods along the path of direct action. The *Blaid* had now come to believe that there was no substitute for electoral success in terms of bringing nearer the day when Wales would be self-governing; although the

---

[1] These discussions inside the Liberal Party came to a head in September 1968 at the Liberal Assembly held in Edinburgh. Jeremy Thorpe and a majority of Liberal delegates did not support Jo Grimond's initiatives.

[2] Notably by George Mackie, Chairman of the Scottish Liberal Party, and Emlyn Hooson, M.P., leader of the Welsh Liberal Party.

[3] Dr. P. Williams, *New Outlook*, No. 76 (February 1969), p. 6.

party's spokesman on water policy, Edward Millward, repeatedly warned that *Plaid Cymru* was prepared to take direct action to prevent the Dulas Valley, on the Montgomeryshire–Radnorshire border, from being flooded to make a reservoir.[1] Nevertheless many of the previously rebellious elements became reconciled to the new orthodoxy of constitutional methods, even those who had been Welsh Republicans.[2]

But one question which was rarely faced by the party leaders was why should the British House of Commons necessarily grant self-government to Wales once a majority of the Welsh M.P.s were Nationalists and the majority of votes cast in Wales at parliamentary elections were for Nationalist candidates? The Irish Nationalists failed to achieve self-government in this way, and the Irish had eventually resorted to violence. Gwynfor Evans assumed in his speeches that the British Government would not allow history to repeat itself, and that its requirement for granting self-government to Wales was a majority of the votes and seats won in a parliamentary election by *Plaid Cymru*. He told the party conference in 1968 that Wales would then become a one-party state for up to three years after independence:

> *Plaid Cymru* would hold the reigns of power for one, two or three years after self-government. By then we have no doubt other parties would have emerged, and we could contest elections.[3]

Saunders Lewis challenged the efficacy of these methods in winning self-government for Wales, in an article in the magazine *Barn*, in October 1968. He argued that no British Government was likely to hand over power to Wales once the conditions laid down by Gwynfor Evans had been fulfilled, and that therefore a mixture of constitutional and unconstitutional methods would be required to bring about self-government for Wales; 'you cannot make an omlette without breaking eggs', he wrote. He was roundly attacked on behalf of *Plaid Cymru* by Edward Millward and by Dr. Gareth Evans, who argued that there was not the revolutionary situation in Wales that Saunders Lewis imagined to exist.[4] It was quite plain that Saunders Lewis's

---

[1] E. Millward, Annual Report of *Plaid Cymru*, 1968–9.
[2] In particular, Harri Webb had become prospective *Plaid* candidate for Pontypool and Cliff Bere was a branch official in Barry.
[3] *Guardian*, 23 Sept. 1968.
[4] E. Millward, *Western Mail*, 10 Oct. 1968 and Dr. G. Evans, ibid., 7 Nov. 1968.

views did not reflect those of the vast majority of the party, and that the party leadership was more than a little annoyed that the issue of the use of violent methods had been broached once more, at a time when a spate of explosions attributed to Welsh nationalists was in progress in Wales, and when the party seemed on the verge of a major electoral breakthrough.[1] The party leadership placed its trust in the British Government to do the decent thing should the occasion arise.[2]

The general election of 1970 crushed the hopes of success that the *Blaid* had nurtured since 1966. The party raised its vote substantially, from 61,000 to 175,000, and contested every Welsh constituency. Yet it emerged without a single M.P., Gwynfor Evans losing his seat at Carmarthen by 3,900 votes. With Labour again in opposition, the *Blaid*'s room for manœuvre in Wales was once more restricted. The loss of its sole M.P. did not foreshadow a return to the party's pre-Carmarthen position. As a lone M.P. Evans was relatively powerless in the Commons. He had not served on committees and never succeeded in moving a bill of his own construction. His usefulness to the *Blaid* while in the House of Commons was primarily as a publicist for Welsh nationalism in the communications centre of Britain. Evans was able to probe the social and economic condition of Wales by tabling many hundreds of parliamentary questions. He also succeeded in making thirty-five speeches in four years on the floor of the House. Yet nothing he could do there could equal the impact caused by his original election victory. Evans proved once and for all in 1966 that *Plaid Cymru* could win a parliamentary seat. His defeat in 1970 could not alter this fact nor the chastening effect it has had on the other political parties in Wales.

[1] There were about a dozen explosions in Wales, July–July 1968–9.

[2] This trust was partly encouraged by the moderate tone of James Callaghan's speech on the subject of devolution to Scotland and Wales. As Home Secretary, he told the Labour Party conference on 1 Oct. 1968: 'I take the view myself that a country, even if it is established that the consequences of its total separation from another country will result in a lower standard of life for it, is still entitled to choose it, if it wishes to do so.' *Report of the Sixty-Seventh Annual Conference of the Labour Party* (1968), p. 185.

7

SOCIOLOGICAL ASPECTS OF WELSH
NATIONALISM SINCE 1945 (I)

DESPITE the reappearance of nationalism as a substantial political force in Wales after 1965, very little attention was paid to the sources of *Plaid Cymru* support. Parliamentary election results since 1945 and local election results since 1960 have given broad indications of the quality of *Plaid*'s electoral support, as have the personal backgrounds of the party's local and national leaders. The expansion of the party's membership and organization since 1965 noticeably affected the composition and political outlook of the *Blaid*. These facets of *Plaid Cymru*'s development are analysed and discussed in this Chapter and in Chapter 8.

The Prevalence of Political and Cultural Nationalism in Wales

It is not possible to give an exact assessment of the prevalence of nationalist political attitudes in Wales since 1945, or in the period 1966–70. However, it is possible to sketch the strength of *Plaid Cymru* support in the different parts of Wales in this period, as revealed by the voting in parliamentary elections. Unfortunately, statistical evidence concerning the level of support for *Plaid Cymru* or for nationalist attitudes, based on voting in local elections or the findings of opinion surveys in Wales, exists only for the 1960s. Before 1960 *Plaid Cymru* rarely fought local elections as a political party, and the first published sample survey of Welsh political attitudes, with a large number of informants, was not conducted until 1967. Thus, the emphasis in time of this section inevitably falls on the later, better documented, and more politically significant part of the period under study. The data that have been used in this section can be divided into three categories: parliamentary election results, local election results as reported over the years in Welsh local newspapers, and several opinion surveys. Most of the opinion surveys concentrated on the determination of current Welsh voting intentions and on

Welsh attitudes to devolution; and in most respects their findings on these points were similar.[1] Only two of the nine opinion surveys undertaken in the period were comprehensive in their treatment of political and cultural nationalism in Wales.

General Political Attitudes in Wales

Most of the surveys of Welsh political attitudes in the period 1967–9 concentrated on ascertaining the attitudes of Welsh electors towards devolution. There were few surveys where informants were asked about their attitudes towards Wales, the Welsh language, socio-economic issues, or the monarchy—all of which have been matters of political controversy in recent years.

Ostensibly, the surveys of the views of Welsh electors on devolution were the most relevant and valuable to the interpretation of Welsh nationalism in the late 1960s, in that it was the issue of self-government for Wales which was the centrepiece of *Plaid Cymru*'s platform.

These surveys rarely asked their interviewees the same questions twice on this topic so that the responses were not strictly comparable. A summary of the evidence produced by the opinion surveys of 1967–8 on Welsh political attitudes is given in Table 7.1. What emerges from these findings is that in the period 1967–8 Welsh public opinion appeared (i) to favour devolution of some sort; (ii) to be divided on the question of a parliament handling domestic and

---

[1] The surveys whose findings have been considered in this Chapter are:

(*a*) N.O.P.'s survey of nationalist attitudes in Wales published in the N.O.P. Bulletin, Nov. 1967. Sample size = 100.

(*b*) Gallup Poll's survey (CS 8433) on the Sunday Entertainments Bill, Jan. 1968. Sample size = 400 (Wales only).

(*c*) *Daily Express* Poll of Public Opinion in Wales, published 1 Mar. 1968.

(*d*) The B.B.C.'s surveys on Welsh and Scottish Nationalism, conducted by Market Information Services Ltd., and broadcast in June 1968 on the programme 'The Disunited Kingdom'.

(*e*) The O.R.C.'s survey of Welsh political attitudes, published in the *Western Mail*, 26–8 Sept. 1968. Sample size = 760.

(*f*) Gallup Poll's survey (CS 8935) on Welsh and Scottish Nationalism, some of whose findings were published in the *Daily Telegraph*, 21 Sept. 1968. Sample size = 658 (Wales only).

(*g*) N.O.P.'s survey of opinion in Wales, published in a special supplement to the N.O.P. Bulletin, Oct. 1968. Sample size = 516.

(*h*) O.R.C.'s survey of social life in Wales conducted in Sept. 1968. Sample size = 1381. (Strathclyde survey.)

(*i*) Survey of Welsh attitudes published in *Primary Education in Wales* (H.M.S.O., 1968). Sample size = 1222.

I am greatly indebted to Humphry Taylor, of O.R.C. Ltd., and Prof. R. Rose, Strathclyde University, for making so freely available the data collected in the two O.R.C. Surveys.

internal Welsh affairs; and (iii) to be decidedly against a completely
separate or independent Welsh parliament or government.[1] The

TABLE 7.1

Welsh Attitudes towards Devolution

(A) Attitudes of Electors towards some Measure of Devolution

	B.B.C.	O.R.C. (*W. Mail*)	O.R.C. (Strathclyde)
	%	%	%
Favourable	70	78	47
Unfavourable	25	14	20
Don't know	5	8	22
It depends	*	*	11
	N = 500	N = 760	N = 1,381
	(June 1968)	(Sept. 1968)	(Sept. 1968)

(B) Attitudes of Electors towards a Domestic Parliament for Wales

	O.R.C. (*W. Mail*)	Gallup	N.O.P.
	%	%	%
Favourable	59	29	49
Unfavourable	31	50	45
Don't know	10	21	6
	N = 760	N = 758	N = 516
	(Sept. 1968)	(Sept. 1968)	(Oct. 1968)

(C) Attitudes of Electors towards Completely Separate or Independent
Parliament/Government for Wales

	Express	O.R.C. (*W. Mail*)	N.O.P.	O.R.C. (Strathclyde)
	%	%	%	%
Favourable	17½	18	19	20½
Unfavourable	72	73	75	45½
Don't know	10½	9	6	24
It depends	*	*	*	10
		N = 760	N = 516	N = 1,381
	(Mar. 1968)	(Sept. 1968)	(Oct. 1968)	(Sept. 1968)

* = Alternative response not open to informants.

[1] It is interesting to note that the O.R.C. (*Western Mail*) survey asked informants
whether or not they favoured 'complete independence for Wales *with dominion status*'
(my emphasis). The response to this question did not differ from that given to other
surveys in answer to questions which were unqualified by a dominion status provision.
Plaid Cymru's policy for Wales insists on dominion status, now Commonwealth
status.

findings of the largest poll (the Strathclyde survey which alone sampled opinion from every county in Wales) were less clear-cut in possible interpretation—showing less sympathy with mild devolution but more sympathy with a completely separate Welsh government than other polls. Both the Strathclyde and *Western Mail* surveys found Welsh-speakers to be more favourable to devolution and to complete separation than those who did not claim to speak Welsh.[1]

The Strathclyde survey revealed interesting differences between the regions of Wales. Welsh-speakers living in mid-Wales were found, for example, to be more decided about the issue of complete separation, and on balance more opposed to the idea, than non Welsh-speakers living in industrial South-east Wales. Those living in industrial Wales, whether Welsh-speaking or not, did not seem to differ greatly on this issue. Omitting the large number of informants who gave equivocal answers[2] to the question, 'Do you think it would be a good idea or a bad idea if Wales had its own government, completely separate from England?' the responses to the Strathclyde survey on this point were as shown in Table 7.2.

Informants living in industrial Wales were less sure of their minds on the issue, and not divided by language. But informants in the other parts of Wales were divided by language, and were more decided on the issue of complete separation. Nevertheless a majority in all parts of Wales of those who expressed preferences were opposed to the idea. The Strathclyde survey found strongest support for complete separation in West and North Wales—with some exceptions (see Table 7.3). Monmouthshire, excluding Newport, emerged in the survey with as many firm supporters of complete separation as Caernarvonshire; the strongest support for complete separation was found in the Llanelli and Cardigan constituencies while, surprisingly, the Carmarthen constituency informants proved relatively unsympathetic to this idea—despite having a *Plaid Cymru* M.P. at the time of interview. There seems little reason why support for complete separation should be strong in some traditionally and strongly Welsh parts of West and North-west Wales but not in others —Pembrokeshire, with its English outlook, being an expected exception. Neither the Carmarthen constituency nor the county of

---

[1] The *Western Mail* survey found that 85 per cent of Welsh-speakers, but only 75 per cent of non Welsh-speakers, were favourably disposed to devolution. Twenty-five per cent of Welsh-speakers in their sample favoured complete independence, compared with 16 per cent of non Welsh-speakers.

[2] i.e. replying 'It depends', or 'Don't know'.

Anglesey revealed in this survey the level of expected support for the idea of complete separation when compared with responses from neighbouring constituencies. It is, however, more reliable to group these survey results according to regions rather than individual

TABLE 7.2

Strathclyde Survey, September 1968

	Separate govt. A good idea	Separate govt. A bad idea	Differ- ence	No. of informants
Furthest Wales (Welsh-speakers*	29%	46½%	−15½%	222
Industrial Wales (non Welsh-speakers)	20%	42%	−22%	263
Industrial Wales (Welsh-speakers)	18½%	41%	−22½%	129
Mid Wales (Welsh-speakers)	23%	52%	−29%	357
Furthest Wales (non Welsh-speakers)	21%	55%	−34%	104
Mid Wales (non Welsh-speakers)	16½%	56%	−39½%	293

* *Furthest Wales* is defined as Anglesey, Caernarvonshire, Merioneth, Cardigan, and Montgomery; *Mid Wales* is defined as Denbighshire, West Flintshire, Brecon and Radnor, Carmarthenshire, and Pembrokeshire; *Industrial Wales* is defined as Glamorgan, Monmouth, and East Flintshire. These demarcations were made on sociological rather than on geographical grounds.

TABLE 7.3

Attitudes in Welsh Counties to Complete Separation:
Strathclyde Survey, September 1968

Question: Do you think it would be a good idea or a bad idea if Wales had its own government completely separate from England?

	Llanelli consti- tuency	Cardigan	Mont- gomery	Caer- narvon- shire	Merioneth	Mon- mouth- shire (excl. Newport)
Good idea	38%	37%	30%	27%	27%	27%
Bad idea	51%	51%	50%	39%	69%	56%
Difference	−13%	−14%	−20%	−12%	−42%	−39%
	N = 72	N = 54	N = 46	N = 126	N = 39	N = 82

TABLE 7.3 (*cont.*):

	Carmarthen constituency	West Flints.	Glamorgan (excl. Cardiff and Swansea)	Cardiff	Pembs.	Denbighshire
Good idea	20½%	20%	18%	18%	17%	17%
Bad idea	46%	61%	33%	49%	54%	63%
Difference	−25½%	−41%	−15%	−31%	−37%	−46%
	N = 98	N = 118	N = 185	N = 57	N = 99	N = 173

Notes. (i) Where the number of informants is less than 50, as in Merioneth or Montgomery, the results are much less reliable than the others. All the above data may be subject to significant sampling error.

(ii) The figures for Glamorgan are not very valuable as only 51 per cent of informants expressed a firm opinion.

constituencies. Support for separation was found to be generally stronger in West and North-west Wales than in other areas. Those regions where the Welsh culture is still strong also tended to have stronger views on the separation issue than South Wales despite the general public controversy on the subject. The non Welsh-speaking minority in Welsh Wales appeared to be as strongly antipathetic to complete separation as non Welsh-speakers in anglicized Wales.

Another issue with which some of these opinion surveys were concerned was the Investiture of the Prince of Wales, and attendant attitudes towards the British monarchy. The surveys confirmed the opinion of commentators that Welsh opinion overwhelmingly approved the institution of the Prince of Wales although younger voters and those who identified themselves with the *Blaid* were least enthusiastic (see Table 7.4).

TABLE 7.4

Welsh Attitudes to the Monarchy

(A)   Attitudes towards the Institution of the Prince of Wales

	All voters		21–34		Welsh Nationalists	
	(*W. Mail*)	(N.O.P.)	(*W. Mail*)	(N.O.P.)	(*W. Mail*)	(N.O.P.)
	%	%	%	%	%	%
Favourable	74	75	61	69	42	55
Unfavourable	15	18	24	24	46	33
Don't know	11	7	15	7	13	12
	N = 760 (Sept. 1968)	N = 516 (Oct. 1968)				

TABLE 7.4 (*cont.*):

(B) 'Which of these statements about the monarchy do you most nearly agree with?' (O.R.C./*W. Mail* Survey, Sept. 1968)

	All voters	Aged 21–34	Welsh Nationalists
	%	%	%
Monarchy should continue as it is now	53	47	33
Monarchy should be abolished	9	11	28
Monarchy ought to change with the times	35	39	34
Don't know	3	3	4

(C) 'Do you think that the Investiture of the Prince of Wales next year and the celebrations that go with it will be money well spent, or will be a waste of money?' (O.R.C./*W. Mail* Survey, Sept. 1968)

	All Voters	Aged 21–34	55+	Liberals	*Plaid*
	%	%	%	%	%
Well spent	50	40	61	45	20
Waste of money	44	53	33	48	72
Don't know	6	7	6	6	8

A substantial number, but still a minority of *Plaid Cymru* voters wanted to see the monarchy abolished, according to one survey taken in 1968; but this was very untypical of most Welsh people, including the young. What did divide Wales in 1968 was the question of the cost of the Investiture and its accompanying celebrations. Almost equal numbers of the Welsh sample agreed or disagreed with the view that the cost of the celebrations would be money wasted, including a majority of Liberals and Nationalists and those under 35 years of age. It is doubtful whether so many would have questioned the cost of the Investiture after the event.

Another aspect of Welsh political attitudes which was probed by opinion surveys for the first time in the late 1960s was the extent of the Welsh electorate's identification with Wales and of its support for the Welsh language. There was no doubt that the overwhelming majority of informants interviewed for the Strathclyde survey conceived of themselves as being Welsh—the test used for identification with Wales. Those higher up the social scale in Wales described themselves as Welsh less frequently than those at the lower end.[1]

[1] As defined by the following classifications of social grade A to E: AB representing the professional and upper middle classes; C1, other non-manual workers; C2, skilled manual workers; DE semi-skilled and unskilled manual workers.

However, at least 55 per cent of those interviewed, in every social group and region of Wales, described themselves as Welsh—as opposed to British or English or some other description (see graph). The Strathclyde survey found that for the whole of Wales, 69 per cent of informants described themselves as Welsh—much the same proportion as the number of Glaswegians calling themselves Scottish (see Table 7.5).[1]

TABLE 7.5

National Identity of Wales, Scotland, and Northern Ireland

	Wales	Glasgow	Northern Ireland
Proportion (%) of samples thinking of self as:			
Welsh	69	1	..
British	15	29	29
English	13	..	..
Scottish	1	67	..
Irish	1	*	43
Ulster	*	*	21
Other, Mixed, Don't know	..	4	7

Table reproduced from R. Rose, *The United Kingdom as a Multi-National State*, p. 10.

* = Alternatives not offered.

This level of identification with Wales did not apparently extend to support for the Welsh language. Those opinion surveys that examined Welsh attitudes to their national language all found only mixed support for the language, especially regarding educational matters. On the question of the availability of official forms and signs, a majority of voters in the *Western Mail* survey wanted *all* official forms and signs in the whole of Wales to be in both English and Welsh, but support for this was found to be uneven between different groups (see Table 7.6). Conservative voters in the sample did not want to see official forms and signs in Welsh in all parts of Wales, but *Plaid* supporters, those over 55 years of age, and Welsh-speakers all wanted this to be so. Non Welsh-speakers were, however, evenly divided on the question, and so—surprisingly—was the 21–34 age group, which showed most support for *Plaid Cymru.*

[1] Richard Rose, *The United Kingdom as a Multi-National State*, Occasional Paper No. 6, Survey Centre, University of Strathclyde (1970), p. 10.

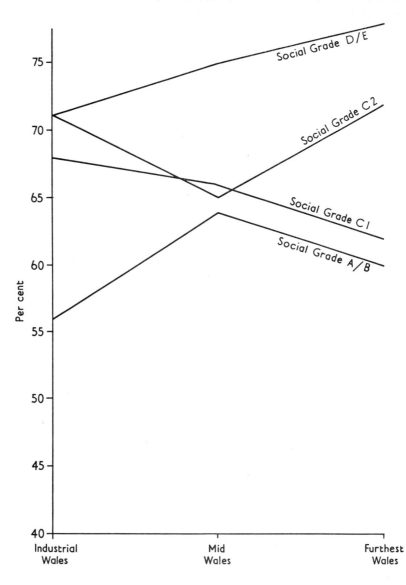

IDENTIFICATION WITH WALES BY SOCIAL GROUP

(% *of sample calling themselves Welsh*)

Strathclyde survey, 1968

Social Grade D/E

Social Grade C2

Social Grade C1

Social Grade A/B

Per cent

75
70
65
60
55
50
45
40

Industrial
Wales

Mid
Wales

Furthest
Wales

TABLE 7.6

Welsh Attitudes towards the Welsh Language

(A) 'Do you think that all official forms and signs should be in English and Welsh in the whole of Wales or only in the strong Welsh-speaking areas?'

	All voters	Aged		Welsh-speaking		Party	
		21–34	55+	Yes	No	Con.	*Plaid*
	%	%	%	%	%	%	%
Whole of Wales	52	49	59	68	47	39	68
Welsh-speaking areas only	44	46	38	39	48	55	31
Don't know	4	5	3	3	5	6	1

Source: O.R.C./*Western Mail* Poll, Sept. 1968.

(B) 'Do you think that the schools should or should not teach Welsh to all the children around here?'

	All voters	Non Welsh-speaking			Welsh-speaking		
		Industr. Wales	Mid Wales	Furthest Wales	Industr. Wales	Mid Wales	Furthest Wales
	%	%	%	%	%	%	%
Definitely should teach	46½	33	41	49½	50	66	77
Leave children/ parents to decide	30	30	40	23	36	26	15
Definitely should not teach	10½	14	7	11½	5½	2	1
Depends	8	12	8	7½	3	4	4
Don't know	5	6½	3	8½	5½	1	3

Source: Strathclyde Survey, Sept. 1968.

(C) 'Do you think it should be compulsory for the Welsh language to be taught in schools, or do you think it should be voluntary?'

	All voters	Aged			Intended vote			
		21–34	35–54	55+	Con.	Lab.	Lib.	*Plaid*
	%	%	%	%	%	%	%	%
Compulsory	28	28	25	31	18	29	31	43
Voluntary	71	72	75	68	82	70	69	57
Don't know	1	..	..	1	..	1	..	..

Source: N.O.P. Bulletin, Oct. 1968, Special Supplement.

Note. The question asked of informants is misleading in that it does not make clear whether the 'compulsory' element applies (i) merely to the availability of facilities for teaching Welsh in every school, allowing children an option to use them, or (ii) to the teaching of Welsh to every child in every school.

It would be rash to place too much reliance on the findings of one opinion survey alone. In fact, only the *Western Mail*'s survey (already quoted) examined electors' views on the question of forms and signs in the Welsh tongue. However, two opinion surveys investigated in 1968 the attitude of Welsh electors to one topic of considerable dispute in contemporary Wales—whether children should be taught Welsh compulsorily in the local schools. The concurrent findings of these surveys are more certain than those of the single *Western Mail* poll. The National Opinion Poll found in September 1968 that a majority in all age groups and of *all* party affiliations thought that the Welsh language should be taught on a voluntary basis in Welsh schools.[1] Less than thirty per cent of the N.O.P. sample in this poll thought that it should be a compulsory subject in school (see Table 7.6). The Strathclyde survey, which also dates from 1968, asked its interviewees a different question, which provoked a different type of answer. The results of this survey suggest that there is more support for the compulsory teaching of Welsh in the schools of Wales than the N.O.P. survey suggests. Again, it must be pointed out, that the Strathclyde survey was twice as large as the N.O.P. survey and sampled opinion in every county of Wales. Strathclyde's findings are, however, not easily summarized. There is no doubt from this survey that Welsh-speakers, wherever they live, favour compulsory Welsh in their local schools; as for the non Welsh-speakers, opinion was divided but more of them favoured compulsory Welsh in their local schools than favoured any other suggested policy. Opinion in each linguistic group was surer on this point outside industrial Wales, especially in North-west Wales (see Table 7.6). Only a small minority throughout Wales (about 10 per cent) disagreed with the teaching of Welsh in local schools. The real division occurred on the question of whether the language should be a compulsory or an optional subject for school children.

Other attitude surveys in Wales have tended to cast doubt on the enthusiasm that many Welsh parents show for the teaching of Welsh in school. The survey of Welsh parents carried out for the Gittins Report showed that parents of children who were taught Welsh as a subject in English-medium schools often could not see any advantage in their children learning Welsh but that, at the same time, they saw no disadvantage either[2] (see Table 7.7). Many more of these parents

[1] N.O.P. Bulletin, Oct. 1968; Special supplement on 'Welsh Nationalism', p. 3.
[2] *Primary Education in Wales* (H.M.S.O., 1967), p. 237.

saw advantages rather than disadvantages in the teaching of Welsh, with parents in South-east Wales the most unclear as to the advantages of their children learning Welsh in school. Parents in the five strongest Welsh-speaking counties of Wales (Anglesey, Caernarfon, Merioneth, Cardigan, and Carmarthen) were most aware of the

TABLE 7.7

Parental Attitudes to the Place of Welsh in the Education System

(A) Attitudes of parents whose children were being taught Welsh in English-medium schools

	All Parents	Anglesey Caerns. Cards. Carms. Merioneth.	Denbs. Flints. Brecs. Montg. Pembs.	Glam- organ County	The County Boroughs
	%	%	%	%	%
Parents saw advantages in child learning Welsh	52	67	60	49	45
Did not see advantages, Don't know/not stated	48	33	40	51	55
Parents saw disadvantages in child learning Welsh	11	22	10	7	14
Did not see disadvantages, Don't know/not stated	89	78	90	93	86
	N = 537	N = 63	N = 100	N = 282	N = 92

Source: *Primary Education in Wales*, p. 237.

(B) 'Which do you think ought to have the highest priority in schools in Wales?'

	All voters	Aged		Welsh-speaking		*Plaid Cymru* voters
		21–34	55+	Yes	No	
	%	%	%	%	%	%
Having more teachers	50	55	43	43	53	33
Improving school buildings	35	34	31	29	36	32
Better teaching of the Welsh language	15	11	25	28	11	35

Source: *Western Mail* Survey, Sept. 1968.

disadvantages as well as the advantages of their children learning Welsh. An opinion survey in 1968 revealed that Welsh did not figure highly in the scale of people's educational priorities, but again Welsh-speakers were greater supporters of the language than non Welsh-speakers, as were the over-55 age group, the nonconformists, and *Plaid Cymru* supporters—although the bulk of these were found to be under 55 (see Table 7.7). This affords us a slight index of the nationalism of *Plaid Cymru*'s support. Attachment to the Welsh language whether for cultural or purely nationalist reasons was super-seded by greater support for other educational objectives in two cases out of three on their part. The 21–34 age group from which the *Blaid* drew its greatest response in the late 1970s was found consistently to be the age group least interested in the Welsh language. Even when interviewees were offered a second choice of priority, more than three quarters of them considered that adding to the number of teachers and improving school buildings had higher priority than better teaching of the Welsh language.[1] When offered a choice of a second language to be learned in school, Welsh informants preferred their children to learn French (49 per cent) rather than Welsh (42 per cent) —although Welsh-speakers and *Plaid Cymru* voters preferred Welsh to French.[1]

To summarize, this sketch of Welsh opinion in the late 1960s on salient nationalist issues such as forms of devolution, the Welsh language, and the monarchy suggests, not unexpectedly, that the Welsh-speaking community is the main source and bastion of nationalist attitudes in Wales, and of *Plaid Cymru* support. On most nationalist issues there was a clear difference in the distribution of opinions of Welsh-speakers compared to non Welsh-speakers. The surveys also suggested that a minority of the non Welsh-speaking section of Wales shares the nationalism of the Welsh-speaking com-munity, especially in areas where the Welsh-speakers dominate. In neither the case of Welsh-speakers nor non Welsh-speakers does this nationalism run to principled disapproval of the institutions of monarchy as they affect Wales.

The surveys also give rise to the hypothesis that *Plaid Cymru*, as a political party, may be falling between two stools in its appeal to Welsh electors. Its stands on the monarchy and dominion status secured much support from the 21–34 age group, but *Plaid*'s sympathy for the language did not. As far as the over-55 age group is concerned,

[1] *Western Mail*, 26 Sept. 1968.

the exact opposite was the case. As a result *Plaid Cymru*, the main expression of political nationalism in modern Wales, looked in danger of gaining firm support in neither age group. Because the language is not a factor in Scottish politics, it is not an issue which has both divided Scotland and provided firm support for the Scottish National Party—as it has done in Wales. Here is a crucial difference which lies at the root of the differing performance of the nationalist parties in Scotland and Wales before and during the 1960s.

Plaid Cymru's *electoral support*

It is only since 1959 that the *Blaid* has given the appearance of having an all-Wales base by fighting more than half the Welsh parliamentary constituencies. Even in 1969 there were still seven constituencies, all in Glamorgan and Monmouthshire, which had never seen a *Plaid Cymru* candidate at a parliamentary election. This late development of the party helped create the aura of youth and novelty the party cultivates. *Plaid Cymru* in its day as a small minority party, essentially cultural–nationalist in outlook, tended to regard Gwynedd (North-west Wales) as its base. Caernarvonshire was the scene of its main electoral campaigns until 1945, and the place of its only headquarters until 1943.[1] Even after 1966 and the rush of nationalist support in South Wales, the *Blaid* kept its headquarters divided, at some considerable cost, between Bangor and Cardiff, for reasons of internal and political convenience.[2] In the late 1960s the higher constituency memberships and the largest number of individual donations to the party were still being achieved in north-west Wales.[3]

The prime indicator of the extent of support for the *Blaid* is the number of votes cast for its candidates in the parliamentary constituencies. The average share of the poll received by each *Plaid* candidate tended to rise in 1955 and 1959 and to fall in 1964 and 1966 (see Table 7.8). Until 1967, the *Blaid* would normally poll its best in the strongly Welsh-speaking parts of Wales, although it has never polled uniformly well or highly in Welsh Wales. Anglicized areas such as the Merthyr and Caerphilly constituencies also gave the

---

[1] In this year *Plaid Cymru* opened an office in Cardiff (*Cyflog Gwaseidd-Dra* [Caernarfon, 1944], p. 13).
[2] Between 1968 and 1971 the arrangement was that the Bangor office was run by the general secretary and the Cardiff office by his deputy.
[3] See below, pp. 174–6.

Blaid candidates about one-tenth of the votes cast. The best election results the *Blaid* has achieved in parliamentary contests have all been at by-elections. Before 1955 these were at Ogmore in 1946 (29·4 per cent of the poll), Aberdare in 1946 (20·0 per cent of the poll) and again in 1954 (16·0 per cent of the poll). The *Blaid*'s share of the vote has normally been higher at by-elections than at general election

TABLE 7.8

Welsh Parliamentary Elections since 1945: Plaid Cymru
Candidates' Performance Compared

(A)   Average percentage of poll gained by all *Plaid* candidates

Year	%	No. of candidates
1945	8·1	8
1950	6·8	7
1951	6·1	4
1955	10·4	11
1959	10·3	20
1964	8·4	23
1966	8·6	20
1970	12·1	36

(B)   *Plaid* performance in constituencies fought successively at general elections

Elections compared	Average % *Plaid* poll in the later election	Average % poll change compared with earlier election	Number of contests compared
1950 and 1951	6·1	+1·05	4
1950 and 1955	14·4	+7·0	6
1955 and 1959	13·2	+2·2	10
1959 and 1964	8·6	−1·9	19
1964 and 1966	9·0	−0·2	19
1966 and 1970	16·3	+7·7	20

contests in the same constituency, with two exceptions.[1] Political commentators in recent years attributed this to protest voting at by-elections on the part of electors, whereas *Plaid* leaders accounted for this difference in terms of the relatively large share of publicity and limelight that their candidates attract at by-elections as compared

[1] *Plaid Cymru* fought 14 out of 16 by-elections held in Wales between 1945 and 1970. In three cases it did not field a candidate at the subsequent general election. Of the remaining eleven cases, only two seats (Swansea East and Montgomery) saw a rise in the *Blaid*'s share of the poll at the following election.

with general elections, when the character of the London government is at stake.

Until 1959 the *Blaid* found its support in terms of share of the poll gained was strongest in the following parliamentary constituencies: Merioneth (23·0 per cent), Caernarfon (21·2 per cent), West Rhondda (17·0 per cent), and Llanelli (13·8 per cent)—the percentages cited are all maxima and were all obtained in the 1959 general election. These named constituencies were clearly a mixture as far as social and occupational composition was concerned, but they all had a strong active or residual Welsh tradition. From the 1959 election onwards, the *Blaid* fought twenty or more of the thirty-six seats at each election, but found that its vote was declining in what had been its best constituencies. Only in Caernarfon did its share of the poll remain at the 1959 high in the 1964 and 1966 general elections. However, in Carmarthen—another bastion of Welsh culture—the *Blaid* succeeded in raising its share of the poll, with the aid of its President, Gwynfor Evans, as candidate, from 5 per cent in 1959 to 16 per cent in 1966. In addition, Caerphilly and Merthyr, two East Glamorgan constituencies lacking a Welsh cultural tradition, gave *Plaid* candidates a ninth share of their election poll—thus pointing to an evenness in the potential support for *Plaid Cymru* which had previously been lacking.

Another indicator of the location of strength of the *Blaid* is the distribution of its candidates at parliamentary general elections since the end of the Second World War (see Table 7.9). This shows that the *Blaid* have always invested a large amount of their electoral effort in North Wales and the Glamorgan Valley seats— where they did best in the 1970 election. It was not until the late fifties that the west and mid Wales seats were areas of sustained *Plaid* activity; Monmouthshire and the Glamorgan coast remained fallow areas until after the Carmarthen by-election in 1966. Absence of large numbers of candidates in anglicized and south-east Wales until the end of the 1960s is clear evidence of the *Blaid*'s long weakness in densely populated, urbanized, and anglicized industrial Wales. This conclusion is confirmed when Welsh parliamentary constituencies are placed in a series defining their characteristics, and the votes of *Plaid Cymru* in those constituencies are compared (see Table 7.10). There is no strong correlation between *Plaid Cymru* voting strength and parliamentary constituencies with a high or low proportion of electors in professional or managerial occupations. There is some correlation between *Plaid Cymru* strength and the proportion of electors employed in extractive industries (agriculture, mining, and quarrying). There is also a moderately good correlation between *Plaid Cymru* voting strength and the proportion of the population in a constituency claiming to speak Welsh. There exists a high correlation between high *Plaid Cymru* voting strength and high membership of the nonconformist churches and the prevalence of sabbatarianism in most constituencies (Merthyr Tydfil is again an exception). These conclusions are based on voting figures in the 1964,

TABLE 7.9

Regional Analysis of Plaid Cymru *Parliamentary Candidatures 1945–1970*

Proportion of opportunities to fight constituencies used by *Plaid Cymru* candidates*

	1945–50	1954–9	1960–9	1970
	%	%	%	%
North-east Wales	33	57	83	100
North-west Wales	50	90	100	100
Mid Wales	..	..	100	100
West Wales	..	71	100	100
Valley seats (Glamorgan)	40	60	80	100
Coastal seats (Glamorgan)	11	17	32	100
Monmouthshire	..	29	14	100

* Candidatures for the 1951 general election are not included in the table because of inter-party pacts obtaining in the election.

1966, and 1970 general elections, and as such they tell us that the traditional areas of support for the *Blaid* were the sources of most of its new growth since March 1966. It is worth notice, however, that the three Welsh by-elections in the period 1966 to 1968 all occurred in constituencies which had been relatively strong centres of *Plaid* support before July 1966. It is questionable whether the *Blaid* would have done so well if it had been forced to fight a by-election in Pontypridd or Monmouth or Swansea West, where it had never fielded candidates at a previous parliamentary election. But the results in the three by-elections held in Wales between 1966 and 1968 were none the less astonishing in terms of *Plaid Cymru*'s past performance in those same constituencies.[1] Their average poll in these seats rose

[1] Carmarthen (1966), Rhondda West (1967), and Caerphilly (1968).

from 12 per cent of the vote to 40 per cent: the share of the vote acquired by the *Blaid* in each of the three by-elections was astonishingly similar, within 1 per cent of 40 per cent in each case, in constituencies which were so dissimilar in social and occupational structure. Although all the three constituencies shared a mining tradition—now largely extinct—they did not share the same strength

TABLE 7.10

The Strength of Sabbatarianism and Nonconformity in Wales compared with Plaid Cymru *Voting Strength*

(A) Sabbatarianism and *Plaid* voting

County	% of electors voting for Sunday closing (1968)	Average % *Plaid* vote 1964–6	% *Plaid* vote 1970
Merioneth	39·4	14	24
Cardigan	34·8	9½	20
Caernarvonshire	31·1	14	21
Anglesey	28·4	6½	22
Carmarthenshire	27·1	9	23
Montgomery	21·4	8	12
Pembroke	20·2	4	7
Denbigh	19·1	5	8
Brecon and Radnor	12·0	5½	5½
Flintshire	7·2	3	5½
Merthyr C.B.	5·5	10½	9½

(B) Nonconformity and *Plaid* voting

	% of adults nonconformist*	Average % *Plaid* vote 1964–6	% *Plaid* vote 1970
Cardigan	50	9½	20
Merioneth	49	14	24
Caernarvonshire	43	14	21
Anglesey	37·5	6½	22
Carmarthenshire	37·5	9	23
Montgomery	35	8	12
Pembroke	22·5	4	7
Denbigh	15·5	5	8
Brecon and Radnor	13	5½	5½
Glamorgan	11	n.a.	12
Flintshire	10·5	3	5½
Monmouthshire	7	n.a.	5

* Estimated on basis of denominational membership figures 1965–8.   n.a. = not available.

Other comparisons are made in Appendix A.

of support for nonconformity or the Welsh language. It is tempting to conclude that there was nothing endemic in the social fabric of these constituencies that naturally predisposed them to Welsh nationalism. In view of the clear indication from voting patterns and opinion surveys that linguistic/cultural nationalism is strongly related to the Welsh language and Welsh nonconformity, the new support for *Plaid Cymru* in all these areas in the by-elections had, arguably, nothing to do with cultural nationalism, but was more to do with an economic protest not confined to Wales, and a feeling of alienation from centralized government which was common currency in the 1960s. If this was so, the important question is whether the *Blaid* broadened its base in South Wales from 1966.

The bulk of Wales's population, and twenty-two of the thirty-six Welsh constituencies, are in Glamorgan and Monmouthshire. A strong base in these two counties would mean that the *Blaid* was capable of attracting large support from the non Welsh-speaking community which forms 75 per cent of the Welsh population in well populated and industrial parts of Wales. Any party aspiring to win a majority in Wales needed a strong base in the South.

Local elections served as the only gauge of *Plaid Cymru*'s strength in South-east Wales prior to the 1970 election. Local election results, however, were complicated by extraneous factors and were available on a large scale only in Carmarthenshire, Glamorgan, and Monmouthshire.[1] In most local election contests in Wales, *Plaid Cymru* members stood as Independents, and only in South Wales have they donned the party label in large numbers, and then mainly since 1968. This indicates a time-lag between the early Nationalist euphoria induced by the Carmarthen by-election in 1966 and its reward in terms of the formation of effective local party machines needed to organize campaigns for aspiring Nationalist local politicians.

It was not until the 1970 county council elections in South Wales that a clear picture of *Plaid Cymru*'s strength in industrial Wales emerged. In the Llanelli constituency, where the Welsh culture still thrives, twelve candidates were fielded by *Plaid Cymru* in the county council elections in 1967, and fourteen in the 1970 elections. However, the seat at Pembrey which was won in 1967 was lost again, despite favourable local circumstances, in 1970. In the eight county

---

[1] Similar evidence from Flintshire and Breconshire is not cited in this Chapter as *Plaid Cymru*'s intervention in local politics is of too limited and too recent a nature in these areas.

council seats in the constituency fought by the *Blaid* in 1967 and in 1970 the votes were distributed as shown in Table 7.11.

TABLE 7.11

	1967	%	Seats won	1970	%	Seats won
Labour	3,358	35·3	3	4,867	56·8	5
Plaid Cymru	3,300	34·7	1	1,759	20·5	..
Liberals and Independents	2,860	30·0	4	1,941	22·7	3
Total	9,518	100	8	8,567	100	8

In Monmouthshire ten candidates were fielded in 1970 for a total of sixty-six vacant county council seats; only one *Plaid* candidate had contested these elections in 1967. Even after allowing for reluctance among *Plaid Cymru* branches about fighting the county council elections on a wide front with a general election judged to be imminent, an

TABLE 7.12

Plaid Cymru *Candidatures in the Monmouthshire County Council Elections, 1970*

Parliamentary Constituency	No. of council seats	No. of *Plaid* candidates contesting	No. of un-opposed Labour councillors elected	No. of *Plaid* councillors elected
Abertillery	13	2	9	..
Bedwellty	11	2	6	..
Ebbw Vale	11	2	3	1
Monmouth	19	1	..	..
Pontypool	12	3	3	..
Total	66	10	21	1

analysis of the county council contests reveals only slight strength for *Plaid Cymru* in Monmouthshire (see Table 7.12). In no constituency could they be regarded even as the main challengers to Labour,[1] this role falling variously to the Conservatives, Liberals, or Independents.

The position in Glamorgan was somewhat different, affording greater contrasts between the strength and weakness of the *Blaid* (see

---

[1] This was because in many areas local elections at district level were only held triennially and also because in some multi-member wards *Plaid Cymru* often fielded only one candidate.

Table 7.13). In four of the eleven parliamentary constituencies which returned councillors to the Glamorgan County Council in 1970, *Plaid Cymru* did not field any candidates in the county council contests. In only five constituencies did they come near to fighting half the available county council seats. The *Blaid*'s strongest performances were mostly in the valleys—in Ferndale (Rhondda), Treorchy (Rhondda), Gadlys (Aberdare), Ogmore Valley, Dulais Valley, and Llandilo-Talybont (Pontardawe), usually in straight fights with

TABLE 7.13

Plaid Cymru *Candidatures in the Glamorgan County Council Elections 1970*

Parliamentary constituency	No. of council seats	No. of *Plaid Cymru* candidates	No. of *Plaid* councillors elected	Average % of poll gained by *Plaid* candidates in contested seats
Gower	7	4	0	25·1
Neath	7	3	0	28·5
Ogmore	7	3	0	24·5
Aberafan	8	0	0	..
Rhondda West*	6	4	0	26·0
Rhondda East*	6	3	1	35·5
Aberdare	7	1	0	47·5
Caerphilly	6	1	0	40·2
Pontypridd	7	0	0	..
Barry†	6	0	0	..
Cardiff South-east†	2	0	0	..
Total	68	18	1	

* One ward in the Rhondda is divided between the two parliamentary constituencies. In this table, the ward has been included in the figures for each constituency—i.e. it has been double-counted.

† Only parts of these constituencies elect county councillors.

Labour candidates in Labour's traditional strongholds. The *Blaid*'s worst performances in the eighteen seats it contested were recorded in those seats where it opposed sitting Liberal councillors;[1] but it could count on at least a fifth of the votes in a straight fight with a Labour candidate, and in these contests in 1970 the *Blaid* share of the poll averaged 32 per cent of the votes cast. This would seem to

[1] In Gower, the *Blaid*'s candidate polled 13 per cent of the votes cast, and the Liberal 52 per cent. In Maesteg, the *Blaid*'s candidate polled 6 per cent of the vote, and the Liberal 48 per cent.

indicate that in many parts of the valleys the *Blaid* has been able to detach a sizeable minority of former Labour supporters. How far this minority was able to survive the relative failure of the *Blaid* in the 1970 general election, remains to be seen. It may be difficult to keep together a political grouping which has placed a high premium on success in order to maintain morale, now that electoral success has proved so elusive.

Since the *Blaid* has expanded its electoral activity at national and local levels in Wales, it is interesting to speculate where it has drawn its votes from, when it has entered the electoral lists. As far as parliamentary elections are concerned, if one examines how far the share of the poll of the respective parties has fallen when a *Plaid Cymru* candidate has newly intervened, it is clear that the Labour Party has suffered most since 1945. In the seventeen cases where the *Blaid* intervened between 1945 and 1966, the Labour Party was most severely hit in ten cases, other parties in five, and all parties equally in two. This analysis is too crude because it omits the fact that the Labour Party has held most of the parliamentary seats in this period and because it does not take account of the 'swings' between the other parties at each election. If an adjustment is made to allow for this last factor (and it is bound to be a tentative one), then the picture of the *Blaid*'s impact changes. It emerges that in the 1945–66 period the intervention of a *Plaid Cymru* candidate in a given constituency was likely to hurt the smaller parties in the contest in each constituency relatively more than the largest party. Thus the smaller parties tended to lose a *higher proportion* of their votes, although the largest party might lose the largest *actual* number of votes.[1]

Another common consequence of *Plaid* intervention is for the proportion of the electorate recording its votes to rise more than it might otherwise have risen. This was best shown by the rise in turnout in the 1959 elections, which saw a large increase in the number of *Plaid Cymru* candidates contesting the general election, and thus indicated that the presence of a Nationalist candidate in Wales raises the electors' interest in the outcome of the election in the constituency or that some Welsh Nationalists will abstain from voting if they have no *Plaid* candidate to vote for in the election contest. This was not,

---

[1] This is a contentious issue among psephologists and political scientists. See D. E. Butler and D. Stokes, *Political Change in Britain* (London, 1969); Michael Steed, 'An analysis of the results', in D. E. Butler and A. S. King, *The British General Election of 1964* (London, 1965), pp. 337–59; and H. B. Berrington, 'The General Election of 1964', in *Journal of the Royal Statistical Society*, Series A, vol. 128 (1965), pp. 17–66.

however, true of the 1970 election. In no parliamentary election prior to 1970 can it be said that the fresh entrance of a *Plaid* candidate caused the seat to change hands, although it is probable that the withdrawal of the *Plaid Cymru* candidate in Merioneth in the 1951 general election caused the Liberals to lose the seat to Labour.[1]

In the local election arena, the effect of *Plaid Cymru* candidatures is not widely different from that in parliamentary elections. In the forty-two wards where it is possible to measure which political group suffered the greatest harm, relatively-speaking, when a *Plaid* candidate entered the electoral combat anew, it is clear that the Labour Party suffered most, but Ratepayer candidates seemed the most vulnerable, although less numerous.[2]

In the 1967–9 period, *Plaid Cymru* improved its local election poll on its pre-Carmarthen performance most where the turnout of voters rose. Where turnout was reduced, the Labour Party's vote was reduced more than *Plaid Cymru*'s vote. The 1967 local elections found Labour's votes reduced in contests with the *Blaid* regardless of whether the turnout of voters rose or fell, which suggested that the reduction of Labour's vote was in part due to abstentions. The 'swing' back to Labour in 1970 and the rise in turnout in the 1970 elections also indicated this.

Where the *Blaid* entered local election contests afresh there were different effects, summarized in Table 7.14. In eighteen of the fifty cases cited electoral turnout rose very considerably—indicating that people voting Nationalist in the late 1960s had previously abstained from voting in local elections. In the context of the Scottish National Party's dramatic victories in Scottish local elections in 1968, it has been suggested that this large rise in electoral turnout in the wake of a Nationalist candidate reveals that it is the previously non-political electors who were drawn to Nationalism in the 1966–9 period.[3] This could be true of some local election contests held during this period in Wales, but the evidence is less telling. *Plaid Cymru* was almost totally unable to match the Scottish National Party's extensive and,

[1] See Ch. 4.

[2] These figures make no allowances for 'swing' between one year and another. Eight out of ten Ratepayer candidates came off worst from *Plaid* intervention in these 42 wards, compared with 21 out of 40 Labour candidates in these wards. These comparisons are largely confined to South Wales where party political contests are most common.

[3] Iain S. McLean, 'Scottish Nationalism: its growth and development with particular reference to the period since 1961' (unpublished B.Phil. thesis, University of Oxford. 1969), p. 62.

for a time, highly successful forays into local government elections in the late 1960s.

An interesting point concerns the extent to which *Plaid Cymru* candidates in local elections received the votes of those who wished to vote against the Labour Party and were only offered a *Plaid* alternative to Labour candidates. A large number of local election contests in South Wales have been two-cornered fights between the *Blaid* and the Labour Party. But there is evidence that votes for *Plaid Cymru* in local elections are interchangeable with votes for Ratepayer

TABLE 7.14

Plaid Cymru *Intervention in Local Elections in 1960s: Single Most Important Effect (50 cases), 3-cornered contests*

Effect	No. of instances	Comment
Turnout rises	16	especially in 1966–7 and in Swansea C.B.
Minor parties hurt despite 'national swing'	12	especially in 1967–8
'National swing' confirmed	15	especially in Rhymney Valley U.D.C.s, and in 1968–9
Not clear	7	
	50	

candidates. Where Ratepayer candidates intervened to make a *Plaid–Labour* contest three-cornered, the *Blaid*'s vote usually fell heavily, and the *Blaid* candidate in most cases found himself at the foot of the poll (see Table 7.15). To a much lesser extent *Plaid Cymru* local election candidates have frequently performed poorly when fighting established Liberal candidates in local elections; this was also the experience of established Liberal candidates threatened with Scottish Nationalist opponents in Scotland.[1] Thus where a credible third force was in existence in local government politics, the *Blaid* was unable to acquire the same measure of support and success which it gained in areas where it was able to pose as the main, and, possibly, only challenger to the Labour Party. Although almost all the local council wards, which the *Blaid* fought fairly constantly between 1960 and 1970, reported noticeably increased support for *Plaid Cymru* local government candidates after the Carmarthen by-election, by the end

[1] Ibid.

of the decade this increase in support had again fallen away in many areas. It is notable that the Carmarthen by-election appears to have provoked the Nationalist upsurge in local government elections, as this was in no way anticipated by the Welsh local election results in May 1966. However, voting patterns were returning to normal when the 1970 county borough and district elections were held in April and May of that year. In the twenty-three wards or districts in South Wales, where comparisons between the *Blaid*'s electoral performance at local government level before the Carmarthen by-election, following the by-election, and then in 1970 are possible, the position of *Plaid Cymru* after the Spring elections in 1970 was such that in only half

TABLE 7.15

Effect of Intervention of Ratepayer Candidates in Local Election Contests between Plaid Cymru *and Labour Candidates 1960–1970*

		Labour votes	*Plaid* votes	Ratepayer votes	Other votes
Rhondda—Treherbert	(1960)	1,946	804	..	810
	(1961)	2,016	386	1,607	864
Merthyr—Penydarren	(1961)	1,906	1,121	..	..
	(1962)	2,170	1,038	606	..
Rhondda—Treorchy	(1963)	2,954	780	..	..
	(1964)	2,047	266	1,656	..
Merthyr—Dowlais	(1963)	1,780	1,145	..	..
	(1964)	1,489	412	1,168	..
Merthyr—Town	(1966)	1,271	715	..	..
	(1967)	1,452	586	963	..
Cardiff—Whitchurch	(1968)	2,646	1,555	..	..
	(1969)	2,088	484	913	..
Rhondda—Treorchy	(1968)	1,995	1,725	..	..
	(1969)	2,174	1,115	901	..
Merthyr—Penydarren	(1968)	1,333	1,146	..	..
	(1970)	1,541	268	1,352	..

these wards had there been an increase in the party's vote in local elections compared with the position before the Carmarthen by-election (see Table 7.16).

The analysis (Table 7.16) of the comparable wards drawn from all parts of South Wales,[1] which *Plaid Cymru* contested regularly in the

[1] The wards in this sample are distributed as follows: East Carmarthenshire 3, Swansea 2, Rhondda—Ogmore 5, Aberdare—Merthyr—Hengoed 5, Cardiff 1, Breconshire 1, and Monmouthshire 6.

1960s, shows how variable was the *Blaid*'s over-all performance after the Carmarthen by-election, even in relation to the Labour Party's sudden changes of fortune in the same period. The *Blaid* made some real advances at local government level between 1966 and 1970, and succeeded in electing members using the party label to six county councils,[1] as well as to the Cardiff and Merthyr Tydfil county

TABLE 7.16

Twenty-three Ward Districts in South Wales: Local Election Votes Compared Pre-1966 and 1970

Party's vote is	Plaid	Labour
Up by 100% or more	5	..
Up by 25–99%	4	3
Up by 25% or less	2	9
Unchanged	2	..
Down by 25% or less	4	8
Down by 25–100%	6	3
Total	23	23

borough councils, and to eight other borough councils,[2] twelve urban district councils, and four rural district councils;[3] only in three instances (all in Carmarthenshire) did the *Blaid*'s representation on a local council decide its control.[4] The scale of *Plaid Cymru*'s presence in local government was generally very small. Of the thousands of councillors from district to county level in Wales, a mere fifty were elected as *Plaid Cymru* representatives.[5]

The Nationalist Voter: a Profile

Opinion surveys provide considerable evidence as to the numbers and characteristics of Nationalist voters in Wales. Seven opinion surveys conducted in 1967 and 1968 asked the voting intention of

[1] Cardiganshire, Merioneth, Denbighshire, Carmarthenshire, Glamorgan, and Monmouthshire.
[2] Rhondda, Carmarthen, Kidwelly, Burry Port, Tenby, Flint, Llanidloes, Monmouth.
[3] The district councils on which *Plaid Cymru* gained representation were: Ammanford (U.D.), Aberdare (U.D.)., Mountain Ash (U.D.), Abertillery (U.D.)., Ebbw Vale (U.D.), Pontypool (U.D.), Fishguard and Goodwick (U.D.), Ogmore and Garw (U.D.), Brynmawr (U.D.), Rhyl (U.D.), Holywell (U.D.), Mold (U.D.), Pontadawe (R.D.), Llandeilo (R.D.), Carmarthen (R.D.), Ystradgynlais (R.D.).
[4] *Plaid Cymru* councillors held the balance of power for a time on the Carmarthen County Council, Carmarthen Borough Council, and Ammanford U.D.C.
[5] Figures for May 1970.

their Welsh informants; these produced a proportion of their samples intending to vote for the *Blaid* which varied between 7 per cent and 20 per cent. Five of these surveys gave sufficient information about their samples and techniques for them to have some academic value, and their over-all findings are cited in Table 7.17. They show *Plaid*

TABLE 7.17

Opinion Surveys of Welsh Voting Intentions 1968

	Lab.	Con.	Lib.	*Plaid*	Other	Don't know	Sample size
	%	%	%	%	%	%	
Gallop Poll (January 1968)	49	31	11½	9½	x	23	400
B.B.C.–M.I.S. (June 1968)	47	26	12	12	3	n.a.	500
O.R.C.–*Western Mail* (Sept. 1968)	41	33	11	13	x	11	760
Gallup Poll (Sept. 1968)	42	38	10	10	x	15	658
N.O.P. (Sept. 1968)	38	35	12	14	1	n.a.	516

x = alternative not offered   n.a. = information not available.

M.I.S. = Market Information Services Ltd.
O.R.C. = Opinion Research Centre
N.O.P. = National Opinion Poll

Cymru level pegging with the Liberals, with the support—in 1968— of about an eighth of the electorate; less than half the level of support opinion surveys at the time had found for the Scottish National Party in Scotland,[1] but in line with the share of the poll won by the *Blaid* in the 1970 election (11·5 per cent). Few indications of any worth exist as to the class composition of the *Blaid*'s support; what there is does suggest that Nationalist voters are drawn equally from all classes.[2] More information exists as to the distribution of Nationalist support among different linguistic, religious, sex, and age groups; the general picture that emerges is that the most likely supporter of the *Blaid* in 1968 was a Welsh-speaking non-Anglican Welshman, aged between 21 and 35 years, living in North or West Wales. This profile very much confirms the impressions of journalists and observers of the Welsh scene at the time. Some surveys found a divergence in the level of support for the *Blaid* in North and West

[1] The level of voting support recorded by opinion surveys of Scotland between November 1967 and February 1969 for the S.N.P., was never less than 19 per cent and rose as high as 43 per cent of their samples.
[2] A breakdown of the O.R.C. poll for the *Western Mail* found that *Plaid Cymru* had attracted the support of 44½ per cent of the Welsh-speaking electors in the C1 social grade (non-professional, non-manual workers). But the total number in this sub-sample was only 35.

Wales as opposed to south-east Wales; the O.R.C. poll indicated that the *Blaid* had the support of 22 per cent of voters in north-west, mid, and West Wales, as compared with 12 per cent in Glamorgan and Monmouthshire and 9 per cent in north-east Wales. *Plaid Cymru* voters appear not to be Anglicans in religion but to be chapelgoers or of no religion. The O.R.C.–*Western Mail* poll suggested that *Plaid* had the support in 1968 of one in four of the Welsh-speaking

TABLE 7.18

Characteristics of Nationalist Voters

(A)   Social class

	Plaid Cymru	All Welsh
	%	%
AB	15½	14
C1	18	23
C2	37½	34
DE	29	29
	N = 72	N = 561

Source: Gallup Poll (Sept. 1968).

(B)   Regional distribution of *Plaid Cymru* voters: level of support in each area

	Gallup Poll (Jan. 68)	O.R.C. (*W. Mail*) Poll (Sept. 1968)	N.O.P. (Sept. 1968)
N.E. Wales	} 10%	} 9%	} 16%
N.W., Mid and W. Wales		22%	
Glamorgan and Monmouths. (S.E. Wales)	10%	12%	12%
	N = 400	N = 760	N = 516

(C)   Religion as a factor in Nationalist voting in Wales

Informant is of	Denomination		
	Anglican	Chapel	Other/None
	%	%	%
Voting intention:			
Labour	31	43	36
Conservative	39	16	28
Liberal	11	11	5
Plaid Cymru	7	18	19
Don't know	12	12	12

Source: O.R.C. (*Western Mail*) Poll (Sept. 1968).

TABLE 7.18 (*cont.*)

(D) Language as a factor in Nationalist voting in Wales

Informant is	Welsh-speaking	Not Welsh-speaking
	%	%
Voting intention:		
Labour	33	37
Conservative	17	35
Liberal	12	9
Plaid Cymru	24	9
Don't know	14	10

Source: O.R.C. (*Western Mail*) Poll (Sept. 1968).

(E) Age as a factor in Nationalist voting in Wales (level of *Plaid* support in each age group)

Age group	O.R.C. (*W. Mail*) Poll (Sept. 1968)	Gallup Poll (Sept. 1968)
21–34	20%	19%
35–54	9%	9%
55 plus	12%	9%

(F) Sex as a factor in Nationalist voting in Wales

Informants who	Will vote *Plaid* (O.R.C., *W. Mail*)	Will vote *Plaid* (Gallup, Sept. 1968)
Are:		
Men	60%	58%
Women	40%	42%
Total	100%	100%

electors, but of only one in ten of the non Welsh-speakers. *Plaid* supporters were apparently younger than other parties' supporters in Wales, the party gaining twice as much support from the under-35 age group as in the older groups. Men were also much more likely to be *Plaid* supporters than women, the surveys suggested—a finding which supports the experience of nationalist parties in other countries[1] at this time.

The most striking factors to emerge from this profile of Welsh Nationalist voters are that they are so young and so likely to be Welsh-speakers. The Welsh-speaking community is a declining part

---

[1] e.g. in Germany, Flanders, and Scotland.

of modern Welsh society, but is being mobilized on different lines from the non Welsh-speaking community because of its interest in the Welsh language and the preservation of Welsh nationality, which are prime concerns of *Plaid Cymru* in Welsh politics. *Plaid Cymru* identifies itself more strongly with these issues in Wales than the other political parties. It is possible that the more of a minority the Welsh-speakers become, the more politically moblized behind *Plaid Cymru* will they become.

The other striking fact that emerges concerning the structure of *Plaid Cymru*'s support in the late 1960s is the fact of its youth compared with other parties' support. If one-fifth of all new Welsh voters were to be Nationalists, and this continued for some decades, then a major alteration in the political balance in Wales would be achieved. The strength of Nationalist support would then be so great as to change the quality of politics in Wales permanently in a Nationalist direction with all the major parties in Wales trying to bid for Nationalist votes by appearing more nationalist in outlook than they are at present. There is, however, evidence which suggests that *Plaid Cymru* has always since 1925 appealed to younger voters in Wales, but that this loyalty has diminished as voters have aged. The nature of this evidence will be examined later in this Chapter.

The Leaders of Plaid Cymru

The profile of the leaders of *Plaid Cymru* does not differ in many respects from the profile of the *Plaid Cymru* voters sketched above, although it contains greater contrasts. It is also possible to give a more detailed account since it is with individuals rather than with a mass electorate that we are concerned. It is proposed to analyse the background of the leaders of *Plaid Cymru* at different levels of the party, defined as:

(i) All Presidents, Vice-Presidents, and Secretaries of the party between 1945 and 1970.

(ii) All members of *Plaid Cymru*'s Executive in 1969.

(iii) The party's 36 candidates in the 1970 general election, compared with candidates in the 1945 to 1966 period.

(iv) Local councillors elected under *Plaid Cymru*'s label serving during May 1970.

(v) Delegates to the *Plaid Cymru*'s annual conference in September 1968 in Aberystwyth.

(i) *The Leadership*

Between 1945 and 1970 there were fourteen individuals who served as *Plaid Cymru*'s principal officers—defined as President, Vice-President, General Secretary, and Assistant General Secretary. Gwynfor Evans served continuously as President throughout the period, the longest term in office of any party leader this century in Britain. Evans in many ways epitomizes the, as yet, dominant strain in *Plaid Cymru*'s leaders. He comes from a Carmarthenshire family, was educated at grammar school and in the University of Wales, and trained for the legal profession. During the war his pacifism led him to take up market gardening and he became secretary of *Heddychwyr Cymru*,[1] a Welsh pacifist organization. Evans was active in the Union of Welsh Independents (Welsh-speaking Congregationalists) and served as President of the Union in 1954 and later as its Treasurer; he is also a teetotaller. He was brought up in Barry, a very anglicized part of Wales, and he took a second degree at St. John's College, Oxford. He learned Welsh as a second language, and this is also true of other prominent individuals in *Plaid Cymru* since 1945.

The leaders of *Plaid Cymru* have been mostly professional men, often engaged in lecturing or teaching occupations, who have had a Welsh grammar school and Welsh university education. Most of them have known no politics other than Nationalist politics. Only Dr. Phil Williams came to his post as Vice-President a non Welsh-speaker; all the *Blaid* leaders in the 1945–70 period were Welsh-speakers, although four of the thirteen learned Welsh as a second language—an unusually high proportion.[2] Many of the *Blaid* leaders in the 1940s and 1950s were also prominent in nonconformist circles: Gwynfor Evans, Dr. R. Tudur Jones, and J. E. Jones being prominent Independents, W. R. P. George and Wynne Samuel being leading Baptists. But this has been much less true of *Blaid* leaders in the 1960s; growth appears to have secularized the top echelons of the party leadership, but it has made no great difference to the section of society from which this Nationalist élite in Wales is drawn.

(ii) *The Executive*

An examination of the next tier in the Nationalist hierarchy—the

---

[1] Goronwy J. Jones, *Wales and the Quest for Peace* (Cardiff, 1970), p. 152 n.
[2] E. C. Rees, Vice-President 1964–6; E. Millward, Vice-President 1966–8, and Emrys Roberts, General Secretary 1962–4; also Dr. P. Williams, Vice-President 1968–70, has learnt Welsh.

party's Executive—reveals other facets of *Plaid Cymru*'s leadership cadre. Unfortunately, historical comparisons are not possible because of the radical reduction in the size of the Executive early in 1966.[1] Until that time the Executive had been more or less an open quarterly forum for any party activist prepared to travel the distance between his home and the meeting place; the complexion of the Executive paralleled very considerably that of the top echelon of the *Blaid* and of the party's candidates. One feature which has stamped the character of the *Blaid*'s leadership at Executive level is the enormous continuity of personnel stemming from the very foundation of the party in 1925. In 1969 there were still prominent in the party men who had joined the *Blaid* forty or more years previously and who had a record of continuous activity and responsibility for the party's affairs: Dan Thomas, the *Blaid*'s Treasurer, J. E. Jones, the former Organizing Secretary, Elwyn Roberts, the General Secretary, and Dr. D. J. Williams (Fishguard). They formed part of a group which had guided the *Blaid* through the political wilderness for decades. The group, sometimes called 'Gwynfor's Court' by newer members in recent years, also comprised Gwynfor Evans, Wynne Samuel, and Dr. Tudur Jones, all of whom joined *Plaid Cymru* in the 1930s.

The streamlined *Plaid Cymru* Executive in 1969 was notable for the long service to the *Blaid* which most of its members had given. Five of the Executive's twenty members in this year had joined *Plaid Cymru* before 1940. Although half the members on the Executive were new to this body since the restructuring of 1966, only two members had joined the party since 1966, this despite the opportunities afforded to the 'new men' in *Plaid Cymru* by the advent of regional representation on the Executive. The old guard was still very much in control of the party's affairs. Fourteen out of the twenty members of the 1969 Executive had joined *Plaid Cymru* before 1960. Twelve of them had been or were teachers or lecturers in educational institutions. Nearly all the members of the executive had enjoyed a grammar school and then a university education, and at least half were graduates of the University of Wales. Non Welsh-speakers were still a small minority on the Executive, although there were a significant number of individuals on the Executive who had learned Welsh.[2] Few of the members of the Executive were active in Welsh

---

[1] See Ch. 5.
[2] Four out of twenty; i.e. G. Evans, Dr. P. Williams, E. C. Rees, and E. Millward.

religious life, although Welsh Independents were again well represented at this level of the party.[1]

(iii) *Parliamentary Candidates*

In the 1945–66 period, fifty-seven individuals contested parliamentary elections as candidates for *Plaid Cymru*. Most of them were
in their thirties, and in the late 1950s a number were even younger.
Most of these candidates were university educated, and half of them
were teachers or lecturers. Very few had had any local government
experience at the time they contested parliamentary elections and
only just over half of them had contested more than one parliamentary election.[2] In the 1945–51 period when *Plaid Cymru* fielded
very few candidates, a high proportion of those candidates it did
put into the electoral fight claimed to be authors or poets. But this
characteristic has faded very much since 1951. The old adage about
teachers, preachers, and poets being the backbone of *Plaid Cymru*
has had to be modified to exclude the poets.

The candidates that *Plaid Cymru* fielded for the 1970 general election were not markedly different in type from those who had fought
previous elections for the party, although many more in numbers.
They were again drawn overwhelmingly from the professional
classes, and from among those with a university education, usually
from the University of Wales.[3] Fifteen of the thirty-six candidates
were teachers or lecturers, two were students, and five were lawyers.
Only one could claim to be a manual worker. At least six of the
candidates were educated at private schools, although most were
products of the Welsh grammar schools. The candidates tended to
be in their thirties,[4] and several had local government experience—
a change from previous years. Only twelve of the thirty-six had,
however, previous experience of fighting as a candidate in a parliamentary election. One of their candidates had fought a previous
election as a Labour party candidate, and two other candidates were
once active workers for the Labour movement, while one had been
a Young Conservative.[5] About one in six of the *Blaid*'s candidates

---

[1] At least six of the twenty members of the Executive were Independents.

[2] Of the 57, 31 contested two or more parliamentary elections.

[3] Of the 36 candidates, 29 attended a university, seven graduated at Oxford or
Cambridge, and seventeen from the University of Wales.

[4] Fourteen were in their thirties and nine in their twenties.

[5] Known ex-members of the Labour Party were Robyn Lewis (Caernarfon), Harri
Webb (Pontypool), and Dr. Phil Williams (Caerphilly). Brian Morgan Edwards
(Cardiff North) was once a Conservative.

in the 1970 general election had joined the party since the previous election, although most of the candidates had been recruited to the party within the previous ten years. At candidate level, therefore, it is possible to see the impact of the Carmarthen and subsequent by-elections. Yet *Plaid* candidates were still very much drawn from Welsh-speakers—twenty-seven out of the thirty-six, in fact, although in Monmouthshire five out of the party's six candidates were not Welsh-speaking and one of these was not of Welsh origin at all. Eight of the thirty-six candidates had learned Welsh as a second language, whereas no other party in Wales fielded a single candidate who had done this. It is not clear how far this was a factor in the nationalist beliefs of those individuals. Nationalism may have led to an interest in the language or vice versa.

In the last analysis, the profile of *Plaid Cymru* parliamentary candidates in 1970 is not unlike that of Labour's candidates in the same election (see Table 7.19). There were the same proportion of teachers and lecturers among both parties' candidates. Most had been university educated, although older Labour candidates may have had other further education instead. *Plaid* candidates were, however, likely to be Welsh-speaking, even in entirely anglicized areas, and more likely to be involved in religious life in Wales than their Labour counterparts, although this is a diminishing factor among Nationalist candidates.

(iv) *Local Government Councillors*

At the local government level, *Plaid Cymru* appears a more socially heterogeneous political party. The *Blaid* has always claimed to have a large number of party members who sit on local authorities as Independents. No general details exist as to the distribution or the background of these individuals even at *Plaid Cymru*'s head offices.[1] More is known about the fifty or so individuals who were serving in June 1970 as councillors elected with the *Plaid Cymru* label. The majority appeared to be Welsh-speakers although mostly elected in South Wales. Most of them could be described as middle class, but an important number were from a working-class background, particularly in Monmouthshire. A local welder and A.E.U. shop steward was elected to Burry Port (Carms.) U.D.C. as a *Plaid*

---

[1] Most of the information presented in this section has been gathered from local newspapers and informal interviews between 1967 and 1970, but some information was supplied by Lili Thomas, former Director of Elections, *Plaid Cymru*.

councillor in 1970. Similarly, a twenty-seven-year-old printing worker was elected to Monmouth Borough Council in 1969, and another twenty-seven-year-old, an electrician's mate, was elected to serve on Monmouthshire County Council as a *Plaid* candidate for an Ebbw Vale ward in 1970. Most of the *Plaid* councillors, however, were professional people, particularly teachers. Some of those elected as *Plaid Cymru* councillors had only recently joined the party prior to their election and were of uncertain allegiance. A checker at the Hoover factory in Merthyr joined *Plaid Cymru* in March 1968 and was elected a councillor the following May. In September 1969 he applied to join the Labour Party. An ironmonger in Carmarthen joined the party at the beginning of 1968 and was elected unopposed as a *Plaid* borough councillor the following May. Two years later he left the *Plaid* group and joined the group of Independent councillors on the council.

TABLE 7.19

Profile of Wales's 1970 General Election Candidates

	Conservative	Liberal	*Plaid*	Labour
	%	%	%	%
% Education:*				
Private School	47	26	17	3
Grammar School	61	79	83	86
Elementary School	..	..	6	11
University	67	58	81	61
University of Wales	22	32	47	33
Teachers' Training College	..	5	3	8
Other Further Education	8	16	17	25
	N = 36	N = 19	N = 36	N = 36
% Welsh-speaking:				
All candidates	14	68	75	42
Wales A candidates†	36	86	100	86
Wales B candidates†	0	20	59	14
% with Local Government Experience:				
In Wales	17	21	22	28
Outside Wales	25	..	..	3
% Aged:				
Under 30	11	26	25	6
30–39	50	32	39	31
40–49	25	37	28	25
50–59	11	5	8	28
60 and over	3	..	..	11

TABLE 7.19 (cont.):

	Conservative	Liberal	Plaid	Labour
	%	%	%	%
% Occupation:*				
Professions	60	58	64	63
Lawyer	19	26	14	22
Teacher	8	16	11	17
Lecturer	14	..	31	25
Other	28	16	8	6
Farmers	14	16	6	..
Company Executives	17	21	14	..
Other Administrative or				
Managerial	6	5	8	28
Engineers	..	5	3	3
Miners	..	..	..	3
Other Manual	3	..	3	3
Students	..	11	6	..
	N = 36	N = 19	N = 36	N = 36

Sources: Party officials and *The Times Guide To The House of Commons 1970* (London, 1970).

* Where a candidate has had more than one kind of occupation or education there has been an element of double counting. Totals do not add up to 100 per cent.

† Wales B is defined as the 22 constituencies in Glamorgan and Monmouth; Wales A comprises the remaining 14 constituencies.

Occasionally, sitting councillors have renounced previous loyalties to join *Plaid Cymru*. Two councillors did so in 1968, leaving the Labour Party to join *Plaid Cymru*. One, an alderman on Flint borough council, was deprived of his aldermanic seat at the next aldermanic elections. The other, who was a past chairman of the Ebbw Vale branch of the Labour Party, failed to be re-elected to the urban council in the 1970 elections. It is noticeable, however, that no such defections to *Plaid* were reported in the party's bulletins in 1969 or 1970.

(v) The Party Activist

Finally, there is the background of the *Plaid* activists to be considered. It has become a maxim in some Welsh circles that *Plaid Cymru* is a party of generals without an army, that it commands the active support of large numbers who are very conscious politically, without being able to attract the mass electorate. Such claims are virtually impossible to verify and do not find backing in the fact that one in nine of those in Wales who voted in the 1970 general election cast their vote for *Plaid Cymru*. Nevertheless the ability of *Plaid Cymru* to field a large and often mobile body of political workers in most of Wales is of political, and possibly electoral, significance. The *Plaid* activist, in a party with a handful of full-time staff or leaders, is the lynch-pin of the movement. Some information about the background of *Plaid Cymru*'s active workers was revealed by a survey conducted by the writer at *Plaid Cymru*'s annual conference (*cynhadledd*) in the autumn of 1968.[1] Those delegates who completed replies were largely Welsh-speaking and chapelgoers. They were more likely to have supported another political party at some time if they were recent recruits, but the majority of informants claimed never to have supported any party but *Plaid Cymru*. Nearly half of those who completed the questionnaire had belonged to the party for ten years or longer. The largest occupation represented amongst these delegates was the knowledge industry: teachers, lecturers, and students comprised nearly half of those answering the survey. Of the twenty-six teachers and lecturers in this sample, twenty-three were Welsh-speaking, twenty-two were under forty-five years of age, nine were active in *Urdd Gobaith Cymru* (the Welsh League of Youth), and five were members of *Cymdeithas Yr Iaith Gymraeg* (the Welsh Language Society).[2] There was some evidence in this sample that newer recruits among *Plaid* delegates in 1968 were more secular, less Welsh-speaking, and less middle class, but this evidence was small and must be treated with extreme circumspection. Those who replied to the questionnaire were probably not wholly representative of the body of delegates at the conference. Personal observation at the 1968 and 1969 conferences of the *Blaid* confirmed the general direction of these findings. There were few indications that the party had recruited to its ranks many active workers in the period since 1966 who did not belong to the student age group. Most of the teachers and lecturers present had been nationalists since their student days. It was impressive how many *Plaid* activists first came into the party in the 1930s and 1940s. The continuity of personnel which was noticeable at the executive level of the party from its foundation in 1925 was equally true of *Plaid*'s active workers. In many ways the leadership and the activists in *Plaid Cymru* sprang from the same Welsh, chapel, and often teaching backgrounds. Signs of change towards a more

[1] The survey took the form of a bilingual questionnaire circulated to all delegates at the conference. After 82 replies were received the survey had to be abandoned, although half the delegates had not completed their replies. Thus the validity of the aggregated survey results is open to question.   [2] See Ch. 9.

anglicized and working-class recruit existed but were small in comparison with the over-all picture of the party. *Plaid Cymru* was clearly a larger party in 1970 than it was in 1945 but the balance within the party had not changed very much in this time, as far as active workers were concerned.

Changes in Party Composition

The expansion of *Plaid Cymru* between 1966 and 1970 was almost certain to cause political and organizational changes within the party. Investigation of the composition of the party as an organization affords a greater insight into these changes and into the sources of the *Blaid*'s strength, old and new, and its prospects for the future. Changes in the pattern of distribution of the party's branches, in the age and linguistic ability, occupations, and size of branch memberships provide reasonable gauges of the nature of the party's expansion. So too do the lists of contributors to the St. David's Day Fund —the party's annual appeal for financial support. Few of the records of those changes, however, are complete or generally available. Much of the analysis which follows is of varying reliability, although the data presented has a value in itself.

The Distribution of Plaid Cymru Branches

No information has been published concerning the geographical distribution of *Plaid Cymru*'s branches past or present, but a picture of the party's branch structure in the period 1945–50 can be pieced together by reference to *Plaid Cymru*'s journals and pamphlets at this time.[1] This can then be compared with the private official records of the *Blaid* in the late 1960s, which were made available for this purpose (see Table 7.20). The comparison shows some interesting changes in the balance of the party in the course of a quarter of a century. Most importantly there has been a shift in favour of South Wales as a result of the recent growth in *Plaid Cymru*. North Wales still had at the end of the 1960s a disproportionate number of branches, viewed in terms of population, although the rural areas, with less density of population and more settlements, are always likely to have more branches than urban areas.[2] In 1945–9 one-half of *Plaid*

---

[1] The main source is *Welsh Nation* which carried regular reports of branch activity in this period, and which J. E. Jones informed the writer were fairly complete.

[2] Another difficulty in this analysis of branches is that in the 1945–9 period the minimum membership of a recognized *Plaid* branch was six, while in the 1965–9 period it was twenty. One would therefore expect some bias in favour of the South, with its larger centres of population, to have developed in the branch structure.

Cymru's recognized branches were situated in the five most northerly counties of Wales; in 1965–9, one-third of the *Blaid*'s branches were found there. Similarly, in the 1945–9 period, one-fifth of *Plaid*'s branches were located in Glamorgan and Monmouthshire; between

TABLE 7.20

Distribution of Plaid Cymru *Senior Branches*

	1938	1945–9	1957	1965–9	1965–9 (Youth branches and university or college branches)
N.W. Wales	45	70	93	54	10
N.E. Wales	22	17	25	27	7
Mid Wales	2	12	16	18	1
West Wales	16	28	51	57	14
Glamorgan	18	31	}57	66	13
Monmouths.	1	2		19	7
Outside Wales	7	6	n.a.	4	3
				245	55

n.a. = not available.

TABLE 7.21

Distribution of Plaid Cymru *Branches 1965–1969 Compared with Distribution of Population*

	% of population	% of *Plaid* branches
N.W. Wales	8	22
N.E. Wales	13	12
Mid Wales	4	6
W. Wales	12	24
Glamorgan	46	27
Monmouths.	17	9

1965 and 1969, one-third of *Plaid*'s branches lay in these two counties —although five-eighths of the population of Wales live in these two counties. Comparing 1945–9 with 1965–9, the expansion of the *Blaid* in terms of branches was greatest in the Carmarthen constituency, Pembrokeshire, Cardiganshire, Flintshire, Monmouthshire, and the Cardiff and Caerphilly areas of Glamorgan. Between 1966 and 1969 the number of *Plaid* senior branches in Gwynedd rose from 17 to 46, in West Wales from 29 to 57, in Glamorgan from 24 to 55, and in Monmouthshire from 5 to 17. In the Carmarthen constituency the number of active branches in 1966 was four, and in 1969, twenty-three. The expansion of *Plaid*'s branch structure in the 1966–70 period did not seriously get under way until 1967, and in North and mid Wales it came to a halt in mid 1968; in South Wales the expansion continued through to 1969. Even then a number of centres in Wales were without a *Plaid* branch, including Prestatyn, Llangollen, Abergele, Cardigan, Haverfordwest, Gower, Porthcawl, Llantrisant, and most of the Vale of Glamorgan. The drive to expand *Plaid*'s organization was encouraged by the desire to channel the tide of nationalism to the benefit of the party, and to prepare for the next general election. With head-office approval, new branches were set up, constituency committees formed, and prospective parliamentary candidates adopted. Branch officials were urged by headquarters to raise money for the party, to organize local social and political activities, to start to canvass their area and to contest local elections, under the party label. The expansion of the *Blaid* after the Carmarthen by-election in July 1966 is illustrated by the progress revealed in Table 7.22.

TABLE 7.22

Growth of Plaid Cymru'*s Organization: 1967–1970*

Year (Aug.)	Branches	Youth sections	Constituency	
			C'ttees	Candidates
1967	128	25	18	6
1968	202	55	27	23
1969	243	45	32	29
1970		300	36	36

Sources: Annual Reports and interviews with *Plaid* officials.

This represents a degree of organizational sophistication previously unheard of in the *Blaid*. Nor do these statistics appear to reveal a situation on paper alone. As the number of paid-up members of the party rose, so did the number of people inside the party willing to take on organizational responsibility; local branches were thus able to expand their activities. 'The transformation in our branches is a marvel' was one official comment in 1967.[1]

The new branch structure should not be judged entirely at face value since the number of branches in an area varied according to whether it was rural or urban in character, and because a good

[1] Annual Report of *Plaid Cymru*, 1966–7.

organization was no guarantee of widespread electoral support. The Carmarthen constituency had been organizationally derelict when *Plaid Cymru* won the by-election. The Aberdare constituency saw the *Blaid*'s vote rise from 9 per cent to 30 per cent between 1966 and 1970, but it had only three branches in 1970 compared with two in 1966. In the same period Pembrokeshire raised its total of branches from four to twelve, but the *Blaid* vote in the county rose only 2 per cent to 7 per cent. Branch structure is nevertheless an important gauge of *Plaid Cymru*'s activity and the way in which this increased at local level. It is also important in that the composition of the party's annual conference is, in practice, largely determined on a branch, rather than a membership basis. The fact of the expansion of *Plaid* branches in South Wales relatively more than North Wales may well be germane to the change of attitudes so noticeable in the party's annual conference debates in the late 1960s.

Age and Linguistic Ability of Branch Members

Information as to the age and linguistic ability of the members of *Plaid Cymru* should in theory be fully documented by the membership records of the party; every membership card issued by the *Blaid* in the last ten years had asked for this information. Very often this information has not been supplied by individual members so that the records suffer from incompleteness. Indeed some branches did not send any of their duplicate membership cards to the *Blaid*'s central headquarters on several occasions. But given the records that have been made available to the writer, at local and national level, there are some indications as to the change in the age and linguistic composition of *Plaid Cymru*'s membership which deserve to be noted.

The membership records all showed a definite increase in branch membership in the later sixties as compared with the early part of the same decade, and a rapid expansion in all parts of South Wales was evident. Everywhere the balance of youth versus adult members of the *Blaid* seemed to be shifting towards more youth members. Membership records for Monmouthshire in 1967–8 showed that at the very least just under half the *Blaid*'s members in the county were under eighteen years of age, and that a quarter of the total membership in Monmouthshire was under sixteen years of age. But there was also some evidence that in the 1968–9 period the *Blaid* was maturing as a political force in this area with less youthful recruits coming into the party in larger numbers than in 1967–8. The records of the party for 1962–3 show that as many as seven out of ten of the party's youth members were new recruits that year. Of the 591 youth members the *Blaid* enrolled in the year 1962–3, 416 were also new members (see Table 7.23). Of the total youth members, at least 223 were students and at least 192 were still at school. Whereas youth members formed about one-quarter of the *Blaid*'s total membership, in Glamorgan and Monmouth youth members accounted for more than a third of the total recorded membership. No such comprehensive figures exist for *Plaid Cymru*'s membership in subsequent years, but such records as have been made available still point to youth members—students and school children—as a high proportion of the members of the party, especially among new members. In the year 1968–9, for example, nearly seven out of every ten youth members in Monmouthshire were new members, and nearly four in every ten full members of the *Blaid* in Monmouthshire were youth members aged below 20.

TABLE 7.23

Plaid Cymru *Membership in 1962–1963*

	Adult members	Youth members	Total members
New members	238	416	654
Old members	1,714	175	1,889
Total	1,952	591	2,543

Clearly, when a political party draws such a large proportion of its support from the young it is reasonable to expect the young *Plaid* members to affect the style of the party as a whole. Throughout the 1960s this youthfulness of the party members was one of its most significant features. Nationalism has often held a special lure for youth, and Welsh nationalism is no exception. Nationalist allegiance frequently originated in the schools. Denbigh Grammar School had a branch of its own in 1962 which used to meet in the dinner hours.[1] St. David's School in Pembrokeshire had its own branch and activities in 1969.[2] One grammar school in Glamorgan was reported to have enrolled 95 new members of the party at the end of 1964,[3] and the Aberdare branch claimed to have 233 members in 1966 with all the branch officers in their teens.[4] Not surprisingly the chairman of the *Blaid*'s youth committee claimed at the outset of 1966 that the party

[1] *Welsh Nation*, Mar. 1962.   [2] *Plaid Cymru*, List of Branches, 1969.
[3] *Welsh Nation*, Jan. 1965.   [4] *Welsh Nation*, July 1966.

had 'plenty of school pupils who are more than prepared to give of their time in distributing literature'.[1] Nevertheless it is strange that with so much youth support evident throughout the decade of the sixties the party's membership did not rise quickly, at least in the period 1960–6.[2] The reason for this was that for many years the *Blaid* was losing members—youth members and adult members—almost as quickly as it recruited them. In the *Blaid*'s annual report for 1963–4 the youth committee admitted that of the 574 youth members known to it in July 1964 only 75 had rejoined from the previous year, a wastage rate of more than 80 per cent per annum. There is some evidence from the late 1960s suggesting that the *Blaid* was able considerably to reduce this wastage of recruits, but officials still admitted that the turnover of youth and adult members was high. This fact also suggests a reason why the *Blaid* was constantly unable to co-ordinate its youth movement's activities at an all-Wales level.[3] While *Plaid* leaders welcomed their large following among the young as a portent for the future, they knew from past experience that youth support can be very temporary.

The *Blaid*'s appeal to youth caused some embarrassment on occasion to the party. Not only has the party suffered in credibility because it has sometimes given the appearance of a 'children's crusade', but individual party members who were school teachers have been accused of abusing their position to benefit the party. One London newspaper gave prominence to a report in the summer of 1968, that 75 members had been recruited in one Caerphilly boys school after 'a boy joined *Plaid* after talking to a school teacher'.[4] Accusations of indoctrination in the schools were plentiful in the late sixties and, although never substantiated, seem to have been generally pointed in the direction of *Plaid Cymru*.[5]

---

[1] Dafydd Evans, 'Plaid Youth are Hopeful', in *Cronfa Gwyl Dewi 1966*, p. 15.
[2] See below, pp. 203–5.   [3] See Ch. 9, *Cymdeithas Yr Iaith Gymraeg*.
[4] *Sunday Telegraph*, 11 Aug. 1968.
[5] See discussion in Ch. 10, *Undeb Cenedlaethol Athrawon Cymru*. Accusations of indoctrination of school children by some of their teachers began to be made at the time of the Investiture, and were keenly felt by all the teaching unions. A notable case concerned a sit-in against the Investiture which occurred in a class at Ysgol-y-Gader Comprehensive School, Dolgellau, Merioneth. The county education committee warned all teaching staff in the county not to use their position to further their politics, and the committee's chairman was reported as saying: 'We have plenty of evidence of indoctrination of a political nature and of staff taking part in sign-daubing' (*Western Mail*, 11 July 1969). Both George Thomas and Cledwyn Hughes warned teachers in 1969 against exercising political influence over their charges (*Western Mail*, 29 Aug. and 8 Dec. 1969). The teaching unions have all strongly defended their members against accusations of indoctrination.

Less is known of the language structure of the *Blaid* in the years from 1945 than of its age structure. The *Blaid* in the year 1962-3 was very much a Welsh-speaking party in terms of its membership. A large majority of its members were Welsh-speakers and its main strength lay in the Welsh-speaking counties. More of its members in Glamorgan in this year were recorded as Welsh-speaking than as non Welsh-speaking.[1] No branch in Wales was entirely non Welsh-speaking, and Welsh-speakers were over-represented in all parts of Wales.[2] Not one member from the Caernarfon constituency was registered as a non Welsh-speaker. Even in anglicized Wales there were striking examples of the Welsh language influence in the party. The Welshpool branch was entirely Welsh-speaking, as was the Swansea University branch. The Rhiwbina branch in Cardiff was 95 per cent Welsh-speaking.[3]

The records from the late 1960s still showed consistent over-representation of Welsh-speakers in *Plaid Cymru* but it is evident that in South Wales there have been great changes in the proportion of Welsh-speakers in many of the party's branches. The scantiness of the records do not permit any firm conclusions. In North Wales, the heavy preponderance of Welsh speakers may have generally continued—but in South Wales the Welsh-speaking influence seems to have waned dramatically with the large influx of new members after the Carmarthen by-election. In 1969 there were branches of *Plaid Cymru* which contained no Welsh-speakers at all, in Monmouthshire in particular. Newly enrolled members were less likely to be Welsh-speakers than longer standing members of the party. This is partly to be expected when Welsh-speakers are a declining part of the population of Wales, especially among the young. The growth of the *Blaid*, if it was to occur in the 1960s at all, had to be based on the non Welsh-speaking community in South Wales for it to be significant politically. The importance of the erosion of the Welsh-speakers' dominance of the party in South Wales is that *Plaid Cymru* widened its political base considerably and could be seen to have an all-Wales appeal regardless

[1] 41 per cent were Welsh-speaking, 37 per cent were not Welsh-speaking; no information was available concerning the remaining 22 per cent.

[2] Over-representation being defined as occurring where a larger proportion of *Plaid* members was known to be Welsh-speaking than the general population of the locality.

[3] In view of the difficulties which can arise in organizations where large numbers of people wish to converse in different languages, it is surprising there are only two instances on record in the *Blaid*'s history since 1945 of attempts to organize branches on a segregated linguistic basis—in Cardiff and in the Rhondda. However, complaints have often been made by non Welsh-speakers who have come into the party about the predominance of Welsh in some branches or party activities.

of language or geographical position. If the *Blaid* remains still as much a Welsh-speaking party as ever in North Wales, as some evidence suggests, this would denote a failure in this part of Wales on the part of the *Blaid* to transcend the language barrier, and would augur a widening split within the councils of the party as to the emphasis and attention to be paid politically to the Welsh language. The evidence available does not point conclusively in this direction; it points only to the danger of this situation developing. Historically the non Welsh-speaking community in Wales has not been so upset by the decline of the language as the Welsh-speakers themselves, and Nationalists in modern times have been no exception to this rule.

Class and Occupational Composition of Branch Members

In any analysis of the class and occupational composition of *Plaid Cymru* based on membership records there are two factors which prevent accurate or meaningful conclusions. First there is the incompleteness of the records themselves; second is the extreme youthfulness of so many of the *Blaid*'s paid-up members in the period under review whose age means that their class or occupational position is indeterminate. The records on which this analysis is based span the decade of the 1960s and encompass the periods in which the *Blaid* was a very small minority group and in which it began to expand its membership quickly. Because the evidence available is incomplete for the whole of Wales, only the evidence provided by individual branch records which appear nearly or wholly complete in individual years has been used for the following account. But there is no knowing whether the duplicate cards of all the members of these local branches cited were returned to *Plaid* headquarters.

The general picture which emerges of the *Blaid* in the early 1960s was of a party strongly dominated by the middle class in Wales, with a leaven of non-manual workers drawn from the stratum of post-mistresses. Ministers of religion and school teachers were very prominent in the party's ranks (see Appendix B). About half the recorded members of the *Blaid* in the year 1962–3 revealed their occupation. Of these just under a third were non-manual workers, just under a fifth were manual workers, and three in every eight *Plaid* members were either students or at school. The party relied in the early sixties on the devotion of one or two stalwarts in scores of Welsh communities to keep the branches going. The branches would naturally reflect the occupational structure of their localities, with the minister or the teacher as a frequent source of support throughout Wales. Often there was little development in these branches, with no youth or new members being enrolled. Other branches would experience a large and sudden influx of members, often still at school, engulfing the branch. A youth section would materialize which might act as a focus for the youth of a small town or village for a while. The Nationalist craze would then fade and the young people would drift away to college, to find work, or other activities.

Almost no records exist which permit a comparison of the composition of a given *Plaid* branch in 1962–3 and then in the late 1960s, but in the case of one Glamorgan town such records do exist.[1] Whereas the branch in the town had no new or youth members in the year 1962–3, its membership in 1967–8, which had doubled in five years, was now half composed of youth members, and half of adults. Four out of every ten members were newly enrolled in 1967. The town branch had in addition found many new members in the villages and townships around the main town, which previously had been fallow ground for *Plaid Cymru*. Welsh-speakers still accounted for at least half the membership of the branch in 1967–8, but in 1962–3 seven out of every ten members had been Welsh-speaking. In the period after 1967–8 further expansion took place, and wastage of new recruits was low. Although the education industry was still strongly represented in the branch, the striking changes were in the number of manual workers and young people who had become members of the *Blaid* locally.

In the case of a town in Monmouthshire, comparable membership records for the years 1967–8 and 1968–9 were inspected.[2] The change in the branch was enormous in this short time. A branch which in one year was composed of 90 per cent students and school children had transformed itself the following year into a mature and enlarged branch with a strong base of manual workers. The wastage among members who joined in 1967–8 was large, but was more than compensated for by the new recruits of 1968–9.

In general, where comparisons between the membership of a branch in different years have been made possible, it appears that throughout the 1960s the rank and file of the *Blaid* was becoming both more youthful and drawn more from the manual-worker section of the population than previously. In many branches, school children and students seemed to form the bulk of the membership. The

---

[1] Town A in Appendix B.   [2] Town J in Appendix B.

example of Town J shows how much of a passing phase this could be. The turnover of the membership in the branches was a constant feature throughout the 1960s, although showing signs of falling off at the end of the decade.

The Growth in the Membership at Large of Plaid Cymru

Plaid Cymru officials have always set great store by the ability of the party to recruit members, and they have shown a constant desire to demonstrate that the Blaid's membership has climbed inexorably higher every year. In order to do this Plaid Cymru officials have tended to redefine 'a member' of the party in order to make their publicly announced membership figures grow. Only in the period 1963–5 did the Blaid, following the initiative of its general secretary Emrys Roberts, publish accurate figures of its paid-up membership— which possibly, for the only period, understated the strength of the party. Normally the party's spokesmen and published reports have tended to overstate, often very considerably, Plaid Cymru's membership; this is well illustrated by the figures presented in Table 7.24. All these figures (except one) have been put forward at various times in Plaid publications or by Plaid Cymru officials, and yet there are some important clashes of evidence. The Blaid's annual report in 1962 disclosed paid-up membership of the party at just over 2,500, but the Blaid's general secretary from 1930–62 claimed in a book published subsequently that membership of the party at that time stood at 24,000![1] In the late 1960s the party claimed to have raised its membership to over 40,000. This represents an average membership of 1,100 per constituency in Wales, but few constituency associations of Plaid Cymru were able to boast of a membership of over 500 at this time, and in 1969, for example, the total membership of the party in Monmouthshire which contains six parliamentary constituencies (out of the total of thirty-six for Wales as a whole), was at the highest estimate considerably less than two thousand.[2]

The doubt surrounding the claims of Plaid Cymru's actual membership inevitably complicates interpretation of the published figures. It is probable that the actual membership of the party corresponds fairly closely to the claims made for actual paid-up membership in any given year from 1957, although the reliability of these figures is in doubt. The party's director of organization commented in 1966 that 'it is difficult to assess total paid-up membership of the Party

[1] J. E. Jones, Tros Cymru, p. 308.   [2] Private information.

because often people who contribute to the Election and St. David's Day Fund often regard themselves as members, without indicating to Central Office that they wish to be so. Similarly local officials do

TABLE 7.24

The Membership of Plaid Cymru *1939–1969*

Year	Paid-up membership for the year	Official *Plaid* claims as to total party membership	J.E. Jones's book *Tros Cymru*
1939		2,000 (1)	3,750 (2)
1945		2,500 (1)	6,050 (2)
1948		25,000 (3)	
1950		6,000 (1)	9,000 (2)
1955		10,500 (1)	15,000 (2)
1957	7,750 (4)		
1958		14,000 (5)	
1961		15,000 (1)	
1962	2,543 (6)		24,000 (2)
1964	2,199 (7)		
1965	3,475 (8)		
1966		16,000 (9)	28,000 (2)
1967	13,000 (10)	27,000 (10)	
1968		40,000 (11)	
1969	est.19,000 (12)	est. 42,000 (13)	40,000 (2)
1969	est.19,000 (12)	est. 42,000 (13)	40,000 (2)

Sources:
(1) *Gweithio Tros Cymru (Plaid Cymru*, 1961), p. 18.
(2) J. E. Jones, *Tros Cymru* (Swansea, 1970), pp. 97 and 308.
(3) Circular issued in Dublin by *Plaid Cymru* (Hydref, 1948).
(4) Report to Pwyllgor Gwaith, Easter 1957.
(5) Annual Report of *Plaid Cymru*, 1958.
(6) Membership record for 1962–3.
(7) Annual Report of *Plaid Cymru*, 1964.
(8) Annual Report of *Plaid Cymru*, 1965.
(9) *Welsh Nation*, May 1966. *Welsh Nation* (Dec. 1966) put the figure at over 20,000.
(10) Annual Report of *Plaid Cymru*, 1967.
(11) Annual Report of *Plaid Cymru*, 1968.
(12) Author's estimate based on constituency and officials' reports.
(13) Official estimate given by Dr. G. Morgan Jones.

not always forward details to Central Office.'[1] Another problem raised by the examination of party membership records is the question of the turnover in the membership. Two views of the vast turnover in *Plaid Cymru* membership card-holders were publicly

[1] Glyn John, 'Report on Organization', in Annual Report of *Plaid Cymru*, 1965–6, p. 10.

expressed by those responsible for central membership records. The director of organization in 1966 noted that 'The membership turnover . . . is enormous. As I see it the prime reason is that Branch Committees do not make a habit, at the beginning of their membership year, of calling on members for their renewal application. This means that literally thousands of sympathizers are lost yearly and do not become active nationalists simply because they are not asked.'[1]

A few years earlier, the general secretary of *Plaid Cymru* had made some different points on the question. 'At present there is a vast turnover of people who pay an initial membership fee and scarcely ever pay again.' This, he said, cluttered up the administration and was costly in terms of the expense of sending circulars to these people. He concluded that 'many more new members are needed, but they must be of the right calibre'.[2]

Nevertheless some trends are discernible through all the doubt about the state of the party's membership. One is that the proportion of members of the party who live in south-east Wales has been rising since 1957. In that year, the party calculated that a fifth of its members came from Glamorgan and Monmouthshire. In 1962, a quarter of *Plaid*'s members came from this part of Wales. The indications are that in 1969 four in every ten *Plaid* members came from south-east Wales. That still meant that West Wales and North Wales were heavily over-represented inside the party, but the prospects for a balanced and broadly based party looked brighter in 1969 than ever before. The general secretary of the party noted that the increase in the *Blaid*'s membership over the previous year was 'not confined to any particular areas nor to certain classes or age groups but is spread throughout Wales amongst people of all ages and groups'.[3] Nevertheless although the proportion of party members living in Caernarvonshire and Merioneth had dropped from 40 per cent in 1957 to less than 20 per cent in 1969, those two counties only contained 6 per cent of the population of Wales; but the shift in the balance of the *Blaid* towards South Wales was incontrovertible.

Another discernible trend is the rise in new memberships of *Plaid Cymru* that were taken out in the late 1960s. The *Blaid* had long been willing to publish detailed figures of the numbers who join the party for the first time. The records kept by the party organizers may have been inaccurate in some details, but the general picture presented

[1] Glyn John, loc. cit.   [2] Annual Report of *Plaid Cymru*, 1962–3.
[3] Annual Report of *Plaid Cymru*, 1968–9.

carries a ring of truth. The figures for new membership which were published between 1957 and 1964 show considerable evenness ranging from between 500 and 1,070 each year; but whereas in 1956–7 they accounted for only one in ten of *Plaid* members in the period 1962–4 new members formed more than a third of the party in each of those years. Evidently many of these new members did not stay in the party very long; for example, the figures given for all new members in the period 1962–4 exceeds the total paid-up membership in 1964 (see Table 7.25). The number of new members joining *Plaid Cymru* each

TABLE 7.25

New Recruits to Plaid Cymru *1957–1967*

Year		New members enrolled	Total membership claimed
1956–7		750 (1)	7,750 (1)
1957–8		700 (2)	14,000 (2)
1958–9		500 (3)	14,440 (3)
1959–60		1,070 (4)	15,000 (4) approx.
1960–1		927 (5)	15,000 (5) approx.
1961–2		1,019 (6)	2,537 (6)
1962–3		851 (7)	2,422 (7)
1963–4		744 (8)	2,199 (8)
1964–5		n.a.	3,475 (9)
1965–6		n.a.	16,000+ (10)
1966–7	at least	6,500 (11)	27,000 (11)

n.a. = not available.

Sources:
(1) Report to the Pwyllgor Gwaith, Easter 1957 (N.L.W. Papers).
(2) Annual Report of *Plaid Cymru*, 1957–8.
(3) Annual Report of *Plaid Cymru*, 1958–9.
(4) Annual Report of *Plaid Cymru*, 1959–60.
(5) Annual Report of *Plaid Cymru*, 1960–1.
(6) Annual Report of *Plaid Cymru*, 1961–2.
(7) Annual Report of *Plaid Cymru*, 1962–3.
(8) Annual Report of *Plaid Cymru*, 1963–4.
(9) Annual Report of *Plaid Cymru*, 1964–5.
(10) *Welsh Nation*, May 1966.
(11) Annual Report of *Plaid Cymru*, 1966–7.

year rose in leaps and bounds after the Carmarthen by-election, at least until the close of 1968. Officials suggested that the rate of enrolment in March 1968 was between eighty and one hundred new members each week—a rate of 5,000 per annum. Two-thirds of these new members were claimed as under twenty-five years of age; two-thirds as white collar/executive class in occupation. By the early summer of 1969 the rate of new enrolments was down to about 2,000 per annum, and this decline was reflected in the caution of the party's officials in giving up-to-date total membership figures. The total membership of the *Blaid* in 1969, according to its organizers, was about 42,000, an increase of only 2,000 on the previous year. Thus, it is not clear how far the proportion of new members inside the *Blaid* has changed since the early sixties. The estimates given in the 1966–7 Annual Report of the party suggest that new memberships in that year accounted for more than half the actual paid-up member-ship (*not* the total claimed membership) of the party. That would represent a big increase, which was not to be continued, as the new members were assimilated into the party. The rate of enrolment of new members since 1966 appears to have tailed off steadily—from over 6,500 per annum in 1966–7 to around 2,000 per annum in 1968–9. It must, however, be conceded that the special circumstances of Investiture year in 1969 may have artificially reduced new enrolments by reducing *Plaid* activity while the celebrations continued; this must remain an open question, but reports from individual branches in this year suggested that many were not affected in this way at all by the Investiture.

Contributions to the St. David's Day Fund

A final, and very individual, index of the fortunes of *Plaid Cymru* in the 1960s was the number of contributions given to the party's annual appeal fund, the St. David's Day Fund. The total contributed to this fund has risen in the course of time in line with inflation and the expansion of the party. The fund remains, as it has done for forty years, the principal source of revenue for the *Blaid* at central office level. Whereas £3,500 was raised through the fund for the party in 1948–9,[1] a total of £10,500 was collected for it in 1964–5;[2] in 1968–9 the figure raised was £24,000.[3] The signs of growth in the party already mentioned also revealed themselves in terms of its finances; but if the total sum of money raised for the fund increased in the late 1960s, was it also true that the number of contributors was raised?

Until 1968, *Plaid Cymru* itself published annually a list of those who had contributed to the previous year's Sr. David's Day Fund. The practice was discontinued in that year because of the high cost and the amount of time required to do so. But such lists as were pub-

[1] *Welsh Nation*, Feb. 1949.   [2] Ibid., Jan.–Feb. 1965.
[3] Annual Report of *Plaid Cymru*, 1968–9, p. 7.

lished offer a unique record of the source of *Plaid*'s financial support. Every contribution was recorded, with the name and place of residence of the contributor. Clearly the individuals who contributed to the fund cannot be treated as representative of the party generally. Some may not have been members of the *Blaid* at all. It is to be expected that middle-class and professional people who were members of the party would be more able and willing to contribute to the fund than pensioners or factory workers. The curious fact that emerges from an analysis of the number of contributions to the St. David's Day Fund in the period 1965–7 is that the growth in contributors was so limited, and apparently so temporary (see Table 7.26). One complication to the picture of contributors that emerges is the fact that *Plaid Cymru* was also trying at this period to expand activities such as raffles—the Cambria Draw, in particular—designed also to benefit its central funds. Some people may have chosen to contribute to the raffles rather than to the St. David's Day Fund. The same general pattern of a shift in the balance towards south-east Wales is shown in the fund figures, as in the figures for membership of the party; but this change, though obvious, is not so striking as could have been expected in view of the West Rhondda and Caerphilly by-election performances. In the whole of the Rhondda in 1967 only thirty people contributed to the St. David's Day Fund. There was a slump too, in the same year, in the number of contributions received from Gwynfor Evans's constituency in Carmarthen. Over all, the number of contributions rose noticeably between 1965 and 1966, but fell back again in 1967. The number of contributors in 1967 was still above that for 1965, but 1965 had been a particularly poor year, financially, for the party. Evidence for the dramatic expansion of the *Blaid* in the post-1966 period does not exist in the records of contributions to the St. David's Day Fund. One interpretation of this is that the expansion of the party at this time did not occur among the middle-classes, but amongst the working-class families who could not be expected to contribute to the fund. This is contradicted by the impressions of those active in the *Blaid* who found increased support in every section of the population, but particularly among white-collar workers. Whatever the social class of the contributors to the fund the total number of contributions to the fund—never more than 3,000—was still small, especially when a number of these contributions were from expatriates.

An interesting sidelight on the composition of the party is shown in the St. David's Day Fund lists. Among the wealth of prominent names in Welsh life, particularly from the universities and the literary world, are also mentioned a striking number of ministers and clergy.

TABLE 7.26

Number of Contributors to the St. David's Day Fund 1965–1967

	1965	1966	1967
Anglesey	56	96	72
Caernarfon (Const.)	244	375	315
Merioneth	244	310	218
Conway (Const.)	95	190	178
Denbighs.	140	274	161
Flints.	71	92	77
Montgomery	67	130	69
Brecon and Radnor	15	29	19
Cardigan	153	258	169
Pembroke	167	210	252
Carmarthen (Const.)	95	224	132
Llanelli (Const.)	69	109	95
Swansea	48	72	60
Cardiff and Barry	120	150	234
Caerphilly (Const.)	18	23	33
Rhondda	18	36	30
Rest of Glamorgan	100	228	152
Monmouthshire	24	41	39
Total	1,744	2,847	2,269

Note. Const. = parliamentary constituency.

Geographical Distribution of Contributors

	1965	1966	1967
5 North Wales Counties	49%	47%	45%
Mid and West Wales	33%	33%	31%
Glam. and Mon.	18%	20%	24%

Analysis of the lists of contributors to the fund between 1965 and 1967 reveals that in any of these years, ministers and clergy accounted for between 5 per cent and 7 per cent of contributors to *Plaid Cymru.* In view of the small number of clergy and ministers in the population of Wales, less than 0·1 per cent of the total, this must be regarded as a very high proportion. In the period 1965–7, 223 ministers and clergy made contributions to the St. David's Day Fund. Few of these were Anglicans; the vast majority were nonconformists, including at least 93 Presbyterian ministers—particularly from Caernarvonshire—and nearly 60 ministers belonging to the Union of Welsh Independents— concentrated particularly in Carmarthenshire, the base of Gwynfor Evans, Treasurer of the Union of Welsh Independents. One *Plaid* sub-agent in a West Wales town claimed that all the ministers in his town were supporters of *Plaid Cymru*, a view confirmed by a North Wales M.P. who was discussing the politics of the ministers in an important town in his constituency. Ministers of religion have long been active in *Plaid Cymru*; the nationalist revival in 1966 seems to have encouraged more ministers to be so.[1]

[1] See Chs. 3, 9, and 10.

8

SOCIOLOGICAL ASPECTS OF WELSH
NATIONALISM SINCE 1945 (II)

THE political success of *Plaid Cymru* after 1965 not only changed the face of Welsh politics; it also changed the face of *Plaid Cymru*. The expansion of any organization, if it leads to the formation of new supporting branches and the sudden involvement of extra individuals and recruits in its work, is likely to shift the balance of forces within the organization and to induce structural and political strains which are neither anticipated nor easily remediable. The growth of *Plaid Cymru* is an interesting case-study in the reaction of a voluntary body to such a situation. The party transformed itself, in the course of two years, from an isolated pressure group, whose strength was the strength of the individuals working independently within it, into an organized political movement with a momentum of its own.

Changes in Party Policy
Economic Policy

One major area which bears examination in the light of *Plaid Cymru*'s growth in the late 1960s is the development of its policy, especially with regard to the Welsh economy and to linguistic affairs. These two areas of policy witnessed important developments in *Plaid*'s thinking and were subject to most criticism from other political parties in Wales in the period under review.

Until the post-Carmarthen period *Plaid*'s economic policy was founded more in theory than in practice. Nationalists in Wales in the last fifty years have sought a number of often conflicting objectives which they have then applied to economic policy. In particular, they have sought an economic structure for the country which would provide the strongest support for the Welsh language and culture. The Welsh rural way of life, notably the small family farm, has been idealized as the most desirable state of economic activity in Wales, and Saunders Lewis is known to have advocated the return of the Glamorgan mining valleys to their earlier pre-industrial state of nature.[1] A devotion to the small family farm is one that is shared by many politicians in Wales who are not Nationalists, but the intensity of this devotion among *Plaid* supporters derives from their belief that the farms and their farmers have been the source of most of what is great in the history of modern Welsh literature and culture. A strong identification with the traditional pattern of agriculture is not the first thing an observer would expect from an avowedly radical party (some would claim socialist), but the explanation is cultural rather than economic. This is illustrated by *Plaid Cymru*'s furious opposition to periodic plans to turn Welsh farming valleys into water reservoirs. Again the preservationist streak in *Plaid* thinking has tended to dominate radical modernizing thought amongst Nationalists in South Wales.

Thus the pattern of agriculture has always been the special concern of *Plaid Cymru* since 1925, although few suggestions for preserving this traditional farming structure on an economic basis were ever made.

The other principal concern of *Plaid Cymru* in the field of economic policy since its foundation has been the feasibility of managing the Welsh economy from Cardiff. The very phrase 'the Welsh economy' only became accepted in economic and political circles in Wales in the 1960s. Even then it was still disputed on grounds such as that there was no cohesion between the various economic activities of the Welsh people and that these activities were integrated more with parts of the English economy than with other parts of the Welsh economy. *Plaid Cymru* has always had to show proof that the Welsh economy would be viable if Wales were governed independently from Cardiff. For decades this remained a completely academic question which not even academic economists were concerned to answer. Lacking independent and expert corroboration that Wales would not suffer from political independence, *Plaid* leaders were forced to rely on the (inevitably favourable) researches of their own members on this point. Such findings never carried much weight, and the claim that Wales would be impoverished if it ever became independent remained a substantial weapon in the armoury of *Plaid*'s political opponents. When the social accounts of Wales came to be investigated in the late 1950s, the issue of the viability of Wales began to be treated realistically in academic circles. The work of Professor Nevin and others on this question, in relation to Scotland and Wales, brought to light

[1] Sir R. Coupland, *Welsh and Scottish Nationalism* (London, 1954), p. 375.

advantages and disadvantages of Welsh economic autonomy. Thus the idea itself became a matter of common argument, and even the *Blaid* changed its ground a little. No evidence was adduced in the 1960s which indicated that a politically independent Wales or Scotland was certain to be either an economic success or a failure.[1] Gradually *Plaid* spokesmen altered their tone on the question. Until 1960, the party's economic policy had remained virtually unchanged for a quarter of a century. The party was principally concerned with the planning aspects of such a policy; it wanted to set up independent Welsh boards to manage the nationalized industries and natural resources such as water, and to initiate and co-ordinate economic development. The Tennessee Valley Authority was regarded with particular favour as an example in developing the rural areas.[2] Budgetary and financial questions were generally overlooked by the *Blaid* until Gwynfor Evans published his pamphlet *Self-Government for Wales and a Common Market for the Nations of Britain*.[3] Evans elaborated the importance of continuing the close economic relationship between England and Wales in this pamphlet, whatever Wales's future political status, and recommended a British Common Market as the best institutional framework through which economic co-ordination could be achieved. This pamphlet was exceptional in view of the general lack of concern among *Plaid* activists about the economic arrangements obtaining in Wales after self-government is achieved.

Economic discussion mainly centred on the issue of the viability of the Welsh economy to the exclusion of what should be done with the economy once Wales was politically autonomous. Interest in the potential of the Welsh economy did not become marked in *Plaid* circles until 1967, after the Rhondda West by-election. The by-election campaign had been fought principally on the issue of pit closures and local unemployment, but it became clear to some *Plaid* intellectuals in the course of the campaign that their party did not have an over-all plan for the Welsh economy—short or long term. This provided the main impetus for the formation of the party's Research Group later in the year.[4] The influence of the Research Group on the

---

[1] See, for example, E. T. Nevin, *et al.*, *The Structure of the Welsh Economy* (Cardiff, 1966); Gavin McCrone, *Scotland's Future* (Oxford, 1969); and J. N. Wolfe (ed.), *Government and Nationalism in Scotland* (Edinburgh, 1969).

[2] See *TVA for Wales* (Caernarfon, ?1944) and *TVA Points the Way* (Caernarfon, ?1946).

[3] Cardiff, 1960.

[4] See Ch. 6.

party's economic policy was paramount from the outset, and *Plaid Cymru* in its own way became attached to the economic jargon and to the extreme confidence placed in governments' ability to manage the economy which had characterized Harold Wilson's approach to the problems of the British economy in 1963–4. No economists were, it seems, members of the Research Group, although the *Blaid* claimed academics and businessmen as their advisers.

The advent of a Labour Government from 1964 to 1970 which implemented a policy of deflation, introduced the Selective Employment Tax which penalized the service industries, and which at the same time planned the inevitable decline in the coal industry gave *Plaid Cymru* its opportunity to attack the Government's economic strategy in Wales. *Plaid Cymru* adopted a position which the Labour Party had so long occupied while in opposition. The *Blaid* spokesmen, especially Dr. Phil Williams, took up the grievances of the Glamorgan valleys, as well as those of the *cefn gwlad* (countryside), and related these grievances to the actions of the Government and the system under which it operated. Instead of pondering the viability of a Welsh economy once self-government was granted, *Plaid Cymru* took self-government for granted and revealed what it would then do. *Plaid Cymru* became the party of economic grievance and succeeded to some extent in carrying its point across to the electors. In the late 1940s, under a Labour Government, it had not succeeded: in the late 1960s, with all of Wales's three major industries (coal, steel, and farming) showing a contracting demand for labour, the *Blaid* was able to fan the feelings of insecurity and despair of valley people.

The Rhondda West by-election showed that the *Blaid* could exploit the grievances of the Welsh valleys with political profit, but the party's new men felt that they must be honest with themselves and their supporters by setting out an alternative policy for Welsh industry in the context of an over-all economic plan for Wales. This, in theory, was what successive Governments had been trying to do since 1963—but the resulting plan for Wales, published in 1967, failed to list priorities or targets or a timetable for action,[1] and increased doubts as to the Government's capacity to tackle the peculiar problems of the Welsh economy. The *Blaid*'s Research Group therefore set about producing its own plan for Wales, admittedly based on inadequate figures and projections because of the dearth of

[1] *Wales: The Way Ahead* (H.M.S.O., 1967), Cmnd. 3334.

available statistical information. An economic plan for Wales was gradually hammered out by the Group in 1968 and 1969, in conjunction with the party's annual conference and its national council—a representative body of the rank and file meeting quarterly. Similarly the Group prepared estimates of receipts and payments made to and from the London Government in connection with Wales, and drew up a budget accordingly. The kernel of the party's plan for Wales, its 'growth centre' policy for development, came under severe attack from those branches whose own area had not been designated as such, and the national council's meeting in Newtown at the beginning of 1969 referred the plan back to the Group. Compromises were effected, and the plan was adopted in outline at the *Blaid*'s 1969 annual conference in Aberystwyth the following September. At the same conference, the party's budget for Wales was approved, but it was made obsolete by an earlier decision of the conference to oppose S.E.T.—a key component on the income side of the budget for Wales that delegates favoured.[1] In fact, this incident illustrated the lack of understanding among the bulk of the party faithful of the issues involved, despite two years of assiduous education by the party's leaders and spokesmen. The *Blaid* put much effort and resources into the production of these economic prospectuses, but attention inside the party had begun to shift from such enterprises before they had completed all the necessary stages of approval. The national council's meeting in Newtown had shown how the authority of the Research Group—at its outset almost undisputed—had been eroded once its main economic proposals were known. As the year 1969 progressed a different economic issue came to dominate the discussion inside the party—the application by the Wilson Government to join the European Economic Community. *Plaid Cymru* found itself served with a tactical advantage it dearly needed, for 1969 was also the year of the Investiture, which the party conspicuously ignored or shunned and which, in the short term, earned the *Blaid* considerable unpopularity. The *Blaid*'s attitude to the E.E.C. was somewhat ambiguous in that it gave the appearance of total opposition to the signing of the Treaty of Rome, while in fact reserving its position until Wales could be separately represented at the negotiations with the Common Market countries. In 1969 both *Plaid Cymru* and the Scottish National Party adopted a strongly critical attitude to the Wilson Government's European initiative while the three

[1] *Liverpool Daily Post*, 15 June 1970.

major parties found themselves committed to a greater or lesser degree to entry to the E.E.C. 'if the price was right'. Little political mileage could be made of the Common Market issue prior to the opening of negotiations at the end of June 1970, by which time the 1970 general election had been held and a new Government, strongly committed to joining the E.E.C., had been returned to power.

The issue of what should be the economic strategy in the development of Welsh industries could not, however, be overlooked, and the *Blaid* still made much in the 1969–70 period of the apparent lack of co-ordination and strategy in the Government's declared plans for Wales. The *Blaid* was able to do this both because of the vague nature of the Government's declared intentions and because, in the period 1967–70, its political success had enabled it to enlist the help of 'experts' in the preparation of policy (for the first time). The main spadework was done by the party regulars, Dr. Williams and Dafydd Wigley, and it was they who took the responsibility for it and steered it through the annual conference. The experts were never publicly named, and, as was pointed out by Emlyn Hooson, the Welsh Liberal leader, during the 1970 election campaign, not a single economist of any standing had by then come out in favour of an independent Wales.[1] Nevertheless the changes in policy effected by the *Blaid*'s attention to economics in the late 1960s were considerable. Political success forced party leaders to be more responsible and realistic. Talk of workers' control and co-operative socialism almost vanished and was substituted by talk of planning. The close economic links between England and Wales were increasingly stressed and the limits on any Welsh government's actions in the economic sphere—especially with regard to taxation—were slowly realized by party spokesmen; a new and more short-term economic programme was developed in detail, whose several parts were co-ordinated into a coherent whole.

Linguistic Policy

In the field of linguistic policy, too, certain changes in the *Blaid*'s official attitudes were instituted as a result of the changing balance in the party following its growth. *Plaid Cymru* in the 1960s still betrayed strong overtones of the party which in 1925 had been founded 'to save Wales from her present state, and to make her a

[1] *Western Mail*, 17 June 1970.

Welsh Wales'.[1] In fact, the party's attachment to the language was being changed over time, but the change was slow. J. E. Daniel, President of the *Blaid* from 1939 to 1943, wrote in 1938 that *Plaid Cymru*'s policy was to make Welsh the first language in Wales;[2] but this was not exactly the pledge repeated by Gwynfor Evans after the Second World War. In the 1950 election Gwynfor Evans wrote in his election address that 'Our national language, which is denied official status in Wales, must be restored to its position as the language of the whole of Wales for all purposes . . . Wales can again become a Welsh-speaking Wales.'[3] This statement is compatible with the post-war official policy of the *Blaid* which was to favour bilingualism. Although bilingualism was propounded by *Plaid*'s leaders as the party's official view on the language, it was a policy which was never put to the party's conference, or ratified by it—until 1968.[4] This partly reflects an old division of opinion on the language which developed before 1939, as to whether the Welsh language could survive in a bilingual situation, or whether the only circumstance in which it could survive was one in which large numbers of people spoke only Welsh.

J. E. Daniel wrote in 1937 that he envisaged a time, after transition, 'when Welsh alone will be the language of government, law and education in Wales. Then only will the evil effects of the Act of Union be undone.'[5] On bilingualism, Daniel had this to say:

> The normal thing in Wales surely should be that Welsh be essential and ignorance of it a handicap . . . Bilingualism we regard as a transitional necessity, not as a final ideal. The theory, so popular in Wales, of the inherent superiority of a bilingual to a monolingual nation, i.e. of Welshmen to Englishmen, is nothing but a bit of face-saving on the part of an inferiority-conscious nation.[6]

Given this division, perhaps *Plaid Cymru* in the 1950s and 1960s did not feel confident enough to expose it publicly at its annual conference. Only in 1968 and 1969 did debates on bilingualism materialize, and then they were brief and unanimous. The official policy of bilingualism was a very radical one, and the consequences of its implementation were likely to be enormous.[7] This was in recent years

[1] Gwynfor Evans, 'The Twentieth Century and *Plaid Cymru*', in A. W. Wade-Evans, *et al.*, *The Historical Basis of Welsh Nationalism* (Cardiff, 1950), p. 142.
[2] J. E. Daniel, *Welsh Nationalism: What It Stands For* (London, 1937), pp. 52–3.
[3] Election address in the possession of the Gladstone Library, National Liberal Club, London.   [4] J. E. Jones, private interview, 6 Aug. 1969.
[5] J. E. Daniel, op. cit., p. 52.   [6] Ibid., p. 53.
[7] *Legal Status of the Welsh Language* (H.M.S.O., 1965), Cmnd. 2785, para. 270.

spelled out by *Plaid*'s opponents, while *Plaid Cymru*'s spokesmen tended to debate the language's immediate position of disadvantage, rather than the consequences for education and the public services of making it possible (and in many cases compulsory) for Welsh to be used as freely and widely as English in public life. Some observers even claimed that in the post-Carmarthen situation, when the party was making its thrust into the South Wales valleys that *Plaid Cymru* deliberately soft-pedalled the language issue. This was a charge that could not easily be substantiated.

There was a close link between *Plaid Cymru* and the Welsh Language Society, which was born out of the party at its 1962 conference. The link continued, and many of the *Blaid*'s young activist supporters, especially the teachers and students, became regularly involved in Welsh Language Society protests.[1] Among older *Plaid Cymru* members and workers concern for the language remained generally strong and many prominent leaders of Welsh culture were connected with the Nationalist movement, including almost all the Welsh-language authors and dramatists. Of more immediate significance was the fact that the future of the Welsh language has been more of an issue in Wales in the 1960s than at any time in its previous history. The rising Nationalist temper of the country, the increased research into the question, and the activities of the Welsh Language Society made it so. *Plaid Cymru*'s views on the language inevitably came under greater public scrutiny than ever before. However, the change in the fortunes of the party gave rise to some changes of tone in *Plaid Cymru*'s attitudes to the language question. For instance, the 1968 resolution on language at the *Blaid*'s annual conference noted 'the impossibility of creating a bilingual Wales overnight',[2] and the original motion, before it was amended, stressed that 'the Welsh education system under self-government will teach both languages so efficiently that we shall have a bilingual generation throughout Wales by the end of the century'.[3] This long time-scale in the achievement of a bilingual society in Wales was echoed by many *Plaid* leaders at this time, and was a new feature of *Plaid*'s policy on language. Criticism of the activities of the Welsh Language Society also came to be voiced by *Plaid* officials and party workers, both on grounds of policy and because of the political embarrassment caused to *Plaid Cymru* by the Society. Dr. Phil Williams, when

[1] See Chs 7 and 9.
[2] *Plaid Cymru* Annual Conference Programme, p. 13.   [3] Ibid., p. 11.

Vice-President of the party, made some strong attacks on the Welsh Language Society accusing the Society of 'alienating increasing numbers of the population' and of creating 'hostility to the Welsh language'.[1] Letters critical of the actions of the Society were published in *Welsh Nation*, and a few *Plaid* branch officers in South-east Wales publicly condemned the language militants.

Meanwhile the party generally was concentrating its fire on the Labour Government's economic policy. For example, economic issues—local and national—dominated the by-election campaigns in West Rhondda and Caerphilly. This reflected a fair appreciation on the part of the *Blaid*'s campaign managers of the salient issues in these areas. The *Blaid* was talking more of pit and rail closures than of cultural affairs. This could not be regarded as a new departure, however, as some commentators suggested. *Plaid* candidates did not consistently pay great attention to the language issue in election campaigns after 1945. The *Blaid* candidates in the two constituencies of Rhondda West and Caerphilly, did not mention the language issue in their 1959 election addresses, but did mention it in their 1966 election addresses. Nor was it the case that the *Blaid* only mentioned the language issue in Welsh-speaking strongholds to the exclusion of the non Welsh-speaking parts of Wales.[2] The evidence available from election literature suggests that the Welsh language was not an issue in many election contests involving the *Blaid*, whether in Welsh Wales or in anglicized Wales, while it was an issue in other contests throughout Wales.

However, it is not clear how far the general change in the *Blaid*'s policy towards the language was the result of long-run trends in Wales towards anglicization or the consequence of a change of tactics among the party's leaders. The sharp decline in the strength and use of the Welsh language in the 1920–70 period was not unnoticed by *Plaid Cymru*. If the party had aimed its appeal entirely at the Welsh-speaking section of the community it would have had an ever-diminishing potential clientele. The party would have had to make relatively more and more converts among a declining part of Wales's total population in order to keep its membership and support at the same level. In practice, *Plaid Cymru* never aimed its appeal exclusively to Welsh-speakers, although before the Second World War

[1] Dr. Phil Williams, speech to *Plaid* Youth Conference in Aberystwyth, 4 Apr. 1969.
[2] This was alleged by George Thomas, Secretary of State for Wales, during the 1970 election: *Daily Telegraph*, 17 June 1970.

non Welsh-speakers who supported the *Blaid* were a comparative rarity. The *Blaid* saw increasing numbers of non Welsh-speakers join its ranks after 1945. In part this was the party's express wish, in part a natural reflection of the changing balance of the two languages in Wales. By the late 1960s, *Plaid* leaders were claiming that a majority of their members were not Welsh-speaking, although no evidence was adduced and no firm evidence existed for such statements.[1] It was, however, clear that more and more of the *Blaid*'s business and campaigning was being done through the medium of English and that interest in the language issue was stronger in North and West Wales than in South-east Wales.[2] There were complaints in the *Blaid*'s annual conferences that such little use was being made of the Welsh language. The electoral breakthrough in South Wales that the *Blaid* had waited so long to see, when it came in the 1966–70 period, was bound to mean a further influx of non Welsh-speakers into the party and further erosion of the hold of the language over the *Blaid* as a whole; this was because there were so few Welsh-speakers remaining in South Wales by this time. It was noticeable how several candidates in the 1966 general election had stressed that *Plaid Cymru* was a party for all who live in Wales,[3] although that did not prevent the *Blaid* trying to emphasize its special appeal to the Welsh-speaking voter— often only in the Welsh-language sections of its propaganda. The *Blaid* candidate for Caernarfon in 1964 issued a pamphlet arguing that 'Plaid Cymru yw'r unig Blaid Gymraeg'—that *Plaid Cymru* was the only Welsh-speaking party. Another candidate, Trefor Morgan in Brecon and Radnor in 1966, wrote in his address, 'Y mae pleidlais i Blaid Cymru yn bleidlais dros y Gymraeg'—a vote for *Plaid Cymru* is a vote for the Welsh language. (Curiously, this candidate was not a native Welsh-speaker.) Thus the *Blaid* tried to ride two horses at once, and was largely successful in doing so. The pressures to do so may continue for some years, as the non Welsh-speakers increase their dominance in the party and the Welsh-speaking minority becomes ever more strident in its demands for the protection of the

[1] This is because of the incomplete nature of the party's membership records. The O.R.C. opinion survey published by the *Western Mail* in Sept. 1968 suggested Welsh-speakers formed a majority of *Plaid Cymru*'s supporters; the 1970 general election results pointed in the same direction (see Appendix A).

[2] This contrast was especially highlighted by certain incidents in the Caerphilly by-election and which provoked a heated correspondence in the *Liverpool Daily Post*, July–Aug. 1968.

[3] See, for example, election addresses of *Plaid* candidates for West Flintshire, Conway, Caernarfon, and Rhondda West in the possession of the Gladstone Library of the National Liberal Club, London.

language. The Welsh language lobby remains a large and important section of the party's active workers, often with a personal vested interest in the language; but if the *Blaid* were ever to give this lobby its full platform, the party would condemn itself to complete political isolation and perhaps condemn Wales to a lasting communal division which would cease only with the extinction of the Welsh language.

The Dynamics of a Political Organization:
Plaid Cymru *1945–1970*

The Pursuit of a Strategy

Since 1930, *Plaid Cymru* has been committed to a parliamentary strategy for the achievement of self-government for Wales. In that year the party reversed its *Sinn Fein* stance towards parliamentary elections because it was judged to have lost it electoral support. Despite occasional flirtations with direct action and confrontation tactics the aim of the *Blaid* has remained the securing of a majority of seats and of votes in a parliamentary election in Wales in order to bring about self-government. Whether self-government would be achieved in this way has been disputed, notably, in recent years, by Saunders Lewis.[1] The *Blaid*'s official spokesmen have claimed that the British Government would be forced to hand over power to a government in Cardiff in this situation. The efforts of the party's organizers have thus been directed for nearly fifty years towards the capture of nineteen parliamentary seats. Their first success came in 1966 at the Carmarthen by-election; but this was overturned in 1970 when the seat was regained by Labour. The first task of *Plaid Cymru*'s organization was to build up an organization in Wales which could contest elections, and to supply to local branches and constituency committees the necessary advice and literature to enable them to do this successfully. Since 1966 the party's paid officials have also been concerned to alter the party's image, with very limited resources at their disposal. Experts in public relations and the design of publications were put to work for the *Blaid*'s benefit, and to some extent succeeded in giving the party a 'trendy', modern, and radical appearance. There was, however, very little the *Blaid*'s advisers on publicity could do about the disastrous image that accrued to the party as a result of the series of bomb explosions which rocked Wales between 1966 and 1969.

[1] See Saunders Lewis, *Barn*, Oct. 1968.

The *Blaid*'s organizers saw that every by-election was contested in the 1966–70 period and succeeded in forming constituency committees in every constituency in Wales, persuading them all to field candidates in the 1970 election. The number of candidates fielded by the party in that election was nearly twice the number put up in the 1966 election, the party's vote was nearly trebled, reaching 175,000, and eight of the *Blaid*'s candidates finished in second place (see Table 8.1). The net result of these efforts was that *Blaid* polled one in

TABLE 8.1

Plaid Cymru's *Performance in General Elections*

(A) Number of constituencies where *Plaid* candidate was second in the Poll

1945	0	
1950	0	
1951	0	
1955	1	(Rhondda West)
1959	1	(Rhondda West)
1964	0	
1966	1	(Rhondda West)
1970	8	(Rhondda West; Rhondda East; Aberdare; Caerphilly; Carmarthen; Llanelli; Merioneth; Caernarfon)

(B) Number of constituencies where *Plaid* candidate polled 20 per cent of the votes cast, or more

Candidate polling	1945	1950	1951	1955	1959	1964	1966	1970
20–24%	..	..	..	1	2	1	1	3
25–29%	..	..	..	..	..	..	..	1
30% or more	..	..	..	..	..	..	..	3

nine of the votes cast in Wales at the election, but lost its only parliamentary seat. The party was also losing ground in the local government elections, with some exceptions, throughout 1970. Local autonomy was, however, much stronger than the party's central staff would have liked, although the production of posters in the general election for individual candidates was centralized, and a party manifesto was issued centrally for the first time. The theme of the party's election campaign was also centrally determined. Between 1969 and 1970 a major change was effected within *Plaid Cymru* concerning the theme on which they chose to fight the general election. Originally planned as the need for a Welsh legislature, it was suddenly changed to stress the party's effectiveness as a pressure group for Wales in the eyes of any Government. This proved a most effective platform for the party. It tacitly assumed that the Labour Government would be returned to power, which proved to be erroneous, and minimized the contentiousness surrounding the *Blaid*'s main platform plank, the granting of self-government to Wales. It was a line of attack that was readily adopted by candidates and agents of the party throughout Wales. Between the two general elections of 1966 and 1970 *Plaid Cymru* had transformed its appeal. Whereas in 1966 it was a pressure group claiming to be a political party, in 1970 it was a political party claiming to be a pressure group. The *Blaid*, however, gained votes but no seats in the 1970 elections. Frustration with the party's performance in parliamentary elections has led in the past to severe internal dispute as to the party's over-all strategy,[1] while parliamentary success has tended to confirm the strategy and the position of the leadership. In 1970, the party's expectations had been raised immeasurably by by-election results in 1966–8, but the party did not repeat these. Once more, disappointing general election results raised doubts about *Plaid*'s parliamentary strategy.

Party Structure

There is room for doubt as to whether the term 'political party' was an apt description for the *Blaid* for most of its long life. Only after the Carmarthen by-election in 1966 did *Plaid Cymru* really come to terms with contemporary political circumstances in Wales—the change in the outlook of its leaders and its workers being forced upon it by sudden success in a parliamentary election. The members of *Plaid Cymru* had previously borne some of the characteristics of a sect: they had an extreme devotion to a Utopian Wales; they idealized their own paucity of numbers; and they had virulently and self-righteously attacked those Welshmen who did not hold their own faith in Welsh Nationalism. *Plaid Cymru*'s leaders saw their movement as more of a pressure group than as a party that would gain power or that could be itself the instrument of political change. Every concession made by Governments to Wales was seen as a concession extracted by and made to *Plaid Cymru*. With electoral success proving so elusive, political success for the party became linked with the success of Wales in the political field. Indeed the *Blaid*, by setting itself up as the sole guardian of Wales's conscience and true interests often seemed to be regarding itself as the Welsh nation. One National-

---

[1] See Ch. 5.

ist writer, not prominent in the party, said as much in the columns of *Y Faner*: 'We, *Plaid Cymru* are the Nation of the Welsh. Without us there is no Nation. Nor for our Nation a path.'[1]

Whatever the proper description of the *Blaid* as an institution, its organizational structure remained remarkably stable despite the changes in its political fortunes. In essence, the party was only as strong as its branches. The branches recruited the party's members and raised its money for use centrally as well as locally. It was the branches which had to co-operate to form constituency committees, and with which much of the political initiative of the party lay. Above the branch level—with its attendant women's and youth sections—was the constituency committee. For most day-to-day purposes the top layer of the party was the central office—of which there were two, one in Bangor and one in Cardiff. In 1968, six regional councils were also set up to co-ordinate and develop the party's work between constituency and national level, but it was some time before they achieved a life of their own. Each regional council had one representative on the *Blaid*'s Executive committee.

The branches were all entitled to be represented at the annual conference which decided the party's policy, and its constitutional arrangements, and to which the party's officers were responsible. The conference elected the party's President, Vice-President, and Treasurer. In between conferences the party's national council containing constituency representatives met quarterly to review progress and policy. The party's officials—officers and full-time staff—reported to the national council and to the conference. These arrangements obtained in *Plaid Cymru* between 1968 and 1970. The method of election of some members of the Executive was altered to suit the formation of the regional councils in 1968, but the major change in the Executive came in 1966 when its membership was much reduced in size to about twenty persons,[2] and the national council, a representative body of the *Blaid*, was set up to compensate for this. Unconsciously, the party streamlined itself the better to meet the new situation later in the year. But the key relationship between the branch and central office remained much as it had been since the foundation of the party. It was at the intermediate level that the structure had to be changed because of party expansion. So many constituencies had met the qualification for a separate constituency

---

[1] J. Legonna, *Y Faner*, July 1962, quoted in *The Nationalist*, vol. 1, No. 1.
[2] See Ch. 6.

committee after 1966 that the old 'district committees', which were sub-regional groups of branches in weak constituencies, had almost died out by 1968. The need was felt for some formal regional grouping nevertheless, and this was how the regional councils of the *Blaid* emerged. Party officials foresee that these councils, particularly in densely populated areas of Wales, will gradually acquire an authority of their own. At present the main exercisers of authority within the party remain the party's full-time officials.

In theory, the highest authority inside the *Blaid* is its Executive committee which meets every three or four weeks. In 1960, the Executive—then a much larger body—would meet only quarterly, but in the late 1960s the volume of business had grown so considerably that despite the increased frequency of its meetings it was rarely able to give detailed consideration to many of the items on its agenda. The Executive appeared in practice to execute very little; it was more of a council to which committees and sub-committees, officers and full-time staff reported, and where some decisions of principle were made or ratified. For example, the Executive had power to disapprove of the selection of a parliamentary candidate by a constituency committee or to expel a member from the party; in practice, it left the full-time *Plaid* officials to do this. Again, the Executive had to approve the appointment of staff, but it could not make the appointment itself; that was the role of the Finance committee.

In a situation where the power of the Executive committee was limited by an overloaded agenda and by the authority of its attendant committees—especially the Finance committee—much power inside the party rested in the 1960s with its full-time officials, in particular the general secretary and, after 1958, the assistant general secretary. This is not to ignore the immense personal authority of the President of the *Blaid*, Gwynfor Evans, acquired over more than thirty-five years active service in the party; but this authority was more informal than formal, deriving from the respect and charisma surrounding the man rather than from the office he held.

Although the *Blaid* has had its main office in Cardiff, which was the base of its general secretary, since 1944, it was agreed in 1964 with the appointment of Elwyn Roberts as general secretary of the *Blaid* that the general secretary would be based in Bangor. Problems of communication between Bangor and Cardiff inevitably meant that whoever had day-to-day charge of the Cardiff office would have much responsibility and initiative. The electoral success of the *Blaid* and the appointment of an assistant general secretary in charge of the Cardiff office complicated the chain of command inside the *Blaid*. The assistant general secretary, although responsible to his superior in Bangor, found himself in charge of a larger and better equipped establishment than the general secretary; he was directly responsible to the Executive for activity in the majority of Welsh constituencies, and the chief spokesman for the party, by virtue of his being located in the principal communications-centre in Wales. Not unnaturally tension developed between the Cardiff and Bangor offices, and within the Cardiff office, following the party's expansion. These tensions seemed often to follow a division between long-standing party officials and newly appointed officials, whose methods and ideas departed from the conventional.

In effect, therefore, these two officials, of nearly equal power, carried the burden of ensuring the consolidation of *Plaid Cymru* as an organized force in Welsh politics following the by-election successes. They were assisted in this by three other high-ranking officials—two assistant organizers and the women's organizer—and four full-time and three part-time clerical and ancillary staff. These individuals managed the party from day to day in the late 1960s. For over a year, in 1968–9, the Cardiff office also had over-all charge of the publication of the party's English-language monthly, *Welsh Nation*.

With a larger complement of full-time staff, the party, at branch level or at the Executive level, expected to see results; but the new staff soon found that their room for manœuvre was severely curtailed by the relative inertia and independence of the party at branch and constituency level. Certainly, the publicity of the party was improved —in design, content, and frequency, as was its public relations. Circulars to local party workers were dispatched more frequently containing a wealth of information and advice. The party conference was transformed into a serious political occasion, and separated from the traditional summer school, which was itself radically altered. But in the task of building up the party at the grass-roots the party's organizers found they faced an uphill struggle. There were enthusiastic supporters in the branches, but they lacked leaders who were either locally respected or politically experienced. Often branches had maintained a precarious existence for many years thanks to the efforts of possibly cantankerous but determined stalwarts who were set in their ways and who did not care for new methods of electioneering (such as canvassing or fund-raising). Some could not be persuaded that local elections should be fought politically and, perhaps, could not even be convinced of the urgency of setting about adopting a parliamentary candidate. Years of political education and manœuvring were required to make the party, which had suddenly come in from the political wilderness, into a cohesive unit. The greatest political failure on the part of the organizers was in the field of local government. Many councillors who were members of the party but who sat as Independent members of various councils would not declare their allegiance and fight for election using the party label. Perhaps more important, in those areas where local government elections were already politically contested, *Plaid* branches still did not see the value of fighting these elections—with a view to building up the party's local organization and support. The *Blaid* did not therefore capitalize immediately on the first flush of its increased support in 1967, when many triennial county and district elections were held. By the time these areas had the occasion for elections again, the *Blaid*'s fortunes had taken a turn for the worse, and results were disappointing. The more the party's officials saw the shortcomings of the party at local level, the more they wanted to step in to remedy the defects—but they had neither the time nor the authority to do so. They were trying to professionalize the party when working in a complete vacuum.

Other problems also arose as the party organization expanded. It became increasingly difficult for the central organization to keep in close contact with local officials, owing to pressure of work at headquarters; complaints of the remoteness of the party's paid officials began to be voiced. In some branches, positions of responsibility were given to those who might have joined the *Blaid* more because they had fallen out with other political parties than because they were Nationalists, and this caused internal friction.[1] Other branches were so successful in their money-raising efforts that they assumed a degree of independence of the party headquarters that was embarrassing to party officials. 'We know of at least two branches who have something like £1,000 each in their local banks, and one of them has not so far contributed a brass farthing to central funds', wrote the party's director of finance in 1969.[2] Some branches in 1969 did not even bother to circulate their members with the annual St. David's Day appeal for party funds.[3] But it is perhaps to be regarded

[1] Private information.
[2] H. Heulyn Roberts, Annual Report of *Plaid Cymru*, 1968–9.
[3] *Forward* (a bulletin to officials of *Plaid Cymru*'s organization), Jan. 1970, p. 10.

as natural that the highly centralized structure of the party should begin to break down as the party's branches began to grow strong locally. It was a sign of strength which party organizers had not anticipated. Repeated exhortations from headquarters through the normal channels of communication often seemed to draw a half-hearted response at local branch level. The central party organization found itself fighting a long-drawn-out battle to get accurate membership details of branches and to persuade branches of the importance of house-to-house canvassing and of fighting local elections using the party label.

One area where the intervention of the central office did become pronounced was in the selection of parliamentary candidates—this for the first time in the party's history. The power to select a parliamentary candidate rested entirely with the constituency committees of *Plaid Cymru*; it remained to the Executive only to approve or disapprove each committee's choice of candidate. However, soon after the Carmarthen by-election the party committed itself publicly to fighting every constituency in Wales, and it was left to the central office staff to see that this commitment was fulfilled. Frequently the party's organizers had to suggest to constituency committees that it was time to look for a candidate. The central office influence would be felt most at the stage when the constituency committees were looking for names of possible candidates. Sometimes the organizers would dispatch a list of possible candidates without the prompting of the local constituency committee involved. In cases where there were local disputes about the selection of a candidate, a party organizer might be called in to settle the matter. In one or two cases the central office was keen to see a prospective candidate replaced, because of inattention to duty; and in at least one case the party organizers and a constituency committee came into direct conflict over the choice of a person as prospective candidate. Central office was by no means certain, in such cases, of having its own way; but in most cases this is what resulted. It was, of course, highly indicative of the state of the *Blaid* that there were more volunteers than vacancies for prospective candidatures, and that such care should be taken in candidate selection. It was a tribute to the central offices that the party's organization was in a sufficiently good position at constituency level to mount a campaign in every parliamentary seat in Wales in the 1970 election.

Mobilizing Nationalist Support

Plaid Cymru's organization at national level faced from 1967 the twofold task of mobilizing Nationalist support in Wales and of pursuing a deliberate strategy in preparation for the oncoming general election, as a means of achieving the objectives of *Plaid Cymru*. The full-time staff had neither the machinery nor the resources nor the time sufficient for the job in hand. At every level of organization they faced the inevitable hazards and delays of a part-time and inexperienced force of active workers who were masters in their own cabbage-patches. The party organizers saw their plans fail to some extent, because there was no way in the circumstances of carrying their plans out. Party workers cried out for 'professionalism' in the organization of the party but power was too widely diffused inside the party for its officials to control it.

Mobilizing Nationalist sympathizers and generating new support the party's full-time organizers counted their greatest successes—largely because their aims in this area were very widely shared and quite intelligible to the rank and file. The organizers in several respects continued the work done by the general secretary since 1930, which had developed into established patterns. Written propaganda had long been a key method of putting *Plaid Cymru*'s case to the people of Wales and beyond. The party devoted considerable effort and resources to the production of pamphlets and leaflets which developed the party's ideals and policy; pamphlets were also issued which commented on current events and political topics, because the usual channels of mass communication were denied to the party in any great measure. In the first thirty years of *Plaid*'s existence the written word, printed and published by the party itself, was for many Nationalists the only way of keeping in touch with nationalist thinking; for them the party's pamphlets and newspapers were a political lifeline, especially during the Second World War.

If it was important for the party to keep open lines of communication between the central office and its members in the field, it was also important that members should meet one another in order to emphasize unity, solidarity, and their common aims. The production of literature was the party's principal method of political education for Nationalists and non-Nationalists in Wales. The public meetings held by the party were also a means of political education, but were more important as instruments for the socialization of Nationalists and sympathizers one with another and with the party. At local level, the public meetings were a way of presenting the Nationalist case to a wider audience, and of introducing *Plaid* leaders to local supporters. At national level, rallies, conferences, summer schools, and marches were organized, as well as a big meeting at the annual conference and, more recently, at the National *Eisteddfod*. These events served a different purpose. They were essentially for the converted Nationalist, allowing him to assert a common personality in a communal activity. This emphasized the strength and numbers of the normally scattered and fragmented party, and raised morale by pointing to progress made by the *Blaid* without dwelling on the setbacks. The activist would be inspired with a sense of loyalty to stick to his beliefs and to continue to make sacrifices on the party's behalf; in addition, his stock of political argument would be supplied with extra sophistication. In this way the Nationalist was equipped with the means, the will, and the vision to see him through months of heartbreaking political work. After 1967, the party developed another technique for rallying the faithful among the young generation. This was the holding of occasional mass *tribannau pop*, Welsh-language pop festivals, at which patriotic and nationalist songs in various singing styles were rendered by well-known Welsh stars. Frequently, the festival would be interrupted half way through for a political speech from a *Plaid Cymru* parliamentary candidate. Thus, the *Blaid* linked itself to a new fashion for Welsh pop songs. Thousands of teenagers and young people would attend these festivals from miles around the scene of the concert.[1] Their political significance lay in the way in which the whole tenor of the *tribannau pop* endorsed or reinforced Nationalist political attitudes among people who were at a very impressionable age, politically. Gradually these concerts came to be held in localities with smaller audiences and were established features of local *Plaid Cymru* activities throughout Wales. At this branch level the *tribannau pop* were not so far removed from the cultural evenings, often involving traditional music and singing, which the *Blaid* had long been in the habit of organizing. Both types shared a common emphasis on patriotism, love of one's country, and of the Welsh language. The scale and intensity and fervour of the *tribannau pop* were new phenomena, and the tide of Nationalism that swelled out

---

[1] The largest of these pop festivals was held at the Pantyfedwen Hall, Pontrhydfendigaid, Cardiganshire, in Sept. 1968; three thousand people filled the hall. The festival coincided with *Plaid Cymru's* annual conference in Aberystwyth. A similar festival in 1969 was not nearly so well attended.

in these festivals was hard to resist. It was on occasions such as these, and at the big meetings held by the *Blaid*, that the symbols used by the *Blaid* were at their most effective. The *Blaid* had for decades adopted the usual trappings of nationalist parties throughout the world by presenting the flag of Wales on formal occasions, by closing its meetings with the singing of the Welsh national anthem, and by adopting an emblem (in 1933)—the *triban*, or three mountains which characterized Wales.[1] The *triban* was used on most of the *Blaid*'s publications and was also made into lapel badges and car-stickers. It was used as a way of identifying Nationalists to one another, and as a way for individual Nationalists to declare to their friends and neighbours where they stood politically. The symbols of the Nationalist movement thus served to differentiate its individual members from the rest of society and at the same time were a means of bringing together fellow Nationalists.[2] The *Blaid* used other more subtle ways of keeping its supporters mobilized for the cause. In many branches—less so now than in the past—the very use of the Welsh language in the conduct of business served to emphasize the distinctiveness of the movement and to boost the pride of its members in belonging to it. The three aims of the party as stated on the *Blaid*'s official membership card served too as a member's creed.

In some ways the *Blaid* tended to take on the air of a large family with an extended kin network functioning throughout Wales and beyond. In part this was the consequence of being a small party in a small country. Personal connection has always been a strong force in Welsh life, and politicians in the *Blaid* (and other political parties) have been able to utilize it fully as they have become established and experienced. There also existed the subconscious sentiment amongst many Nationalists in Wales that they alone, as members of the *Blaid*, were members of the nation, a great family of Welsh people. On occasion Nationalists have themselves seen this parallel of family and nation—if a little humorously. The Reverend Stanley Lewis of Llanwrtyd was once reported as explaining that one of the reasons he was a member of the *Blaid* was that it was a family matter as he had nineteen cousins, all members of the party.[3] And the well-known Welsh pop singer, Dafydd Iwan, the son of a minister, claimed in

---

[1] See J. E. Jones, *Tros Cymru*, p. 92, for a description of how the *triban* was chosen as the party's emblem.

[2] See W. B. Cameron, *Modern Social Movements* (New York, 1966).

[3] *Welsh Nation*, Dec. 1961.

1966 that at a guess one hundred and twenty members of his family were 'in the *Blaid*'.[1]

A clearer parallel exists between the operations of the *Blaid* and the development of a revivalist religious movement in the nonconformist tradition. Wales has had notable religious revivals in the past, in particular in the nineteenth century and culminating in the 1904 revival.[2] The Welsh Nationalist revival in the 1960s bore much of the stamp of nonconformity and revivalism. One editor in North Wales wrote to the author at the close of 1968 that 'it is not true nationalism (if there is such a thing) that we have here but an aspect of nonconformity—still confused with echoes of the "Irish Question"'. The link between nonconformity and nationalist politics in Wales was first forged in the late nineteenth century over the issue of disestablishment.[3] There were signs of its renewal following the incident of the burning of the Penyberth bombing school in 1936.[4] Comment on the link between the two in modern times was made more recently by a sociologist after working in North Wales. 'The close ties in the past between Welsh culture, religion and politics have led some religious people to hope for a revival of Welsh culture by means of specifically Welsh politics. They believe that the weakening of the chapel is a sign that the Welsh culture is moribund. The Welsh Nationalist Party "*Plaid Cymru*" is a movement of people who despair of the Welsh culture surviving and see political separation as the only remedy.'[5] It would not be accurate to see the source of the new Nationalist support as being mainly in the nonconformist churches, although nonconformity has certainly a strong hold on older members of the *Blaid*. Much of the new support that the *Blaid* generated came from the young age groups which nonconformist leaders almost despaired of keeping within the chapel fold; even many sons of the manse in the party were not practising Christians. There was a curious alliance in *Plaid Cymru* between the older nonconformists and the irreligious young, both intent on saving Wales and her culture. The longstanding nonconformist elements in the party have carried into its very heart much of the terminology and the attitudes of their religion and their denominations. In one important aspect,

[1] Ibid., Mar. 1966.

[2] See E. T. Davies, *Religion in the Industrial Revolution in South Wales* (Cardiff, 1965); C. R. Williams, 'The Welsh Religious Revival 1904–5', in *British Journal of Sociology*, 1952; and Eifion Evans, *The Welsh Revival of 1904* (Port Talbot, 1969).

[3] See Kenneth O. Morgan, *Wales in British Politics*.

[4] Ibid., p. 303; see also Ch. 1.

[5] I. Emmett, *A North Wales Village* (London, 1964).

the revivalist atmosphere that Nationalists have sought in Wales has been encouraged by the individual distinction of Gwynfor Evans. In searching for the 'promised land' of an independent Wales, the Nationalists needed a leader for guidance. 'Gwynfor' was heralded—by young and old among Nationalists—as a new Messiah for Wales; his qualities of integrity and dedication marking him out from other men. Indeed his victory in the Carmarthen by-election was regarded by Nationalist supporters as something akin to a Second Coming, so miraculous it seemed at the time. One ex-trade union leader, at least, saw the parallel when he referred to *Plaid Cymru*'s President as 'the prophet Gwynfor'.[1] The party's affinity for religion was confirmed by leading Nationalists who preached the essential link between Christianity and nationalism, from Saunders Lewis to Gwynfor Evans.[2] In the latter's view, 'The idea of Welsh nationality has from the very beginning been bound up with Christianity.'[3]

Plaid leaders have imagined that a major transformation in the mental outlook of the Welsh people towards Wales and its place in the world would be required before Nationalism could take firm root. The anglicized parts of Wales, in particular, seemed to Nationalists to be inhabited by lost sheep who had strayed from the true path. Gwynfor Evans wrote after the Aberdare by-election in 1946 that 'anglicized East Glamorgan can be won for the cause of Welsh freedom. Its people, many of whom resent having been despoiled of their cultural heritage, need only an effective lead to become conscious again of their membership of the Welsh nation....'[4] A new awakening of Nationalism among the people would come to pass in the same manner as a religious awakening. Nationalists in Wales have actively sought to create a revivalist atmosphere in their movement in order to foster their cause, and in so doing they have adopted the language, the mentality, and the methods of the Welsh nonconformists of the past. The packed meetings, the communal singing, the banners, and the cavalcades arranged by the *Blaid* were all weapons from the old nonconformist armoury. The extreme devotion to the cause among its supporters made Welsh Nationalism a religious form of politics as opposed to the old nonconformists' political form of religion. An early manifestation of this phenomenon

---

[1] Wil Whitehead, lecture at Gregynog, Montgomeryshire, 6 Dec. 1969.
[2] See Saunders Lewis, *Canlyn Arthur* (Aberystwyth, 1938) and *The Party for Wales* (Caernarfon, 1942).
[3] O. D. Edwards, G. R. Evans, *et al.*, *Celtic Nationalism* (London, 1968), p. 224.
[4] *Welsh Nationalist*, Jan. 1947.

in the *Blaid* occurred in 1937 when the three Nationalists who had set
fire to the bombing school in Penyberth were released from prison.
'A revival atmosphere welcomed the three back to Wales from Wormwood Scrubs', Gwynfor Evans has written.[1] Mrs. Catrin Daniel also
compared the packed meeting at Caernarfon pavilion to celebrate
their return to the atmosphere at a revival meeting.[2] Thirty-one years
later, the Caerphilly by-election occurred in Wales—the third by-
election in as many years in which the *Blaid* was to make a dramatic
impact. The atmosphere in which the contest was fought was itself
dramatic and unique, and strange to political agents and journalists
alike. One elderly Labour worker commented that 'There has not
been anything like this in this valley since the 1904 revival. All you
have to do is to substitute Welsh Nationalism for Christianity and
Phil Williams for Christ, and there you've got it.'[3] Referring to the
Aberdare by-election in 1946, Gwynfor Evans wrote that he counted
it as a permanent result of the by-election that 'Ministers of religion
throughout the valley said that the awakening was to them incredible
and had made *their* work easier. . . . Perhaps, indeed, one will find that
industrial divisions . . . and not the rural constituencies will pioneer
the way to Welsh freedom.'[4] In the same article, Evans pointed out
that 'The basic appeal of *Plaid Cymru* is not material but moral, to
the Welshman's sense of *what is right*.' Here is illustrated another
facet of the nonconformist influence on the *Blaid*—on its language
and political outlook. In the 1960s this was still clearly to be seen in
Plaid campaigns and speeches. Dr. Pennar Davies, a leading nonconformist, in discussing the future of the *Blaid* in 1965 and prospects
for reviving national consciousness in Wales called for 'a sacrificial
campaign for the recognition of the language'.[5] Likewise one of the
party's 'new men', Dr. Phil Williams, stressed the importance, in the
by-election in Caerphilly, of Wales bearing the responsibility for
regenerating her economy and her way of life. The *Blaid*, he said,
wanted 'to build a society that represents the aspirations of Wales'.
'We have always lacked confidence in ourselves', he said. 'Now there
is a new confidence especially among young people. . . . If we have
problems, it is our duty to solve them.'[6] Such is also the nonconformist philosophy.

[1] Gwynfor Evans,'The Twentieth Century and *Plaid Cymru*', in A. W. Wade-Evans,
et al., op. cit., p. 146.
[2] Mrs. Catrin Daniel, interview for'Yesterday's Witness', broadcast on B.B.C. 2,
1 Mar. 1970.   [3] Private interview, 12 July 1968.
[4] *Welsh Nationalist*, Jan. 1947.   [5] *Welsh Nation*, Jan. 1965.
[6] Dr. Phil Williams, speech in the Ystradmynach Workers' Institute, 13 July 1968.

If the language of the *Blaid* bore strong traces of nonconformity—
and this was not so surprising in view of the background of so many
Plaid leaders, so too did the mentality of the Nationalist match that
of the nonconformist. One senior member of the party described it
in this way: 'The *Blaid* had for many years, since 1950 to 1951, the
feeling that they were on the point of a "breakthrough". Their public
meetings were so enthusiastic. But it did not seem to come. Then
there was Tryweryn. It was a very successful propaganda point; the
mass media were very interested too.' The breakthrough was indeed
slow in coming, but the prospect of the imminent arrival of the
'promised land' gives a small group remarkable confidence and stay-
ing power. That is why Carmarthen was so important to Nationalists
and sympathisers in Wales, for it made their dreams, after forty years
in politics, look as if they might soon be realized. Alongside the idea
of the 'breakthrough' ran the ideal of a self-governing 'free Wales'.
In the early days of the *Blaid* this meant a Welsh-speaking, property-
owning Welsh democracy. One of the party's pamphleteers wrote in
1938 that 'A thoroughly Welsh education in Wales is the Beautiful
Gate to self-government.'[1] One former member of *Plaid Cymru*
sceptically suggested to the writer that *Plaid Cymru* thought of Wales
as a nation between heaven and earth. There was a strong streak of
Utopianism about the *Blaid*'s conception of a self-governing Wales.
Every Nationalist conceived of it as ideal in his own lights: for some
it was a Christian Wales, for some a socialist Wales, for some a Welsh-
speaking Wales. In addition, there was the idea that Wales, as a
national state in its own right would be able to act as a moral force
for good in an evil and turbulent world. This view was reinforced by
the notion that every nation had a natural right to self-government,
and a duty to take upon itself the responsibility of its own government. This was not something that a Nationalist would argue about.
It was a belief which he accepted as unchallengeable, justified by the
natural order of things. Consequently, Wales was to him a nation
without the rights due to a nation, a nation deprived of its nationhood and therefore suffering from a great injustice. This idea of a
nation deprived of God-given rights and of recognition—although
not substantiable in fact—nevertheless has great political and
spiritual power, if it is accepted, and is an important factor in evoking
the zeal and determination transparent in so many Nationalists.
Somehow the natural law seemed to be violated because Wales has

[1] *Cymru Rydd: Braslun o Bolisi'r Blaid Genedlaethol.*

not got its freedom. The very word 'freedom' was invested with a moral, spiritual, and individualistic quality which Nationalists in Wales did not find in the word 'independence'. The *Blaid*'s leaders have made this distinction between the two words since 1926. They have never been statists or Hegelians in their view of 'the nation'. Instead they saw the Welsh nation as an entity with a personality of its own, currently shackled by an alien government. Their concern was to give that nation 'freedom', freedom to develop in its own chosen way, freedom to be responsible for itself in the world and in the eyes of its own people, freedom to exercise its own personality. Allied to this view was the nationalist doctrine that attributes nearly all the things that are wrong with the country to the absence of its own government. This is a simplistic doctrine which permits of almost universal application. It can become a complete mental framework, entirely governing the logic of those who cling to it. It is also a political concept which is easily understood and thus can be grasped by the very young.

The youthfulness of the *Blaid* is largely a new phenomenon which could have enormous consequences for Wales and Britain. If the party continued to recruit at the same rate the numbers of young people it did recruit in the period 1966–9, and if it held the allegiance of all those who were in its ranks already, then by 1990 it might well form the government of Wales. The picture that emerges from analysis of the membership records of the party is that the high turnover of members applies at least as much to youth members as to adults, and in the early sixties it was the youth members who were particularly prone to drop quickly out of the *Blaid*. This is an important fact concerning the quality of allegiance on the part of many young people to the *Blaid*. There are some who join when young and become confirmed for ever as stalwarts of the party. But for many others the Nationalist movement has a particular appeal only for a relatively short period of their lives. W. B. Cameron has commented that 'The casual exploitation of romantic youngsters is frequent among subversive movements. In the rather unsatisfactory world that young folk have been entering for several thousands of years many things make for such an appeal. . . . Many social movements offer things he can be against. As he ages the youngster may and often does become disenchanted with the movement either through wisdom, the attraction of a secure place in conservative society, the accumulation of responsibilities. . . .'[1] Religious revivalism is also known to appeal

---

[1] W. B. Cameron, op. cit., p. 84.

most strongly to people at the beginning of their teens;[1] and the evidence is clear that many people in this age group were joining *Plaid Cymru*. The attraction of a nationalist political movement is sociopsychological for such young people. They are at the stage of growing away from the authority and the influence of the home and their parents and seek a new system of beliefs in the wider world in which to place their trust—as de Grazia has put it, to relieve them of their 'separation-anxiety'.[2] The political–religious climate of society first impinges on the child as his parents' limitations are discovered. De Grazia argues that in the nation-state the religious symbolism imparted by the home or the school is matched by the personalized symbols of nationalism; thus 'the nation becomes an expanded home'.[3] At a later stage of adolescence, difficulties experienced in finding work after leaving school may encourage a radicalism that finds an effective voice in Wales in Welsh nationalism. For the qualities of *Plaid Cymru*, of being a nationalist, radical, and quasi-religious movement make it attractive to different youthful aspirations. One particular quality of the *Blaid* which is important, especially to the young, is the aura of friendship and comraderie it conveys. The emotionalism and brotherliness of the Welsh Nationalist movement can also be compared with the revivalist's demand for return to the security of a simple settled life, as provided in agricultural villages or 'communities of early industrialism after they had settled into committed Methodism'. 'It is a recurrent demand for the fraternal society, found still among religious radicals in the mid twentieth century.' The demand of the revivals 'was often for the persistence of relationships and community structure which were often no longer possible in the rapidly changing conditions of industrial society. . . . Revivalism promises a return to the decencies of the past through the reassertion of fundamental truths.'[4] This gives a significant insight into the Welsh Nationalist's plea for the Welsh way of life and the preservation of the Welsh language. Traditionally the Welsh Nationalist cause has attracted the Welsh-speaking religiously inclined intellectual or idealist, in the main professional people. For the professional men who do not leave Wales have conflicting pressures on them. Anglicized by university education, they still have an intellectual appreciation of Welsh culture. The practice

---

[1] Bryan Wilson, *Religion in Secular Society* (London, 1966), Ch. 1.
[2] S. de Grazia, *The Political Community* (Chicago, 1948), Part I, Ch. 1.
[3] Ibid., Part I, Ch. 2.   [4] Bryan Wilson, op. cit., pp. 27–8.

of a profession can often estrange a man from others, making his relations special and unequal; he tries to compensate by being Welsh 'from the top'—politically as a nationalist. By his very conscious affiliation to Welsh life, he goes a step further in cutting himself off from it. Thus has Emmett described the professional man who is a Nationalist supporter in a North Welsh village.[1] The intellectuals who form the leadership of the *Blaid* are in the main romantic radicals trying to re-establish communion with a fading Welsh way of life. The fact that several Nationalist leaders and candidates have gone out of their way to learn the Welsh language also points to this, as well as to genuine nationalist convictions. But the main appeal of the *Blaid* is to the young and the insecure, whether in their jobs or in their community or in their personal life. This is to be seen particularly in communities whose industry has been made redundant by industrial change and where depopulation is rife. In such circumstances, Welshness is helpful but not essential to the generation of Nationalist support. The *Blaid* in these areas—in the valleys of Glamorgan and Caernarvonshire especially—combines protest with the restoration of hope and confidence. It cannot avoid a material appeal to the people, but it adds a moral tone to its appeal that seems lacking in modern socialism. Whereas the revivals recurred in the type of church that was 'the church of the poor, the church of the dispossessed'[2] so the *Blaid* offered to be the party of the poor, the party of the dispossessed and the forgotten. The *Blaid* has acted as much as a political church as a political party.

If the appeal of the *Blaid* strongly resembled the appeal of nonconformists and revivalists, there were also striking organizational parallels between the *Blaid* and the chapels owing largely to the chapel background of so many Nationalist activists. Two of the main marks of the chapel on the *Blaid* were its lack of formal procedures and its extreme reluctance to debate matters publicly. One former senior official of the party complained that '*Plaid* was organized like a chapel meeting'. Nowhere could this more clearly be seen than at the annual conference of the party. Until 1968, this would take place at the same time as the summer school which was a rather unstructured event. This changed considerably from 1968: the conference of the *Blaid* became organized, with a detailed timetable, standing orders, and rules of procedure, if the chairman needed to apply them. On the whole, the *Blaid* had relied on working out

---

[1] I. Emmett, op. cit., Ch. 3.   [2] E. T. Davies, op. cit., p. 60.

difficulties within the party on an *ad hoc* and highly personal basis, but this was less successful in the late 1960s and the subject of some criticism. In particular there was no distinction made between the role of political leader and chairman of the party organization in the case of the President of the *Blaid*, and this caused friction and left a political vacuum.[1] The relationship of Gwynfor Evans to the party was akin to that between a minister and his congregation, in this respect as in others. Decisions inside the party for a long time were taken by 'Gwynfor's court', a group of trusted advisers and party stalwarts acting in the manner of chapel deacons. The effect of growth on the party was to formalize procedures, but the machinery for taking decisions became so overloaded that much informal decision-taking still occurred. Thus there were demands for the democratization of the party from within—from any 'out-group' at leadership level, and from those who wanted more formal procedures and those who resented some of the bureaucracy which had crept into the party since 1966.

A reluctance to bring arguments out into the open and to disagree with one's colleagues in public was another striking example of the influence of the chapels on the *Blaid*: dissatisfactions tended to be expressed in private and rarely to those in a position of responsibility. There were other manifestations, which were relatively unimportant: the St. David's Day Fund list of subscribers to the *Blaid* was clearly modelled on the detailed list of donations that local chapels still print and publish and circulate to members; the way in which population statistics were regarded so significantly by Nationalist debaters and pamphleteers probably owed its origin to the nonconformists' emphasis on increasing or preserving the numbers of members and hearers in their congregations. The reluctance to disagree with fellow-Nationalists in public was a marked characteristic of the party, and was potentially dangerous and embarrassing. Perhaps it stemmed from the insecurity engendered in members of a small group which feels its existence threatened by internal disputes. Politically, the consequence for the *Blaid* has been that large items of policy presented to the party in conference have been accepted without much debate.[2] Thus the party workers gained little under-

---

[1] A special conference of *Plaid Cymru*, held in March 1970, did finally decide to institute a separate office of chairman of the party. The first person elected to hold this position was Dr. Phil Williams.

[2] During the 1968 conference less than 10 hours were provided for the discussion of 41 motions and attendant amendments. At the 1969 conference, 15½ hours were allocated for the discussion of 47 motions and attendant amendments.

standing of the reasoning behind a policy, and only later would some of the policy's implications become clear; this was, typically, the result of some of the resolutions of the conference in 1968 concerning economic planning in Wales. The lack of debate also led to situations where conflicting resolutions were agreed in conference, without the contradictions being pointed out. The sabotage of the *Blaid*'s budget for Wales at the 1969 conference by its approval of a motion calling for the complete abolition of the Selective Employment Tax has already been noted. At the same conference a motion on local government was passed which opposed all amalgamation of local government units and proposed instead that 'the present Councils should be given more authority and responsibility, particularly in financial matters, so that the principle of local government can be strengthened and not diminished'.[1] This contradicted the view of the *Blaid*'s spokesmen that some reorganization was necessary, which was expressed both before and after, but not during the conference. The local government motion was hardly debated at all, and the *Blaid*'s previous official view was at no stage of the debate explained or mentioned. In effect, this decision was ignored by the party leadership because it is so out of line with their thinking. This fact in itself shows too how powerful the bureaucracy and the leadership of the *Blaid* have become as the party has expanded. However much the party tended to add formality to its discussions and decision-taking processes, the distribution of power within the party did not change substantially. The leadership possibly became stronger in relation to the rank and file, as a result of improved organization and an increase in full-time officials.

[1] *Plaid Cymru* Annual Conference Programme, 1969, p. 21.

9

THE PLACE OF NATIONALISM IN SOME WELSH
INSTITUTIONS AND PRESSURE GROUPS (I)

NATIONALISM, defined as the belief in the supreme importance of the interests of the nation, has many sources and buttresses in Wales. Nationalist attitudes find support from people in all walks of Welsh life in all parts of Wales. The political goal of national self-determination is *Plaid Cymru*'s main platform, but national consciousness is asserted in the outlook and attitudes of the majority of Welsh people. The Investiture of the Prince of Wales in Caernarfon Castle in 1969 was one of the most nationalist events held in Wales in the twentieth century, yet it was not supported by Welsh Nationalists, who regarded it as politically motivated. Welsh nationalism which supports the interests and identity of Wales is a more subtle, complex, and widespread phenomenon than *Plaid Cymru*. It is such a nationalism that colours the approach and the decisions of politicians and administrators because it is so general a feeling, and because those who feel themselves to be Welshmen often wish to see the individuality and the special needs of their nation recognized.

In Wales since 1945 there have been many groups and organizations which have sought to promote and defend Welshness and the Welsh culture. Many have chosen constitutional methods; a few, however, have chosen unconstitutional methods by which to further their objectives. Some have been overtly political, while others have concentrated their attentions on such fields as the educational system or broadcasting. These bodies have each had an influence on, and have each been influenced by, the state of the nationalist temper of Wales at any one time. *Plaid Cymru* has used and has been used by some of these bodies. The discussion in this Chapter will centre on the extent to which the *Blaid* and various Welsh pressure groups and institutions have interacted, how far the success of one may have conditioned the success of another, and what impact they have had on the attitudes of the élite and of the general population in Wales. National consciousness is a force which permeates all Welsh life;

but it is not an autonomous or self-regulating force. It has its own sources and supports, including many of the organizations, usually non-partisan, which are described in this Chapter. The intention of such organizations has been to foster nationalism among the Welsh people in different aspects of their life.

Undeb Cymru Fydd (*The New Wales Union*)

Undeb Cymru Fydd was set up in 1941 after the merger between two bodies formed to foster the Welsh culture, the National Union of Welsh Societies[1] and the National Conference for Safeguarding Welsh Culture which was formed on 1 December 1939 as a result of the outbreak of war and the stresses that war was placing on Welsh society.[2] The aims of *Undeb Cymru Fydd* were to safeguard Welsh social, linguistic, and educational interests, and to co-ordinate and develop the activities of Welsh societies in and out of Wales. Its methods were always constitutional. It initiated conferences of delegates from all sections of Welsh life on issues of national importance, such as devolution or the television service in Wales. It made representations to public and private bodies on behalf of Welsh interests, and encouraged its branches to do so. It was also responsible for a number of publications such as *Yr Athro*, a magazine in Welsh circulating to Welsh teachers;[3] *Cofion Cymru*, a monthly newsletter in Welsh for those serving in the forces during the war;[4] *Llythyr Ceridwen*, a journal circulating to Welsh women;[5] and *Yr Anghor*, which started in 1964 as the official magazine of the *Undeb* giving news of its activity. Among the most important of its occasional pamphlets was the publication in 1963 of the proposals for a Central Welsh Council set out by Gwilym Prys Davies, who was advising the Welsh Council of Labour on questions of devolution and local government.[6]

[1] The name *Undeb Cymru Fydd* was suggested by Gwynfor Evans (*Undeb Cymru Fydd 1939–1960* (Aberystwyth, 1960), p. 2). The National Union of Welsh Societies, *Undeb Genedlaethol y Cymdeithasau Cymraeg*, was founded in 1911 to support Welsh causes. E. T. John, one-time M.P. and ardent devolutionist, was a prominent member and became its President.

[2] This was the result, principally, of a letter to the *Manchester Guardian* published on 8 Sept. 1939 which suggested that an advisory committee be set up to watch the effects of the war on Welsh life. The authors of the letter were Saunders Lewis and J. E. Daniel.

[3] *Yr Athro* was published from 1952 under U.C.F. auspices. Its circulation in 1960 was about 1,600 (U.C.F. Minutes).

[4] *Cofion Cymru* had a monthly circulation of 25,000 and ceased publication in 1946, after sixty-two editions.

[5] *Llythyr Ceridwen* was produced by U.C.F.'s women's committee under Mrs. T. I. Ellis, and was published between 1958 and 1968.

[6] G. Prys Davies, *A Central Council for Wales* (Aberystwyth, 1963).

The main work of *Undeb Cymru Fydd* in the period 1941 to 1965 was to focus the attention of the civil authorities on to some of the acute problems facing traditional Welsh life in the course of rapid social and industrial change. A host of memoranda, submissions, and delegations were presented to ministers, M.P.s, civil servants, and local government officials. The main co-ordinator of these efforts was T. I. Ellis, son of the famous Tom Ellis, Gladstone's Whip in the 1892–5 Parliament.[1] Ellis was secretary of the *Undeb* from its foundation until 1967, and through his many contacts—and those of other *Undeb* members—secured access for the *Undeb*'s viewpoint at every level of government at a time when little special attention was given to Welsh affairs. Without Ellis the *Undeb* would probably not have lasted much beyond the 1940s when it was at its most active. But his capacity for organization and hard work ensured that the *Undeb* aired its nationalist views on a wide variety of issues, which included the size of the War Office's holdings of land in Wales for defence purposes, the education system, the position of the Welsh language, radio and television services in Wales, and Welsh water and electricity supplies.

The most important single act of *Undeb Cymru Fydd* was its decision to call a conference on the question of a Parliament for Wales at Llandrindod Wells on 1 July 1950.[2] Towards the end of 1949, Liberal M.P.s from Wales had called for a Covenant in Wales along the lines of the Scottish Covenant for a Scottish Parliament, which had attracted mass support in Scotland. Since October 1949 *Plaid Cymru* had called for a campaign for a Parliament for Wales.[3] *Undeb Cymru Fydd*—T. I. Ellis in particular—acted as honest broker between these two parties, and was considered by them the best medium through which to launch a campaign for a Welsh Parliament. Emrys Roberts, the Liberal M.P. for Merioneth, committed the Welsh Liberals to a Welsh Covenant organized by *Undeb Cymru Fydd* early in January 1950. 'I think this would be excellent', he wrote. 'I think we [the Liberals] would gain the kudos of having launched the campaign but avoided a stunt or a flop.'[4] On 13 January the *Undeb*'s council decided, on Ellis's suggestion, to convene a National Con-

---

[1] T. I. Ellis (1899–1970) was formerly headmaster of Rhyl Grammar School. He was educated at Westminster School and at Jesus College, Oxford. His education gave him many contacts which he used later in the service of *Undeb Cymru Fydd*. Ellis wrote a number of books about Welsh history and the Welsh countryside.

[2] See below, pp. 257–61.   [3] *Welsh Nation*, Oct. 1949.

[4] Emrys Roberts to Hywel Rhys, secretary of the Liberal Party of Wales, 8 Jan. 1950 (letter in Liberal Party of Wales MSS.).

ference as soon as possible to consider promoting a petition in favour of parliamentary self-government for Wales.[1] Despite the importance of the decision, only twelve members of the *Undeb*'s council were at this meeting; nineteen sent apologies for absence.[1] Of those present, three were prominently associated with *Plaid Cymru*.[2] Thus the campaign was begun, with the *Undeb* as midwife. It was many months before the *Undeb* could hand over its responsibility to the organizers of the Parliament for Wales campaign, and some *Undeb* members later regretted that it had done so. Many *Undeb* members were involved in the campaign until it was wound up in 1956—its objective unattained.

Undeb Cymru Fydd asked the Lord Mayor of Cardiff to call another National Conference of Wales in 1959, to consider the television services available in Wales.[3] The conference set up a continuation committee to keep up the pressure on the authorities. Its members included Dr. B. Haydn Williams, Sir Cennydd Traherne, and T. I. Ellis, all later involved in the abortive television enterprise 'Wales West and North' which failed in 1963.[4] When the I.T.A. and the B.B.C. each gave extra time and money to Welsh-language television broadcasting in 1963–4, *Undeb Cymru Fydd* could take some of the credit for this, having for many years drawn attention to deficiencies in the television service in Wales.

Undeb Cymru Fydd was, therefore, largely the organization of one man, T. I. Ellis, who held it together for twenty-five years. It acted as a nationalist pressure group of a non-partisan character, bringing together men and women in many walks of life and focusing their attention and the attention of the mass media on the social and cultural changes in Wales. Its outlook was that of the Welsh-speaking intelligentsia; it was never a grass-roots movement. It helped legitimize the nationalist viewpoint among the civil authorities because of the respectability of its spokesmen. There were, naturally, several well-known *Plaid Cymru* members in its ranks, but this did not matter for most of the *Undeb*'s life as a political pressure group.[5] The *Undeb* was for decades a voice on its own when the voice of

---

[1] Minutes of U.C.F. Council meeting, 13 Jan. 1950 (N.L.W., U.C.F. MSS.—*Tachwedd* 1960 (presentation) No. 268, Minute Book 1949–1955.)

[2] They were Gwynfor Evans, Dr. Gwenan Jones, and the Reverend Dr. R. Tudur Jones.

[3] *Undeb Cymru Fydd 1939–1960*, p. 24.   [4] See below, pp. 249–50.

[5] *The New Wales Union 1941–1948* (Aberystwyth, 1948) notes that M.P.s were initially suspicious of U.C.F. until Sir Henry Morris- Jones, a National Liberal, became chairman of the Welsh parliamentary party.

Wales was hardly heard in Britain as a whole. It 'did not really have a long-term strategy, but pursued issues according to events and the interest of its members'.[1] It was never a particularly large or effective body, and often its viewpoint carried little weight. Finance was always a worry, and when *Undeb Cymru Fydd* became an educational charity in 1965 in order to qualify for grants from Welsh Church funds from county councils (under the 1919 Welsh Church Temporalities Act), it had severely to limit its forays into the political arena. Yet since 1966 the climate of opinion has changed so greatly that 'other bodies have taken over the role of *Undeb Cymru Fydd*'.[2] In 1969, *Undeb Cymru Fyndd* decided to suspend its general public activities and to try to establish a new organization charged with over-all responsibility for Welsh cultural affairs.[3] At the outset of 1973 no such body had materialized.

Urdd Gobaith Cymru (*The Welsh League of Youth*)

Like *Undeb Cymru Fydd*, *Urdd Gobaith Cymru* has tried to stimulate and to preserve Welsh-consciousness among the people of Wales, but in a broader and younger context. The *Urdd* is the largest youth movement in modern Wales, with over forty thousand members.[4] Initially it was a movement for children and grew out of the magazine *Cymru'r Plant* (The Children's Wales), founded by O. M. Edwards, first chief inspector of the Welsh Department of the Board of Education.[5] His son, Ifan ab Owen Edwards, continued the magazine after his father's death in 1920, and in January 1922 he invited readers of *Cymru'r Plant* to become members of *Urdd Gobaith Cymru Fach* (League of Hope of Young Wales). A recent *Urdd* publication explains:

> It was January 1922. Interest in small nations was at a premium and almost every section of the Welsh community had for several years been persistently demanding a parliament for Wales within the British federal system. It is little wonder, therefore, that *the Urdd was primarily a nationalist movement, though non-political*. It was a children's movement, and its aim was to foster Welsh awareness, Welsh culture and the Welsh language.[6]

---

[1] T. I. Ellis, private interview, 31 July 1969.
[2] T. I. Ellis, private interview, 30 July 1969.
[3] *Liverpool Daily Post*, 17 Nov. 1969.
[4] Much of the information about the *Urdd* which appears below has been provided by J. Cyril Hughes, now Director of *Urdd Gobaith Cymru*, to whom I am greatly indebted.
[5] David Williams, *A History of Modern Wales* (London, 1950), p. 283.
[6] *Urdd Gobaith Cymru*: press handout in English issued by the movement in 1969 (author's emphasis).

The *Urdd* adopted a threefold pledge of loyalty to Wales, to fellow-man, and to Christ (in that order)—a pledge which every member still has to take before admission to the League. In its early days, the *Urdd* acquired an internationalist as well as a nationalist outlook, and it soon became co-sponsor with the League of Nations Union of the annual 'Goodwill Message of the Children of Wales to the Children of the World'. The *Urdd*'s development as a youth movement paralleled the development of youth movements elsewhere in Europe between the wars.

National youth movements arose in many other European countries soon after the first World War. The *Urdd*, having based its ideals on the concept of brotherhood, avoided their errors.[1]

Nevertheless the *Urdd* was highly nationalistic in inspiration. It too had its own uniform, and its own youth camps; but the hand of non-conformity exercised a strong influence on the movement, and there was no question of the *Urdd* straying into politics. Part of a statement of aims dating from 1930 reads thus:

Wales is today, mainly because of her traditions, in a better position to work out the ideals of peace in the world than any other nation. For small nations have served the world—need Canaan be referred to—and we see in Wales today a small country which can serve mankind.

But to keep these traditions true and her ideals pure, she must develop them in a language of her own. If Wales is to live as Wales, her language is essential to her existence. . . . The only way to keep alive Welsh traditions and ideals is to develop them in a separate language, the language in which they have ever been developed.

When Wales loses her language, she will be assimilated to England, she will lose her ideals and thus cease to be a nation, for a nation without ideals is valueless—a nation lives not for itself but for mankind.[2]

This was the guiding philosophy of the *Urdd* in its first fifty years as a youth movement; these were the ideals of its founder, Sir Ifan ab Owen Edwards.[3]

Soon after war broke out in 1939, the role of the *Urdd* was considerably changed. The Board of Education decided that boys and

---

[1] *The Urdd (The Welsh League of Youth): What it is: What it does: How to Help: How to Join* (Aberystwyth, 1947).

[2] *Yr Urdd: Its Aims: Its Ideals: Its Work* (Llanuwchllyn, 1920s).

[3] Sir Ifan ab Owen Edwards was, like his father, a Liberal in politics. In 1945 he was short-listed along with Roderic Bowen, J. Morgan Davies, Alun Talfan Davies, and Jenkin Alban Davies for the Liberal nomination in Cardiganshire (letter from Raymond Jones, of the Liberal Central Association, to Hywel Rhys, secretary of the Liberal Party of Wales, 16 Oct. 1946, in Liberal Party of Wales MSS.).

girls in the 16 to 19 age group must join either a voluntary youth organization or a pre-service military organization.[1] The *Urdd* decided to widen its age span to take in this older age group. Pacifist ministers of religion, for example, did not want their children to be in service units. Many parents in Wales felt similarly about the Board of Education's requirements. So the *Urdd* expanded and qualified for grants from the Board and from local education authorities.[2] The *Urdd* realized at the time that a great opportunity had come its way, and willingly altered its structure for the older age groups. So the *aelwyd* (the hearth)—the *Urdd* youth club for the 16 to 25 age group —became a standard part of Welsh life. The *Urdd*'s expansion was naturally greatest in the Welsh-speaking areas because of its Welsh ethos and emphasis on the Welsh language.[2] Many *aelwydydd* and new *adrannau* (junior groups) were formed, and new publications were begun.

Coinciding with the outbreak of war in ·1939 was the opening of the first *Ysgol Gymraeg* (Welsh School) in Wales, in Aberystwyth with Miss Nora Isaac as headmistress. The purpose of this private primary school was to provide an education mainly in the medium of Welsh, which was not available in the town's schools. Although the school was forced to close in 1951 because it was losing money, its example was followed by several local authorities from the end of the 1940s with Ministry of Education encouragement. It is interesting that the *Urdd* at this point of time made little official effort after 1952 to further the growth of *Ysgolion Cymraeg*. This was left to individual parents and teachers, principally in the Welsh Schools Parents' Association which the *Urdd* set up in 1952.[3] Another achievement of the *Urdd* (in the war years) was to found the Union of Welsh Publishers and Booksellers in 1943.[4]

Once the war was over, the *Urdd* gradually reduced the scale of its operations, when the requirement that 16 to 18 year olds should join a recognized voluntary or military organization was relaxed. The *Urdd* maintained its structure almost unchanged, however, the movement being founded on the *aelwyd* for older members and the *adran* (often a class in school) for younger children. From a peak, in the war years, of more than 80,000, membership fell to a stable

---

[1] Circulars 1577 and 1585 (Board of Education).
[2] *Adroddiad Blynyddol 1941–1942 (Cwmni Urdd Gobaith Cymru).*
[3] See below, 'The Welsh Schools Movement', pp. 220–6.
[4] *Urdd Gobaith Cymru: Hanner Canmlwyddiant 1922–1972* (1968).

42,000 to 44,000.[1] In the meantime, the *Urdd* had become a recognized part of the government's youth service, and it extended its age limits still further to include boys and girls between the ages of ten and twenty-five. Its regular activities continued to be the holding of *eisteddfodau* and sports competitions for young people, the publication of magazines in Welsh, and the holding of camps, which encouraged non Welsh-speakers learning Welsh to use the language,[2] and which were supposed to give a taste of the Welsh way of life.

Because of its emphasis on the Welsh language, the *Urdd* has been strongest in the Welsh-speaking parts of Wales. Most of its members in the 10–16 age range have been attached to branches in schools, and for most of them Welsh was a second language. The *Urdd* thus had to cater for different ages and different states of linguistic development, and this accounts for the large range of its magazines. In this sphere the *Urdd* worked hand in hand with local education authorities in Wales, who paid for the bulk of the orders, which came from schools. The total annual sale of its seven magazines exceeded 500,000 copies by the late 1960s.[3] Magazines, however, were not the only source of help from the local authorities to the *Urdd*. They also financed the purchase of premises at local level, and made grants to the *Urdd* centrally. In particular, they subsidized the salaries and expenses of the *Urdd*'s full-time county youth organizers.[4] One of the prices of accepting government and local authority money was the placing of limits on where the *Urdd* could develop. Although their objectives were rather different, there was a tacit understanding between the *Urdd* and the Young Farmers' Clubs not to try to rival each other in a locality where one of these organizations was already established. Some clubs were even run jointly by the *Urdd* and the local education authority.

Despite this substantial support, the *Urdd* came to appreciate the vulnerability of its own position in the 1960s, and set up a number of

[1] *Adroddiadau Blynyddol*, 1963–4 to 1969–70 (*Cwmni Urdd Gobaith Cymru*) and *The Urdd* (*The Welsh League of Youth*): *What it is: What it does: How to help: How to join* (1947).
[2] The permanent camps are at Llangrannog, Cardiganshire and Llanuwchllyn, Merioneth.
[3] *Urdd Gobaith Cymru: Hanner Canmlwyddiant 1922–1972*. The subscriptions for October 1969 totalled 18,000 for *Bore Da*, 9,150 for *Mynd*, 6,940 for *Deryn*, 6,350 for *Cymru'r Plant*, and 2,340 for *Hamdden* (J. Cyril Hughes, private interview, 29 Sept. 1969).
[4] The annual report for 1951–2 showed six counties giving subsidies in this way. The report for 1969–70 names nine county councils as giving such grants; Pembrokeshire, Carmarthen, Cardigan, Merioneth, Caernarfon, Anglesey, Denbighshire, Flintshire, and Montgomery.

working-parties to review its activities and future strategy. The strength of the *Urdd* lies in Welsh-speaking rural Wales, which is fast losing its isolated character. Increasingly, the *Urdd* has had to cater for those learning the Welsh language rather than native-speaking Welsh youngsters. In addition, the organizers of the *Urdd* recognize that the activities of each *aelwyd* are much more likely to appeal to the highly intelligent, academically-oriented children with middle-class backgrounds, rather than more practically-minded youngsters; but it is the academically successful who are in the van of the emigration from rural Wales, while the less successful, who are more likely to remain in the communities in which they were brought up, are left to keep the Welsh culture and way of life going. Depopulation and the consequent closure of schools has itself taken a toll of *aelwydydd* in the Welsh countryside, as the *Urdd's* private report on its activities revealed in 1969;[1] but the shortage of leaders was an even more common cause of closure of an *aelwyd*.[1] In eight counties fifty *aelwydydd* were closed between 1957 and 1967 for these reasons. Even so the total number of *aelwydydd* in September 1969 was still 193, and there were 566 *adrannau*.[2] Thus the *Urdd* is still a substantial movement with a wide appeal to the youth of Wales.

The rise of Nationalism as a political force in Wales posed testing problems for *Urdd Gobaith Cymru* in the 1960s. The whole inspiration of the movement has been cultural-nationalist from its foundation, but the *Urdd* has also rigorously sought to be non-political, as well as non-denominational. The fact that governments have been prepared to give large grants to the movement shows that the *Urdd* has succeeded in appearing non-partisan over the years. This non-political stance became harder to maintain in the 1960s when one of the central features of Welsh politics was the rise of *Plaid Cymru*. The boys and girls in the movement were, not surprisingly, caught up in these developments, or at least most interested in what was happening; the same was true of the *Urdd's* full-time officials and local leaders, several of whom made no secret of where their sympathies lay. The fact that the politics of many of the *Urdd's* leaders were known to boys and girls in the movement itself provoked their curiosity. The *Urdd's* leaders at local level were overwhelmingly schoolteachers and ministers, the two occupational groups already

---

[1] *Comisiwn Bywyd A Gwaith Urdd Gobaith Cymru* (unpublished internal *Urdd* report), p. 46.
[2] J. Cyril Hughes, private interview, 29 Sept. 1969.

identified as providing the most active support for *Plaid Cymru*.[1] In many cases it was the nationalist beliefs of these individuals that drew them into being *Urdd* leaders. The *Urdd* has always claimed to be a movement that promoted nationalism in Wales, and thus it is not surprising that many *Plaid Cymru* supporters have become involved in its work; men and women of other political allegiances have also been prominent in the *Urdd*'s activities.[2] The nationalist upsurge following the Carmarthen by-election certainly caught the *Urdd* unawares. It was, however, the Investiture of the Prince of Wales which caused the *Urdd* the greatest public embarrassment in its whole history. The tension in the *Urdd* between its nationalism and its status as an officially-supported youth movement was for the first time publicly exposed.

The occasion for this temporary crisis in the *Urdd* was the invitation it received along with many other Welsh organizations to send representatives to attend the Investiture of Prince Charles as Prince of Wales. The Council of the *Urdd* met late in October 1968 and decided, with some misgivings, to accept the invitation to send representatives.[3] The rank and file of the *Urdd* did not take this decision lying down. Thus:

. . . it became obvious that there was a difference of opinion on this subject between the ranks of the *Urdd* and those in other institutions and bodies in Wales. Two young members of the Council resigned because of the decision, and some young members of the staff felt unhappy with the position. The Executive Committee decided that it would be appropriate to call a special meeting of the Council to study the matter again in view of the position which had arisen. In the meantime the opinion of the County committees was sought, but their replies too were very divided.[4]

When the special meeting of the *Urdd*'s Council took place on 14 December 1968 it was 'much better attended than the October Council meeting'.[5] It decided that the *Urdd* should not send representatives to the Investiture ceremony, but that the Prince of Wales

---

[1] See Chs. 7 and 8.

[2] In modern times, these have included Cledwyn Hughes and Goronwy Roberts, two leading Labour politicians in Wales, as well as Emlyn Hooson, the Welsh Liberal leader.

[3] *Western Mail*, 28 Oct. 1968.

[4] *Adroddiad Blynyddol 1968–69* (*Cwmni Urdd Gobaith Cymru*), p. 30 (author's translation).

[5] J. Cyril Hughes, private interview, 23 July 1969. The *Urdd* Council is comprised of officers of the movement, twenty members elected by the annual general meeting, the representatives of the county youth parliaments, and forty-seven representatives of the county committees. At least one-quarter of the Council's members were identifiable to the author as *Plaid Cymru* supporters.

would be welcome to visit the *Urdd*'s camp at Glanllyn, Merioneth.[1] This decision was arrived at in order to keep the movement united, and the founder of the movement, Sir Ifan ab Owen Edwards, was reported as commenting that:

> We are a youth movement, a loyal youth movement, but we don't want to get into politics. We will help the Prince, but we are not going to help a political stunt invented by Lloyd George in 1911. That is what the investiture is. It has no tradition behind it, it does not belong to Wales.[2]

Government circles were surprised, if not shocked, by the *Urdd*'s reversal of its decision, and the position of Sir Ifan ab Owen Edwards on the Duke of Norfolk's Investiture committee became curious in the extreme.[3] Whichever way the *Urdd*'s decision had gone, politics would have been involved, and it is idle to pretend that politics did not enter into the *Urdd*'s final decision not to be represented at the Investiture. It was the young teachers, the students, and the sixth-formers in the *Urdd* who forced the movement to make a stand on the issue. That they succeeded in overturning the decision of the *Urdd*'s Council is evidence of how far political nationalism had pene-trated the grass-roots of the movement.

The involvement of individuals prominent in the *Urdd* in some of the manifestations of political nationalism in the late 1960s in Wales presented other problems for the movement. The evidence of the impact of the three by-elections held in Wales in 1966–8 on the *Urdd*'s members can be seen in the tone of some of its publications. The *Urdd*'s own working-party found that members of the movement were in some difficulty at local level in keeping the movement out of politics.[4] To some members, the *Urdd* seemed only to go half-way in trying to keep the Welsh language and culture thriving. Young mem-bers were reported to be very interested in the activities of the Welsh Language Society, and of *Plaid Cymru*, and yet the movement had no way of discussing such subjects. But it was plain that a principal ingredient in the *Urdd*'s success over the years had been its ability to stand outside politics. As other voluntary organizations, such as Shelter and Oxfam, found in the late 1960s, politics and politicians can do much to advance the objectives of a non-partisan organiza-tion: the tensions in the *Urdd* concerning politics and the movement

---

[1] *Adroddiad Blynyddol 1968–69*, p. 30.   [2] *Western Mail*, 17 Dec. 1968.
[3] The *Liverpool Daily Post*, 17 Dec. 1968, suggested that R. E. Griffith, director of the *Urdd*, was also on this committee, although his name does not appear in the list published in *Cymru 1967* (H.M.S.O., 1968), App. I.
[4] *Comisiwn Bywyd A Gwaith Urdd Gobaith Cymru*, pp. 57–62 especially.

were similar. It could not avoid being influenced by the climate of nationalist success and controversy in Welsh politics. Indeed, some of the most prominent members of the Welsh Language Society were recent products of the *Urdd*.[1] The impact of this change of mood in politics on the *Urdd* was confusing for the movement. In some ways it seemed to be outflanked by other nationalist organizations striving to support the Welsh culture, and the *Urdd* was attacked for its complacency by the Welsh Language Society, in particular. Thus the *Urdd*'s headquarters' staff tried to seize the initiative a little more. The *Urdd* intervened in 1969 to try to ensure that a Welsh pop-singer would have the right to sing a song on behalf of Britain in the Eurovision song contest.[2] The *Urdd* also secured the first bilingual motor-discs for its transport fleet, some weeks before they were issued to the general public in 1970.[3] This was in addition to the stand finally adopted by the *Urdd* Council concerning the sending of representatives to the Investiture. In return for the *Urdd*'s stronger identification with the spirit of nationalism running through Wales at the time, the movement found that its objectives were becoming commonly confused with those of nationalist political extremists, even to the point of being accused of responsibility for the incidents of sabotage occurring in Wales between 1966 and 1969. Surprisingly, the size of membership of the *Urdd* has not benefited from the rise of political nationalism in Wales since 1966, nor do individuals appear to be any more willing to give service to the movement as leaders of *aelwydydd* and *adrannau*. But the *Urdd* does believe that there is more willingness among non Welsh-speaking children to learn the Welsh language and it thinks that this is the way in which the *Urdd* can help Welsh national consciousness in the 1970s.

The achievement of the *Urdd* is already great, regardless of its uncertainty about the future. The mishandling of the Investiture issue was of only temporary significance when compared to the *Urdd*'s impact on the political attitudes and the cultural consciousness of hundreds of thousands of Welsh boys and girls who have passed through its ranks. The *Urdd*, with government and local authority support, has consciously attempted to imbue generations of Welsh children and young people, at highly impressionable ages, with a fierce love of Wales and its cultural and linguistic heritage.

---

[1] Dafydd Iwan offers the clearest example. See below, *Cymdeithas yr Iaith Gymraeg* (The Welsh Language Society), pp. 231–45.

[2] *Western Mail*, 25 Sept. 1969. The singer was Mary Hopkin.

[3] *Y Cymro*, 25 Mar. 1970.

It may not have succeeded in every case in doing this. It may not have been able to penetrate the minds of non-academically oriented children or children outside the rural and Welsh-speaking parts of Wales, but as a force for the promotion and activation of nationalism and national consciousness in Wales it has been of the first importance. There is no single organization in Wales that has conditioned so many minds to sympathize with Welsh nationalism as *Urdd Gobaith Cymru*, and this is an achievement of which it is proud. The problem for the *Urdd* remains how to continue as a modern youth movement in style and appeal without becoming over-identified with nationalist forces in Welsh politics.

The Welsh Schools Movement

It was *Urdd Gobaith Cymru* which launched the first *Ysgol Gymraeg* (Welsh School) and which gave the impetus to the movement for setting up 'Welsh Schools' in anglicized parts of Wales, described by the Gittins Report as 'one of the most significant developments of the last 30 years' in Welsh education.[1] The movement represents both the growing awareness among Welsh parents that the Welsh language is in danger of extinction and the demand that the principles governing the treatment of Welsh in the schools, which have been set out in numerous official educational reports and circulars since 1927, be at last applied in the schools of Wales. The basis of the Welsh schools movement is the spontaneous desire of many Welsh parents for their children to receive a truly Welsh education. Parents have often had to fight local authorities hard and long before officialdom has recognized their demands and tried to meet them. In general the Welsh Department of the Ministry of Education has been more interested in trying to make the schools of Wales major defences of the Welsh language and culture than have local education authorities in Wales itself, but experience has varied between authorities in Wales. In Flintshire, it was the Director of Education, Dr. B. Haydn Williams, who led the parents;[2] but in Glamorgan it was the parents who led the educationalists. After many years of pressure they convinced Glamorgan education committee (whose chairman since 1945 had been Lord Heycock) of the need for Welsh-medium secondary schools in the county.

[1] *Primary Education in Wales*, pp. 220–1, para. 11.5.2.
[2] Dr. B. Haydn Williams was also chairman of the Welsh television company, 'Wales West and North'; see Chs. 3 and 10.

The Welsh schools movement has operated to date in anglicized parts of Wales, for the simple reason that in those areas education through the medium of Welsh is rarely provided by the schools. The purpose and development of these schools, commonly known as *Ysgolion Cymraeg*, was summarized in the Gittins Report:

> The original aim of these schools was to provide a focus of Welsh instruction, traditions and life in areas which could make no provision for a minority of Welsh-speaking children whose parents wished them to be educated in their mother-tongue. They have been consciously modelled on the rural school in the Welsh-speaking areas and are motivated by the traditional Welsh emphasis on literature, *penillion* singing, music and institutions such as the *eisteddfod*. Their strength is their strong relationship with parents, and their close connection with local chapels and the *Urdd*. Their staffs are committed and dedicated . . .
>
> Although *Ysgolion Cymraeg* were first suggested in 1927 in 'Welsh in Education and Life', the idea did not at first receive much official support and it was not until 1939 that the first school, a voluntary foundation, was opened by *Urdd Gobaith Cymru* at Aberystwyth. The first Local Education Authority *Ysgol Gymraeg* did not appear until 1947, at Llanelli. Many have since been established mainly because of parental enthusiasm and pressure. Education authorities were on the whole reluctant at first to make the necessary provision, possibly because they doubted the viability of these schools and were unconvinced of the need for them.[1]

The Gittins Report noted how the movement had made its greatest impact in the period 1947 to 1951, when thirteen such schools were set up, and that in Glamorgan 'some of these, with between 30 and 50 on roll initially, have increased six and seven-fold over 16 years, and the average increase over the same period has been three-fold'.[1] But the Report went on to say that 'the rate of establishment appears to have slackened recently and evidence offered by authorities suggests either that demand has been met in present circumstances, or that it would be difficult to respond to further requests for such schools because of the small scattered number of children involved'.[1]

At the beginning of 1970 forty-one Welsh schools or departments offering primary education in mainly English-speaking areas of Wales were known to the Department of Education and Science. The total number of pupils receiving instruction in these schools was between 5,000 and 6,000.[2] This was nearly twice the number recorded

---

[1] *Primary Education in Wales*, p. 221, para. 11.5.2.
[2] Letter from Miss Olive Arnold of the Department of Education and Science to the author, 2 July 1970.

by the Gittins Report in 1967,[1] although the number of schools was only two more in 1970 than in 1967.[2] Contrary to the expectations of the Gittins Report, this indicates that a considerable growth in the demand for this type of education occurred between the years 1966–7 and 1969–70, probably associated with the rising Nationalist temper in most of Wales at this time.[3] A similar expansion of the schools occurred in 1959–60, at least in Glamorgan, but here the reason was not so obvious.[4] As for secondary schools, six of these were functioning as essentially Welsh-medium schools at the beginning of 1970—at Llanelli, Ystalyfera, Rhydfelin, Wrexham, Mold, and Rhyl;[5] another Welsh-medium secondary school in Glamorgan was scheduled for 1971, but otherwise no additional Welsh-medium schools were in prospect. These schools had nearly 2,500 pupils on their books in 1970.[6]

A study of the origins of *Ysgolion Cymraeg* in the administrative county of Glamorgan has shown that while four of the schools in the late 1960s had well over a hundred children, nearly all of them started as nursery classes with fewer than twelve children, some with five or six.[4] Parents had to prove to the local authority from the size of the pre-primary demand for Welsh-medium education that provision of Welsh-medium teaching at primary level was also needed. But none of the parents and ministers of religion involved in the setting up of these schools were aware at the outset that it was only as a result of the 1944 Education Act that they had a right to demand that local education authorities provide Welsh-medium education.[4] The impetus for founding these schools had come from a common feeling that communication in personal relationships between one generation and another was being permanently impaired as the hold on the young of the Welsh language and culture faded. In addition, there was the feeling of urgency in the face of grave danger to the whole structure of Welsh society. In the words of one parent interviewed (wife of a minister of religion): 'It's the end of the road for the Welsh way of life unless the present generation does more than the last for the Welsh language.'[4] The demand for this type of education

---

[1] *Primary Education in Wales*, p. 221, para. 11.5.2.
[2] Forty-one in 1970 as compared with 39 in 1967.
[3] Figures for the numbers of pupils in *Ysgolion Cymraeg* compiled by *Undeb Cenedlaethol Athrawon Cymru* suggest that most of the increase was registered between 1965 and 1967.
[4] Iorwerth Morgan, private interview, 4 Dec. 1968.
[5] Letter from Miss Olive Arnold to the author, 2 July 1970.
[6] Statistics supplied by the Department of Education and Science.

given in the *Ysgolion Cymraeg* has typically come from the Welsh-speaking section of the professional and middle classes in anglicized Wales. The leaders of the parents' societies in Glamorgan associated with founding these schools have invariably come from the highest social grades, and the children of the middle class (especially from social class II in the Registrar-General's classification) have always been heavily over-represented in these schools.[1] But the success of the schools has depended on attracting working-class parents and children to the schools to make up sufficient numbers. 'Nevertheless the schools often reflect a new educated and urban Welsh-middle-class, aware of their language and traditions, and keen to continue them in modern life.'[2] For some parents the attraction of the *Ysgolion Cymraeg* has been the high academic standards of the schools, low staff–pupil ratios, and the commitment and dedication of their staff, rather than Welsh-medium education.

The Gittins Report noted that in many instances, 'children leaving *Ysgolion Cymraeg* are transferred to English-medium secondary schools, few if any of which provide for teaching through the medium of Welsh'.[3] Insufficient facilities exist at secondary school level to provide courses through the medium of Welsh, and this situation is likely to continue—a factor which itself will tend to hinder the development of *Ysgolion Cymraeg* at primary level.

The development of Welsh-medium secondary schools has been, in recent years, a matter of some political controversy at local authority level. Some authorities have been torn between trying to put through a comprehensive system of education following the D.E.S. Circular 10/65, and trying to find a place for special projects to help Welsh-medium education. Carmarthen County Council decided to make all comprehensive schools bilingual in its area.[4] In general, the standstill in the opening of Welsh-medium secondary schools in anglicized areas seemed attributable to the large building programmes involved in making schools comprehensive, and to the greater effort being put into Welsh teaching and courses at English-medium secondary schools.[5] With limited resources, the

---

[1] Iorwerth Morgan, private interview, 4 Dec. 1968; Gwilym Humphries, private interview, 2 Dec. 1968; and information supplied by Moses J. Jones, private interview, 15 Oct. 1969.

[2] *Primary Education in Wales*, p. 221, para. 11.5.2.

[3] Ibid., p. 222, para. 11.5.2.

[4] At the prompting of Gwynfor Evans, this was agreed in 1969, after many years of debate.

[5] Wales Circular 2/69 (Department of Education and Science).

priorities of making education comprehensive and of improving the knowledge and teaching of Welsh conflict in their claims on county education budgets. In addition, it appears that a large majority of parents, Welsh-speaking as well as English-speaking, do not wish to see the learning of subjects through the medium of Welsh in secondary schools;[1] this must be a limiting factor in the introduction or expansion of Welsh tuition at secondary level.

Politics have never been far away from the Welsh schools movement, both because education policy and education budgets are politically controlled, and because of the ideals of many of those who have pressed for *Ysgolion Cymraeg* and started nursery classes for them. These educational and cultural ideals have often found a political outlet in *Plaid Cymru*, both among parents of pupils and among the teaching staff of *Ysgolion Cymraeg* whose ideals for Welsh education have led them to this special type of school. At secondary level, the pupils of Welsh-medium schools have become involved in the Nationalist movement, sometimes to the severe embarrassment of sympathetic staff when accusations are made that Welsh-medium schools were a breeding-ground for Welsh Nationalists. Such charges are not without substance, although, given the strong Welsh background of many of the children attending these schools, it is arguable that it is the parents, not the schools, who are disposing the pupils towards nationalism. Nevertheless, a very large number of individuals who have been and are connected with Welsh-medium education in anglicized areas have been and are connected with *Plaid Cymru*.[2] Frequently their whole life is the pursuit of Welsh nationalism; in politics, this means working for *Plaid Cymru*; in education, this means working in the schools to promote Welsh-consciousness and to bolster the Welsh language and culture. Ministers of religion have also had an interest in the Welsh schools movement. In order to keep their congregations Welsh-speaking and the language of their services Welsh, they have seen the need to make sure that the young generations have a good knowledge of the language in order to induce them to remain within the fold of the chapel. With so many anglicizing pressures at work in Welsh society, the minister has sometimes become a prime mover in shielding children of a Welsh back-

---

[1] *Primary Education in Wales*, p. 238, para. 11.10.12.
[2] One headmaster estimated that in the late 1960s 95 per cent of his staff and all of the pupils in his *Ysgol Gymraeg* supported *Plaid Cymru*. Many teachers in Welsh-medium schools have been candidates for the *Blaid* at local and parliamentary elections.

ground from anglicization by promoting a Welsh school. Very many of the nursery classes have been started off in chapel vestries as a prelude to the foundation of an *Ysgol Gymraeg*.[1]

But the Welsh schools movement will only have real political and social significance if it can imbue all the children from Welsh backgrounds and some of the children from anglicized backgrounds with a Welsh-consciousness, and a love of Wales. The evidence of the language surveys of children of school age carried out by the Welsh Joint Education Committee suggests that the knowledge of Welsh among school children has consistently decreased in Welsh Wales and has increased in very few of the anglicized parts of Wales.[2] In most areas the expansion of Welsh teaching has not compensated for the effects of mixed marriages between Welsh- and non Welsh-speakers, and of depopulation. Where the Welsh schools movement thrives, the liveliness of the Welsh culture is impressive, and the consequences for political nationalism are significant. James Griffiths, the first Secretary of State for Wales, pinpointed this when he wrote that 'the young people who are the products of the "all-Welsh schools" ' were one of 'the three sections of the Welsh community' forming the membership of *Plaid Cymru*.[3] *Plaid Cymru* can only gain strength from the intensity of devotion to Wales that these schools inspire, but there is a real danger that the segregation at school level of those whose parents are interested in their Welsh heritage from those whose parents have no such ties may only serve to deepen the cleavage between the two linguistic communities in Wales. This cleavage was becoming increasingly apparent and troublesome in Welsh society in the 1960s. A change of attitude amongst a section of the Welsh middle class towards favouring the Welsh language and insisting on its use where possible must be judged mainly responsible; and it is from this section of Welsh society that the momentum for Welsh-medium education has been achieved. However, given the current pattern of development of Welsh-medium schools at primary and secondary level, there is a real prospect that the effect of setting up *Ysgolion Cymraeg* will have been to strengthen the attachment of a minority to the Welsh language and culture, and to strengthen the apathy and lack of interest towards it among the remainder of the population. This may

[1] Iorwerth Morgan, private interview, 4 Dec. 1968.
[2] i.e., Newport C.B., Cardiff C.B., Merthyr Tydfil C.B., and Flintshire C.C. (*Language Survey 1961*, Welsh Joint Education Committee, pp. 4 and 5).
[3] James Griffiths, *Pages From Memory*, p. 200.

eventually defeat the original purpose of many in the Welsh schools movement which is to extend Welsh-consciousness amongst the Welsh population, as well as to preserve it among the minority.

The Defence of the Federal University of Wales

The anglicization of the University of Wales was a cause of great concern to its students and its staff during the 1960s.[1] The issue of anglicization arose in three particular contexts: there was the expansion of numbers attending the University's colleges before and after the Robbins Report;[2] there was the place of the Welsh language in the University's curricula, and the need to follow through at university level the work of the Welsh schools movement; most critically, there was the controversy about the continuance of the University's federal structure.

The University of Wales owes its foundation in the late nineteenth century to the fusing at that time of two tides of Welsh opinion: the desire for greater educational opportunity in Wales, and the nationalist movement, which led to the foundation of a number of Welsh national institutions of which the University is the most celebrated. The University of Wales, founded partly with money raised in small subscriptions from the people of Wales for the people's improvement, 'forms perhaps the most glorious monument to the national revival which revitalised Wales in the later Victorian era'.[3] It was therefore not surprising that, when a proposal was made in 1960 that the four main constituent colleges of the University[4] should be made independent universities in their own right, thus defederalizing the University of Wales, there was considerable oratory from academics and from nationalists against what was seen partly as an assault on the Welsh nation and its past.

The Senate of the University College at Cardiff had suggested back in 1918 that the University of Wales should be defederalized, and

---

[1] The development of the University of Wales is also discussed in Ch. 3.

[2] An early and typically spirited reaction to this expansion in the University came from Alwyn D. Rees, Warden of the University's Guild of Graduates. He wrote in the *Western Mail*, 12 Dec. 1962, that: ' . . . some of the English students in the University of Wales are here as a matter of choice. But what has turned this English trickle into a flood is the failure of the Government to make adequate provision for the education of English students in England. The rejects of English universities come knocking at our doors, and some of them have qualifications well above the minimum.'

[3] Kenneth O. Morgan, 'The People's University in Retrospect', in *University of Wales Review* (1964), p. 7.

[4] At Cardiff, Swansea, Aberystwyth, and Bangor.

this idea had not been laid to rest when it was rejected by the Haldane Committee in 1918.[1] It is not clear that there was any general feeling developing inside the University colleges on the issue of federalization when the initiative of Professor Emrys Williams brought the question to the attention of the Court of the University in 1960. When the Court, which is the highest authority in the University, met in July 1960 forty local authorities had sent resolutions to it urging university status for the four constituent colleges of the University, representatives of the local authorities having nearly half the seats on the University Court. The Court did not hold much brief for the initiative of Caerphilly Urban District Council and its allies, but since problems in administering the federal University were generally admitted, a further discussion on these matters was arranged for the next meeting of the University Court in December 1960. Meanwhile considerable support for the idea of defederalization was mobilized inside the University colleges, and thus the proposal of the University Council to set up an internal committee to review the organization of the University was accepted by the Court. The findings of this committee proved not to be unanimous, and it submitted two reports to the University Court, offering conflicting advice. It was left to the Court to decide which report to accept; the one report, signed by fourteen members of the committee (including five co-opted members), suggested the splitting up of the University into four separate universities; the other report, signed by twelve members of the committee, recommended certain internal reforms but the preservation of the federal structure of the University. The defederalist case rested mainly on the administrative and governmental difficulties of running the federal University when each of its constituent colleges had greatly enlarged numbers of students. The federalist case was based on optimism that the University structure could adapt itself to cope with the problems of college expansion and that the co-operation between the colleges and the interchange of ideas between different parts of the University enforced by its federal structure improved the climate of the academic environment. The argument as to which structure, federal or defederalized, would best serve the Welsh nation and express its distinctiveness underlay much of the discussion surrounding the reports of the committee, and some observers saw the dispute as representing a choice between the University as an

[1] Most of the following account is based on evidence provided in the *University of Wales Review* (1964).

expression of Welsh nationhood and the University as a modern seat of higher education.[1]

The federalists were a minority on the University's committee, although they included a majority of the Welshmen on the committee, and a large majority of graduates of the University on it. The defederalists on the committee comprised all the nine non-Welsh members, in addition to five Welshmen. Three college principals emerged as defederalist; the fourth principal, Dr. Parry of Aberystwyth, did not subscribe to either report. When the University Court met in April 1964 to decide the issue it was clear that the defederalists had lost the battle. The vote went against them by three to one, the bulk of their support coming from principals, senates, and registrars of the colleges.[2] The federalists claimed the support of most of the representatives of the University's Guild of Graduates, the College courts and councils, local authorities, and many of the cultural and educational institutions represented on the Court. The University of Wales preserved its federal structure but had still to come to terms with a world of 'large international units and assimilated cultures'.[3]

The federal structure of the University ceased to be an issue of importance among academics, although it was raised again in 1965 when the College of Advanced Technology in Cardiff became attached to the University. Student leaders in the University, however, remained hostile to the federal structure and again in 1969 claimed that it was a source of weakness in the Welsh system of higher education.[4]

Undeb Cenedlaethol Athrawon Cymru (*The National Association of Teachers of Wales*)

A further source of nationalism in the Welsh education system has been *Undeb Cenedlaethol Athrawon Cymru* (U.C.A.C.), formed in 1940 to represent the interests of Welsh teachers in every type of educational institution.[5] Its aims are, broadly, to ensure that Wales

---

[1] This was the view of *The Times*, 25 Apr. 1964. An editorial noted that during the controversy 'an impression is had that Welsh nationhood, having been balked by the English of a proper deliberative assembly, finds in the Court of the University of Wales a substitute of which it will not be deprived. The Welsh have in their university a modern seat of learning and an institution of higher education. They also have an instrument and emblem of Welsh-consciousness. It seems that they must now decide which they want more of.'

[2] The voting in the Court was 103 for the University of Wales and 33 for four unitary universities.

[3] Kenneth O. Morgan, op. cit., p. 10.   [4] *Western Mail*, 19 July 1969.

[5] *U.C.A.C. Handbook for Welsh Teachers* (Lampeter, undated).

has an independent educational system, to promote the teaching of the Welsh language and Welsh subjects, to unite the teachers of Wales into a single professional body, and to safeguard the welfare of professional teachers.[1] Like the Farmers Union of Wales, it claims to offer teachers benefit schemes which are more attractive than those offered by other unions in the field, but U.C.A.C. is strongly nationalist in outlook. It argues that Wales as a separate country should have its own separate institutions, including its educational system and teaching unions; all U.C.A.C.'s investments are made in Wales.[2] Like the F.U.W., it has had to battle for recognition, and while it has not been entitled to representation on the Burnham Committee in London, it has secured the right since 1967 to sit on the Welsh Joint Education Committee;[3] and the Welsh committee of the Schools Council offered U.C.A.C. similar facilities in 1968.[4] In 1968 the union had about 1,600 members drawn from lecturers, teachers, and students about to join the profession;[5] the membership showed a rise of 15 per cent in 1967, and it is tempting to suggest that this was not unrelated to the rising tide of Welsh nationalism at this period.[6] But U.C.A.C. is still very small; it represents less than 10 per cent of the teachers of Wales, and does not really compare with the National Union of Teachers or even the National Association of Schoolmasters for support in Wales.[7] The union has a strong *Plaid Cymru* element in its leadership and represents the growing Welsh-language interest in the Welsh education system, which is always in danger of being overlooked by the larger teaching unions.[8] If not recognized in England, it is recognized in Wales and its membership of the Court of the University of Wales and of other official bodies has served to advance the cause of Welsh-medium education.

[1] *Arolwg 1968* (Liverpool, 1969), p. 101.
[2] *Why U.C.A.C.?* (Cardiff, undated).
[3] *Western Mail*, 9 Dec. 1967.
[4] *Bwletin* No. 25 (U.C.A.C., 1968), p. 6.
[5] Iorwerth Morgan, private interview, 4 Dec. 1968.
[6] *Arolwg 1967* (Liverpool, 1968), p. 78.
[7] About 24 per cent of male teachers in Wales (2,203 teachers) were members of the National Association of Schoolmasters in 1967 (G. Latta, 'The National Association of Schoolmasters', unpublished M.Sc. thesis, University of Warwick, 1969).
[8] The National Union of Teachers has, however, maintained a permanent sub-committee of its Executive to deal with Welsh matters since 1909. A full-time regional official for Wales became part of the N.U.T. establishment after the First World War. The union has also set up a Secondary Committee for Wales, and an Advisory Committee for Wales, comprising county and borough union representatives (Letter from Alan Evans, secretary to the N.U.T. Welsh Committee, to the author, 7 Jan. 1970).

Merched Y Wawr

Merched Y Wawr (Daughters of the Dawn) was formed early in 1967. Its founder, Mrs. Zonia Bowen of Parc, near Bala, had been in dispute with the Merioneth County Federation of the Women's Institute over the use of Welsh in its administration. The County Federation insisted that reports of branch activities be in English when sent to county headquarters.[1] Mrs. Bowen who had learned to speak Welsh as a second language[2] registered her protest by breaking away from the W.I. to form the first branch of *Merched Y Wawr*, a women's movement in which the Welsh language would have an honoured place.

Merched Y Wawr is effectively a Welsh-speaking equivalent of the Women's Institute movement. Aiming to span differences of town and country, political party, and denomination, it organizes at county and branch level varied programmes of entertainment, and educational and cultural activities which interest its members. The only stipulation is that Welsh is the official language of *Merched Y Wawr* and that the Welsh language is given a 'dignified place' in all the activities of the movement.

The idea of a Welsh-speaking Welsh women's movement corresponded with the rising nationalist mood at large in many parts of Wales after 1966. Within two years of the foundation of *Merched Y Wawr* about seventy branches had been set up in Wales, and the movement appeared to have considerable impetus. Between August 1969 and May 1970 a further thirty-two branches of *Merched Y Wawr* were formed bringing the total number of branches to 109.[3] The great strength of the movement lies in Anglesey, Caernarvonshire, and Merioneth where 58 per cent of the branches were situated in August 1969.[4] Inter-branch *eisteddfodau* were already being established, and a well-produced periodical, *Y Wawr*, with a sale of over three thousand copies per issue, circulated through the branches, keeping them in touch and offering articles of feminine interest.[3] One branch of the movement was even set up in Patagonia in 1969.[5]

Merched Y Wawr, like the breakaway Farmers Union of Wales,[6] seems to have quickly established a place for itself in Welsh society. Although confined very much to the small towns and villages of

---

[1] *Liverpool Daily Post*, 25 May 1967.
[2] A. Le Calvez, *Un Cas de Bilinguisme: Le Pays de Galles* (Lannion, 1970), p. 183.
[3] *Y Cymro*, 13 May 1970.   [4] *Y Wawr*, No. 5 (Aug. 1969).
[5] *Liverpool Daily Post*, 13 Nov. 1969.   [6] See below, pp. 268–71.

Welsh-speaking Wales, it appears to have a stronger appeal to the younger women than the Women's Institutes. It is difficult to assess accurately which is the more significant factor in the success of *Merched Y Wawr*, the youthfulness of the movement, or its nationalism; both are important to its survival. *Merched Y Wawr* represents a division in Welsh society, between those who enthuse about the Welsh language and those who do not, which threatens the peace of many communities in Wales. The rivalry between *Merched Y Wawr* and the Women's Institutes may only serve to exacerbate this linguistic cleavage by forcing the two movements to adopt contrasting and entrenched attitudes concerning the Welsh language.[1]

Cymdeithas yr Iaith Gymraeg (*The Welsh Language Society*)

The Welsh Language Society (*Cymdeithas yr Iaith Gymraeg*) was founded in 1962 at *Plaid Cymru*'s annual summer school and conference, which was being held in Pontardulais at the beginning of August that year.[2] Its aims were to 'attain official status for the Welsh language equal with that of English in Wales', and to see that the Welsh language could and would be used by public bodies throughout Wales.[3] These demands were seen as a first and essential step towards saving the Welsh language from extinction. The Society was to use 'non-violent democratic methods, wherever possible', but was 'prepared to break flagrantly unjust laws when all other methods fail'.[4] Originally the Society's membership comprised only those who were prepared to do this themselves, but this condition has not always been enforced. The Society was founded in response to a lecture given on the B.B.C.'s Home Service by Saunders Lewis in February 1962, in which he had called for a movement to insist on the use of Welsh in forms and business by public authorities in the Welsh-speaking parts of Wales;[5] Lewis cited particularly the efforts of Mr. and Mrs. Trefor Beasley in refusing to pay their rates, and going to prison, until their rate demands appeared in the Welsh language. In many ways, the birth of the Welsh Language Society signified the hiving-off of one particular kind of activity from *Plaid Cymru*. But whereas the *Blaid* had been lukewarm about civil disobedience and non-violent direct action, and had given no lead to its members to challenge the

---

[1] However, Mrs. Zonia Bowen has claimed that many women are members of both the Women's Institutes and *Merched Y Wawr* (*Western Mail*, 1 Oct. 1970).
[2] An account of the formation of the Welsh Language Society is given in Ch. 5.
[3] *The Welsh Language Society* (Cardiff, 1966), p. 3.
[4] Ibid., p. 4.   [5] *Tynged Yr Iaith* (1962).

inferior position of the language in their localities, the Welsh Language Society, as a separate and autonomous organization, could engage in its own activities without directly involving the *Blaid*. The fact remains that, in its early days, hardly a member of the Welsh Language Society was not also a member of *Plaid Cymru*, and among those were Saunders Lewis, Dr. Huw T. Edwards, and Gwynfor Evans.

The history of the Welsh Language Society in its first eight years is a history of growing frustration, and extremism towards the authorities. The Society was and is largely based on the University Colleges in Wales; each generation of students produced leaders of the Society who appeared more despairing and extreme on the language question than the last. However, it is impossible to separate the development of the Welsh Language Society in the 1960s from the wider development of student protest movements in Europe and North America. The spirit of protest, the techniques of their protest, and the progression towards extremism and activism, the Welsh Language Society shared with other protest movements which were based on the student population.

The Society concentrated throughout the 1960s on trying to persuade government and local authorities to provide bilingual official forms and road-signs, although many outside the Society doubted whether this was the best way of helping the Welsh language. Latterly the Society also tried to focus attention on the inequitable treatment of the Welsh language in the mass media.

The first protest by this Society arose after a founder-member of the society was caught giving a lift to his girl-friend on his push-bike. He decided he had a right to a Welsh summons, and spent a night in the cells at Aberystwyth for his novel request. Out of this trivial offence developed the first organised protest, the sit-down in Trefechan Bridge, Aberystwyth, in order to win Welsh summonses.[1]

The upshot of this protest was that translations of the English summons became available in some parts of Wales. The Society then moved on to two other campaigns—for bilingual signs on Welsh post offices, and for bilingual road fund licences and application forms. Sit-ins and imprisonment of individuals followed as a result of the campaigns involving considerable self-sacrifice and publicity. Another campaign, launched by members of the Society, was to secure registration of births in Welsh. The passage of the Welsh

[1] *The Welsh Language Society*, p. 5.

Language Act in 1967, following the report of the Hughes-Parry committee in 1965, together with pressure from the Welsh Language Society secured this right at the start of 1968.[1] Other campaigns followed: sit-ins, hunger strikes, refusals to pay fines were all part of the campaign to win equal status and use for the Welsh language. But after July 1967, the Society had an important shot in its locker, the Welsh Language Act. This Act of Parliament was apparently designed to embody in the law the principle of equal validity of Welsh with English in the courts and in the provision, for example, of statutory forms. But the Act did not make the principle of equal validity effective as of right, nor did it implement fully the recommendations of the Hughes-Parry Report whose concept of 'equal validity' was the inspiration of the Act.[2] Much still depended on the willingness and liberalism of individual government Ministers and local authorities in following up the Welsh Language Act.[3] The first months of the working of the Act revealed that it was being interpreted conservatively by most authorities, and the Welsh Language Society decided to call attention to the situation. In January 1969 the Society launched a campaign to obliterate with paint (usually green in colour) selected road-signs, especially in Welsh-speaking counties, which carried only English-language details.[4] This followed largely unsuccessful approaches to the Welsh Office and the County Councils concerned on the question of introducing bilingual road-signs. At Penmachno, Caernarvonshire, Society members undertook each to daub ten such signs.[5] All over North and West Wales the actions of the Society quickly became obvious, and there was a scandalized reaction in the Welsh press. Nor was it clear how such activities could help the Welsh language.[6] It was some months before legal action was taken, but eventually eighteen members of the Society were fined a total of £111 (including compensation) at Betws-y-Coed, Caernarvonshire, in April 1969 for wilfully damaging

---

[1] *The Times*, 3 Jan. 1968, reported that many of the Society's members had 'waited up to two years before registering names for their children. Somerset House had had dozens of entries that read: "Baby Jones, female" or "Baby Davies, male"'.

[2] *Legal Status of the Welsh Language*, Cmnd. 2785.

[3] The Welsh Language Act, in *Public General Acts and Measures 1967* (Eliz. II), ch. 66, pp. 1305–7.

[4] An account of part of the campaign is given in Robyn Lewis, *Second-Class Citizens* (Llandysul, 1969), pp. 88–101 especially.

[5] No road-signs were painted out that were thought to be essential to safety.

[6] The *Western Mail*, 4 Jan. 1969, commented in an editorial that the Society's actions 'will antagonise the vast majority of Welshmen and do nothing to promote the true interests of the Welsh language'.

road signs by daubing them with green paint.[1] The campaign, however, continued, although it did not gain the approval of the Welsh people as a whole, whatever their language. In May, *Plaid Cymru*'s general secretary blamed his party's poor local election showing on the activities of the Welsh Language Society, among others. 'The campaign by the Welsh Language Society to obliterate road-signs where they are in English only, has done us a great deal of harm', he said.[2] In June the *Blaid* asked the Society to call a truce to allow time for more representations to be made.[3] In fact, in July the Society announced that 'members will not continue to delete English signs in counties where a positive assurance is given by councils to put money on one side during the next year to provide bilingual signs'.[4] By this stage it was clear that many of those authorities who originally had cold-shouldered the Welsh Language Society's written requests for bilingual signs,[5] were beginning to make more friendly responses to the Society's campaign. In August 1969, the Secretary of State for Wales, George Thomas, gave guidance to local authorities on the question of bilingual road-signs, permitting them to put up certain bilingual signs without Welsh Office approval, but vetoing bilingual directional-signs on grounds of the risk to safety.[6] At the beginning of October 1969, the Welsh Office followed this up with a circular to all local authorities noting that 'all local authorities will no doubt now wish to consider what further action can properly be taken, having regard to what is being done by the Government itself to implement the recommendations of the Hughes-Parry Report'.[7] This was the first occasion ever on which the Welsh Office had issued a circular on the use of the Welsh language, although the department had been in operation for five years. Although most opinion in Wales was hostile to the daubing of road-signs by members of the Welsh Language Society, some important bodies did view the Society's activities sympathetically. *Plaid Cymru*, although politically embarrassed by the Society, nevertheless supported the aims of its campaign. More unexpectedly, the churches came to the defence of the Society. Associations of Independents and Presbyterians, and the committee of the Welsh section of the Church in Wales

---

[1] *Daily Telegraph*, 12 Apr. 1969.   [2] *Liverpool Daily Post*, 10 May 1969.
[3] *Western Mail*, 23 June 1969.   [4] Ibid., 18 July 1969.
[5] See *Pam Peintio?* (Aberaeron, 1969) for the initial responses of the local authorities.
[6] *Western Mail*, 29 Aug. 1969. Further advice was reported in ibid., 7 Apr. 1970.
[7] Circular 82/69 (Welsh Office) issued 1 Oct. 1969.

publicly declared support for the Society's objective of bilingual road-signs.[1] Shortly after the Betws-y-Coed fines were imposed on Welsh Language Society members Dr. Glyn Simon, the Archbishop of Wales, wrote to the *Western Mail* expressing the view that it was not unreasonable that Welsh-speakers 'should expect to see these [Welsh] names on the sign-posts of their country' and that 'it would be a pity if unreasonable and stupid official attitudes to reasonable demands should seem to encourage the violence we all deplore'.[2] In fact, the Society's campaign must be judged a relative success in that a number of local authorities in 1969 began seriously to consider replacing old road-signs in English only with bilingual signs. Yet a very great deal of public goodwill towards the Welsh language had also been lost by the time that the Society finally called off its daubing activities in November 1969.[3]

The road-signs campaign was not the only activity of the Welsh Language Society in the late 1960s. The year 1967 had seen a curious suspension of campaigning, pending the passage and implementation of the Welsh Language Act. The Society emerged from the shadows in August 1968 when it complained to the National *Eisteddfod* Court that insufficient use was being made of the Welsh language in the displays on the *Eisteddfod* field.[4] The complaint was ignored. In November, the Society turned its attention to the B.B.C. in Wales and promised unlawful non-violent action against the corporation.[5] Simultaneously, parties of the Society's supporters invaded and occupied by means of a sit-in B.B.C. studios in Bangor and Cardiff. At least eighty students were involved; their complaint briefly was that the B.B.C. gave more broadcasting time to Arabic languages and many foreign languages than it gave to the Welsh language.[6] This was not, however, a campaign that was immediately followed up. The Welsh Language Society moved on to other issues—such as road-signs and the Investiture—but returned to the B.B.C. in the

---

[1] *Y Cymro*, 7 May 1969 (Church in Wales, Welsh section). Ibid., 28 May 1969 (Independents, Dyfed area conference). Ibid., 20 Oct. 1969 (Presbyterians, South Wales Association). Ibid., 26 Nov. 1969 (Presbyterians, North Wales Association).
[2] *Western Mail*, 14 Apr. 1969.
[3] *Y Cymro*, 12 Nov. 1969. This decision was revoked early in 1970. The Bowen Committee set up by the Secretary of State in 1970 to investigate the question of bilingual road-signs reported in November 1972 that all authorities responsible for traffic signing should be required to provide bilingual traffic signs on all roads in Wales and that direct Government aid should finance the provision of such signs on all classes of road.
[4] *Western Mail*, 8 Aug. 1968.   [5] Ibid., 20 Nov. 1968.
[6] *Guardian*, 30 Nov. 1968; *Western Mail*, 30 Nov. 1968.

autumn of 1969, when sit-ins inside the B.B.C.'s Cardiff studios and outside the B.B.C.'s studios in Bangor were arranged. Again this was not followed up. Attention was turned to the position of Dafydd Iwan, the chairman of the Society and a leading Welsh pop singer, who was sent to prison for refusing to pay the fines imposed on him at Betws-y-Coed. A number of protests followed, including several sit-ins in January 1970 in various court-rooms around Wales.[1] The impact of this campaign was very much overtaken by the dispute that arose when it was revealed that twenty-one J.P.s had together paid Iwan's fine anonymously.[2] Even this controversy seemed small compared to virtually spontaneous protest involving the Welsh Language Society which occurred on 4 February 1970. This was the invasion by twenty-two students of the University College of Wales, Aberystwyth, of one of the Royal Courts of Justice in London while it was sitting; many of the students were reading Welsh at the University. Much to the surprise of those involved, this protest received enormous publicity throughout Britain; some of the students were not even members of the Welsh Language Society. Eight of the students who apologized to the court were fined, but the remaining fourteen who refused to do so were imprisoned for three months.[3] Eleven of the gaoled students appealed against this sentence and were released. In a memorable judgment, the Master of the Rolls, Lord Denning, noted that the students had wanted to preserve the Welsh language, of which they might well be proud, and stated that 'on high authority it should be equal in Wales with English'.[4] For most people the interruption of the High Court by a demonstration bore little relation to helping the Welsh language, and much more publicity was given to the students and the enormity of their action, than to the cause they sought to sponsor.[5] The leaders of the Welsh Language Society claimed that support for the Society increased dramatically as a result of all the publicity it received from the incident.[6] On the initiative of the Welsh Liberal leader, Emlyn Hooson, a special

---

[1] Including Caernarfon, Llangefni, Shrewsbury, and Aberystwyth.

[2] The Lord Chancellor, Lord Gardiner, later reprimanded the justices for their action. Only two of the J.P.s involved, both from Cardiganshire, revealed their identities.

[3] Children of well-known *Plaid Cymru* figures were involved, including the daughter of Gwynfor Evans, the daughter of the Revd. Dr. Tudur Jones, and the son of Trefor Morgan.

[4] *The Times*, 12 Feb. 1970.

[5] The protest was planned to call attention to the imprisonment of Dafydd Iwan for his non-payment of fines.

[6] *Y Cymro*, 11 Feb. 1970.

meeting of the Welsh Grand Committee (consisting of Welsh M.P.s) was subsequently called to discuss the Welsh language.

Certainly the extent of the activities of the Welsh Language Society seemed to be growing considerably from 1968 onwards. There were more reports from every part of Wales, except Monmouthshire, of its exploits. The product of this militancy was to make it the focus for other protests from the young generation in Wales not specifically connected with the preservation of the Welsh language.

The clearest example of the Society's usefulness as an umbrella-movement for unconnected protests was the lead it gave in the campaign against the Investiture of the Prince of Wales from 1968. This was partly because the Society's chairman, Dafydd Iwan, was the most prominent of the Investiture's opponents, so that the two movements, one opposing the Investiture and the other defending the Welsh language, would in any case have been confused.[1] Nevertheless it was the deliberate decision of the Society to play a part in the protests against the Investiture. Its conference in October 1968 decided to organize a rally to protest against the Investiture, and this rally was staged outside Caernarfon Castle on St. David's Day 1969. Several thousand people attended the rally, which was addressed by the Society's leaders and by Professor J. R. Jones, then Professor of Philosophy in the University College of Swansea, who was effectively the Society's intellectual leader.[2] The anti-Investiture campaign was much helped by the attention given to Dafydd Iwan's song, *Carlo*, which lampooned the Investiture and the Prince of Wales.[3] But when a further rally was held by the Society at Cilmeri, Breconshire, shortly before the Investiture took place, only about one thousand people attended it[4] where five thousand had been expected.[5] Members of the Welsh Language Society were also involved in a protest against the Prince of Wales when he gave a speech to the National *Eisteddfod* of *Urdd Gobaith Cymru* at the end of May. About one hundred protesters began to interrupt the Prince as he

[1] Dafydd Iwan, the son of an Independent minister of religion, was the leading Welsh-language pop singer at this time. Previously chairman of *Plaid Cymru's* Youth Section, he became chairman of the Welsh Language Society in 1968. He holds a degree in architecture from the University College of South Wales and Monmouthshire.

[2] J. R. Jones (1912–70) was Professor of Philosophy at the University College of Swansea and author of *Prydeindod* (Llandybie, 1966) and *Cristnogaeth a Chenedlaetholdeb* (Swansea, undated).

[3] *Carlo* is believed to have sold over 10,000 copies. *Carlo* is a traditional nickname in Wales for a dog.

[4] *Guardian*, 30 June 1969.   [5] *Western Mail*, 27 June 1969.

was about to address the *Eisteddfod* in Welsh—his first public speech in that language. The audience was so infuriated by this interruption that many set upon the protesters. This particular incident earned the Society considerable unpopularity and the Prince gained in prestige enormously for his composure and his success in speaking Welsh on this occasion; thus the Welsh Language Society succeeded in helping the Prince of Wales to find a rapport with the Welsh people.[1] A further consequence was that the Society's actions on behalf of the language were treated with less sympathy because of its role in opposing the Investiture, the equation being commonly made that those who protested about the status of the language were also hostile to the monarchy, and the Prince of Wales in particular. This had been foreseen by some of the Society's members when it decided to run an anti-Investiture campaign; but it is difficult to imagine how any other group in Wales could have arranged protests against the Investiture with comparable success.[2]

The Welsh Language Society at the end of the 1960s had become one of the most publicized and least understood organizations in Welsh life. It expressed in a very individual way the impatience, the frustration, and the nostalgia of the rising generation of Welsh-speaking intellectual youth whose political imagination had been awakened by the Carmarthen by-election result in 1966. Before that date the Society had been only occasionally active, and had taken action very deliberately on behalf of the Welsh language. The nationalist pulse quickened after 1966, and the patience of young students with parliamentary methods was easily exhausted. The Society became very much a student movement combining protest and danger with panache. Although university lecturers and ministers of religion were members of the Society, they were not its leaders. The leadership came from a small group of individuals whose main link was often the University College of Wales at Aberystwyth. Most of these individuals were involved in university or school life, either as teachers (Gareth Miles, Emyr Llewellyn, Gwynn Jarvis) or as students (Ffred Ffransis, Geraint Eckley, and Ieuan Bryn Jones). In this respect they were no different from previous leaders of the Welsh Language Society. Similarly they had mostly spent a period of activity inside *Plaid Cymru,* and were impatient with its inactivity on the language question. Equally, Tryweryn, rather than Carmar-

---

[1] *Sunday Telegraph,* 1 June 1969 and *Liverpool Daily Post,* 2 June 1969.
[2] See below, pp. 263–8.

then, was their inspiration. The leadership of the Welsh Language Society represented a strain of middle-class radicalism, not unlike that found in the Campaign for Nuclear Disarmament.[1]

As the Welsh Language Society developed and grew in size it became less moderate in its tone and its activities. The size of the Society has never been easily determinable, as many who were not registered as members would have claimed to be so. But press reports estimated the Society's membership as about 300 in 1963,[2] 400 in 1967,[3] about 825 in 1968,[4] and about 1,500 in 1970.[5] The methods of the Society have not changed substantially since its foundation in 1962, and have usually included challenging the law in a non-violent way, and playing upon the emotional reactions of a section of the public by incurring prison sentences (for non-payment of fines, typically) or by going on hunger strike. What has changed is the intensity of the Society's activities, its political timing, and its ability to win the sympathy of the Welsh public. All of these are probably the result of the increased numbers in the Society. Less control over activities can be exercised, and there is less unity of strategy, more individuals making for less cohesion. In a sense, this autonomy amongst its members has been encouraged by the Society's leaders.[6] This, in itself, goes only some way towards explaining the capacity the Society has had for ignoring or misjudging the political consequences of its actions. Spontaneity of action among the Society's members has led to vehement reaction among the public. Three examples illustrate the position. First, the protest at the *Urdd Eisteddfod* in 1969 succeeded in antagonizing the Welsh public about the Society in general, not simply its stand against the Investiture but also its general activities on behalf of the Welsh language. At the same time it served to revive a fading loyalty to the Crown. Secondly, the invasion of the Law Courts in London won little sympathy for the language but angered many Welsh people because it seemed to be an offence against justice itself.[7] This particular action contributed substantially to the loss of *Plaid Cymru*'s only seat

---

[1] See below, pp. 242–3.
[2] *Western Mail*, 4 Feb. 1963.
[3] J. I. Daniel, 'The Welsh Language Society', in *Celtic Advance in the Atomic Age*, Annual Volume of the Celtic League, 1967 (Haverfordwest).
[4] *Sunday Telegraph*, 13 Oct. 1968.
[5] *Guardian*, 14 Nov. 1970.
[6] For example, the sign-daubing campaign left activity very much to the whim of individual members.
[7] *Guardian*, 5 Feb. 1970; *Western Mail*, 5 Feb. 1970.

in the House of Commons later in the year.[1] Thirdly, there were the incidents in Rhayader, Radnorshire, in February 1969 and in Dolgellau, Merioneth, in January 1971 when scuffles broke out between local townspeople and supporters of the Welsh Language Society.[2] It is tactlessness of this kind which did not endear the Society to the Welsh public, yet the very antagonism it has stimulated in Welsh society is an important ingredient in its appeal to the alienated Welsh-speaking student. This may have been one cause of the Society's increased disregard for public opinion, and of its deteriorating relations with *Plaid Cymru*.

It has already been noted how the desire of the *Blaid*'s leadership to interfere with the policy platform of its Youth committee appears to have led to a redirection of its leaders' efforts into the Welsh Language Society.[3] The price of trying to control the youth of the party was the denial to the *Blaid* of an organized youth movement on an all-Wales level. The activities of the mobile student population, particularly, have been channelled into the Welsh Language Society. Nevertheless what actions the Society engaged in still contrived to embarrass *Plaid Cymru*. Most members of the Welsh Language Society are supporters of *Plaid Cymru*, and the general public seems to know this. Thus the *Blaid* could not control the activities of its vociferous young supporters, could not canalize much of their activity into work for the party (except at election time), but had to share in the opprobrium which only the Welsh Language Society knew how to attract to it. On certain occasions, individual members of the Welsh Language Society were asked not to help the *Blaid* at election time because they were too well-known to the public and might thus embarrass the party. This desire for respectability inside *Plaid Cymru*, while very understandable, has nevertheless provoked antipathy between the *Blaid* and the Society. While the *Blaid* has seemed more wedded to constitutional methods and more cautious about the language as each year passes, so the Welsh Language Society has seemed

---

[1] This was the view of *Plaid* workers in the Carmarthen constituency. Gwynfor Evans's daughter, Meinir, had been directly involved in the Law Courts protest and her actions received considerable local publicity.

[2] At Rhayader, the scuffles occurred when Society members began painting out road-signs in broad daylight (*Western Mail*, 17 Feb. 1969). At Dolgellau, the scuffles occurred during a public meeting held by the Society; it was alleged that Dafydd Iwan was thrown to the ground and kicked while making a speech (ibid., 4 Jan. 1971).

[3] Dafydd Iwan was a former chairman of the *Blaid*'s Youth committee. Dyfrig Thomas was once the *Blaid*'s Youth organizer. Geraint Eckley and Morys Rhys both held office on the party's Youth committee.

more intent on direct action as a way of achieving results. The immediate effect was that major splits occurred in at least two university branches of *Plaid Cymru*, at Bangor and at Aberystwyth, in 1969. In Bangor, Ieuan Bryn Jones led a break-away from the *Blaid* because he regarded the party as too constitutional; many members of the branch followed suit and resigned their membership. Many students active in the Welsh Language Society shared their views, although some *Plaid* activists were happy that 'extremists' were leaving the party because this would help to emphasize the *Blaid*'s moderation.

The Welsh Language Society developed from 1966 into the principal protest movement for the youth of Wales, not excluding those who were unable to speak Welsh. It served as the rallying-point for those who were anxious to defend the Welsh culture, or who traced their alienation from society to its decline. The Welsh Language Society expressed the disillusion of certain Welsh middle-class people with the performance of the Labour Government in office and with the prospects for the future of the Welsh language. It served to mobilize a stratum in Welsh politics which has always existed, those alienated from the norms of Anglo-Saxon Britain, anti-establishment, anti-cosmopolitan, anti-militarist, and anti-monarchist. Added to this stratum was the Society's following amongst the young, those who wished to rebel and those attracted to its 'youth culture', two strands clearly linked in the person of Dafydd Iwan. For these people, the Welsh Language Society provided a cause and a movement in which they could join to express their discontents, which concerned more than the Welsh language. This perhaps explains how the Society came to spearhead the protests against the Investiture in 1969. The Investiture offered it a chance to attack the establishment in Wales, as well as in England, in addition to protesting against the assault on Welsh nationality that the Society conceived the event to be. Nowhere does this come through more clearly than in the trenchant columns of the Society's monthly magazine, *Tafod y Ddraig* (The Dragon's Tongue). The Society was also fortunate in that it developed at a time when young people in most Western democracies, particularly students, were becoming disillusioned with the normal process of parliamentary democracy. Members of the Welsh Language Society were quick to question the impact of electoral success on the behaviour of *Plaid Cymru* after 1966. The Society was able to exploit a common demand for action in politics. It is fair to say that the Society has consciously used the Welsh language as a political weapon. Its protests about the status of the Welsh language have been a means of asserting Welsh nationalism and of expressing their disgust with political leadership in Wales and in Britain. Their emotive appeal is well encapsulated in the Society's slogan 'Cenedl heb iaith, cenedl heb galon' (A nation without a language is a nation without a heart).

The Welsh Language Society offers an excellent example of a movement which is concerned with 'expressive politics'.[1] The Society is concerned to defend the Welsh language in some public, tangible, and principled way. It seeks to express its political views and is not so concerned with 'instrumental politics' which is 'primarily concerned with the attainment of power to bring about desired ends, even if this means some compromise of principles'.[2] The Society has often seemed not to care about the effects of its actions on Welsh opinion and Welsh authorities, but simply to be seen to be doing something for the causes it espoused. Outstanding evidence of this tendency was provided by the Society's sign-daubing activities. The act of painting out a road-sign in English is a simple one, but one which, for the individual dauber, expresses his concern for the Welsh language yet jeopardizes his relations with authority, in particular the police, and the establishment. It is also a spontaneous act which can be performed anywhere by any individual given stealth and bravado. As such the sign-daubing campaign was brilliantly conceived, for it caught the mood and the personal needs of members of the Welsh Language Society publicly to proclaim their protest, regardless of the consequences. Yet the extensiveness of the daubing gave also an exaggerated sense of the Society's strength, even though relatively few individuals were involved.

A clear comparison can also be made between the social base of the support for the Welsh Language Society and that of the Campaign for Nuclear Disarmament. They were both movements whose political goals were not materialist, but moral: this is a common characteristic of middle-class-based radical movements. Nor did either of these movements have an over-all ideology to explain the social problems with which they were confronted, preferring instead

---

[1] I owe this concept to Frank Parkin who develops it in *Middle Class Radicalism: The Social Bases of the Campaign for Nuclear Disarmament* (Manchester, 1968).

[2] Parkin, op. cit., p. 34. The contrast between the achievements of the Society's campaigns, and the success of the Bilingual Road Fund Licence Disc Campaign is striking in this respect.

to consider such problems as 'social isolates each requiring a particular solution'.[1] The moral concerns of the two movements tran-
scended class-politics and class-preoccupations. Most of C.N.D.'s
members were, like the Society's members, socially marginal—that
is to say, they were occupying a place in society (often in fact a
privileged position) while not conforming to certain of its values.
This is common among intellectuals (who are often teachers by profession) and the young—students being a combination of the two.
(It is also true that this description fits many who are members of
Plaid Cymru and, arguably, many other Welshmen who are 'socially
marginal' in relation to British society.) The Welsh Language Society
thus offered to socially marginal individuals in Wales a chance to be
an organized deviant minority, mobilized behind a counterculture,
the Welsh culture—the culture of the rebel and more recently the
pop culture of the Welsh youth. In one important respect this comparison between C.N.D. and the Welsh Language Society does not
hold. Whereas the outlook of C.N.D. was essentially internationalist,
the outlook of the Welsh Language Society was essentially local,
confined to Wales.[2] The Society brought its attacks to bear on
authorities—local councils, not nuclear super-powers—more vulnerable than those C.N.D. attempted to influence. Hence the relative
success of the Society in getting more bilingual signs displayed and
in helping to persuade government authorities at all levels to consider how to extend the use of Welsh in their work. Yet the tendency
of the Welsh Language Society was, like C.N.D., to make 'gestures
which stress moral absolutes, but which tend to have little practical
effect on outcomes'.[3] Their opponents were for the most part not
alien ministers in Whitehall, but Welshmen in Wales: so much for
Home Rule!

Nevertheless the Welsh Language Society could claim success in
securing some of its immediate objectives, such as bilingual road-
signs and official forms, despite the resistance of public opinion in
Wales to its methods. Above all the Society made the language an
important political issue and compelled the authorities to take a view
on matters of detail affecting the Welsh language. It also showed
every sign of failing to get the public to understand that a more
fundamental change than a change of signs was needed to ensure the

---

[1] Parkin, op. cit., p. 41.
[2] One drawback of this localist outlook on the part of the Society was that it
showed little appreciation of the problems of other countries which have linguistic
cleavages in their political life.   [3] Parkin, op. cit., p. 37.

survival of the Welsh language. The reaction of many politicians to the Society's activities ranged from incomprehension and incredulity to violent antipathy. The editor of *Plaid Cymru*'s monthly, the *Welsh Nation*, wrote early in 1970 that:

> . . . Society members must now talk, and talk, and talk to make sure that their real ideas, and not twisted versions of them, are being put across.
>
> Unless they do so, their activities will come more and more to be seen as sheer hooliganism.[1]

The Secretary of State for Wales, George Thomas, was more outspoken when he discussed the activities of the Society and described them as madcaps.[2] His criticisms were shared by several M.P.s when the Welsh Grand Committee came to debate the language issue in February 1970.[3] But Mrs. Eirene White, Minister of State at the Welsh Office, went further in this debate in her criticisms:

> Increasing numbers of Welsh-speaking people are beginning to realise that while some of the protests, particularly from the younger people, are, no doubt, part of the general and worldwide movement of student revolt, which in Wales finds this cause easily to hand, much of it is politically inspired.[4]

Other M.P.s echoed this condemnation with attacks on Saunders Lewis whose lecture in 1962 effectively launched the Welsh Language Society.[5] But one of the most telling facts to emerge from this debate was that in 1969 only twenty-eight copies of six of the most common Welsh forms had been issued from the wide range of official forms which had been made available in the language.[6] This pinpointed both the limited demand for forms in the Welsh language (however badly the facility was publicized) and the doubts shared by many Welsh leaders as to the importance of bilingualism in official forms and signs, as a means of guaranteeing the survival of the Welsh language. Evidence from the Welsh press in the summer of 1970 suggested that members of the Welsh Language Society were themselves looking for new ways of supporting the language. The Society

---

[1] *Welsh Nation*, Apr. 1970.   [2] *Guardian*, 10 Feb. 1970.
[3] The debate on the language issue was arranged at the instigation of Emlyn Hooson, the Welsh Liberal leader, largely because of the Law Courts' protest earlier in the month.
[4] Official Report, Welsh Grand Committee (25 Feb. 1970), c. 50.
[5] *Tynged yr Iaith*.
[6] Official Report, Welsh Grand Committee (25 Feb. 1970), cc. 11–12. The Secretary of State for Wales also disclosed that bilingual registrations of births in Wales represented 1·81 per cent of total registrations; the corresponding figure for deaths was 0·22 per cent.

gave practical help to Bryncroes primary school in Caernarvonshire when it was resisting closure by the county council. Emyr Llewellyn suggested that a fund be created to help young families set themselves up in farms or in trade in the Welsh countryside.[1] One journalist suggested that Welsh *kibbutzim* might be the answer.[2] The Society was beginning to realize the need for constructive action, as well as protest action. Apolitical activism may yet be discarded in favour of political pragmatism, even if a retreat to the *cefn gwlad*, which has also underpinned the thought of Dafydd Iwan,[3] does offer a pessimistic view of the ability of the Welsh language to survive in a modern, urban, and industrialized society. Whatever turn the Welsh Language Society may take in future it has already made an important impact on Welsh politics. It has made the Welsh language an issue in politics and it has forced politicians and civil servants to attend to that issue; but it has probably also served to deepen and exacerbate the linguistic cleavage that exists in modern Wales. By the extremism of its language alone *Cymdeithas yr Iaith* has succeeded in dividing Welshman from Welshman, Welsh-speaker from Welsh-speaker. One journalist caught the mood of Wales shortly before the Investiture with these remarks: 'It is easy in Wales today to be a traitor, and easy to feel you are one. . . . The time has come when even the faithful and true must feel themselves traitors if they accept an invitation to take part in any event allied to the Investiture's hilarity.'[4] It was this attitude that confronted the Prince of Wales when he spoke to the *Urdd Eisteddfod* at the end of May 1969, and which provoked Owen Edwards, son of the founder of the *Urdd*, to make these remarks at the National *Eisteddfod* in Flint later the same year:

I should like to delete three ugly words which have become fashionable to use these days—*Bradwr* [traitor], *Taeog* [serf], and *Cynffonnwr* [sycophant]—three words used by a vocal minority to describe anyone whose form of service to Wales does not conform to a certain pattern. . . . I find it difficult to understand how anyone who sincerely cherishes the wellbeing of Wales and wants to see it united as it goes into the seventies can use such words. They are signs, I fear, of that pettiness and immaturity which account for the fact that we in Welsh-speaking Wales find it so easy to divide and bicker.[5]

[1] *Tafod y Ddraig*, Apr. 1970 and 'Sbardun' in *Y Cymro*, 1 July 1970.

[2] Ned Thomas, 'Survival of the Welsh Language', *Western Mail*, 23 June 1970.

[3] Dafydd Iwan, 'Wales: Review of Cultural Life 1968–9', in *The Significance of Freedom*, Celtic League Annual 1969 (Dublin, 1969). Iwan saw some hope for the language's future in Wales generally.

[4] T. Glynne Davies, 'Welsh Traitors All', *New Statesman*, 30 May 1969.

[5] Owen Edwards—now Head of B.B.C. Programmes, Wales—speech to the Royal

The Bilingual Road Fund Licence Disc Campaign

The campaign to secure a bilingual road fund licence disc was launched through the columns of the Welsh-language monthly, *Barn* (Opinion), and occurred in the summer of 1969. The campaign was brief and successful. The magazine *Barn* had received in April of that year a letter from the Welsh Office which indicated that it was unlikely that a bilingual disc would ever be issued, the computerization of the issue of licences for the whole of Britain being a major factor in this decision.[1] This provoked *Barn* to follow up its request. At the beginning of June, it announced that two hundred Welsh people in prominent positions in Welsh life had agreed to join its campaign for a bilingual disc.[2] The campaign consisted of the individuals concerned pledging themselves, as from a certain date, not to display their English-only road fund licence disc on their cars, but to display instead a specially-prepared disc stating that the owner had paid the licence tax but would not display the disc until it was issued bilingually. The success of the campaign depended partly on the venerability and prestige of many of the individuals who undertook to take this action, which in turn would have led to imprisonment if they refused to pay fines for not displaying the disc. This is fully what the organizers had intended. The prospect of sending hundreds of schoolmasters, and dozens of university lecturers and ministers of religion, to prison was more than most politicians could bear. After making a special approach to the Ministry of Transport, the Secretary of State for Wales announced at the end of July 1969 that the bilingual disc would be available in 1970.[3] Within eight weeks of the start of the campaign, the politicians had bowed to Welsh pressure.

The campaign illustrated very well the extent to which the Welsh-speaking intelligentsia could be mobilized on the language issue, and it showed, too, which sections of the intellectual élite were most concerned and determined to strike a blow for the Welsh language. *Barn* published for four successive months lists of those individuals who had undertaken not to display the regular disc and to take the consequences.[4] An analysis of these lists shows that 642 individuals took the *Barn* 'pledge', discounting names which appeared twice.

National *Eisteddfod*, 7 Aug. 1969 (translated from the official press handout by the author).

[1] *Western Mail*, 14 Apr. 1969 and *Y Cymro*, 16 Apr. 1969.
[2] *Western Mail*, 2 June 1969 and *Y Cymro*, 4 June 1969.
[3] *Western Mail*, 26 July 1969.   [4] *Barn*, Nos. 80–3, June to Sept. 1969.

Of these 263 gave their profession as schoolteachers (41 per cent of the total), 90 said they were university or college lecturers (14 per cent of the total), and 91 were clergy or ministers of religion. In addition seventeen senior members of the staff of the B.B.C. were listed as having taken the 'pledge', including several producers and the Head of the Entertainments Department. Nine officials of *Urdd Gobaith Cymru* were also listed in this way by *Barn*. Other signatories included a member of the University Grants Committee, a member of the Welsh Joint Education Committee, two Archdruids, and two members of the Government's advisory panel on the translation of Welsh for official forms. Several members of the teaching staffs of Welsh secondary schools were listed, including the headmasters of Ysgol Glan Clwyd (Flintshire) and Rhydfelen School (Glamorgan)— two of the five Welsh-medium secondary schools. Not unnaturally *Plaid Cymru* supporters were also well represented in these lists, including several prospective parliamentary candidates. Of the ministers and clergy who promised to protest against the disc, Independents (32) and Presbyterians (18) were most numerous. The geographical distribution of the individuals named in the *Barn* lists followed closely the proportions of Welsh-speakers in the different parts of Wales; the protest was very much a Welsh-speakers' protest and did not bridge the linguistic barrier at all frequently. Once again it was the schoolmasters and ministers who formed the backbone of the protest, as they have formed the backbone of so many aspects of the nationalist movement in Wales. Distinguished names in the Welsh literary world were also a marked feature of the *Barn* lists.

The story of the bilingual disc campaign contained several lessons for Welsh nationalists and Welsh politicians. It showed how quickly a well-judged campaign could achieve its object: the Welsh Language Society had run a similar campaign for four years without success.[1] The campaign showed the increased mobilization into politics of the Welsh intelligentsia, and how quickly and effectively it could respond to a bureaucratic slight to its strong sense of Welsh nationality.

---

[1] The Welsh Language Society did, however, co-operate with and encourage the organizers of the campaign.

10

THE PLACE OF NATIONALISM IN SOME WELSH INSTITUTIONS AND PRESSURE GROUPS (II)

Welsh Broadcasting

Although separate broadcasting services developed in Wales much later than in Britain as a whole, it took a much shorter period for the broadcasting authorities to become entangled in the political arena. Wales has acquired a degree of autonomy in broadcasting over the years as its national claims have been recognized, particularly as regards the Welsh language and culture. As a result of this autonomy the Welsh broadcasting services' treatment of Welsh nationalism has undergone careful scrutiny since the 1950s; politicians in Wales have made this a sensitive issue.

The recognition of Wales's special needs in the field of broadcasting came about after a long struggle with successive Governments and the broadcasting authorities; separate broadcasting facilities for Wales were established piecemeal from 1935 onwards.[1] Shortly after the Second World War an advisory council was set up by the B.B.C. to comment on radio programme policy in Wales. The B.B.C.'s Charters of 1952 and 1964 both gave Wales a National Broadcasting Council with control over programme content and policy, and the Council's chairman became an *ex-officio* governor of the whole Corporation.[2] Following the Pilkington Committee's report in 1962, the B.B.C. television service in Wales became responsible for initiating twelve hours of programmes in Wales each week, and the National Broadcasting Council for Wales was given the same powers over Welsh television as it already retained for radio. The Independent Television Authority had meanwhile set up its own Committee for Wales in 1963; its chairman too was an *ex-officio* member of the nine-member Authority. The Committee for Wales replaced an *ad hoc* committee which had overseen T.W.W.'s programmes.[3]

[1] See Ch. 3.
[2] See the Royal Charter granted to the B.B.C., printed in *B.B.C. Handbook 1970*, section 10, pp. 259–76.
[3] *I.T.A. Annual Reports and Accounts 1962–3* (H.M.S.O., 1963), p. 13.

The impact of these advisory bodies is difficult to assess since their work is carried out on a confidential basis. Among the problems with which they have been faced are the over-all broadcasting structure in Wales, the questions raised by political broadcasting, and the role of the broadcasting services in the wider context of Welsh life.

One of the principal concerns of the I.T.A. in Wales has been the allocation of frequencies for the commercial companies which have a Welsh audience. In the late 1950s two independent television companies based in Lancashire and in Bristol controlled programmes for Wales, but the efforts of many Welsh people, led by Jenkin Alban Davies, the Welsh member of the I.T.A., secured in 1960 the promise of another independent company to produce television for Wales.

The widespread demand within Wales, however, for a broadcasting organisation owned and controlled by Welshmen persuaded the Authority to create a separate service area on the basis of three transmitters. . . .[1]

The I.T.A. was very wary of this experiment, especially as 70 per cent of those who would receive the new company's transmissions were already receiving programmes put out by rival companies. Yet the case for an all-Welsh television company was too strong to be resisted when other medium-sized companies were proving financially successful at the time. The licence for the new franchise was given to the Wales Television Association, whose chairman was Dr. B. Haydn Williams, the director of education for Flintshire, in competition with three other consortia. The board of the new company was stacked with prestigious names in Welsh life, especially Welsh politics and culture, but none of them had had much experience in the entertainments industry.[2] Transmissions began in September 1962, but the company never survived the financial difficulties and handicaps it had to face. Its ambition to be the bilingual service for Wales and a bastion of Welsh culture foundered on its initial extravagance,[3] and the problems of having such a sparsely populated,

---

[1] Ibid., p. 14.

[2] The board consisted of Dr. B. Haydn Williams, chairman; Col. Cennydd Traherne, vice-chairman; S. Kenneth Davies; Gwynfor Evans; Lady Olwen Carey Evans (daughter of David Lloyd George); Alderman Llewelyn Heycock (chairman of Glamorgan County Council Education Committee); Tom Jones, J.P.; Sir David Hughes-Parry; Dr. Thomas Parry, Principal of the University College of Wales, Aberystwyth; Emrys Roberts, a former Liberal, M.P. for Merioneth; Eric Thomas, editor of Y Cymro; Dr. W. Thomas; David Tudor; Peter O. Williams; Sir Thomas Parry-Williams; Col. J. Williams-Wynne; T. I. Ellis; and Moses Griffith.

[3] One example was the building of a new and expensive studio for the company in Cardiff. The B.B.C. had been content to use two disused chapels for its studios in Wales.

poor, and mountainous service area which was largely overlapped by other commercial companies' transmissions. In addition, the company suffered from having too many people on the board with so many other commitments that they were unable to give sufficient attention to the company's affairs. It was also alleged that the directors were not often given the chance to discuss the finances or the strategy of the company; their discussions were usually confined by Dr. Haydn Williams to minutiae. By 28 July 1963 the company had lost £283,485 after being 'on the air' for ten months.[1] It was salvaged by T.W.W., the company with the South Wales and West of England television franchise. The I.T.A. concluded laconically that:

It proved impossible for the company to continue to operate as an independent unit. . . .[2]

This experience showed that two programme companies could not be expected to operate successfully in Wales. The Authority therefore decided, during the new contractual period, to treat the two areas as one. Wales is thus for the first time in Independent Television to be regarded as a single unit.[3]

But whereas *Teledu Cymru* (as the Wales Television Association's service was known) tried too hard to sponsor and represent Welsh life and culture, T.W.W. did not go far enough. It produced an undistinguished service, although it made money for its shareholders in London and Lancashire. Thus neither company was allowed to survive in independent television: Harlech Television replaced T.W.W. early in 1968 on the understanding that it would be more sympathetic to Welsh ideas. Major criticisms of T.W.W.'s performance were current in the I.T.A. Committee for Wales from 1966,[4] although T.W.W. was completely surprised when it lost its programme contract in 1967.

Political broadcasting has long presented problems for broadcasters in Wales as in London, such as how to strike a balance in the reporting of news and views, and how to remain independent of political interference. The issue of the allocation of time between political parties is peripheral to this, but has acquired much of the limelight in Welsh politics. There was, however, one occasion when the impartiality of the Welsh Region of the B.B.C. as a whole was

[1] I.T.A. Committee for Wales, Secretary's Report, 9 Oct. 1963.
[2] *I.T.A. Annual Reports and Accounts 1963–4* (H.M.S.O., 1964), p. 7.
[3] Ibid., p. 8.
[4] Memorandum to the I.T.A. Committee for Wales, CW 13 (66), dated 26 Sept. 1966.

publicly challenged. Allegations were made that there was 'a distinct bias on the Welsh Region of the B.B.C. in favour of Welsh National-ism and *Plaid Cymru*, in favour of the Parliament for Wales campaign, and in favour of the individuals who support those move-ments';[1] the charge was made by David Llewellyn, the Conservative M.P. for Cardiff North, in the House of Commons at the end of January 1956. George Thomas, who was later to be Secretary of State for Wales, supported Llewellyn's plea for an inquiry, as did six other Welsh M.P.s.[2] There had in fact been an internal inquiry conducted by the B.B.C. in 1950 concerning a claim made by the Welsh Regional Council of Labour that the Corporation was biased in favour of *Plaid Cymru*; the explanations of various incidents referred to this inquiry which the Director-General of the B.B.C., Sir William Haley, offered to the Council of Labour were not accepted, and the points raised by the Council in 1950 were raised again in 1956. The Conservative Government accepted Llewellyn's demand for an inquiry, much to the astonishment of the Welsh staff of the B.B.C., and a committee was appointed under the chairman-ship of Sir Godfrey Ince to look into the allegations made in the House of Commons.[3] The committee completed its report to the Postmaster-General in November 1956, and in most particulars it vindicated the conduct of the B.B.C.[4] It did, however, make some criticisms concerning the presentation of news: while rejecting charges of deliberate or distinct bias, the Ince report found that some criticism of the lack of balance in news reporting on the Welsh Home Ser-vice of the B.B.C. radio was justified.[5] This, it explained, was the result of institutional factors such as the B.B.C.'s large dependence on local correspondents and its difficulty in finding qualified Welsh-speakers to take part in cultural and social programmes.[6] The political impact of this report was shortlived, but the inquiry seems to have left a permanent scar on some of the officials of the B.B.C. in Wales who were involved in its proceedings. The B.B.C. in Wales was so inclined to caution in the treatment of *Plaid Cymru* and Welsh nationalism in the 1960s that the National Broadcasting Council for Wales had

---

[1] 548 HC. Deb. Fifth Series, c. 618, 30 Jan. 1956.
[2] They were Garner Evans and Raymond Gower (Conservative), and Arthur Pear-son, Ness Edwards, James Griffiths, and Cledwyn Hughes (Labour).
[3] The members of the committee of inquiry were Sir Godfrey Ince, G.C.B., K.B.E., John Beavan, and H. V. Lloyd-Jones, Q.C.
[4] *Report of the Committee of Inquiry into Welsh Broadcasting*, Cmnd. 39 (H.M.S.O., 1956).
[5] Ibid., para. 46, p. 20.   [6] Ibid., paras. 48–52, pp. 20–2.

informally to push B.B.C. Wales's officials into giving the *Blaid* a special programme report on its annual conference.

Much more attention has been given in Wales to the question of party political broadcasts. This has been a point of contention between *Plaid Cymru* and other political parties almost continuously since 1945, for the allocation of broadcasting time to political parties has never been the responsibility of the broadcasting authorities. Clement Davies, when leader of the Liberal Party and M.P. for Montgomery, was the only one of the three major party leaders to urge that the *Blaid* and the Scottish National Party should be given broadcasting time at all.[1] The Ince report revealed that an exploratory meeting was held in 1953 between the political parties and the broadcasting authorities to discuss the possibility of local party political broadcasts in Wales. The Welsh Regional Council of Labour was later to adduce the B.B.C.'s suggested basis for discussion at this meeting that equal time be given to all four parties as evidence of B.B.C. bias in favour of *Plaid Cymru*.[2] When the National Broadcasting Council for Wales made a proposal in 1955 for local party political broadcasts in Wales for all parties, this was vetoed by Dr. Charles Hill, the Postmaster-General, with the approval of the Conservative and Labour Party organizations in Wales.[3] When *Plaid Cymru* applied for a party political broadcast to broadcasting authorities in Wales in 1964, the National Broadcasting Council did not express a view on the question, but the I.T.A. Committee for Wales decided that it would like all political parties fighting one-fifth of the seats in Wales to have facilities for party political broadcasts.[4] Nothing was decided in time for the 1964 election, but soon after this election facilities were offered to the Scottish National Party and to *Plaid Cymru* to the extent of one broadcast of five minutes every year on both television and radio.[5] For the rest of the 1960s this remained the position both during and between general elections. In the 1970 election there was wide dissatisfaction among members of all political parties that so little time was allowed to *Plaid Cymru* to put its case on radio and television, in view of the party's considerable increase in strength since 1966. In this situation the B.B.C. was powerless to

---

[1] Clement Davies to Hywel Rhys, 27 Nov. 1951 (letter in the Liberal Party of Wales MSS.).
[2] *Report of the Committee of Inquiry into Welsh Broadcasting*, pp. 9, 10, and
[3] *B.B.C. Handbook 1961*, p. 110.
[4] I.T.A. Committee for Wales, CW Minutes 9 (1964).
[5] *The Times*, 17 Dec. 1964.

act as the allocation of time was decided by the political parties in London.[1]

A more important issue is the way broadcasters in Wales have seen their role in the choice and content of programmes. It is certainly arguable that the development of autonomous regional broadcasting facilities may have helped to develop regional consciousness in Britain on a mass scale and in a way that had previously eluded regional newspapers. In this respect great importance attaches to the number of hours of separate regional broadcasting beamed in every year, and to the use to which these transmissions are put. Table 10.1 shows how the transmission of television programmes in Wales and the number of television licences bought increased substantially from the end of the 1950s. With the rise in broadcasting time Wales greatly expanded its output of locally produced television programmes; B.B.C. Wales, unlike every other B.B.C. region, increased the proportion of Wales-originated programmes transmitted to viewers in Wales. B.B.C. Wales was producing annually by the end of the 1960s over 690 hours of Welsh-language radio programmes and over 1,200 hours of radio programmes altogether. B.B.C. Wales and Harlech Television usually co-operated with each other so that Welsh-language television programmes on the two networks did not clash;[2] a total of more than six hundred hours of Welsh-language television was transmitted by the two networks in 1969.

Given that the amount of Welsh broadcasting output as well as the size of its potential audience has risen, what have the broadcasting authorities aimed to achieve through the media of radio and television? Productions of Welsh news and comment programmes, as well as drama and entertainment programmes, have all been expanded. Whereas before the war one bulletin of Welsh news a week was broadcast, several such bulletins are now broadcast on radio every day. Since the foundation of its Regional Home Service in 1935, the B.B.C. in Wales has always been Wales-minded in its approach to the production of programmes, and has tried to reflect all aspects of Welsh life and culture. The expansion in broadcasting time gave it greater scope to do this, even though nationally produced programmes from London still heavily dominate the Welsh broadcasting media. Through its own sponsorship the B.B.C.

---

[1] The I.T.A. Committee for Wales took the view that ten minutes' broadcasting time would have been fairer for the *Blaid* (private information).

[2] As urged by the Government in December 1962 in Cmnd. 1893.

TABLE 10.1

Expansion of Welsh Broadcasting Services

(A) Hours of broadcasting

Area and source		1962–3		1968–9	
		Hours	% of broadcast time	Hours	% of broadcast time
(a) B.B.C. TV					
Wales	Wales-originated	342	9·3	815	12·4
	Not Wales-originated	3,328	90·7	5,742	87·6
Scotland	Scotland-originated	319	9·2	494	7·5
	Not Scotland-originated	3,154	90·8	6,110	92·5
All other U.K. regions	Regionally originated	1,064	7·2	1,665	6·2
	Not regionally originated	13,658	92·8	25,052	93·8
(b) B.B.C. Welsh Home Service					
	Wales-originated	n.a.		1,234	19·7
	Not Wales-originated	n.a.		5,022	80·3

Company	Year	Weekly hours of locally initiated programmes	Weekly hours of locally initiated programmes in Welsh
(c) I.T.A.			
T.W.W.	1958	8·5	3·0
T.W.W.	1963	n.a.	3·0
W.W.N.	1963	5·0	2·5
T.W.W.	1965	12·0	5·0
Harlech	1968	12·0	5·5

n.a. = not available.
Sources: *B.B.C. Handbook* and *I.T.A. Guide to Independent Television.*

(B) Television Licence Holders (Wales, Hereford, and Shropshire).

1958–9	549,300
1965–6	667,500
1966–7	861,400
1967–8	908,900
1968–9	932,700

Source: *Digest of Welsh Statistics.*

in Wales effectively became the national theatre in Wales, and it retained the only national Welsh orchestra. Its staff, which in 1969 numbered 850, was recruited mainly from Wales, most of its graduate recruits coming from the University of Wales.[1] Although the majority of its staff are not Welsh-speaking, the majority of programme staff are bilingual, as are the Controller, the Head of Programmes and his planners, and the Information Officer and his staff.[2] Welsh-speaking administrative staff in B.B.C. Wales are paid a proficiency bonus for their command of the language. The staff of the B.B.C. in Wales claim with pride to have a Welsh outlook above all others and see this as part of their task in producing programmes from Wales. There were pressures inside the B.B.C. in Wales to secure a larger share of broadcasting time for Welsh-originated programmes before the publication of the Pilkington Committee's report. Undoubtedly it has been the intention of the B.B.C. staff in Wales to stimulate interest in Welsh affairs; to that extent the B.B.C. has helped develop Welsh-consciousness.

The position of the I.T.A. with respect to Wales is similar to that of the B.B.C., and better documented. Technically and commercially it was found to be difficult to treat Wales as a unit for television.[3] It has already been noted that the Authority refused to renew T.W.W.'s programme contract in 1967 largely because the company had failed to reflect sufficiently the quality and changes in Welsh life in its programmes. The function of the programme company had long been debated in the I.T.A. Committee for Wales, and the possibilities and dangers of television as regards Welsh life have also been considered.

It is probably not too much to say that the coming of television to the Principality could mean the early disappearance of Welsh as a spoken language—the oldest in these islands. On the other hand, television could help to give it a new lease of life and, efficiently and sensibly organised, Welsh language programmes could help to promote and sustain a lively and progressively bilingual society. It is however imperative that the necessary steps are taken before it is too late.[4]

Thus wrote the I.T.A.'s regional officer, Lyn Evans, in a memorandum to the Authority's Committee for Wales in 1963.

---

[1] T. Rowland Lucas, private interview, 28 Aug. 1969.

[2] *Legal Status of the Welsh Language*, para. 154, p. 34.

[3] In 1970 Harlech Television still had to cater for an audience in the West of England as well as Wales.

[4] *Television in Wales*, I.T.A. Committee for Wales, CW Paper 11 (63), para. 17.

He stated the I.T.A.'s policy for Welsh programme output in these terms:

If a Welsh independent television service is to be of any real value to society and to the nation it should reflect that society, not only as it is, but as it ideally has been and could be.[1]

On this evidence the I.T.A. has been more explicitly Welsh-conscious in intention even than the B.B.C. in Wales, although its achievements for Welsh life and culture distinctly failed to live up to these ideals. B.B.C. officials were of the opinion that the independent television companies in Wales had never offered them any real competition in this respect. The B.B.C. Wales television budgets were larger, and the Corporation was not expected to show a profit at the end of each year.

Despite the intentions of the B.B.C. and the I.T.A. to foster Welsh life and culture through radio and television, these media have served much more to integrate Wales with England than to differentiate the two countries. It is the cosmopolitan, anglicized culture that wins the largest audience; it is the Welsh-language programmes that struggle to arouse the viewers' interest, and which draw complaints from television viewers when shown at peak viewing hours. In addition, there is the problem of finding good Welsh-speaking television performers. A paper prepared by T.W.W. in 1963 noted that:

Professional talent among Welsh speaking performers is necessarily limited. To develop further talent, extensive auditions are regularly held and promising artists are given many opportunities.[2]

Some would complain that too many opportunities were given in Welsh broadcasting to too few, because of the limited talent available. The professional broadcasters in Wales generally form a close community, often linked by kinship or marriage, and drawn from the educated bilingual middle class, a small section of Welsh society. Even the high standard of their spoken Welsh is apt to be an obstacle to their performance on the air, since it contains many words and neologisms which Welsh-speakers in general find hard to understand. It is impossible to say how many or how few watch the Welsh-language programmes on television, but many people suspect that the largest Welsh-language programme audience is not greater than

---

[1] *Television in Wales*, I.T.A. Committee for Wales, CW Paper II (63), para. 35.

[2] T.W.W. Welsh Division, 'Notes on the special organisation operated (1958 to 1963) for the particular interests and needs of Wales', Sept. 1963.

100,000 viewers. In this situation, it is ironic that the B.B.C. in particular should have met such severe criticism from the Welsh Language
Society. While several strong arguments for a separate Welsh-
language television channel have been advanced in recent years, the
B.B.C. has done much to help the Welsh language on television, given
the small number of hours B.B.C. Wales has at its disposal. The
National Broadcasting Council for Wales firmly questioned in its
report of 1969 whether the sit-ins arranged by the Welsh Language
Society would in the long run be in the best interests of Wales, and
it maintained that with only twelve hours at its disposal each week
B.B.C. Wales's allocation of seven of these to Welsh-language programmes was fair.[1] However, there is a strong feeling among many
Welsh-speakers that the broadcasting system in Wales is still far
from helpful to the Welsh language, and some of the broadcasters
themselves agree that this is so.[2]

Ymgyrch Senedd i Gymru (*The Parliament for Wales Campaign*)

The campaign for a Parliament for Wales was launched in July
1950 with support from members of all parties in Wales and of none.
Its main activity was to collect signatures for a petition to Parliament
which claimed that 'self-government within the framework of the
United Kingdom should accrue to the good government both of
Wales, and of other parts of the United Kingdom', and which asked
for a 'Parliament with adequate legislative authority in Welsh
affairs'.[3] In order to make better known the case for a Parliament
for Wales, a large number of public meetings with leading speakers
were organized throughout Wales. In addition, a bill legislating for
a Parliament for Wales was introduced in the House of Commons
by a private member, S. O. Davies, the Labour M.P. for Merthyr
Tydfil, but this was defeated by 48 votes to 14 on 4 March 1955.[4]
The petition for a Parliament for Wales was presented in April 1956
by Goronwy Roberts, the Labour M.P. for Caernarfon. The petition
contained 250,000 signatures collected between 1954 and 1956,[5]
which represented about 14 per cent of the electors of Wales; the

---

[1] Annual Report of the National Broadcasting Council for Wales, 1969.
[2] See discussion in *Broadcasting in Wales in the Seventies* (Bangor, 1970).
[3] *Campaign for a Parliament for Wales* (Aberystwyth, undated).
[4] The sixteen M.P.s who supported the bill (including tellers) comprised 13 Labour,
1 Liberal, and 2 Conservatives. Six sat for Welsh, and two for Scottish seats. The
other eight sat for English constituencies.
[5] The figure of 240,652 signatures was given in *Western Mail*, 19 Apr. 1956.

petition organizers claimed that between 70 and 80 per cent of those approached had signed the petition.[1] Nevertheless the Welsh petition did not compare even with the 'Scottish Covenant' on which it was modelled, for the 'Covenant' was supported by more than two million signatures.[2] The Welsh petition failed for reasons similar to those of its Scottish counterpart. The signing of a petition cannot of itself change a political system: it can at best act as a secondary influence on the policy of a government. The Parliament for Wales Campaign did not have much support among M.P.s at Westminster. Of the thirty-six from Wales only six supported it[3]—even the three Liberal M.P.s from Wales were divided in their attitude.[4] One of the campaign's organizers believed that the Welsh M.P.s. were 'the biggest obstacles of all'.[5] Where the local M.P. gave a lead the campaign seemed to go well. The penetration of the campaign was patchy throughout most of Wales; the rural and Welsh-speaking areas showed the strongest support for the petition, but even the Rhondda valleys produced 30,000 signatures.

From its inception the campaign was poorly organized. It was fully three years before the business of collecting signatures to the petition got under way. Just over twelve months after being launched, the campaign was over £500 in the red,[6] and it continued thus until 1956 when the debts were, with difficulty, cleared.[7] Elwyn Roberts rescued the campaign following his appointment as organizer late in 1953; Roberts was later to be general secretary of *Plaid Cymru*, and had already had a varied career as bank official, National Eisteddfod organizer, and, for a time, rat-catcher in Merioneth.[8] The campaign faced many difficulties apart from the inherent weakness of the petition as a political weapon. The chairman of the campaign, Lady

---

[1] Private information.

[2] See H. J. Hanham, *Scottish Nationalism* (London, 1969), pp. 171–2.

[3] These were Cledwyn Hughes, Coronwy Roberts, T. W. Jones, Tudor Watkins, and S. O. Davies—all Labour M.P.s—and Clement Davies, the Liberal leader. Seventeen Welsh M.P.s opposed the bill, including James Griffiths, James Callaghan, George Thomas, and Peter Thomas. Edward Heath and Iain Macleod also opposed the bill, while Philip Noel-Baker and George Wigg voted in favour.

[4] Clement Davies supported the campaign; Roderic Bowen (Cardigan) and Rhys Hopkin Morris (Carmarthen) did not.

[5] Elwyn Roberts, private interview, 4 July 1969.

[6] Minutes of the Parliament for Wales Campaign Executive Committee, 15 Sept. 1951.

[7] At the end of May 1956 the debt was nearly £1,600, half of which was owed to the campaign's two organizers, Dafydd Miles and Elwyn Roberts. Campaign Executive members had to dig deep into their own pockets to pay off the debts.

[8] Roberts was appointed campaign organizer on secondment from the *Blaid*.

Megan Lloyd George, the Liberal M.P. for Anglesey from 1929 to 1951, was a distinguished leader in Welsh life but, although a very popular speaker at meetings, she did not supervise the work of the campaign at all thoroughly and was herself difficult to organize.[1] Again, the campaign suffered from the outset from having too many prominent people on its committee who could not give much time to its work because of other heavy commitments.

There were also political problems facing the campaign. The very breadth of support for the campaign, from Conservative to Communist, was also a weakness when it came to its management and the determination of strategy; the powers of the proposed Parliament for Wales were never defined in detail. No single group, other than *Plaid Cymru*, gave the campaign staunch support, even when officially associated with it, as the Liberals were. One Liberal M.P. refused to support the campaign because there were too many political viewpoints represented.[2] Other Liberals felt they had been dragged into the campaign only because of the enthusiasm of younger elements in the party. Thus the Liberals' support for the campaign was described in the *Welsh Nation* as 'anaemic'.[3]

In Welsh-speaking Wales one of the main problems of the campaign was the widespread fear that a Parliament for Wales would be dominated by representatives from Glamorgan and Monmouthshire, with their different interests and political outlook. Such fears had been a prime cause of the collapse of *Cymru Fydd* in 1896. There was little that the supporters of the campaign could say in answer to this except that the differences between the counties were exaggerated.[4] As for South Wales the difficulty seemed more to convince the people of the benefit of a Parliament for Wales. The campaign itself, although aiming for a broad appeal throughout Wales, in fact had very much a North Wales air about it. Few prominent leaders in South

---

[1] Private information.
[2] This was Roderic Bowen, Liberal M.P. for Cardiganshire 1945–66.
[3] *Welsh Nation*, May 1956.
[4] For example, the Executive Committee's minutes for 15 Dec. 1951 contain this item (my translation):

> 5. *Constitution.* Mr. Shubert Jones said that supporters of the Campaign in Anglesey were finding it difficult to answer the argument that there was a danger of the counties of Glamorgan and Monmouth ruling over any Welsh Parliament, and he asked for the Committee's guidance. Some members suggested that the differences between these counties and the rest of Wales had received too much attention, and that the experience of members of the joint-committee showed that there was nothing to fear from that bogey.

Wales were supporters of the campaign: Aneurin Bevan was not, nor was James Griffiths or Gwilym Lloyd George.[1] The business of the campaign, at its executive level, was conducted entirely in Welsh,[2] again indicating where the locus of its support was to be found. Moreover, it appeared that the bulk of the work of the campaign was done by *Plaid Cymru* activists, and by some who were not otherwise politically involved.[3] Liberal and Labour Party workers were thin on the ground in the campaign, and this must have hindered the progress of the campaign, both because of the generally bad reputation of the *Blaid* at this time, and because of the large gaps in the campaign's coverage of Wales that resulted.

From the political standpoint the results of the Parliament for Wales Campaign are hard to assess, the negative effects on its declared objectives being more apparent than the beneficial effects. The petition, once presented to Parliament, was soon forgotten. Those Labour M.P.s who had supported the Campaign found themselves isolated from their colleagues. Five M.P.s were eventually reported to Labour's National Executive Committee in January 1956 for opposing party policy on the Parliament for Wales issue.[4] The onset of the campaign forced the Labour Party to declare its hand on the whole question of devolution and Wales; there were even rumours that the Conservative Government was about to create a Secretary of State for Wales.[5] Between 1952 and 1954 Labour's policy for Wales was hammered out by the Welsh Regional Council of Labour, the Welsh group of Labour M.P.s, and the National Executive Committee. The eventual policy statement was openly hostile to the Parliament for Wales Campaign and was approved by the party conference in the autumn of 1954;[6] it promised to set up a Welsh Grand Committee, suggested some minor institutional reforms, but did not commit the party even to a Secretary of State for Wales. Thus Labour emerged more hostile to the idea of a Parliament for Wales, largely as a result of the campaign. As for the Liberals, the campaign convinced them that the bulk of the population of Wales was not interested in the Parliament for Wales issue,

---

[1] Glyn Tegai Hughes, speech at Llan Ffestiniog, 29 Sept. 1952.
[2] Minutes of the Executive Committee 1950–6.
[3] Private information.
[4] No further action was taken. The five were Cledwyn Hughes, Goronwy Roberts, T. W. Jones, Tudor Watkins, and S. O. Davies.
[5] *Western Mail*, 18 Nov. 1953.
[6] Printed in full as Appendix I, *Report of the Fifty-Third Annual Conference of the Labour Party* (London, 1954), pp. 186–91.

and for the next ten years they gave the issue of devolution a low priority in their programme.

The Parliament for Wales Campaign, however, did have some positive results. It showed to the political parties that the issue of a Parliament for Wales was not forgotten, and it forced them all to look into the proposal. The campaign kept the issue in the public eye for six years, and helped to educate public opinion as to its consequences; this may have had some long-term effects where the campaign was well organized. The *Blaid*'s involvement in the campaign did the party nothing but good, as its greatly improved showing in the 1955 general election demonstrated. But many of the campaign's leaders were forced to rethink their views on devolution as a result of their own unhappy experiences between 1950 and 1956 in the cause of a Welsh Parliament.

Mudiad Gweriniaethol Cymru (*The Welsh Republican Movement*)

The Welsh Republican Movement grew out of *Plaid Cymru* in the late 1940s, the product of frustration among some party members (especially students in the University College of Wales, Aberystwyth) with the tameness and lack of urgency in the party's leadership. This frustration was crystallized under the influence of some Irish writers into the demand for a Welsh republic, and the idea found support among a number of individuals who, for various reasons, were at odds with the leaders of the *Blaid*.[1] About fifty disaffected party members met in the Cory Hall, Cardiff, in 1949 prior to the *Blaid* summer school which was to be held in Duffryn Ardudwy, Merioneth. A motion urging a republican platform on the *Blaid* was discussed at the summer school and was defeated. The republicans then left the party and began to organize on their own. The *Blaid* expected this revolt to be temporary, but it was not to be so. The republican movement was never strong in Wales. At its peak it probably had no more than a hundred members. It was essentially a movement run by a handful of individuals—Gwilym Prys Davies, Cliff Bere, Huw Davies, Ithel Davies, and Harri Webb—who under the banner of republicanism offered a distinctive nationalist appeal, which differed sharply from *Plaid Cymru*'s at that time. They received support from other *Plaid* quarters. Mair Saunders Lewis, daughter of the former

---

[1] Information in this section was mainly supplied by Gwilym Prys Davies, private interview, 4 Dec. 1968.

Plaid President, Dr. Ceinwen Thomas, and Dr. D. J. Davies, the architect of the *Blaid*'s early economic thinking, all contributed to *Welsh Republican*, a bi-monthly broadsheet which the movement published between August 1950 and May 1957.[1] The *Welsh Republican* was one of the few tangible results of the movement. One parliamentary candidate was fielded in the 1950 general election: Ithel Davies contested the Ogmore constituency and was rewarded with 613 votes and a lost deposit. The movement set up a branch at Bargoed, along the Rhymney valley, but the 'latent republicanism' which the organizers expected to materialize did not develop. One of the Republican leaders commented much later that they had been naïve and that few of them had previously lived in the valleys.

The tone of the Republicans' utterances was a mixture of the extreme and the reasoned. They were more overtly anti-English, but more interested in the economic reconstruction of Wales than their *Plaid* counterparts. They were also notably less interested in preserving the Welsh culture, and had little sympathy for the Christian pacifist elements in the *Blaid*. Mair Saunders Lewis wrote in 1951 that:

> The prevalence of Pacifism in Wales is but another manifestation of a slave mentality. One has only to compare the Welshman's timidity with the courage of the Israelite.
>
> . . . A Welshman's conscience is no concern of England. Only too often has a Welshman's patriotism been a simmering stew of pacifism, sectarianism, vegetarianism, teetotalism, and chronic respectability. Welsh history teaches us no such rag-bag nationalism.[2]

Dr. D. J. Davies, writing in the first number of *Welsh Republican*, had called upon the movement to 'develop a more dynamic type of strategy, unfettered by pacifist commitments . . .' and wanted it to 'adopt a more realistic language policy . . . conducting all its political activities in English'.[3] As for the strategy of the movement, this was from the outset left deliberately vague. It sought 'the direction and tactics which may produce the desired result in the quickest way'.[4] This led the Republicans both to contest a parliamentary election and to disrupt the proceedings of the House of Commons.[5]

---

[1] Altogether thirty-seven issues of *Welsh Republican* were printed; nearly all of them can be found in Swansea Public Library.
[2] *Welsh Republican*, Aug.–Sept. 1951, vol. 2, No. 1.
[3] Ibid., Aug. 1950, vol. 1, No. 1.
[4] Ibid., Oct.–Nov. 1950, vol. 1, No. 2.
[5] During the 'Welsh Day' debate on 24 Nov. 1949.

Welsh Republicans burned Union Jacks in public, caused uproar at political meetings, and were even found in possession of quantities of explosives.[1] But the movement made no impression at all in Wales, and its leaders began to recognize that the whole undertaking had been a mistake, and that it would be more effective to operate within the political system than to try to create a revolutionary situation. A meeting was held at Pontypridd in 1954 to decide future strategy. The decision of the nine or ten individuals present was, unanimously, to try to advance their views within the Labour Party. Gwilym Prys Davies remained inside the Labour Party and became a leading adviser on devolution to its Welsh leaders. Cliff Bere was involved for a while as an organizer of the Parliament for Wales campaign. Harri Webb, Ithel Davies, and Cliff Bere all found their way back to *Plaid Cymru*; Webb was to become one of the most outspoken advocates of moderation among *Plaid* candidates after 1966. The *Welsh Republican* limped on until it ceased publication early in 1957, having become steadily more hostile to the *Blaid*. But, in one important respect, despite its evident failure, the Welsh Republican Movement could claim long-term success. *Plaid Cymru* in the 1960s was surely changing into the sort of party the Republicans had wanted it to be in 1948; that is, a party that was more secular, and more interested in the Welsh economy than in the Welsh culture in isolation. Whereas in 1948 *Plaid Cymru* was unable to keep within its ranks men and women who wanted to see these changes, such people were in 1968 the moving spirits in the Nationalist movement.

Miscellaneous Nationalist Groups

More formidable than the Welsh Republicans were a number of extremist organizations reported by the press and broadcasting services to have been formed in Wales in the 1960s. All of them led a shadowy existence, and any activity of theirs was usually well reported. The most important aspect of the operations of these groups was their occasional use of violent methods, particularly in the period 1966 to 1969, reaching a peak in the days immediately preceding the Investiture of the Prince of Wales in July 1969. The impact on public opinion of the violent exploits of these organizations was severely to discredit all nationalist politics and politicians in Wales and, in connection with the Investiture, to rally previously apathetic Welsh feelings around the Prince and the monarchy.

[1] *Welsh Republican*, Apr.–May and June–July 1953, vol. 3, Nos. 5 and 6.

Although this violence did not cause loss of life to the general public, two individuals were wounded by explosives said to have been planted by extreme nationalists, and two men who were planting explosives at Abergele on the morning of the 1969 Investiture were killed by their own devices. *Plaid Cymru* always denounced these activities, but certain individuals in Welsh cultural circles gave moral support to some of those connected with these events. Saunders Lewis came to the defence of the accused in the Free Wales Army trial;[1] Dr. Bobi Jones, who tutored Prince Charles in Welsh culture, dedicated a poem of praise to those killed in the Abergele incident, as did the Reverend Euros Bowen of Llangywair.[2]

Not all the organizations on the nationalist fringe used violent methods, although many condoned others' use of them. The Free Wales Army claimed to have used violent methods on several occasions, but it is doubtful whether the F.W.A. did anything more than stage exhibitions of its violent intentions to eager reporters and film cameramen. The question of who was responsible for the bomb explosions has yet to be fully established in a court of law. The main feature of these activities was that it was three years before any individual was prosecuted in the courts on charges relating to them; many of the legal proceedings instituted proved eventually to be unsuccessful.

The Free Wales Army (originally known as the Welsh Freedom Army) emerged in 1963 and became the best known of the fringe nationalist groups formed in the 1960s. Its aim was to do for Wales what the I.R.A. had done for Ireland, to initiate a revolution which would lead to independence for Wales. The leadership of the F.W.A. appeared to rest in the hands of a young and able publicist, Julian Cayo Evans, member of a well-known Cardiganshire family and breeder of Palomino stallions. Publicly associated with him was a motley collection of individualists, some with a chequered past. They occasionally held F.W.A. 'manœuvres' for the benefit of the press, and made appearance in uniform at extreme nationalist demonstrations. Every activity of the F.W.A. was reported at length in the Welsh press, and often in London newspapers and periodicals. The F.W.A. claimed responsibility for most of the explosions which rocked dam sites and public buildings in Wales between 1963 and 1969. Late in February 1969 the police finally decided to round up most of the individuals prominently connected with the F.W.A. Nine

---

[1] *Barn*, Aug. 1969.   [2] *Baner ac Amserau Cymru*, 24 July 1969.

individuals were charged under the Public Order Act with organizing and training the F.W.A.; other charges concerning firearms and explosives were laid against some of those concerned. The nine men included Cayo Evans, Anthony Lewis, founder of the National Patriotic Front, and Dai Bonar Thomas, who had been a *Plaid Cymru* candidate in the Carmarthen County Council elections in 1964. The staging of the Free Wales Army trial struck many observers as being connected with the approach of the Investiture. The trial finally started in the middle of April 1969, and the sentences for those convicted were announced on 1 July 1969, the very day of the Investiture. The explosions did not cease while the nine accused were held in custody during the course of the trial. Three of the accused, including Bonar Thomas, were found not guilty on all charges against them, and the cost of the trial to the taxpayer and to the rate-payers of South Wales was put at about £130,000.[1] Cayo Evans received the longest sentence of fifteen months' imprisonment, and two others among the accused served prison sentences following conviction. Amidst the celebrations surrounding the Investiture, one London journal concluded that the F.W.A. trial was 'a perfect illustration of that mixture of amused condescension and *force majeure* with which the English habitually treat their Celtic subjects. (It was the defence, not the prosecution, which spoke of English sledgehammers to crack Welsh nuts.)'[2] The 'boys' in the F.W.A. were essentially disillusioned with the parliamentary methods of *Plaid Cymru*, as were most of those on the extreme nationalist fringe in Wales; but the cause of Welsh freedom which they advertised so brilliantly was much harmed in Wales by their antics. Although they claimed thousands of members, the F.W.A. probably numbered less than a hundred. However, its impact on the climate of Welsh politics, and on the fortunes of *Plaid Cymru* in particular, was substantial and out of all proportion to its strength.

The National Patriotic Front, formed in 1966, set out to be the political arm of the Free Wales Army, although relations between the two groups sometimes seemed to be strained. Its aim declared in its newsletter *Front* ('not for sale or resale to the public') was:

> To unite within one organisation all patriotic movements and societies, affiliated together in an alliance to form a truly national patriotic front. The object of this alliance will be to put pressure on the English government and native quisling institutions to reach agreement with the aims of

[1] *Y Cymro*, 9 July 1969.   [2] Editorial in *New Statesman*, 4 July 1969.

this patriotic front. The aims being—an independent Welsh republic within a confederation of Free Celtia.[1]

The N.P.F.'s activities appeared to be very few beyond the rare demonstration and the publication of sporadic and abusive literature. It did also circulate to *Plaid Cymru* delegates to the party's annual conference in September 1968 a leaflet touching on a motion to be debated concerning the Investiture. The N.P.F. asked members of the *Blaid* to beware of 'the Royal Court of Llangadog who will try to persuade you to ignore this insult' (a reference to Gwynfor Evans), and it complained that the *Blaid* itself was 'fast becoming a regional English party'.[2] The personnel of the Front was linked with that of the F.W.A. (Anthony Lewis, Julian Cayo Evans, and Glyn Rowlands) and with that of another group, *Pwyllgor yr Ymgyrch Wrth-Arwisgo*, the Anti-Investiture Campaign Committee, which included Owain Williams and B. ap Ioan. The Anti-Investiture Campaign Committee was, however, non-violent in its methods.[3] Its aim was to form opinion on this issue and 'to inform the people of the facts about this insult, with door-to-door literature drives, and arranging rallies and protests wherever possible'.[4] It also threatened to fight the Caernarfon constituency against *Plaid Cymru* and all other opponents in 1969.[5] This threat was never carried out, and the Committee seems to have achieved very little other than occasional publicity. Certainly it was the Welsh Language Society which organized most of the opposition to the Investiture. The A.I.C.C., like the National Patriotic Front, was the product of a few young people disillusioned with *Plaid Cymru* and its attitude towards constitutional politics and the Investiture; for example, Owain Williams, chairman of the A.I.C.C., had organized the *Blaid*'s youth branch in Pwllheli early in the 1960s. Whereas the Welsh Language Society tried by fashionable militant protests to bring more attention to the plight of the Welsh language, and showed considerable resourcefulness and success in so doing, movements such as the N.P.F. and the A.I.C.C. which were more overtly nationalist in their outlook could not claim to have attracted much attention or support for their aims. This may partly be explained by the nature of the people in charge of these two groups; a more likely explanation is the fact that language protests

---

[1] *Front*, vol. 1, No. 5, Aug. 1968.
[2] Circular issued by the 'Central Committee of the National Patriotic Front', Sept. 1968, in the author's possession.
[3] Owain Williams, letter to *Y Cymro*, 27 Feb. 1969.
[4] A.I.C.C. leaflet in the author's possession.   [5] *Y Cymro*, 9 Apr. 1969.

and the folk and pop culture surrounding them were much more attractive to young radicals in Wales than bitter strident nationalism. In September 1969 both the N.P.F. and the A.I.C.C. united in the newly established non-violent republican movement, *Mudiad y Werin* (The People's Movement),[1] of which little has since been heard.

Since the use of explosives against property was probably not the responsibility of any of the groups so far mentioned it remains to be explained who was responsible. It was not until the spring of 1970 that two men, a regular sergeant in the Royal Army Dental Corps and a former Territorial Army bandsman, were convicted at Flintshire Assizes on charges relating to many of the explosions that had shaken Wales in the previous four years.[2] They were believed to have spearheaded a movement known as *Mudiad Amddiffyn Cymru* (Movement for the Defence of Wales), with which the two men killed by explosives at Abergele were also connected. Further legal proceedings in 1970 revealed that two of the three young men in their early twenties, all attached to Anglesey County Council's planning department, who were convicted of conspiring to cause an explosion at Holyhead at the end of June 1969, had been wrongfully convicted on some counts the previous October. These men had claimed to be attached to a movement called 'The Organization', but in April 1970 the two individuals from *Mudiad Amddiffyn Cymru* were convicted for the same offences.[3]

These were not the only groups of extreme nationalists that were known in Wales in the 1960s, but all of them were small in size, whether constitutional or violent in their methods. The damage done to property was very costly, and many lives were endangered by those groups using explosives. As for Wales and the Nationalist movement generally, the one tangible result of the operations of the extreme nationalist fringe was to ruin *Plaid Cymru*'s political reputation, if only because the *Blaid* and the extremists both claimed to be nationalists; more than one *Plaid* politician publicly speculated whether the Welsh explosions were government-inspired in order to achieve precisely this effect. Extremist activities caused a massive security network to be mounted in Wales, particularly to protect the Prince of Wales during his stay at the University College of Wales, Aberystwyth, and over the period of the Investiture at Caernarfon. The

---

[1] *Y Cymro*, 24 Sept. 1969.   [2] *The Times*, 21 Apr. 1970.
[3] Ibid., 28 July 1970.

inquiries of the hundreds of detectives and of the police Regional Crime Squads concerning security gave rise to enormous resentment and considerable sympathy for the extremist fringe in more orthodox nationalist circles and in the Welsh Language Society. The flood of police seemed to them proof of the heavy fist of alien England keeping down the Welsh and, according to some, using Gestapo methods. Inevitably those nationalists who shared this view in 1969 did not find their spirits crushed by the court convictions of 1969 and 1970; rather their determination and their hatred of the English was heightened and renewed.

Undeb Amaethwyr Cymru (*The Farmers' Union of Wales*)

The Farmers' Union of Wales was formed in December 1955 as the result of a breakaway from the National Farmers Union. The centres of this revolt were Carmarthenshire and Cardiganshire; the secretary of the Carmarthen branch of the N.F.U., J. B. Evans, became the F.U.W.'s general secretary; the vice-chairman of the N.F.U.'s Welsh committee, D. J. Davies, an Aberaeron farmer, resigned his post to join the revolt. The main complaints of the F.U.W. were that the N.F.U. seemed to be dominated by large farmers and that Wales did not have the representation at the annual Price Review negotiations afforded to both Scotland and Northern Ireland. The new F.U.W. was greeted by a hostile press, and the *Western Mail* commented that:

> It is possible to see in this latest insistence on our 'Welshness' the same prickly self-assertiveness, the limiting effects of which can be traced in so many of our relations with England and other countries.[1]

Nevertheless the F.U.W. found a strong response within the Welsh farming community. Within nine months of its formation it claimed 10,000 members on its books.[2]

The objectives of the F.U.W. in the 1960s were to attain for farmers in Wales equal status with farmers in England, Scotland, and Northern Ireland through their respective unions; to co-operate fully and equally with other farming organizations in the United Kingdom and overseas; and to safeguard and protect the interests of Welsh farmers.[3] In particular the F.U.W. has pressed for full Welsh representation on all marketing boards and statutory bodies affecting

---

[1] *Western Mail*, 5 Dec. 1955.   [2] Ibid., 11 Sept. 1956.
[3] *Undeb Amaethwyr Cymru, Ymunwch nawr i gwtogi eich costau* (undated).

Welsh agriculture, for independent consideration of the costs of production in Welsh agriculture, and for a 'realistic' level of farm incomes comparable with those of other industries and other countries within the United Kingdom. By 1969 the Farmers' Union of Wales had 14,000 members, a large full-time staff, and a branch in every county of Wales except Radnorshire.[1] The union has felt bound to refuse membership to small farmers from just over the Welsh border who wanted to join the union.[2] It has attracted to its ranks men of all political persuasions.[3] It claims, too, to have offered the cheapest insurance rates available to Welsh farmers, and to charge a much lower membership fee than the N.F.U.

The F.U.W. emerged in the mid fifties when the farmer started to be penalized for overproduction. It attracted a fair cross-section of the farming community, small farmers particularly, and larger farmers from the hill-farming areas; only estate owners were under-represented in the union. On several occasions the F.U.W. has captured for its candidates seats on marketing boards previously held by N.F.U. representatives, but it has yet to secure full official recognition from the Government. At various points in the 1960s F.U.W. leaders felt that even this barrier would fall. In 1965 they persuaded the Welsh Parliamentary Party to send a delegation to the Minister of Agriculture, Frederick Peart, to urge the Ministry to recognize the union.[4] However, four years later, the Secretary of State for Wales, George Thomas, told the F.U.W. annual general meeting that the union would never be recognized by the Government while it did not co-operate with the N.F.U.[5] Thus the F.U.W. is not represented at the price review discussions or on other government advisory committees; its bargaining position and its effectiveness are consequently much reduced.

The F.U.W.'s relations with the N.F.U. were inevitably antagonistic in the period immediately following the breakaway in 1955, although the F.U.W. has always claimed to be willing to co-operate with the N.F.U. The two unions have constantly queried each other's

[1] *Undeb Amaethwyr Cymru*, Agenda for 13th A.G.M., Aberystwyth, June 1969.
[2] *Western Mail*, 7 Sept. 1965.
[3] J. B. Evans, the first general secretary, was a Conservative candidate in the 1959 election. John Morris M.P., a former assistant general secretary, and D. J. Davies were prominent in the Labour Party. Emrys Bennett Owen, general secretary 1959–66, and Llewelyn Bebb were known *Plaid* supporters. Emlyn Thomas, general secretary 1966–8, left to become secretary of the Welsh Liberal Party, and Geraint Howells stood as a Liberal candidate in the 1970 election.
[4] *Western Mail*, 4 Mar. 1965.   [5] Ibid., 5 June 1969.

membership claims during the F.U.W.'s attempts to secure official recognition. Talks which were initiated unofficially between the unions in December 1957 broke down, and the chief mediator, Col. J. J. Davies of New Quay, resigned from the N.F.U. to join the F.U.W.[1] In 1965 the union rejected an appeal for unity made by the N.F.U.'s deputy president, Gwilym T. Williams, himself a Welsh-speaking Welshman.[2] Attempts were made by both sides to get talks about unity off the ground in 1966, and again in 1968, with little success.

Despite the fact that the F.U.W. cannot function fully as a farmers' union while it is not recognized by the Government, the union has been able to claim many successes in pressing the case of the Welsh farmer. Government departments have never closed their doors to the F.U.W., and the union claims that the Farm Improvement Scheme of 1957 and the Small Farm Scheme of 1959 were adopted by the Ministry of Agriculture largely on the F.U.W.'s initiative. It also campaigned for the publication of separate Welsh agricultural statistics, which occurred in 1967 for the first time. The F.U.W. has made a number of policy stands on questions relating to Wales generally. It has supported proposals for an elected council for Wales,[3] and for a Welsh Water Board. It has also helped farmers to fight plans to establish water reservoirs in their areas. The F.U.W., unlike the N.F.U., contested very strongly government plans to set up a Rural Development Board in mid Wales from 1967. It criticized, particularly, the proposed board's powers to interfere with sales of farm land. A large part of the evidence taken at the public inquiry in 1968 was supplied through the F.U.W., and was presented by Emlyn Thomas, formerly the general secretary of the union. The F.U.W. was able to claim a large amount of the credit for so delaying the launching of the new board that it still had not become operational when the change of government occurred in June 1970 and the board quickly dissolved. Thus the F.U.W. has certainly found a role in Welsh agricultural politics, but many observers have wondered whether this is not a role that could have been played even more successfully if the F.U.W. and the N.F.U. had merged. In the late 1960s the N.F.U. seemed to have learned some of the lessons arising from the F.U.W. breakaway; sometimes the antagonism between the two unions seemed only to emphasize the absence of real differences

[1] *Western Mail*, 28 Apr. 1958.   [2] Ibid., 30 Oct. 1965.
[3] Ibid., 15 Jan. 1966.

between them. Nevertheless, the F.U.W. has successfully adopted independent courses of action which have received the support of many small farmers in Wales. It still remains doubtful whether the N.F.U. in Wales could ever represent effectively the interests of the small farmer. It is the difference of interest between different types of farmer rather than a difference between England and Wales that is the real explanation of the success of the Farmers' Union of Wales; nationalism has played a subordinate but a cohesive part in ensuring the union's survival.

The Trade Unions and the Idea of a Welsh Trades Union Congress

The principal manifestation of nationalism inside the trade union movement in Wales has been the discussion surrounding the idea of a Welsh Trades Union Congress, similar to the existing Scottish Trades Union Congress. There have been no other signs that nationalism has made an impact on the union movement since 1966 or before. A handful of *Plaid Cymru* members have held offices in trade unions at branch or lodge level. No members of *Plaid Cymru* were known in the late 1960s to hold any senior post in any trade union in Wales. This impression is confirmed by the experience of the National Union of Mineworkers in South Wales. No organized group existed inside this union to further the cause of Welsh nationalism in the late 1960s, and Nationalist penetration did not appear to the union's officials to be very great or very different before or after 1966. Devolution was not discussed at the annual conferences of the South Wales Miners' Federation in the latter half of the 1960s; although some interest was aroused by the discussions concerning the setting-up of a Welsh Trades Union Congress. Only forty members of the forty-thousand strong South Wales Miners' Federation had contracted out of affiliating to the Labour Party at the beginning of 1970.[1] This appears surprising in view of the disaffection among the miners with the Labour Government's fuel policy after 1964, and in the light of the by-elections held in mining areas between 1966 and 1968 when it became clear that many miners and their families were voting for *Plaid Cymru* candidates.

The idea of a Welsh Trades Union Congress was canvassed many times between 1945 and 1970. The National Executive of the Electrical Trades Union considered, on the initiative of their branch in Pontardulais, whether to make a move inside the T.U.C. in 1954 for

[1] Private information.

a W.T.U.C.[1] Union leaders in Wales were seriously considering the idea late in 1960, but the problems of financing it were deemed to be too great.[2] The Amalgamated Union of Foundry Workers came out in favour of a W.T.U.C. in 1961, and again in 1964.[3] *Plaid Cymru*, at its annual conferences in 1964 and 1968, passed resolutions calling for a W.T.U.C. When the Llanelli Trades Council in 1966 came to endorse the call for a W.T.U.C., the two regional advisory committees of the T.U.C. in Wales were already discussing the idea on the initiative of the South Wales advisory committee.[4] The formation of the Welsh Office and the institution of a Secretary of State for Wales were judged by some to make the argument for a W.T.U.C. more pressing. The South Wales miners in conference the same year unanimously approved proposals for a W.T.U.C., the proposer complaining that the current T.U.C. advisory committees were unable to make policy decisions.[5] However, in December 1966 the idea of a W.T.U.C. was dropped by the T.U.C. advisory committees; the North Wales trade unions were not enthusiastic about a W.T.U.C., and the costs involved in setting it up and running it did not seem to match the foreseeable benefits.[6] The matter of the W.T.U.C. was, however, raised again strongly in 1968 when the South Wales Federations of Trades Councils gave unanimous approval to the idea. It was suggested at their annual conference that pit and rail closures might have been delayed or avoided if Wales had had a T.U.C. to press for more industry to come to Wales and for better planning of the Welsh economy.[7] The West Wales Federation, representing many Welsh-speaking members, was most interested in the W.T.U.C. plan; so were the Welsh sections of the Union of Shop, Distributive, and Allied Workers and the building trade unions.[8] The two regional advisory committees of the T.U.C. in Wales decided to reinvestigate the issue, and a meeting between the chairman and secretary of each committee was held early in August 1968. The South Wales T.U.C. advisory committee had previously estimated the cost of a W.T.U.C. to be over £12,000 per annum, a cost which they were willing to share.[9] Contrary to their expectations, the South Wales representatives found their North Wales counterparts as hostile as ever to the plan for a W.T.U.C. when they met in

[1] *Western Mail*, 29 May 1954.   [2] Ibid., 15 Nov. 1960.
[3] Ibid., 30 May 1961 and 26 May 1964.
[4] Ibid., 12 Feb. 1966.   [5] Ibid., 5 May 1966.
[6] Ibid., 6 Dec. 1966.   [7] Ibid., 24 Apr. 1968.
[8] Private information.   [9] *Western Mail*, 25 June 1968.

Newtown, Montgomeryshire, to discuss it. It was pointed out that most unions administered their Welsh membership in three regions— from the north-west of England, the Midlands, and from South Wales, and that most of the nationalized industries in North Wales were linked with Merseyside; the proposed Dee barrage would naturally strengthen the ties between the two areas.[1] Thus North Wales effectively buried the idea of a W.T.U.C.—a rare example of the South being more keen on treating Wales as a single unit than the North. Economic ties between North Wales and the north-west of England still proved to be too strong to admit the claims of national unity and national recognition for Wales in the late 1960s.[2]

Conclusion

This analysis of the place of nationalism in Welsh institutions and pressure groups, although incomplete, demonstrates how various are the means by which movements and organizations in modern Wales have been affected by Welsh-consciousness and Welsh nationalism. Yet it is difficult to assess how significant has been the contributions to the cohesion and character of modern Wales of those bodies which have directly or indirectly fostered nationalist thinking, and how far their efforts have affected the fortunes of *Plaid Cymru*.

It seems fair to conclude that it is only in organizations with a cultural orientation that real results have been achieved in engendering a sense of nationalism and Welsh identity. Nationalist arguments failed to establish a Welsh Trades Union Congress or even a Welsh National Union of Students. Important regional criticisms of the operation of their larger British-based organizations proved insufficient to provoke a nationalist breakaway. The example of the Farmers' Union of Wales is exceptional; it has been noted that the cause of the F.U.W. break with the N.F.U. was the frustration of the small farmers with their union, *qua* small farmers rather than *qua* Welshmen. The union's identification with Wales has added to its cohesion, but it is doubtful whether the F.U.W.'s origins owed much to nationalist inspiration.

Among the organizations and groups on the cultural side of Welsh life, five of those surveyed have had and are having a considerable effect on the attitudes of numbers of Welsh people. The

---

[1] *Notes of a meeting held to consider proposals to establish a Welsh Trades Union Congress*, T.U.C., Aug. 1968.
[2] A Welsh Trade Union Congress was, however, formed in January 1973.

broadcasting organizations in Wales see their role as being to foster Welsh culture and Welsh national identity. The broadcasters have certainly reduced the mental distance between the four corners of Wales, but they have at the same time assisted in the integration of Welsh with English culture. The University of Wales has, since its creation, given Wales an intellectual unity. The desire to advance the frontiers of knowledge has not always been compatible with the desire to serve Wales and to retain a Welsh ethos. The refusal of the Court of the University to countenance defederalization in 1964 showed that a nominal nationalism was still strong in its ranks, even if not present among the colleges' principals. Despite the revival of interest in the Welsh language in the community at large, the departments of Welsh in the University Colleges have tended to contract while the rest of the University has expanded.

The Welsh Language Society, which finds its main support from within the University of Wales, especially in the departments of Welsh, has aimed to redirect the attention of Welsh people to their heritage more overtly. The achievements of the Society from 1962 cannot be compared with those of the University. The Society opted for the political arena and established itself as an administrator's gadfly. More than any other body the Welsh Language Society made the language a matter of political dispute, and added substantially to the pressures which earned the Welsh language greater status in the 1960s. In the course of mobilizing student and other political support for the Welsh language, the Society also created plenty of hostility and has probably diminished permanently the extent of goodwill that once existed throughout Wales towards the language.

The Welsh Schools movement and *Urdd Gobaith Cymru* have both aimed to spread a love of Wales and its language among generations of children and young people in Wales. It would be impossible to assess how far these two movements have affected the socialization of tens of thousands of children within the schools of Wales. Few politicians or educationists can dismiss the impact of these two movements. The *Urdd* in particular has had a cumulative and continuing effect on the attitudes of countless young people in every part of Wales. Its activities may not attract the limelight, but its influence has been pervasive, radical, and subtle. It is an avowedly nationalist body which owes much of its past success to generous subsidies from national and local government. The *Urdd* had probably changed the social attitudes, and indirectly the political climate of Wales, more so than any other single Welsh institution. The Welsh Schools, however, may yet prove to be more significant still in moulding the attitudes of present and future generations. The intensity of devotion to the heritage of Wales which those schools encourage has already led several of their ex-pupils to adopt militant attitudes in public which are commonly associated with the Welsh Language Society.

11

WELSH NATIONALISM AND THE OTHER POLITICAL PARTIES IN WALES SINCE 1945

ALL political parties in Britain which have attempted to secure the support of the Welsh people have had to reckon with the challenge of Welsh nationality ever since the extension of the franchise under the 1867 Reform Act. It has already been noted how Welsh nationalism, as expressed in the *Cymru Fydd* movement and underpinning the campaign to disestablish the Anglican Church, was one of the major themes of Welsh politics before 1914. The Liberal Party has always been friendly to the political demands of Welsh nationalism and so, in its early years, was the Labour Party. Since 1945, the Conservative Party has also paid attention to the problems raised by the Welsh people's desire to assert their nationality, and at times has been better disposed towards its claims than has the Labour Party. For the first time in more than half a century Welsh nationalism became an issue of major importance throughout Britain during the period of the Labour Government between 1966 and 1970. In conjunction with the success of the Scottish National Party, *Plaid Cymru* for a time appeared to be an immediate and permanent threat to the balance of the political parties in the United Kingdom, and thus forced all political parties at Westminster to give the problem of Scotland and Wales special and renewed attention.

The Labour Party and Welsh Nationalism

In its early days in Wales the Labour movement was nationalist in its outlook both with regard to Welsh economic and social problems and to the question of Home Rule. When Keir Hardie was elected in 1900 the first independent Labour M.P. from Wales, in the Merthyr Tydfil constituency, he claimed to be a Welsh Nationalist.[1] This outlook was carried over into the programme of the Labour Party; in

---

[1] Kenneth O. Morgan, 'The Merthyr of Keir Hardie', in *Merthyr Politics* (Cardiff, 1966), p. 70.

1918 the Labour Party conference suggested that 'along with the grant of Home Rule to Ireland, there should be constituted separate statutory legislative assemblies for Scotland, Wales, and even England, with autonomous administration in matters of local concern . . .'.[1] Despite equivocation by MacDonald while the Labour Party was in office in 1923–4 and in 1929,[2] Labour claimed throughout the 1920s to favour Home Rule all round; this pledge was endorsed in the Labour Party's manifesto for the 1929 general election.[3] Increasingly this policy pledge was treated as a dead letter. The newer leaders of Welsh Labour had themselves been schooled in the cause of international social democracy, notably at the Central Labour College in London.[4] When the Welsh Parliamentary Party, half of whose members were Labour M.P.s, approached Neville Chamberlain on the question of Welsh devolution in 1938 it was to ask only for a Secretary of State for Wales and for the establishment of a Welsh Office.[5] This proposal was re-endorsed by the Welsh Regional Council of Labour in 1943, and at the party conference that same year James Griffiths attempted without success to insert into the Labour Party programme a pledge to support the setting-up of Regional Authorities in the context of local government reorganization.[6] Winston Churchill, the Prime Minister, rebuffed the attempts of Welsh M.P.s to bring pressure on him to adopt the Secretary of State proposal, and the demand was quietly dropped.[7] Labour's election manifesto in 1945 made no specific pledges concerning Wales although many Labour candidates in Welsh seats reaffirmed their commitment to the idea of a Secretary of State.[8] However, the

---

[1] Resolution XIII on 'Constitutional Devolution', *Report of the Eighteenth Annual Conference of the Labour Party*, p. 70.

[2] Sir Reginald Coupland, *Welsh and Scottish Nationalism*, pp. 398–401.

[3] 'Labour's Appeal to the Nation', manifesto printed in *Report of the Twenty-Ninth Annual Conference of the Labour Party*, p. 307.

[4] e.g. Aneurin Bevan, Ness Edwards, James Griffiths, Dr. J. H. Williams, Revd. Llewelyn Williams, Morgan Phillips, and W. H. Mainwaring were all connected with the Central Labour College which closed down in 1928. See W. W. Craik, *The Central Labour College* (London, 1964).

[5] James Griffiths, *Pages from Memory*, pp. 158–9.

[6] *Evidence of the Labour Party in Wales to the Commission on the Constitution* (Cardiff, 1970), p. 19. See also *Report of the Forty-Second Annual Conference of the Labour Party* (1942), pp. 190–5, 197–8.

[7] P. J. Randall, 'The development of Administrative Decentralisation in Wales from the establishment of the Welsh Department of Education in 1907 to the creation of the post of Secretary of State for Wales in October 1964' (unpublished M.Sc. Econ. thesis, University of Wales, 1969), pp. 209–10.

[8] For example, Cledwyn Hughes (Anglesey), Tudor Watkins (Brecon and Radnor), Goronwy Roberts (Caernarvonshire), R. M. Hughes (Carmarthen), W. Mars-Jones (Denbigh), and Arthur Pearson (Pontypridd).

prospect of a Secretary of State for Wales receded the longer Labour was in office. When in 1946 the Welsh Parliamentary Party put forward a demand for a Secretary of State for Wales, Attlee rejected the proposal in a letter to D. J. Grenfell and suggested several small changes of practice including a Welsh Day each year in Parliament. The Welsh Parliamentary Party replied that Attlee's letter seemed 'to repudiate entirely the claims of Wales as a nation';[1] but later that year the Welsh Regional Council of Labour 'came to the conclusion that the proposal for a Secretary of State for Wales was no longer practicable and could not be fruitfully pursued'.[2] The Attlee Government, however, created an opening for further progress in January 1948 with the publication of a white paper on Scottish affairs which suggested that a consultative body on Scottish economic affairs be set up.[3] When a Welsh Liberal M.P., Emrys Roberts (Merioneth), suggested in the Commons three days later that a similar body for Wales was needed, Attlee said he was prepared to examine the idea.[4] The Welsh Labour M.P.s and the Welsh Regional Council of Labour set to work to prepare a scheme and in June they came forward with a proposal for a Welsh council to advise the Government.[5] This met with some dissent among more devolutionist Labour leaders in Wales, but Herbert Morrison announced in October 1948 that the Government would set up a nominated advisory council, along the lines suggested, although considerably modified in scope; for example, the Council was not to be given any statutory powers nor was its chairman to be a Minister with a Welsh constituency.[6] Morrison refused to amend his scheme despite pressure from the Welsh M.P.s and thus the Council for Wales and Monmouthshire was launched in May 1949 with Dr. Huw T. Edwards, the respected North Wales Labour and trade union leader, as chairman. The response to the new Council was hostile both inside and outside Wales. The Times commented that 'a debating society meeting in camera once a quarter implies no step towards the control of Welsh affairs by the Welsh'.[7] Dr. Huw T. Edwards recorded some years later that he could not imagine that 'any other Council in the history of our (the Welsh) nation ever had

---

[1] The Times, 15 Oct. 1948.
[2] Welsh Regional Council of Labour, Report to Annual Conference (Cardiff, 1948).
[3] Scottish Affairs 1948, Cmnd. 7308 (H.M.S.O., 1948).
[4] 446 HC Deb. Fifth Series, cc. 1468–9 (2 Feb. 1948).
[5] Western Mail, 21 June 1948.
[6] See E. L. Gibson, 'A Study of the Council for Wales and Monmouthshire' (unpublished M.A. thesis, University of Wales, 1968) and P. J. Randall, op. cit., p. 219.
[7] The Times, 21 May 1949.

such a cold reception';[1] however, he believed that this was exaggerated opposition and that in private Welsh leaders were favourable towards the Council.[2] The Council for Wales and Monmouthshire produced a number of detailed reports on Welsh problems and continued to advise the Government, with occasional changes in composition, until 1966; one authority has concluded that in this period it 'was important because it provided something not available elsewhere—direct consultation and specialist advice in some detail, aside from the party conflict'.[3]

Nevertheless the Council for Wales and Monmouthshire was no solution to Welsh demands for devolution so far as many Labour supporters in Wales were concerned, and when the Parliament for Wales Campaign was launched in 1950, S. O. Davies was not alone among the Labour M.P.s in offering the campaign his support.[4] Cledwyn Hughes, Goronwy Roberts, T. W. Jones, and Tudor Watkins were the other Labour M.P.s from Wales who supported the campaign throughout its six years. Their actions forced the Labour Party to reconsider its position on Welsh devolution, and many motions were received by the Welsh Regional Council of Labour before its 1952 conference calling for the formulation of a definite socialist policy for Wales.[5] Since 1949, the Labour Party had seemed to be even less interested in Welsh devolution than has the Conservative Party; at least the Conservative manifesto in 1959 promised that 'a special responsibility for Wales should be assigned to a member of the Cabinet'.[6] While the Labour Government was in office between 1945 and 1951, a Cabinet Minister was given, to uncertain effect, a watching brief over Welsh affairs.[7] When the Conservatives regained office in 1951 they designated the Home Secretary as Minister for Welsh Affairs—although the title meant less than it sounded;[8] David Llewellyn, the Conservative M.P. for Cardiff North, was

[1] H. T. Edwards, *Hewn From The Rock* (Cardiff, 1967), p. 125.
[2] Ibid., p. 126.
[3] E. L. Gibson, op. cit., p. 234. Gibson also points out that the Council for Wales served as a model for the council for the mid West region of Nigeria set up in the 1960s.
[4] See Ch. 10.   [5] *Western Mail*, 27 May 1952.
[6] *The Times*, 25 Jan. 1950.
[7] The ministers responsible were successively Morrison (Lord President) until 1950, Bevin (Lord Privy Seal) during 1950, and Chuter Ede (Home Secretary) 1950–1. Ness Edwards claimed in 1952 that when the Cabinet was going to discuss Welsh matters, 'a meeting over which the Home Secretary presided' would be held in advance at which Welsh members of the Government would be present (495 HC Deb. Fifth Series, c. 719, 4 Feb. 1952).
[8] See below, pp. 297–8.

appointed Under-Secretary at the Home Office at the same time. The 1952 conference of the Welsh Regional Council of Labour called for 'a Labour Policy for Wales' and the Council's Executive committee set up a sub-committee without time limit to formulate this policy.[1] This sub-committee accepted that Wales had its own special problems and listed these in *order of priority* as education, the economy of Wales, government and administration, and the Council for Wales.[2] The Welsh Labour M.P.s meanwhile investigated the idea of a Welsh Grand Committee of the Commons.[3] The findings of the sub-committee were not ready until 1954; in the meantime there was some confusion in Wales because of the public expression of Labour's divided counsels. At the end of 1953 the Welsh Regional Council of Labour, the Welsh Labour M.P.s, and members of the National Executive Committee of the party, including Herbert Morrison, Labour's Deputy Leader, met to discuss the new policy in draft. The *Western Mail* reported that Labour leaders were alarmed at the 'progress of the Welsh Nationalist movement and the effect upon Socialist policy and membership'.[4] It soon became clear that all three parties to these discussions were predominantly opposed to any scheme for home rule within the United Kingdom, but the full policy was not announced until March 1954. The new document, *Labour's Policy for Wales*, was mainly concerned to attack the idea of a Parliament for Wales and to defend Labour's record in office. Very few new specific proposals concerning the handling of Welsh affairs were made, although it was suggested that the constitution of the Council for Wales and Monmouthshire be altered to make it 'a more representative and more effective organ of Welsh opinion'.[5] The new policy agreed to keep unchanged the post of Minister for Welsh Affairs, with a seat in the Cabinet, which had been created by the Conservatives in 1951. The Minister would remain without departmental responsibilities.[6] When the Regional Council of Labour met for its annual conference, 'Labour's Policy for Wales' was approved by 154 votes to one, but for various reasons sixty-two delegates did not take part in the vote.[7] The Labour Party was at this

---

[1] Welsh Regional Council of Labour, *Report of the Annual Conference* (Cardiff, 1952).
[2] Welsh Regional Council of Labour, *Report to the Annual Conference* (Cardiff, 1953).
[3] P. J. Randall, op. cit., p. 231.   [4] *Western Mail*, 11 Nov. 1953.
[5] *Labour's Policy for Wales* (Cardiff, 1954), p. 12.   [6] Ibid., p. 11.
[7] Welsh Regional Council of Labour, *Report of the Annual Conference* (Cardiff, 1954).

time particularly antagonistic towards the claims of Welsh nationality, and once this new policy was approved by the whole of the Labour movement in Scarborough in the autumn of 1954, the Welsh Regional Council's Executive Committee was in a position to challenge the activities of those Labour M.P.s involved in the Parliament for Wales campaign. This was achieved by reporting the five M.P.s concerned to the National Executive Committee in January of 1956.[1] However, no action seems to have materialized.

The Labour Party's position on Welsh devolution remained unchanged until 1959, but the issue was reopened by the report issued in 1957 by the Council for Wales and Monmouthshire on government administration in Wales.[2] The report was the product of two years work between 1954 and 1956 and was published in January 1957. The Council's main criticisms of the administrative position affecting Wales were that there was still too little co-ordination between government departments despite the quarterly meetings of heads of civil service departments in Wales; that the grading of civil servants in charge of offices in Wales was too low to enable them to take decisive action concerning Welsh problems facing their departments or to carry enough weight in Whitehall; and that the position of Minister for Welsh Affairs lacked any specific executive authority with regard to Wales alone. The Council's report suggested two principal remedies: that some heads of offices in Wales should be given a higher grading and additional responsibilities; and that there should be a Cabinet Minister with specific and sole executive authority in specified fields in Wales. The impact of this weighty report on public opinion in Wales and on the Welsh M.P.s was considerable; nearly every Welsh M.P. who spoke in the Welsh affairs debate in the House of Commons shortly after the report was published supported the proposal for a Secretary of State.[3] Opposition within the Labour group of Welsh M.P.s did, however, grow as the year progressed, and by the end of July 1957, the group was reported to be sharply divided on the issue.[4] The Welsh Regional Council of

[1] Welsh Regional Council of Labour, *Report to the Annual Conference* (Cardiff, 1956). See above, Ch. 10.

[2] *Government Administration in Wales*, Third Memorandum of the Council for Wales and Monmouthshire, Cmnd. 53 (H.M.S.O., 1957).

[3] Of the fourteen M.P.s from Welsh constituencies who gave their views on the proposal for a Secretary of State in this debate, twelve were in favour (8 Labour, 3 Conservatives, and a Liberal); Walter Padley, Labour M.P. for Ogmore, was sceptical, and David Llewellyn, a Conservative, opposed the idea.

[4] *Western Mail*, 24 July 1957.

Labour merely reaffirmed the policy it had adopted in 1954, but discussion continued within the party. The Welsh group of Labour M.P.s
met representatives of the Welsh Regional Council of Labour and of
the National Executive Committee of the party to discuss ministerial
responsibility for Welsh affairs. In May 1957, Gaitskell and the Chief
Whip, Herbert Bowden, met the Labour group of Welsh M.P.s for an
informal exchange of ideas.[1] The matter was then allowed to rest as
far as the policy of the whole party was concerned. As the year 1958
drew to a close and as no further Welsh policy statement appeared
to be forthcoming, certain Labour M.P.s, especially from North
Wales, began to raise objections. A meeting of the Labour group of
Welsh M.P.s late in November produced no unanimity on the idea
of a Secretary of State, but the advice of Gaitskell and James
Griffiths was sought, and a further discussion was held early in
December.[2] The upshot was the setting up of a tripartite committee
containing four representatives from each of the Welsh Labour
M.P.s, the National Executive Committee, and the Welsh Council of
Labour.[3] It was this committee which finally determined the Labour
Party's policy on devolution—much in the shadow of an approaching
general election. Reports and leaks in the following months suggested
that Welsh Labour M.P.s were becoming less enthusiastic about a
Secretary of State.[4] In fact, key changes of view on the part of certain
leading Labour politicians and the chance fact that the Deputy Leader
of the party and chairman of its home affairs policy committee was a
Welshman meant that opinion in the leadership was swinging in
favour of the proposed Secretary of State despite the divisions of the
Welsh backbenchers. Aneurin Bevan had criticized the humbug of
believing that a Welsh Day in the Commons had the slightest
relevance to any important Welsh problem,[5] and had denounced
in 1946 the idea of a Minister with full responsibility for Wales
sitting in the Cabinet as one that would create 'nothing but a
messenger boy'.[6] Like Morrison, Bevan was never opposed to all
forms of devolution. He did, however, believe it was impossible to

---

[1] Welsh Regional Council of Labour, *Report to the Annual Conference* (Cardiff, 1958).
[2] *Western Mail*, 26 Nov. 1958.
[3] Ibid., 16 Dec. 1958, and J. Idwal Jones, private interview, 17 July 1968. Seven of the twelve members of the committee were M.P.s, including James Griffiths and Aneurin Bevan.
[4] *Western Mail*, 6 July 1959.
[5] 403 HC Deb. Fifth series, c. 2312 (17 Oct. 1944).
[6] 428 HC Deb. Fifth Series, cc. 403–4 (28 Oct. 1946).

isolate important problems for Wales from those of Britain generally; in his view they required common treatment. In the 1940s he scoffed at the proposal for a Secretary of State for Wales because he considered that Scotland had benefited little from such an appointment. Bevan wanted at that time 'a more effective constitutional device for enabling Welsh life to be articulated at a national level'.[1] However, in December 1958, when the Welsh Labour M.P.s again debated the Secretary of State proposal, Bevan did not urge opposition, only caution.[2] His change of attitude was crucial to Labour's acceptance of the idea, as he was one of the party's most prominent leaders. He is credited with having told one Welsh M.P., 'I think you might as well have it'.[3] James Callaghan is also believed to have changed his mind on this issue at this time, because he was convinced that it was because Scotland had had a Secretary of State in the Cabinet that the Conservative Government had given priority in 1957 to the Forth Bridge rather than to one over the Severn.[4] But, most important, it was the substitution of James Griffiths for Herbert Morrison as Deputy Leader of the party and Chairman of the Home Affairs committee which brought forward the proposal for a Secretary of State. Morrison had once said that 'to have a special Minister for Wales would introduce delays and confusion of responsibility which would make it harder and slower'.[5] Griffiths had, with varying intensity, been an advocate of a Secretary for Wales for decades. He saw that there was now a new opportunity to push the proposal forward. The Labour Party was in need of a new policy. It was going into an election with a new leader for the first time in twenty years; and Griffiths was chairman of the tripartite committee which was to settle the new policy. Gaitskell did not resist the proposal for a Secretary of State, and thus to the surprise of some Welsh Labour M.P.s, when the policy statement on Welsh affairs was issued early in August 1959 the proposal was included.[6] The Labour manifesto at the ensuing general election said simply that 'the time has now come for the special identity of Wales to be recognized by the appointment of a Secretary of State'.[7] The Labour Party Conference subsequently ratified the new policy. Gaitskell meanwhile offered

[1] Aneurin Bevan, 'The Claim of Wales: a Statement', in *Wales*, Spring 1947.
[2] *Western Mail*, 9 Dec. 1958.
[3] Private information.
[4] Private information. See *The Times*, 11 Oct. 1957.
[5] *News Chronicle*, 20 May 1949.
[6] *Labour's Policy for Wales* (London, 1959).
[7] *Britain Belongs To You* (London, 1959).

Griffiths the Secretaryship for Wales if Labour were returned to power.[1] Such was not to be the outcome of the 1959 election, but the Labour Party found itself once more ahead of the Conservatives in its commitment to devolution in Wales.

An early success for Labour in the 1959–64 Parliament was the decision to set up a Welsh Grand Committee made in March 1960 by Henry Brooke, the Conservative Minister for Welsh Affairs. Ness Edwards, the Labour M.P. for Caerphilly, persuaded both the Select Committee on Procedure and the Minister to support the idea.[2] The principal concerns of the Labour movement in Wales in this period were with the Welsh economy and with local government reform. It was through consideration of various schemes for local government reform that the next development in the attitude of the Labour Party in Wales towards devolution occurred. Both Gaitskell in 1961[3] and Wilson in 1963,[4] confirmed the official Labour pledge to set up a Secretary of State for Wales and a Welsh Office, and in April 1963 Transport House issued a comprehensive policy document for Wales, *Signposts to the New Wales* (a companion volume to *Signposts to the Sixties*), which was welcomed in Wales by the Liberals and the *Blaid*. The new document did not touch on questions related to local government reform and promised only to 'review the position of the Council for Wales in the light of the constitutional changes we propose'.[5] However, moves had been made by Labour in 1962 shortly after the commission to inquire into Welsh local government had been appointed in 1961. A working party on local government in Wales was set up with representatives of the Welsh Council of Labour, Welsh M.P.s, and Labour councillors in Wales;[6] James Griffiths acting as chairman, and Cledwyn Hughes as secretary.[7] One of their principal advisers was Gwilym Prys Davies who had become a friend of Griffiths, and it was he who produced, on the initiative of Cledwyn Hughes, a draft plan for a central council for Wales as a measure of local government reform; this was later published by *Undeb Cymru Fydd*.[8] In the process of centralizing the administration of certain Welsh local government functions, Davies argued that a single all-

[1] James Griffiths, op. cit., p. 164.
[2] Ibid., pp. 163–4 and Lord Brooke of Cumnor, private interview, 19 Nov. 1968.
[3] *Western Mail*, 8 May 1961.
[4] Ibid., 23 Feb. 1963.
[5] *Signposts to the New Wales* (London, 1963), p. 22.
[6] Welsh Council of Labour, *Report to the Annual Conference* (Cardiff, 1963).
[7] Gwilym Prys Davies, private interview, 4 Dec. 1968.
[8] Gwilym Prys Davies, *A Central Council for Wales* (Aberystwyth, 1963).

Wales authority could be created which would provide a structure for further devolution from central government. This scheme was not entirely welcome in Welsh Labour circles; it was attacked as being too nationalistic, for example, by Cliff Prothero, then Secretary of the Welsh Council of Labour. Although it was discussed throughout the party, the plan for an elected council for Wales did not make much progress. The election of Labour to power in 1964 and the succession of Emrys Jones to the secretaryship of the Welsh Council of Labour early in 1965 changed the balance inside the party. The plan was discussed at every level of the Labour movement, and Emrys Jones sent out an additional brief to the constituencies tactfully entitled 'A Welsh Regional Council'.[1] The idea of an elected council was finally given the blessing of the Welsh Council of Labour at its conference in Llandudno in May 1966.[2] The proposal was not taken to the National Executive Committee of the party, so that the Labour Party as a whole was not committed to it.[3]

In the meantime, a Labour Government had been elected to power at the general election in October 1964. Labour in Wales had fought the election on an attractive platform which included the promise of a Secretary of State and leasehold enfranchisement, a burning issue in South Wales especially. The party improved its position in Wales slightly and captured Swansea West from the Conservatives. The twenty-eight Welsh Labour M.P.s at Westminster during the 1964–6 Parliament found themselves well placed to exercise leverage on a Government with an infinitesimal majority. In 1965 intensive lobbying by Welsh Labour M.P.s, with the support of James Callaghan in the Cabinet, secured the Government's adoption of proposals for leasehold reform against the wishes of the Minister of Housing, Richard Crossman.[4]

Within hours of his appointment as Prime Minister, Harold Wilson announced the formation of the Welsh Office, headed by a Secretary of State with a seat in the Cabinet.[5] James Griffiths was the first to hold this office, and he was succeeded by Cledwyn Hughes following the 1966 election. Hughes was replaced by George Thomas, M.P. for

---

[1] Duplicated brief issued by the Welsh Council of Labour entitled 'A Welsh Regiona Council', p. 10.
[2] Welsh Council of Labour, *Report of the Annual Conference* (Cardiff, 1966).
[3] Private information.
[4] Private information. The leasehold bill was drawn up by Leo Abse and Samuel Silkin.
[5] A 'Welsh Office' of a limited nature was set up by the Conservative Government in 1963 under the Ministry of Housing and Local Government.

Cardiff West, in 1968 and Thomas remained in this office until the defeat of the Labour Government in June 1970. At first one junior minister assisted the Secretary of State at the Welsh Office, but this was increased to two early in 1968. The Secretary of State was given responsibility in 1964 for housing and local government, trunk roads, and economic planning for Wales, as well as oversight within Wales for the general policy of several other ministries.[1] Responsibility for agriculture and health services in Wales was transferred to him in April 1969. At the start of 1965 a Welsh Planning Board and a Welsh Economic Council were set up as part of the over-all Department of Economic Affairs regional planning structure; the one was an administrative body and the other a broadly representative body. The Board and the new Council were to advise on and to co-ordinate the economic planning of Wales. The Council for Wales and Monmouthshire was wound up in 1966, so that the Welsh Economic Council was from 1965 until 1968 the main representative body advising the Government on Welsh affairs. Under the aegis of Cledwyn Hughes it was decided to reconstitute a Welsh Council of an advisory kind; at the same time the whole issue of an elected council for Wales was naturally raised under the banner of local government reform.[2] The Secretary of State was under pressure from local authorities in Wales to state his proposals for reform, and was anxious not to delay doing so while the issue of an elected council was being settled. The crucial decision on the elected council was being taken by a ministerial committee in November 1966 when the Welsh Labour M.P.s intervened and showed how divided they were; the M.P.s were believed to have been evenly split on the issue, broadly on a Welsh-speaking versus non Welsh-speaking basis.[3] This considerably weakened the position of Hughes who was having to fight opposition from the Scots inside the Government who believed that Scotland should have priority over Wales. Whereas previously the battle which James Griffiths had had with other government departments to transfer powers to the Welsh Office had been settled at Prime Ministerial level,[4] the row over the elected Council for Wales was taken to the Cabinet, apparently several times. Hughes believed that time was the crucial factor as it was likely that

[1] 702 HC Deb. Fifth Series, cc. 623–32 (19 Nov. 1964). S.I. 1965, No. 319, Secretary of State for Wales and Ministry of Land and Natural Resources Order, 1965.
[2] *Local Government in Wales*, Cmnd. 3340 (H.M.S.O., 1967).
[3] Private information.
[4] James Griffiths, private interview, 19 July 1968.

he would soon be transferred to another ministry. This all but happened in August 1967, but it was in the event delayed until January 1968.[1] Hughes therefore decided to publish his local government proposals without the issue of the elected council being determined. The white paper published in July 1967 promised only that:

. . . further consideration will subsequently be given, in the light of the Royal Commissions' reports and other developments, to the possibilities of a further strengthening of all-Wales machinery by giving it additional powers and responsibilities and by making appropriate changes in its membership and constitution.[2]

At the same time, Hughes pushed through two other important decisions before the summer recess of Parliament in 1967. The economic plan for Wales, which, like the project for an elected council, had suffered from under-preparation in the early part of the Labour Government, was published amid widespread criticism.[3] And the Welsh Language Act passed through Parliament and enacted some of the recommendations of the Hughes-Parry report.[4] The urgency over local government reform proved short-lived, both because of the controversy caused by the 1967 proposals and because of the imminent publication of the Maud Report on Local Government in England, published eventually in 1969. The new Welsh Council set to work in 1968, however, under the chairmanship of Professor Brinley Thomas.[5] Yet the question of an elected council for Wales did not rest; many local authorities had taken a strong line on the elected council issue in 1968, some threatening not to co-operate with any nominated Welsh council.[6] In 1969, the elected council was discussed once again by the Welsh Council of Labour and its study group as part of its preparation of evidence for the Crowther Commission set up by the Labour Government at the end of 1968 to suggest, *inter alia*, constitutional changes to satisfy the

---

[1] Private information.
[2] *Local Government in Wales*, p. 21, para. 57.
[3] *Wales: The Way Ahead*, Cmnd. 3334 (H.M.S.O., 1967).
[4] *Legal Status of the Welsh Language*, Cmnd. 2785 (H.M.S.O., 1965).
[5] Professor Thomas was Professor of Economics at University College of South Wales and Monmouthshire, Cardiff, and was once a prominent member of the Labour Party. He unsuccessfully attempted to secure the parliamentary nomination in the Aberdare constituency in 1946 (*Aberdare Leader*, 23 Nov. 1946).
[6] Two county councils, at least, tried to thwart the formation of the nominated Welsh council by refusing to appoint nominees to it. The county councils of Cardigan and Caernarvon declared strongly in favour of an elected council for Wales (*Western Mail*, 11 and 12 Jan. 1968).

regional and national grievances of England, Scotland, and Wales.[1] In August 1969 the Council of Labour's study group of twelve, including two M.P.s, produced a plan for an elected council for Wales which would give it legislative powers and considerable financial independence.[2] This met with considerable criticism from inside the Welsh Labour movement, from Government ministers in particular, especially from George Thomas, the Secretary of State.[3] The report of the study group was pulled to pieces throughout the autumn and rewritten several times to accommodate the divergent views of Welsh M.P.s, the National Executive Committee, the Welsh Council of Labour, and its study group.[4] At one stage when the N.E.C. appeared to want to make the proposed council only partially elected the study group was preparing to submit separate evidence to the Crowther Commission.[5] The interventions of George Thomas seemed only to make the waverers at different levels of the Labour Party decide to make a stand for an elected council, according to one member of the study group.[6] After several changes of mind, the executive committee of the Welsh Council of Labour decided finally at the beginning of January to support a fully directly elected council for Wales.[7] The approval of the National Executive Committee to the final document was secured. This committed the party to the scheme but not the Government, as was indicated by the absence of any pledge to set up an elected council for Wales in the Labour Party's manifesto issued prior to the general election in June 1970.[8] (Yet at least a third of the evidence had been written by officials in Transport House in London, while the rest had been heavily censored.) Nevertheless the position of the Labour Party in 1970 was still in advance of the Conservatives' on the question of devolution to Wales, the Welsh Conservatives having decided not to present any evidence at all to the Crowther Commission.

---

[1] Special panels of the Commission were set up to study the position of Scotland and Wales. The Welsh panel comprised Sir Ben Bowen Thomas, Alun Talfan Davies, Q.C., T. Haydn Rees, Professor Graham Rees, K. Griffin, and Lord Brecon.

[2] 'Reform of Machinery of Government', unpublished report of the Welsh Council of Labour study group, 1969.

[3] Western Mail, 17 Dec. 1969, and private information.

[4] Emrys Jones, private interview, 10 Dec. 1969, and J. Barry Jones, private interview, 10 Dec. 1969.

[5] Western Mail, 24 Dec. 1969, and private information.

[6] Private information.

[7] Evidence of the Labour Party in Wales to the Commission on the Constitution (Cardiff, 1970).

[8] Guardian, 28 May 1970.

Labour policy on Welsh devolution has reflected the strength of Welsh demands for concessions to nationalism, of Labour's internal politics and of inter-party competitiveness. It was not until 1967 that the Labour Party finally realized the strength of the backing for *Plaid Cymru*, for whereas the latter had always seen the Labour Party in Wales as its principal opponent, the Labour Party in Wales had always regarded the Conservatives as its main opposition. The structure of Welsh politics is, however, highly complex and there are many parts of Wales where the Conservatives are inactive politically and where groups such as the *Blaid* are the only permanent opposition to the Labour Party, however small they may be. In the old mining valleys of South Wales in particular, the Labour Party has held absolute political control over the community since the 1920s. In these areas, the heartland of Welsh socialism, the Labour Party is a trade union party to such an extent that it is the local Trades Councils that often decide local council election nominations and it is the trade union delegates who decide constituency nominations. Even so, there have been occasions, despite the intense loyalty of the valley people to socialism and to the Labour movement, when rival socialist parties have gained an important following in these communities. In the 1930s it was the Communist Party that challenged Labour's hegemony in the valleys, and in the 1960s it was *Plaid Cymru*.

Labour's attitude to *Plaid Cymru* in Wales has normally been to discount its importance, but on occasions since 1945 severe attacks on the *Blaid* have been made by prominent Labour leaders. Suggestions that the Labour Party's decisions on policy for Wales have been influenced by the appearance of the *Blaid* on the political scene have always been strenuously denied. This does not mean that the *Blaid*'s activities have escaped Labour's notice. One familiar charge that the Labour Party seems to have brought against the *Blaid* is that either its message or its activities were akin to fascism. This charge was made at by-elections in 1946,[1] and was repeated by the Labour candidate in the Caerphilly by-election in 1968 when he warned that 'unless we are very careful we shall see an incipient form of fascism'.[2]

These fears concerning *Plaid Cymru* were given their clearest public expression in the early 1950s, culminating in the evidence given by the Welsh Regional Council of Labour to the Ince Committee of

---

[1] *Western Mail*, 6 June and 7 Dec. 1946.
[2] *Guardian*, 17 July 1968 and *Sun*, 17 July 1968.

Inquiry into Welsh Broadcasting.[1] Thus the attractiveness of the *Blaid* to Labour supporters was far from obvious at this time. It was not until the late fifties that the *Blaid* began to claim some prominent constituency Labour activists as converts: the *Blaid*'s most notable convert was Alderman Huw T. Edwards, the North Wales trade union leader and former Chairman of the Council for Wales and Monmouthshire, who left the Labour Party to join the *Blaid* in August 1959.[2] The only evidence which points in the direction of earlier recruitment from Labour circles is an academic study of social change in South-west Wales in the early 1950s which suggested that Welsh Nationalism appeared to be growing in this area. Most of the children in the study's sample of trade union leaders and their families 'were not associated with the Labour Movement. Indeed, a number were active with the Welsh Nationalists.'[3]

It was not until very late in 1955 that *Plaid Cymru* began to make any impact on the local politics of the South Wales communities (in Ynysybwl in fact). Council seats in the Rhondda were fought from 1956 onwards regularly, success coming finally in 1960. But the best results for the *Blaid* in this direction occurred in Merthyr Tydfil in 1961–2, when three seats on the county borough council were won by the *Blaid* from Labour.[4] S. O. Davies, M.P. for Merthyr, doubted the sincerity of local *Plaid* leaders' protests about the Welsh culture and Welsh nationhood and alleged that most of Merthyr's *Plaid* members were not Welsh speaking.[5] The Nationalist breakthrough in Merthyr was short-lived, and appeared to have more to do with the absence of an organized ratepayers' opposition to the council's plans for central redevelopment of the borough, than with Welsh nationhood.[6] After the May elections in 1962 the local newspaper concluded that:

> Merthyr has flattered the Welsh Nationalists only to deceive them. They must now know to their cost that there is a vast difference between piercing the labour defences by infiltration and knocking them out by frontal attack. . . .[7]

There were few signs of Nationalist revival after 1962 at local or national level in Wales until the Carmarthen by-election in July

---

[1] *Report of the Committee of Inquiry into Welsh Broadcasting 1956*, Cmnd. 39 (H.M.S.O., 1956), paras. 24–5.   [2] *Western Mail*, 7 Aug. 1959.
[3] T. Brennan, E. W. Cooney, and H. Pollins, *Social Change in South-West Wales* (London, 1954), p. 171.
[4] *Merthyr Express*, 20 May and 24 June 1961, and 24 Feb. 1962.
[5] Ibid., 6 May 1961.
[6] Ibid., 20 May and 24 June 1961, and 19 May 1962.
[7] Ibid., 19 May 1962.

1966, and little after this until the Rhondda by-election in March 1967 and the county, borough and district elections in April and May of that year.[1] Thereafter at the parliamentary by-election level, the *Blaid*'s progress between 1966 and 1968 was considerable while the Labour Party was reduced to winning West Rhondda and Caerphilly on minority votes for the first time ever.[2] In Carmarthen, a Labour majority of over nine thousand was converted into a *Plaid Cymru* majority of over two thousand. The Labour Party in its campaigns against strong *Plaid Cymru* electoral challenges did not depart from its usual concern with economic prosperity in Wales. Indeed it tended to use such arguments as that the price of Welsh Nationalism was economic impoverishment for Wales rather than tackle the issue of what rights of nationhood should accrue to Wales. Whereas in the Rhondda the *Blaid*'s challenge had not been regarded as a real threat to Labour, it was clear during the Caerphilly by-election that Labour was fighting the *Blaid*, not the Conservatives, from the very beginning. This preoccupation with the *Blaid* in Welsh Labour circles continued until the general election of 1970. In 1968 several local Labour leaders in Wales had severed their ties with the party.[3] When the Welsh Council of Labour reported to its annual meeting in May 1970 about the county council elections, it offered no comment on the Conservative performance but spent several lines commenting on the relative failure of the *Blaid*.[4] One action which the Labour Party did take was to appoint a public relations officer to the Welsh Council of Labour. The post was given to Gwynoro Jones, the Labour candidate for Carmarthen, and it enabled him to give extra attention to nursing his constituency until the general election.

It has often been argued that the presence of the *Blaid* in Welsh politics has helped to gain recognition for the Welsh culture from Governments and other political parties. It is difficult to establish in which decisions of these bodies the presence of the *Blaid* has played such a part, but if this theory is correct, the time when this phenomenon should have been seen at its clearest would have been between 1966 and 1970. It was at this time that the *Blaid* scored the greatest electoral success in its history, when the party most vulnerable to its

---

[1] See Ch. 6.
[2] F. W. S. Craig, *British Parliamentary Election Results 1918–1949* (Glasgow, 1969).
[3] *South Wales Echo*, 29 Apr. 1968.
[4] Welsh Council of Labour Executive, *Report to the Annual Meeting* (Cardiff, 1970), p. 13.

challenge, the Labour Party, was the party in government. On the economic front, it is possible to see considerable efforts being made in Wales from 1966, but it is doubtful whether much of this can be attributed to the challenge of the *Blaid* to Labour's hegemony; for the Government introduced special investment incentives for all development areas in Britain. On constitutional issues, the impact of the *Blaid* may well have been to hinder efforts being made by M.P.s and Ministers to see a measure of devolution implemented. Some politicians have argued that Labour might have taken a stronger line in favour of devolution (with regard to plans for an elected council) but for the *Blaid*'s by-election successes. The explanation for this attitude seems to be that Labour M.P.s from Wales did not wish in any way to appear to be identified with forces of Nationalism after 1966.[1] The Labour Party was naturally suffering from wounded pride as a result of the Carmarthen by-election, and some of its leaders made bitter public attacks on the *Blaid*. There existed a personal animosity between many *Plaid* and Labour politicians which others shared. Even the desire of the Labour Party to help the Welsh language seemed consequently less ardent after 1967, and at the Flint National Eisteddfod in 1969, Mrs. Eirene White, Minister of State at the Welsh Office, condemned the 'self-righteousness' of people who spoke the Welsh language. Too many people, she complained, 'elevated a proper pride in their language to idolatry'.[2] Nevertheless in other important directions, notably in accepting the recommendations of the Gittins Report, Labour's attitude to the Welsh language still continued to be sympathetic.[3]

While the Labour Party in Wales showed that it was able to beat off the *Blaid* challenge in the 1970 general election, winning back Carmarthen from Gwynfor Evans, it still remained vulnerable to attacks from Nationalists and other parties. It certainly established that economic issues were paramount still in Welsh politics. Its trade union base was as secure as ever and its hold on local government in South Wales not very seriously challenged. Just as the Labour Party in Wales survived the onslaught of the Communists in Wales in the 1930s so it appeared to have overcome the threat of *Plaid Cymru* in the 1960s. There remained certain features of the Labour Party in Wales which made its structure in 1970 insecure and its sympathy for the claims of Welsh nationality precarious. Despite the influx of

[1] Private information.   [2] *Guardian*, 4 Aug. 1969.
[3] Circular 2/69 (Department of Education and Science), Mar. 1969.

some new blood in 1969 and 1970, the Labour Party in Wales was an ageing party. Those young college lecturers who came in to advise and radicalize the party in Cardiff were not paralleled by keen youngsters joining Labour organizations at branch level. No longer did the party make much attempt to educate its members politically. There were few Young Socialist groups in evidence.[1] Local parties were 'giving very little attention . . . to the recruitment of new members and to the collection of contributions from existing members'.[2] Party membership had shown an unmistakable tendency to fall off from a peak of nearly 44,000 in 1950.[3] More sobering still was the success of S. O. Davies, M.P. for Merthyr Tydfil, in securing re-election as M.P. for the constituency in 1970. Although deprived of the Labour nomination and fighting as Independent Labour, he made his official Labour opponent look like an also-ran.[4] The rock-hard Labour loyalty was clearly being eroded as the by-elections in 1966 to 1968 had indicated.

The achievements of the Labour Party in securing a Secretary of State for Wales and a Welsh Office were very important but might never have come to pass if James Griffiths had not been chairman of the Labour Party's national policy committee in 1959, and so secured a clear commitment to these proposals.[5] The Labour Party at that time became irrevocably committed to the idea of a Secretary of State largely as a result of an accident of fate. In 1970 it seemed likely that similar accidents of fate within the Labour movement would be needed if the extent of devolution in Wales was to be furthered by Labour, for many of its leaders in Wales were still either uninterested in, or antagonistic towards ideas for devolution. The Labour Party's very dealings with the Welsh Council of Labour over the evidence to the Crowther Commission showed how little devolutionist thinking had penetrated the party. Although the party had progressed from the time in the late forties when it refused the Welsh Regional Council

---

[1] There were fewer than forty Young Socialist branches in Wales in 1969 and 1970.

[2] Welsh Council of Labour Executive Committee, *Report to the Annual Meeting* (1970), p. 13. The party organization in Wales was probably too dependent on trade union activists with a prior loyalty to their union organizations.

[3] Welsh Regional Council of Labour, *Report to the Annual Conference* (Cardiff, 1950).

[4] The process of depriving S. O. Davies of the official Labour nomination in Merthyr and the timing of the general election found the constituency Labour party in disarray. The official Labour candidate was well known in the area, but unpopular. The 1970 result was: S. O. Davies (Independent Labour), 16,701; Tal Lloyd (Labour), 9,234; Edgar Jones (Conservative), 3,169; Chris Rees (*Plaid*), 3,076.

[5] See above, pp. 282–4.

of Labour permission to change its name to the Welsh Council of Labour,[1] many of the members of the study group preparing the Crowther evidence were appalled that the Council of Labour was in such a dependent position *vis-à-vis* Transport House in London. The affair of the Crowther evidence had, curiously, succeeded in raising in Welsh Labour circles the whole issue of the party's internal structure. Another member of the study group preparing evidence for the Crowther Commission later commented that:

> For too long members of the Labour Party in Wales have sat in their front porches, looked up and down the valleys and seen their friends and relations on every Council. Secure in its valley strongholds, the Party, to many outside and to some within, appears in the same way as the enervating Union Nationale regime of Duplessis appeared to the reforming Liberals in the Quebec of the fifties, stale in their eyes in so far as it is no longer fired by idealism, appearing to wield power through patronage, shaped by events rather than shaping them.[2]

and he warned that:

> It is not Labour in Wales which is blind to the challenge of nationalism. But if its representatives at Westminster were to starve the party of an effective policy for devolution, the results may be disastrous.[2]

The Labour Party in Wales was not inflexible on questions of devolution in 1970 but it appeared that mere chance, reflected in the rise and fall in the careers of particular political personalities, might be crucial in determining the party's responses to nationalist aspirations.

The Conservative Party and Wales

In the period when nationalism first played an important part in the politics of Wales, from 1868 to 1914, the Conservative Party was generally hostile to the nationalist movement. This was directed in particular against two institutions which Conservatives wished to defend, the Church and the landowners. Conservatives did not admit that Welsh nationhood was a political reality, although they granted occasional separate legislation for Wales, notably the Welsh Intermediate Education Act of 1889.[3] After 1885 they were proud to call themselves Unionists. The Conservatives took the blame in Wales for the unemployment after the First World War; socialism was at its

---

[1] Welsh Regional Council of Labour, *Report to the Annual Conference* (Cardiff, 1948).
[2] Gerald Purnell, *Socialist Commentary*, May 1970.
[3] Kenneth O. Morgan, op. cit., pp. 307–8 especially.

most militant in the valleys, and in the rural areas the wounds caused by the battles for disestablishment had not yet healed. It was not until after the Second World War that the Conservative Party made any serious attempt to identify itself with Welsh nationality and to evolve a separate policy for Wales. As a result of strong pressures from the Conservative rank and file in Wales, coming to a head in a motion proposed by the Caernarvon Boroughs Conservative Association to the Conservative Party conference held in Llandudno in October 1947, the Conservative leadership in London was called upon to produce a Conservative policy for Wales.[1] Brigadier Enoch Powell, then of the Conservative Central Office's parliamentary secretariat, conducted two fact-finding tours of the rural and industrial areas of Wales in January and in the late Spring of 1948.[2] His report was ready by the end of May,[3] but it was not until November that a panel to advise on policy for Wales was set up, after about a year's pressure from Lt.-Col. Pryce White, M.P. for Caernarvon Boroughs;[4] this panel included Nigel Birch, M.P. for West Flintshire, and Peter Thorneycroft, M.P. for Monmouth. The final policy document was not published until St. David's Day 1949 but a clear indication of the drift of Conservative thinking was given by R. A. Butler in a speech in the House of Commons during the annual Welsh Day debate in January 1948, in which he called for an 'Ambassador for Wales'.[5] The new policy statement (which, significantly, was published in both English and Welsh) acknowledged Wales's 'separateness as a national entity' and suggested that 'one member of the Cabinet should be given special responsibility for Wales'. The statement reminded the Welsh public that Conservatives had been 'responsible for the great education acts of 1902 and 1944, under which the position of the Welsh language in Welsh education has been safeguarded' and promised that a Conservative Government would be sympathetic to 'the preservation of the Welsh language and lore'.[6] Among many reforms proposed was a reform of the law of leasehold.[7] The policy was thus very much in keeping with the liberalizing forces which were reshaping the Conservative Party and philosophy in Britain generally after the landslide defeat of 1945. In particular it accorded with

---

[1] *Western Mail*, 22 Sept. and 6 Oct. 1947.
[2] Ibid., 7 May 1948.   [3] Ibid., 28 May 1948.
[4] Ibid., 11 Dec. 1947 and 29 Nov. 1948.
[5] 446 HC Deb. Fifth Series, c. 693 (26 Jan. 1948).
[6] *The Conservative Policy for Wales and Monmouthshire* (London, 1949).
[7] Ibid., p. 7. See also J. J. Hayward, *What do you think about the Conservative Policy for Wales and Monmouthshire?* (Cardiff, 1949).

Conservative attempts to erode the Liberal vote, which in North Wales was still very strong. The new policy was not universally acceptable in Conservative circles. Lord Merthyr, a former chairman of the Pembrokeshire Conservative Association, condemned the new document as 'simply a further instalment of Welsh nationalism, which has been fostered for years by the *Western Mail* in an ill-judged effort to increase circulation'.[1] Conversely at the Conservative conference in October 1949, one delegate, the Hon. John Grigg (later Lord Altrincham), criticized the new policy for opting for a Minister with a nominated advisory council, rather than for a directly elected Parliament for Wales.[2] Another prominent figure, Sir Henry Morris-Jones, the National Liberal M.P. for Denbigh, had early in 1949 presented a bill to the Commons which would have established a Secretary of State for Wales,[3] but it was not pursued.

The Conservative manifesto produced for the 1950 general election confirmed the policy for Wales set out in 1949;[4] but this was not rewarded by any increase in the number of Conservative or allied M.P.s there. In the intervening period between the defeat in 1950 and the victory in the 1951 election, the party fought strongly against the ideas revived and expounded by the Parliament for Wales Campaign, which claimed some Conservative support.[5] A Parliament for Wales would be a Transport House Parliament was a common line of argument;[6] Lord Woolton was more outspoken on the Home Rule question when he said that 'a country for the whole of which the product of a penny rate fetches less than the City of Westminster cannot be expected to pull itself up by its own bootstraps'.[7] At the same time (and in the same speech) Lord Woolton emphasized that the Conservatives did not wish to treat Wales as a region of England, and he developed his views on the precise arrangements needed to support a Minister for Welsh Affairs. This had also been the theme of a speech by R. A. Butler, the official Conservative spokesman on Welsh affairs, in Haverfordwest in May 1951.[8] It was clear that the Conservatives were in earnest about their pledge to give special treatment to Wales,

[1] *Western Mail*, 5 Mar. 1949.   [2] *South Wales Echo*, 15 Oct. 1949.
[3] 460 HC Deb. Fifth Series, c. 1245 (28 Jan. 1949).
[4] *The Times*, 25 Jan. 1950.
[5] *Western Mail*, 31 Mar. 1951; see also *Some Questions and Answers on a Parliament for Wales* (Cardiff, 1954).
[6] See, for example, *Western Mail*, 21 May 1951. This line of argument caused real concern to the supporters of the Parliament for Wales Campaign—see Ch. 10 above.
[7] Lord Woolton, speech at Bodorgan (Anglesey), 2 Aug. 1951.
[8] *Western Mail*, 26 May 1951.

and thus, for the second time, the Conservatives entered a general election campaign with a policy on devolution that was more advanced than that of their Labour opponents.[1] The Conservatives and their National Liberal allies took 31 per cent of the votes cast in Wales at this election, and gained seats at Conway and Cardiff North. The new Minister of Welsh Affairs was Sir David Maxwell-Fyfe, who was also Home Secretary. Although a Scot, he was personally very popular and earned the nickname 'Dai Bananas';[2] but his powers were extremely limited as he was given almost no direct departmental responsibility for Wales. An occasional intervention, such as over the Towy valley scheme, which would have dislodged local tenant farmers, showed that the new office and title had some value.[3] Maxwell-Fyfe, and his successor, Gwilym Lloyd George, did not initiate much activity in Wales itself, largely because their specific responsibilities for Wales were shared with other departments. At the beginning of 1957, however, when Macmillan succeeded Eden as Prime Minister, responsibility for Welsh Affairs was transferred to the Ministry for Housing and Local Government, initially under Henry Brooke. This arrangement was generally considered more successful because the responsibility for Welsh affairs rested with the Minister already in charge of Welsh planning and local government problems.[4] When Brooke took up the problems of Wales, he found that several thorny issues were awaiting him—notably the planned drowning of the Tryweryn valley in Merioneth, and the Council for Wales's strong support for a Secretary of State for Wales. However, there was a virtually empty file on Wales in Whitehall, and Brooke had to make his own way through the morass. It was not a happy progress. On the Tryweryn issue, Brooke was conciliatory about water policy generally, and set up an Advisory Water Committee for Wales, but he defended the demands of Liverpool Corporation for Tryweryn against the opposition of nearly all the Welsh M.P.s and the bulk of Welsh opinion. The Tryweryn valley was given up to Liverpool by vote of the Commons on 31 July 1957.[5] This provoked a considerable reaction among the Welsh-speaking community and a visit planned by Brooke to the National Eisteddfod in Llangefni the following

---

[1] *The Conservative Party and Welsh Affairs* (Cardiff, 1951).
[2] 'Dai' being short for 'David'; 'Bananas' matching 'Fyffes', the banana importers.
[3] Viscount Kilmuir, *Political Adventure* (London, 1964), pp. 190–221.
[4] Lord Brooke of Cumnor, private interview, 19 Nov. 1968; Lord Brecon, private interview, 25 July 1968; David Gibson-Watt, private interview, 11 July 1968.
[5] 574 HC Deb. Fifth Series, cc. 1331–4 (31 July 1957). The voting was 175 in favour of Liverpool's bill and 79 against (excluding tellers).

week was cancelled 'in view of the likelihood of disturbance to the harmony' of the event.[1] A more important rebuff to the Government arose from its treatment of the proposals of the Council for Wales for a Secretary of State for Wales and other administrative reforms. It was over a year before the Government replied to its suggestions, and the solution of a Minister of State operating from the House of Lords, which Macmillan hit upon was greeted in Wales with a mixture of incredulity and blank despair. Even *The Economist* which was not sympathetic to Welsh demands, was moved to note that:

> The fun Labour has had with last week's announcement lies in the peculiarity of politics, not in rudeness about personalities. How an obscure Brecon county councillor, visiting London (in his tweed suit) for the University Rugger match, was called to Downing Street to be made a baron and a Minister of State, represents one of the most curious political appointments since Caligula made his horse a consul.[2]

The affair did not rest with this new appointment. The Council for Wales was highly displeased by the manner in which the Government had turned down its proposals which had been the product of two years' work. In October 1958, the chairman of the Council, Alderman Dr. Huw T. Edwards, and four of its other members resigned in protest at the Government's treatment of the Council on this issue. Dr. Edwards complained of 'a complete lack of confidence by the Government in the Council' and that this was only one occasion from many 'when the Government could and should have recognized the status of the Council as a Government-appointed advisory committee and brought the Council in on discussions affecting a whole series of Wales issues'.[3] Brooke was forced to reconstruct the Council for Wales, and himself took on its chairmanship while looking for a suitable candidate for the office. He also brought in new members to the Council 'with a wider view of Wales'. Calm was restored to the Council but it had by this time lost too much of its credibility in Wales and in Whitehall ever to become an effective body again.

Even if the Government was not interested in the proposed Secretary of State for Wales, there was more support for it in the Commons among Welsh M.P.s than could have been expected. A debate in February 1957 had produced a chorus of support from Welsh Labour M.P.s, but the Conservative M.P.s appeared divided. David

---

[1] *The Times*, 7 Aug. 1957.
[2] *The Economist*, 21 Dec. 1957, p. 1034.
[3] H. T. Edwards, op. cit., p. 159.

Llewellyn (Cardiff North) opposed the proposal and wanted the Council for Wales wound up;[1] David Gibson-Watt, who was for five years between 1965 and 1970 'shadow' Secretary of State for Wales, was also opposed to the idea of a Secretary of State.[2] The proposal was welcomed by other Conservative M.P.s, such as Raymond Gower, Garner Evans, and also by Peter Thomas, who in 1970 was to become the first Conservative Secretary of State for Wales.[3] One small concession was the decision of the Conservative Government, when Sir Keith Joseph was Minister for Welsh Affairs in 1963, to set up a Welsh economic intelligence unit, known as the 'Welsh Office', to advise him in planning the Welsh economy. It was, however, a headless body, with no Permanent Secretary and only two civil servants of the rank of Assistant Secretary.[4] The difficulty the Labour ministers had in producing an economic plan for Wales after 1964 suggests that this innovation in 1963 was little more than 'window dressing'.

In retrospect, the years 1951 to 1964 during which the Conservatives were in government were strangely blurred concerning the recognition of Wales's needs. Each attempt to show that the Conservatives wanted to help Wales was countered by errors of policy. The Conservatives were remembered not for the issue of circular 15 in 1953 which urged full bilingualism in the schools[5] or for the introduction of a Welsh books grant,[6] but by the Tryweryn episode and the decision in 1960 to appoint Mrs. Rachel Jones, a non Welsh-speaker, as chairman of the Welsh Broadcasting Council.[7] The success of Henry Brooke in keeping part of the new sheet steel and tinplate investment in Wales in 1958 against the claims of Scotland was eclipsed by the reversal of the original decision to give the Forth Bridge priority over the Severn Bridge,[8] and by the Government's lack of success in evolving a policy to revive the economically depressed areas. The high noon for the Conservatives in Wales came briefly in 1959. Tom Hooson, the Conservative candidate in Caernarvon (and brother of the future Liberal member for Montgomeryshire) was busy trying to dispel the image of his party as 'alien to Welsh cultural values'.[9] With Geoffrey Howe he produced a weighty

[1] 564 HC Deb. Fifth Series, cc. 934–45 (11 Feb. 1957).   [2] Ibid., cc. 992–6.
[3] Ibid., cc. 961–4, 968–73, and 1001–5.
[4] H. Noel Jerman, private interview, 12 Dec. 1969.
[5] Wales Circular 15 (Ministry of Education), 24 Feb. 1953.
[6] 523 HC Deb. Fifth Series, cc. 318–20 (2 Feb. 1954).
[7] The Times, 3 June 1960.   [8] Ibid., 12 Sept. and 11 Oct. 1957.
[9] T. Hooson, 'St. David's Day Speech', Wales, No. 7, Mar. 1959.

economic programme for Wales under the aegis of the Bow Group.[1] Even so, the Conservatives polled less than a third of the votes cast in Wales at the general election on October 1959, and gained only one more seat at Swansea West. The liberalism of the Welsh Conservatives continued with two private members' bills, Peter Thomas's Eisteddfod Act, passed in 1959, which allowed local authorities to support the National Eisteddfod from rate revenue, and Raymond Gower's Elections (Welsh Forms) Act of 1964 which made valid the use of Welsh versions of official election forms.[2] Yet the Conservatives reaped few electoral dividends from their benevolent attitude, and at the 1966 general election were reduced to three Welsh M.P.s and 27 per cent of the vote in Wales. In the 1970 election, they made strikingly little progress, securing only 28 per cent of the votes cast. They won seven seats, regaining Conway, Cardiff North, and Monmouth—all lost in 1966—and took Pembrokeshire on a split vote. The Conservative share of the votes cast in Wales at the 1970 election was still lower than it was in 1906, the year of the great Liberal landslide. Conservative policy for Wales showed strains in developing during the Labour Governments of 1964 to 1970. The leadership soon accepted that the party could not dismantle the new Welsh Office and its Secretary of State which had been one of the new administrative creations of the Wilson Government in 1964. Whereas the Conservative policy statement for Wales at the 1964 election had contained few new proposals,[3] the statement issued during the 1966 election was more positive and included, unexpectedly, a pledge to defederalize the University of Wales.[4] This was followed by a statement by Edward Heath during the election campaign that the Conservatives would support the development of Portbury, near Bristol, as a new port, at the probable expense of the South Wales ports.[5] The Conservatives after their election defeat in 1966 were not unmoved by the new Nationalist presence in Welsh politics, and suffered the humiliation of seeing their candidate in each of the three by-elections held in Wales during the 1966–70 Parliament lose his deposit, while in the rest of Britain the Conservative stock was rising very high. The Conservatives accepted the views of the Gittins Report

[1] T. Hooson and G. Howe, *Work for Wales* (London, 1959).
[2] 7 and 8 Eliz. II *Public General Acts and Measures*, ch. 32, pp. 546–7. 12 and 13 Eliz. II *Public General Acts and Measures*, ch. 31, p. 396.
[3] *Wales with the Conservatives* (Cardiff, 1964).
[4] *Action—not Words for Wales* (Cardiff, 1966). The pledge to defederalize the University of Wales was not renewed in 1970.
[5] *Western Mail*, 14 Mar. 1966.

in favour of a bilingual educational policy in 1968. A policy group was set up in 1967, with Gibson-Watt as chairman, to report on Welsh affairs. At their conference in March 1968 the Young Conservatives in Wales supported by a small majority the idea of an elected council.[1] In addition, pressure was growing in Wales, particularly in the North and West, for a clear statement of Conservative policy so that the rank and file could fight the Nationalists more effectively.[2] It was not until the end of January 1970 that the new policy was published (bilingually); a strong protest was made at the Conservative Party conference the previous autumn about the delay.[3] The new policy reaffirmed that the Conservatives would retain a Secretary of State for Wales and proposed that he should be given additional responsibility in the field of primary and secondary education. A reformed Welsh Council to include an elected element was proposed, although the party reserved its position on other schemes for devolution pending the report of the Crowther Commission.[4] The main drawback of the new document was that it seemed to put in jeopardy Wales's position as a development area, and even the Wales region of the Confederation of British Industry was critical of it.[5] When returned to office in June 1970, Edward Heath immediately transferred powers over primary and secondary education to the new Secretary of State, Peter Thomas, but otherwise the Conservatives proceeded cautiously in implementing their proposals for Wales.

Conservative reluctance in the 1960s towards pursuing an active policy with regard to Wales was always tempered with a recognition that times were changing and that Welsh demands could not be ignored. These demands, even within Conservative ranks in Wales, nearly always stressed that Wales required treatment different from the rest of Britain. At the same time Conservatives in Wales, as elsewhere, retained a strongly Unionist outlook which led them to express conflicting attitudes when considering the practical needs of Wales. Conservative leaders clearly recognized the political trend in Wales in the 1960s and were faced with a dilemma. David Gibson-Watt wrote in 1969 that:

If Nationalism gets much support at a General Election, pressure on the Government of the day will drive it to give concessions to Nationalism

[1] Ibid., 1 Apr. 1968.
[2] Private information.
[3] *Western Mail*, 11 Oct. 1969.   [4] *Wales into the '70s* (Cardiff, 1970).
[5] *Western Mail*, 13 Mar. 1970.

and little by little we shall arrive at the situation where Home Rule is inevitable.[1]

It is demonstrable that Conservative policy since 1945 in respect of Wales has assisted in this process of giving 'concessions to Nationalism'. The Conservative view that the economic problems of Wales were more likely to be solved by effective Unionist government than by any Nationalist panacea, did not meet the widespread demand for devolution in many sections of Welsh life, including some Conservative circles. Welsh Conservatives have found it hard to reconcile their sympathy for the Welsh cultural tradition with their strong belief in the constitutional *status quo*.

Essentially the Conservative Party is still regarded in Wales as the party of the Union; in places it is still the party of the Anglican Church—once known as the 'alien' Church, and its parliamentary candidates are often identified with the Church where candidates from other parties in Wales are more likely to have links with the chapels.[2] The party has for a long time suffered from a shortage of local leaders in Wales.

It may be said without any disrespect that many candidates who have sought election in Welsh constituencies have been unfamiliar with Welsh conditions. They have fought magnificently in the circumstances; but the fight has been hopeless; and one of the first essentials of successful political fighting in Wales is to obtain candidates familiar with local conditions, and imbued with the National spirit that animates the vast majority of Welshmen at the present day.[3]

These comments written by a prominent Conservative in 1908 applied equally to the Conservatives in Wales after 1945. They have had great difficulty in fielding candidates who were Welsh-speaking; only five were found for the 1970 election, while the Liberals found

[1] *Progress* (1968–9), Swansea University Conservative Association Yearbook, pp. 22–4.

[2] The political isolation of the Conservatives in Welsh Wales was epitomized in Cardiganshire at the time of the 1970 election. The chairman of the Cardiganshire Conservative Association was concerned that there was no Welsh-speaking farmer in the Lampeter area who was sufficiently sympathetic to the Conservatives to introduce the non Welsh-speaking Conservative candidate to other farmers. The chairman, a Welsh-speaking Lampeter solicitor, announced that he would be translating the candidate's election address into Welsh; at the previous election, this had to be farmed out to a Welsh Nationalist! A burning topic of conversation among constituency activists at the Association's fête held in May 1970 appeared to several observers to be the size of Sunday *church* collections.

[3] 'J.A.S.', 'The Welsh Nation and the Conservative Party', in *Souvenir of the Forty-Second Annual Conference 1908* (National Union of Conservative and Constitutional Associations).

thirteen. Conservatives have also found it necessary to put into the field many candidates who had no connections with Wales at all; this applied to about a quarter of their candidates in Wales in the 1970 election. It was not until 1964 that the Conservatives contested every constituency in Wales, having previously allowed Liberals in some rural areas a free run, while there were many constituencies in South Wales where the Conservative Party was politically inactive between general elections, often completely avoiding politically contested local elections.[1] Such was the precarious nature of the Welsh seats which Conservatives did succeed in winning that many of their abler Welsh politicians, such as Peter Thomas and Geoffrey Howe, have had to find seats in England. It is probable that individual Welsh people of Conservative inclination who have considered a political career have been deterred by the weakness and the stigma attaching to the Conservatives in Wales. Thus the party still wears a very English air. The organization is given only a 'provincial area' status; 'Monmouthshire' is usually added to the description 'Wales'; and English immigrants to Wales are prominent at every level of the party. When it has held an annual meeting in the past it has been as likely to be in Shrewsbury or Chester as in a Welsh locality.[2] Despite assurances that the party is changing at the grass roots, the Conservatives still wear well the image of the party of England in Wales, and are thus appropriately wedded to the union of the two countries. If Conservative voting were to be regarded as an index of the degree of Wales's assimilation with England, then it would be seen that this assimilation has not progressed very far in Wales, and not at all in the last twenty years.

Welsh Liberalism and Welsh Nationalism

Before 1914 the only political voice of Welsh nationalism was the Liberal Party, and the Liberal Party succeeded in identifying itself strongly with campaigns for Welsh Home Rule and Welsh disestablishment. Lloyd George described himself for many years as a Welsh Nationalist, and Liberals in Wales, even in the 1970s, boast of the achievements of Liberal Governments in Welsh affairs, beginning with

---

[1] e.g. Llanelli, Rhondda West and East, Aberdare, Caerphilly, Pontypridd, Ebbw Vale, Abertillery, and Bedwellty constituencies.

[2] The annual meeting of the Wales and Monmouthshire Area Council was held at Chester in 1953 and in 1961, and at Shrewsbury in 1957. The area executive committee met at Ludlow on one occasion in 1952. In more recent years area meetings have almost invariably been held in Wales, perhaps a sign of the times.

the Welsh Sunday Closing legislation of 1881.[1] After 1918, however, the Liberal Party in Wales succumbed quickly to the challenge of socialism and the Labour movement in South Wales, especially when Lloyd George refused to implement the Sankey proposals to nationalize the mines. It suddenly found itself entirely a rural party, and riven with the splits in the party at large; first, the Asquith–Lloyd George split, and later the division in 1931 between Simonites, Samuelites, and the followers of Lloyd George. There was the famous series of Cardiganshire elections between 1921 and 1923 when Liberal fought Liberal;[2] and in 1931 Lloyd George and three members of his family were returned as Independent Liberals opposed to the 'National Government', unlike the rest of the party.[3] *Plaid Cymru* had also arrived on the Welsh political scene and was attracting a section of the Liberal intelligentsia away from the old party.[4] And yet the Liberals were still a substantial force in Welsh politics in the interwar years. In the 1929 election, Liberals polled a third of the votes in Wales and carried ten Welsh constituencies; the Conservatives won one seat only, and polled 22 per cent of the vote. Liberalism was still as Welsh as Wales itself, and was active at student level, where Cledwyn Hughes began his political career as a Liberal,[5] and in the constituencies; as late as 1939 there were over a hundred local Women's Liberal Associations in the five North Wales counties affiliated to the Women's Liberal Federation.[6] In the 1945 to 1950 Parliament, seven out of the twelve Liberal M.P.s sat for Welsh constituencies.[7]

The Liberals did not in this period, or later, always stick to the letter of the Home Rule platform with which they had long been associated. There was some wavering in the 1930s, when Liberals narrowed their sights towards the immediate objective of a Secretary of State for Wales. Few Welsh Liberal candidates in the 1945 general election promised more than support for a Secretary of State. The

---

[1] Emlyn Hooson, *Llythyr at Etholwyr Cymru* (Cardiff, 1970).

[2] See Kenneth O. Morgan, 'Cardiganshire Politics: the Liberal Ascendancy, 1885–1923', in *Ceredigion* V. No. 4 (1967), pp. 331–7.

[3] The four M.P.s were David Lloyd George (Caernarvon Boroughs); Megan Lloyd George (Anglesey) and Gwilym Lloyd George (Pembroke)—daughter and son; and Goronwy Owen (Caernarvonshire)—family relation.

[4] See 'Wales Minor', 'Unrest in Wales', in *Liberal Magazine*, Jan. 1935.

[5] See *The Dragon*, magazine of the University College of Wales, Aberystwyth, vol. LVIII, Michaelmas Term 1935 and Summer Term 1936, and vol. LIX, Michaelmas Term 1936.

[6] Liberal Party of Wales MSS.

[7] Anglesey, Merioneth, Montgomery, Cardigan, Pembroke, Carmarthen, and the University of Wales.

Liberals remained the largest party, in terms of parliamentary representation, in Wales, outside Glamorgan and Monmouthshire, until 1950. They were still very much the expression of the Welsh radical tradition and Welsh nonconformity. At the annual meeting of the Liberal Party of Wales in 1948, for example, two of the four resolutions carried concerned the subject of drink. One called upon the Government 'to introduce legislation prohibiting the sale of intoxicating liquors in clubs in Wales and Monmouthshire'.[1] The old divisions inside the party continued to manifest themselves, and at one point in the 1940s, Hopkin Morris, M.P. for Carmarthen, resigned the Whip. Professor W. J. Gruffydd noted in the House of Commons how the cream of the intellectuals were joining the *Blaid*.[2] But young recruits to the party were forcing it to take up again the question of a Parliament for Wales, and they found support from Emrys Roberts, the young Liberal M.P. for Merioneth, who was in command of Liberal organization in Wales. The Liberal Party Assembly at Hastings in 1949 followed the Assembly of 1947 in supporting the call for separate Parliaments for Wales and Scotland, with only six votes opposing.[3] In the following autumn, the Liberals were making plans to launch a Welsh equivalent of the Scottish Covenant, all of which were merged into the Parliament for Wales Campaign in 1950.[4] The 1950 and 1951 elections were disastrous for Liberals in Wales, more so than for Liberals in the rest of Britain. The party's recommitment to a Home Rule platform[5] did not save it from seeing its representation in Wales halved, with all three M.P.s remaining—in Carmarthen, Cardiganshire, and Montgomeryshire—elected without Conservative opposition. There were grave disputes inside the party about whether and where Liberals should oppose the Conservatives. Clement Davies, the Liberal leader and M.P. for Montgomeryshire, had to disown a Liberal peer, Lord Rennell, who urged Liberals in Brecon and Radnor to vote for the Conservative candidate in preference to the Liberal.[6] The attitude of the Welsh Liberals to the Conservative Party was to bedevil their political direction for at least the next decade, for they were beginning to feel that their survival as a political force in Wales depended on

---

[1] Annual Meeting of the Liberal Party of Wales in Carmarthen, 22 May 1948.
[2] *The Times*, 29 Oct. 1946.   [3] Ibid., 26 Mar. 1949.
[4] See Chs. 9 and 10.
[5] The Liberal manifestos for the 1950 and 1951 elections both contained this pledge. See *The Times*, 6 Feb. 1950 and 4 Oct. 1951.
[6] *The Times*, 20 Feb. 1950.

Conservative help. This was not to be without long-term effect on the fortunes of Welsh Liberalism. Meanwhile the Lloyd George element in the party was sharply reduced. Gwilym Lloyd George, who was defeated in Pembrokeshire by Desmond Donnelly in 1950 as a joint Liberal and Conservative candidate, found a seat in Newcastle in 1951 as a Conservative and became a minister in Churchill's Cabinet. Lady Megan Lloyd George, who lost her seat in Anglesey in 1951, declined an invitation to stand there again as the Liberal candidate on the grounds that she had 'latterly been disturbed by the pronounced tendency of the official Liberal Party to drift towards the Right'.[1] Lady Megan gave most of her political attention in the early fifties to the Parliament for Wales Campaign, and eventually joined the Labour Party in 1955.[2] Most of the public Liberal pronouncements at this time concerned the campaign for a Welsh Parliament, but an occasional theme stressed co-operation between Liberals and Nationalists in Wales, which was already happening as a result of the campaign.[3] Nothing materialized from this dialogue and as the Parliament for Wales Campaign progressed leading Welsh Liberals began to lose interest in the issue of self-government, on which any such co-operation between Liberals and the *Blaid* would have centred. Despite the growing influence inside Welsh Liberal counsels at this time of a young group of recent graduates headed by Emlyn Hooson and Glyn Tegai Hughes, vitality was not restored to Welsh Liberalism, even when elsewhere in Britain a new breeze was beginning to fill out the Liberal sails again after 1955. As one Liberal observed, 'the talent and enthusiasm available to Liberals in Wales . . . is being frustrated by our habit of muddling on'.[3] The nadir was reached early in 1957 with the by-election in Carmarthen which followed the death of Sir Rhys Hopkin Morris. While Labour adopted Lady Megan Lloyd George as their candidate, the Liberals chose as candidate John Morgan Davies who, unlike the party at large, supported the British invasion of the Suez Canal zone[4] and boasted of the support of the Carmarthen Conservative Association.[5] Even so, the Liberal

---

[1] Lady Megan Lloyd George to W. Shubert Jones, J.P., 5 Nov. 1952—Liberal Party of Wales MSS.

[2] *The Times*, 26 Apr. 1955.

[3] *Denbighshire Free Press*, 12 Jan. 1952.

[4] Alan Watkins, *The Liberal Dilemma* (London, 1966), pp. 84–5.

[5] The Liberals published in a leaflet the statement of the chairman of the Carmarthen Conservative Association saying: 'I urge all Conservatives to record their votes in favour of Mr. Morgan Davies who, I am sure, will follow in the very able footsteps of our late beloved Member.'

failed to hold this seat and Lady Megan was returned with a majority of over three thousand. The theme of 'peace and liberty' as against 'the inhuman control of the state'[1] and the intervention of the aged Lord Samuel, the former Liberal leader, urging Liberals not to vote for Lady Megan could not prevent the slow erosion of Liberalism in Carmarthen. The 1959 election did not see the Liberals making much progress in Wales, particularly as many more *Plaid Cymru* candidates opposed Liberals in the contests. The Liberals simply hung on to their ancient citadels in Cardiganshire and Montgomeryshire, despite the presence of a Conservative candidate in the latter seat. It is clear, however, that at this time the Welsh Liberal leadership was becoming ever more aware of the threat of *Plaid Cymru*'s political challenge. They were particularly concerned with the publicity that the *Blaid* attracted to itself, compared with the minimal coverage given to Liberals in Wales, and with the political advantage the *Blaid* gained over the Liberals in being an independent Welsh party. This led the secretary of the Liberal Party of Wales, Madoc Jones, to conclude:

> I believe we have reached a point where we must recognise the Nationalist challenge. We dare not try to ignore it. And I feel sure that a positive and constructive remedy for the situation would be for the Liberal Party of Wales to declare itself an autonomous and quite independent organisation—similar to the Scottish Liberal Party which has no affiliation—financially—with the Liberal Party.[2]

This proposal was well received by many including Emlyn Hooson, but there was spirited opposition to it from within the South Wales Liberal Federation. This concern with the political advance of *Plaid Cymru*, which had put up twenty candidates to the Liberals' eight in the 1959 election, was also strongly voiced by Alun Talfan Davies, a leading barrister who had recently become prominent in Welsh Liberal circles.[3] He noted that it was evidently the *Blaid*'s intention to obliterate the Liberal Party from the Welsh political scene and protested that Dominion Status for Wales was as dead as the dodo,

---

[1] Leaflet printed by Carmarthen Liberals during the by-election campaign (in the author's possession).

[2] G. W. Madoc Jones, 'The Future of the Liberal Party in Wales', unpublished memorandum.

[3] Alun Talfan Davies was associated with *Plaid Cymru* for a time in the 1930s. He contested the University of Wales by-election in 1943 against W. J. Gruffydd and Saunders Lewis, standing as an Independent. He was short-listed in 1945 for the nomination for the vacant Liberal seat of Cardiganshire, and later fought three elections as a Liberal between 1959 and 1966. Davies was for a time Chairman of the Liberal Party of Wales, and was (and is) a prominent figure in Welsh publishing and television, and at the Welsh Bar.

following the election.[1] The Welsh Liberals were evidently in some disarray because the Nationalists appeared to have seized the initiative in the politics of Welsh devolution. It was, however, some consolation that Lord Ogmore, a former minister in Attlee's Government, left the Labour ranks shortly after the 1959 election to join the Liberals; he was to play a major part in their development in Wales in the 1960s.

Liberals in Wales were not unaffected by the Liberal revival in England which became marked in 1957. An annual summer school was initiated and new blood was brought into the party. The early sixties saw new pamphlets and policy being produced, all stressing Welsh nationhood and the need for a Welsh assembly; Patrick Lort-Phillips, Alun Talfan Davies, and Edward Nevin, an academic economist, each made a contribution to the flow of ideas through the Welsh Radical Group.[2] At local government level Liberal candidates, mainly in South Wales, were having some success in securing election to local councils from 1961 onwards, in Cardiff, Newport, and Llanelli especially. Liberals contested Ebbw Vale at the 1960 by-election for the first time since 1929 and narrowly failed to keep their deposit;[3] when another highly industrial seat fell vacant at Swansea East in 1963, the Liberal candidate came second in the poll with 15 per cent of the vote.[4] But the climax to Liberal efforts in Wales came in May 1962, a few weeks after the famous Orpington by-election, when Montgomeryshire voters went to the polls to elect a successor to the late Clement Davies. Emlyn Hooson, as Liberal candidate, scored a notable victory by collecting more than half the votes cast in this four-cornered contest;[5] the *Blaid*'s candidate fared badly and polled only 6 per cent of the vote. Now it was the Nationalists who were in disarray, and they continued thus until July 1966. Yet the Liberal tide did not flow strongly for long; after the local elections in Spring 1964, it was clear that the Liberals in Wales had lost much of the

[1] A. Talfan Davies, 'Some Reflections on the Election', in *Challenge*, No. 2, Spring 1960.

[2] See P. Lort-Phillips, *The Future of Wales* (Carmarthen, 1961); E. T. Nevin, *Wales in the 60s* (London, 1962).

[3] The Ebbw Vale result in November 1960 was: M. Foot (Labour) 20,528, Sir B. Rhys Williams (Conservative) 3,799, P. Lort-Phillips (Liberal) 3,449, E. Roberts (*Plaid*) 2,091.

[4] The Swansea East result in March 1963 was: N. McBride (Labour) 18,909, R. Owens (Liberal) 4,895, Revd. L. Atkin (Independent) 2,462, Miss P. Thomas (Conservative) 2,272, E. C. Rees (*Plaid*) 1,620, B. Pearce (Communist) 773.

[5] The Montgomery result in May 1962 was: H. E. Hooson (Liberal) 13,181, R. H. Dawson (Conservative) 5,632, T. Davies (Labour) 5,299, Revd. I. Ff. Elis (*Plaid*) 1,594.

ground captured since 1959 and this was confirmed by the 1964 general election results. For the first time since the war Liberal candidates were everywhere opposed by Conservatives. The Liberal Party of Wales brought out a detailed policy document for the election for the first time in years, but it modified its devolution proposals to a pledge to support an elected Council for Wales as a first step.[1] This was echoed in the Liberal manifesto, and thus represented a step backwards from full support for a Welsh Parliament which had been the Liberal position in 1959. Lord Ogmore and Lort-Phillips had both emphasized the need for some administrative base, such as a civil service, on which to found any Welsh legislature. The 1964 election in Wales did not reveal the greatly increased Liberal support recorded in England and Scotland, although in Anglesey and West Flint the Liberal showing improved greatly, and creditable results were seen in Pembrokeshire, Monmouth, and Cardiff North. Still, no seats had been gained, and Cardiganshire, for the first time, seemed to be slipping from the Liberals' grasp.

The role of the Liberals in the 1964–6 Parliament was vital to the Labour Government with its majority of three. Much attention was therefore given to Liberal activity in the British press, although the party's strategy of radical re-alignment had been shipwrecked by Labour's victory. In Wales, work was beginning on a Liberal economic plan for the nation, and the first fruit of this was a plan for mid Wales published in July 1965 suggesting how its economy could be built up with agriculture still as the basic industry.[2] A monthly *Welsh Liberal News* was started but only two issues appeared. The main focus of attention in Liberal ranks turned to Roderic Bowen, M.P. for Cardiganshire since 1945, when the Speakership of the House of Commons became vacant in 1965 with the death of Sir Harry Hylton-Foster. Bowen was one of the main candidates for the succession. The Government's majority in the House of Commons looked as if it might be reduced to one vote only, if two opposition M.P.s did not fill two of the three Speakership positions. The Liberals generally were unwilling to lose one of their ten M.P.s in this way or to appear to be propping up the Government. Bowen eventually accepted the second Deputy Speakership, but in March 1966 he lost his seat at the general election. The Liberals were

---

[1] *Liberal Partnership in Wales* (Maesteg, 1964).
[2] H. E. Hooson and G. Jenkins, *The Heartland: a Plan for Mid-Wales* (London, 1965).

thus left with only one M.P. in Wales—Emlyn Hooson in Mont-gomeryshire. The party's manifesto had promised an elected Council for Wales with large powers[1] in the context of a federal Britain, and the Liberal Assembly in Brighton the following autumn approved once more a resolution supporting separate Parliaments for Scotland and Wales.[2] In 1968 Lord Ogmore introduced a Government of Wales Bill into the House of Lords, but only seventeen peers supported it, fifteen of them Liberals, as against eighty-six who opposed, even with the Government taking a neutral view of the idea.[3] In the House of Commons, three Home Rule bills were introduced by Liberal M.P.s in the 1966–70 Parliament but they did not make progress.[4] Immediately after the general election, plans to make the Liberal Party in Wales an independent body were confirmed. The executive of the party in Wales approved the scheme in June 1966 and a full meeting of the party endorsed it in September, with some opposition from South Wales.[5] Thus at the third attempt the Welsh Liberals became masters in their own house, but the path thenceforward was difficult. Although claiming twenty thousand party members in Wales,[6] it was difficult to persuade the more independent constituency Liberal associations to co-operate with the Welsh Liberal Party. Meanwhile the Nationalists were exultant after their victory at the Carmarthen by-election in July 1966; the Liberals had come an indifferent third. Gradually the party pulled itself together after years of neglect and bickering in the relations between Welsh constituencies and Liberal headquarters in London. An office and a full-time secretary were based in Aberystwyth from 1968 to 1970, and a policy directorate met infrequently to decide policy. The party's resources for sustaining activity were still small in comparison with its opponents. Constituency associations were established in about thirty of the thirty-six seats in Wales, and eventually nineteen candidates contested the general election in 1970, eight more than in the previous election, and the largest number of Liberals to fight in

---

[1] *The Times Guide to the House of Commons 1966* (London, 1966), pp. 297–8.
[2] *Guardian*, 22 Sept. 1966.
[3] 288 HL Deb., cc. 702–64 (30 Jan. 1968).
[4] Liberal M.P.s were active throughout the 1966–70 Parliament in pressing for devolution to Scotland and Wales. Russell Johnston, M.P. for Inverness, introduced his Scottish Self-Government Bill on 30 Nov. 1966; Emlyn Hooson followed on 1 Mar. 1967 with his Government of Wales Bill. The Liberal leader, Jeremy Thorpe, introduced a Federal Government Bill on 21 Feb. 1968, and James Davidson, M.P. for West Aberdeenshire, pressed his Scotland and Wales (Referenda) Bill to a second Reading on 14 Feb. 1969. None of these bills made any progress in Parliament.
[5] *Western Mail*, 9 and 13 June 1966.   [6] Ibid., 29 Nov. 1966.

Wales since 1950. It was obvious that the formation of the Welsh Liberal Party was having some effect on the liveliness of the party in Wales, a case of successful devolution in practice, but the political climate in which this counter-attack was made proved distinctly unfavourable. The Welsh Liberals did not have as much energy in their ranks as *Plaid Cymru*, and they did not offer such clear-cut solutions to the problems of Wales. Their traditional vote in rural Wales was still being eroded (in some areas dramatically) by Labour and by the *Blaid*, but they were once more making an impression in some parts of South Wales, notably Pontypridd and Tredegar. The Welsh Liberal Party emerged from this election, blooded but not finished as a political force. The broad-front tactics of *Plaid Cymru* had meant that the Nationalists in Wales had emerged with many more votes than the Liberals who had fought half as many seats. However, the *Blaid* had lost its seat at Carmarthen, while the Liberals had retained Montgomeryshire, and on average Liberal candidates in Wales still polled more votes than their Nationalist opponents. Inevitably, talk of ways in which the two parties could co-operate revived as a result of the election, but the problem of how far the support of these parties is interchangeable remained a major obstacle to co-operation in practice. The two parties each collected strong support from only one section of Welsh society, the small farmer. It was difficult to see how this could act as a secure base for concerted action. And yet there was a strong feeling among many Welsh Liberals that the *Blaid* and the Liberals and the devolutionist wing of the Labour Party had much in common. What had yet to be found was a course of political action which would unite all three groups. In the meantime the three groups remained in conflict, contested elections against each other, and could point only to limited political achievements. The electoral system was certainly a major cause of this disunity but so was the very Welshness of all the protagonists.

The question yet remains as to why the Liberals were unable to pose as the radical-nationalist alternative to Labour in the 1960s in Wales. The Liberal base in Wales has long been eroded by industrialization and anglicization. In addition, the long period of co-operation between Liberals and Conservatives in Wales which lasted until the 1960s was an important factor. Shades of this old alliance remained in Carmarthen and Cardigan even after 1966.[1] This prevented the

---

[1] *Carmarthen Journal*, 22 Nov. 1968, 21 Feb. and 2 May 1969; *Carmarthen Times*, 2 May 1969; *Cambrian News*, 5 June 1970.

Liberals in rural Wales from becoming a radical party in the Grimond image and confined its social base to local establishments. The conservative ethos which the Liberal Party in Wales acquired as a result of this co-operation remained long after the alliance between the parties was terminated. Yet the Welsh Liberals were only able to occupy this conservative ground in Welsh politics because of the failure of the Conservative Party in Wales to acquire a truly Welsh base. While Liberals and Nationalists shared many of the same cultural ideals, they differed in the extent of their tolerance and radicalism. Because the Welsh Liberals allowed themselves to appear as a relatively conservative party, they allowed *Plaid Cymru* to stand out as the one alternative for radicals disillusioned with Labour.

Conclusion

It would be a mistake to assume from the description of the various parties' attitudes to Welsh nationalism that Welsh issues have generally been a major concern of all the political parties active in Wales since 1945. The problems of the British economy and of unemployment, of expansion in the social services, and of world peace have normally dominated the speeches of Welsh politicians and the thinking of the Welsh electorate. Increasingly these problems have tended to be viewed in a specifically Welsh context, at least since the end of the Second World War. The political parties competing with *Plaid Cymru* have made more effort to present themselves as Welsh parties and to promote their policies for Wales separately—usually in the form of special manifestos and pamphlets covering Welsh affairs. In their election addresses, candidates from each of the Conservative, Labour, and Liberal parties in Wales have increasingly devoted more attention to Welsh issues and have more frequently used the Welsh language as a medium for presenting their message. With regard to specific policy for Wales, each of the parties has made more effort to present a detailed programme for Welsh problems, particularly when out of office. The Conservatives issued their most comprehensive policy documents for Wales in 1950 and in 1970. Major changes of policy were effected in 1949 and 1957 concerning Welsh administration—the former while the Conservatives were in opposition, the latter while in office in response to pressure from the Council for Wales. On cultural issues, the Conservatives have developed a sympathy for the special needs of Wales and Conservatives can fairly claim to have helped to support the language from the Butler Education Act of 1944 to the acceptance of the Gittins Report in 1968, although here the fact that the party was in opposition and very much aware of the Nationalist upsurge may have been crucial to its acceptance of so nationalist a report. The Labour Party can equally claim to have modified its policy for Wales in a nationalist direction, at least after 1946 when Attlee rejected the Welsh M.P.s' demands for a Secretary of State for Wales. But the changes of policy have always come slowly and uncertainly. The final change in favour of a Secretary of State came in 1959 fifteen years after the Welsh Regional Council of Labour declared its support for the institution. Again, the fact that Labour was in opposition at this time was probably important in persuading the party to accept the proposal. It appears that whenever either of the two main parties has spent a long period in opposition it has become more responsive to Welsh demands. The Liberal Party has always been a cultural-nationalist party in Welsh politics and continued to be so after 1945, taking up with intermittent enthusiasm calls for a Welsh Parliament and the protection of the Welsh language. So long as it retains an unusually strong following in Welsh Wales, it can be expected to remain an ally of Welsh political nationalism even if the party's political development in Wales has been arrested since the 1940s thus making it uncharacteristically conservative in outlook. There are, however, several signs that the axis of Liberalism in Wales is changing; that the Nationalists have succeeded in taking much of the Liberal support in rural West and North-west Wales, but that in Eastern Wales Liberalism is more secure. The party is becoming anglicized, and to remain a distinct political entity it may well be forced to make its radicalism plainer, in order to occupy different ground from the Conservatives. It was anglicized Wales which recorded the partial Liberal revival in the early 1960s, rather than Welsh Wales and it is anglicized Wales which has shown signs of losing its primordial loyalty to Labour as the fabric of society has been transformed. In these areas, the need for a radical opposition to Labour is strongly felt in many quarters. In places the Liberal Party has begun to provide this, but usually it has been the Nationalists who have offered the only organized opposition. Their image is, however, tarnished by so-called 'extremism' towards the use of force and the recognition of the Welsh language. Nationalist support in north Glamorgan in the 1960s was not simply a demand for devolution; it was a demand for a new society, offering secure employment and the full benefits of modern culture and science. To this extent the attempts of the three major British parties to adopt a more Welsh stance missed the point of the Nationalist protest. The demand for a Welsh government was the expression of a demand for radical change in the conditions of life in the older areas of Wales. It is an open question whether a Welsh government could fulfil this demand for change, and it is clear that if the modernization of the Glamorgan valleys could be achieved without the loss of population and of community so far observed then the demand for a Welsh government in this area would fade. Welsh-consciousness, however, would not be so transient a phenomenon since there remain so many forces in Welsh life which foster it. Support for effective administrative and political recognition of Wales is therefore unlikely to evaporate with full economic prosperity.

The political situation in rural Welsh Wales is very different, and the sources of Nationalist support here have been much more cultural in origin. *Plaid Cymru* mobilized in most of these areas a core of support which was acutely conscious of the decline in the structure of its own community—the chapel, the small farm, the rural school, and the Welsh language which knits them together into a distinct way of life. Nationalist demands were opposed to anglicization and in favour of increased employment opportunities, although these two attitudes often appear to be incompatible. Nationalist voting became a defence mechanism, a protest against a socio-economic process of rationalization which governments and the main political parties could at best delay but never reverse. Essentially *Plaid Cymru* tried to ride the two horses of modernization and of the conservation of Welsh life, the former in urban Wales, the latter in rural Wales. But whereas in rural Wales the *Blaid*'s support is deep-rooted, in urban Wales the Nationalist hold is tenuous. It could easily represent a passing phase if either the Labour Party rekindled the flame of idealism and modernized its machine and its methods in the industrial valleys of Wales, or some other potentially radical force—such as the Liberals—without the negative reputation under which the *Blaid* labours, were to attempt to organize on a wide scale opposition to the frequently apathetic and conservative local Labour and trade union hierarchies in these areas. If neither eventuality were to occur, the Nationalists seem likely to remain a small but tightly organized force in industrialized and anglicized Wales, but with interests increasingly seen to be diverging from those of fellow Nationalists in rural Wales. In the meantime, *Plaid Cymru* has fairly claimed to have played a major part in persuading the other political parties in Wales to show the true colours of their nationalist pretensions and in urging them along the path to devolution. In this respect the *Blaid* compensated for the smallness of its numbers by intense activity and by assiduous political pressure so that, since the mid 1950s, none of the other political parties has been able to ignore its presence and its political challenge. It would, however, be a mistake to credit much of the new nationalism of Conservatives, Labour supporters, and Liberals solely to the competition offered by the *Blaid* to their parties. The same intensification of Welsh-consciousness that allowed the *Blaid* to make a political impact in the 1960s had also been slowly making its mark on the other parties since the 1940s. The effect of the *Blaid*'s new success in 1966 was not to cause the other parties to change their views about nationalism but rather to hasten their identification with demands for separate treatment and the recognition of Wales in British politics.

12

CONCLUSION

THIS survey of modern Welsh nationalism and of *Plaid Cymru* has shown that nationalism has permeated the outlook of many institutions in Welsh social life, and that it found new favour in political circles in the 1960s. By nationalism is meant the active solidarity of a human collectivity which shares a common culture (or a common fund of significant experiences and interests), which conceives of itself as a nation, and which strives for political unity and self-government.[1] Welsh nationalism is formed of three component parts: an ideology, which maintains that a nation has an inalienable right to self-government; a social movement which aims to promote solidarity among the Welsh people and support for national demands; and a group consciousness which extends far beyond the political horizon into the general social and cultural attitudes of the population. In these respects, Welsh nationalism is typical of many nationalisms in world politics.

However, it also suffers from particular disadvantages which arise from the divided condition of Welsh society. The nationalist ideology concerning the nation-state is held by only a small minority of people in Wales, and was not even the inspiration behind the foundation of *Plaid Cymru* in 1925;[2] it was the desire to preserve the place of the Welsh language in Welsh society that gave rise to the Nationalist Party. Thus nationalists in Wales are not sure in themselves about the demand for self-government. Saunders Lewis has argued that it would be a tragedy for the Welsh language if Wales achieved self-government before the language was fully established with official status equal with that of English.[3] *Plaid Cymru* leaders have privately admitted that the time is not right in Wales for self-government to be a success. This uncertainty about the ideal of self-government for Wales stems from the nation's divided self. Nationalists do not want to see Welsh

---

[1] This definition arises from the discussion in K. Symmons-Symonolewicz, *Modern Nationalism* (New York, 1968), pp. 24–8.
[2] See Ch. 1.
[3] Saunders Lewis, *Tynged yr Iaith*.

nationhood in practice until there is a greater consensus in the country about the place of the Welsh language and culture in the community. Immediate independence for Wales would most likely lead to the continued stifling of the language, according to this view, and would thus lose much of its attractiveness to nationalists. The sense of solidarity among Welsh people, regardless of language, has yet to be created. This is seen as one of the functions of *Plaid Cymru*, but the gulf between the communities appears to be widening, and the task of combining their interests within one nationalist movement is inherently difficult. If the *Blaid* emphasizes the larger role of the Welsh language it wishes to see in Wales, it threatens the geographical unity of Wales by alienating anglicized South Wales. If, instead, it emphasizes the economic demands of Wales and plays down the language issue, then it may sacrifice the support of Welsh speakers who form the party's hard core. The *Blaid* has not conceded much to the non-Welsh speaking community in its language policy since 1945; rather it has tried to convince non Welsh-speakers of the merits of bilingualism, and it has not succeeded in allaying the fears many people in South Wales have concerning the implications of bilingualism for employment opportunities and public administration. On the other hand, if there was disagreement about nationalist ideology and an absence of national solidarity in Wales which made the progress of a nationalist party hazardous, there was a large measure of Welsh-consciousness which became pronounced in the 1960s and which was considerably assisted by *Plaid Cymru*. The party's most tangible achievement was to accelerate popular emphasis on the separate identity of Wales at this time, and to establish this as an essential and incontrovertible factor in Welsh politics. Even so *Plaid Cymru* did not find it easy to turn Welsh-consciousness to political advantage.

The spread of nationalist thinking was, however, mainly confined to cultural and political circles. Welsh nationalism, even after 1966, made virtually no impression on the trade union movement, and won no proclaimed adherents from the ranks of academic economists or industrialists. Yet *Plaid Cymru*'s impact on Wales was considerable, and far from confined to party politics. Its political successes after 1965 made the Nationalist viewpoint respectable and encouraged its expression in organizations where it had previously lain quiescent. Welsh nationalism became a subject of free and serious discussion in every stratum of society. In addition, it offered an alternative ideology to socialism, one which also accepted much socialist thinking, at a time when disillusion was rife within the ranks of the Labour Party. Welsh nationalism was not, however, born in a day; it had been an essential feature in the spectrum of Welsh political philosophies for well over a century. The *Blaid*'s relatively poor result in the 1970 general election could do little to halt the progress of nationalist thinking in many Welsh cultural, educational, and religious organizations. *Plaid Cymru* itself revived discussion of devolution at a political level throughout Britain and, although only supported by one-ninth of Welsh voters in 1970, it still showed that it had become a political minority to be reckoned with, and that its political challenge could not be dismissed. The *Blaid* uniquely expresses a viewpoint too intense, coherent, and widely shared to fade away in the near future.

The causes of the new political development of Welsh nationalism are hard to determine with any certainty. Ardent Nationalists believed that the logic of their ideology was bound to be accepted sooner or later by the Welsh people. Implicitly they accepted that Wales could scarcely be counted a nation if its people rejected indefinitely the political consequences of nationalism. A more probable explanation is that the political situation and general conditions in Wales had changed so as to make nationalism attractive in the 1960s where it had not been twenty or thirty years before.

An important reason for this change lies in the transformation of *Plaid Cymru* since 1925. Whereas the party started out almost as a cultural conservationist society, under the dominance of Saunders Lewis, it became increasingly involved with economic issues. Under the leadership of Gwynfor Evans, the party lost its pan-European perspective, while interest in political uses of violence was strongly discouraged. Evans was a more politically acceptable figure than Lewis, and was part of the nonconformist tradition. In time he inspired a devotion from his supporters equal to Lewis's following, and he developed political skills which kept the party united even in times of severe electoral frustration. Although essentially a cultural nationalist, he continued the flexibility of approach towards the political situation which first became apparent in 1945—when the party had campaigned to keep the territorial integrity of Wales intact for planning purposes, and had suspended its demands for self-government. This flexibility was instanced again in 1946 when the party fought the Aberdare and Ogmore by-elections on the issue of unemployment, not devolution, and in 1950 when the party joined the Parliament for Wales campaign and subscribed to a platform which ruled out dominion status. When the *Blaid* came to contest the Rhondda West by-election in 1967, it played upon the economic uncertainty prevalent in the valley without having developed a solution for the Rhondda's economic difficulties. The *Blaid* was clearly not averse to putting on a new face in order to meet new political situations, but after 1945 it was increasingly forced to give more attention to economic issues and policy. It became generally accepted by the public that it was the task of governments to manage the economy. The *Blaid* had traditionally been happy to highlight particular economic grievances in Wales, and it was a long time before it gave such consideration to over-all economic strategy. There was a considerable gap between the contributions of Dr. D. J. Davies in the thirties and the efforts of the Research Group from 1967. A change in the party's development was, however, noticeable from about 1960. South Walians were again coming to play a prominent role in the *Blaid* and Gwynfor Evans was beginning to redefine his ideas concerning the economic status of Wales.[1] The party tried to adopt an integrated, if not very sophisticated, approach to Wales's economic problems. Yet when the *Blaid* came to fight the Carmarthen and Rhondda by-elections it still had little detailed economic policy, beyond the promise of independent Welsh boards to plan the use of the country's resources. The reconstitution of the party's economic programme was not evident until 1968. The *Blaid*'s political impact at the by-elections in Rhondda and Caerphilly was nevertheless achieved by skilful campaigning on economic issues, even if the victory at Carmarthen was *sui generis*. The party devoted much effort to building up an economic plan for Wales, and its continuing interest in the Welsh economy enabled it to make political headway in Glamorgan and Monmouth on an unprecedented scale. Economic affairs dominated the *Blaid*'s annual conferences, even though the ranks of the party activists were still dominated by individuals whose interests in nationalism was cultural in origin.

Major changes in Welsh social life have also helped to swell the nationalist tide. The very fact that people in Wales, and in South Wales in particular, no longer regard the Labour Party with the trust and respect that it knew a quarter of a century ago, points to a recent

---

[1] Gwynfor Evans, *Self-Government for Wales and a Common Market for Britain* (Cardiff, 1960).

change of outlook in many Welsh people. Public attitudes have been conditioned by repeated governmental failure to get to the root of the difficulties of the Welsh economy and by the contraction of major staple industries in Wales in the last thirty years, reflected so tellingly in the depopulation of valley and village throughout the country. Other subtler influences have also changed life in Wales and the perspectives of its people over the past decades. The vast acceleration of communications and the increase in individuals' mobility have meant that Welsh people know more about the world outside the Welshman's own parish. It has led among other things to a greater consciousness and acceptance, on the part of Welsh people, of the interest of Wales as a whole. The traditional bastions of Welsh culture —the chapels, the Welsh press, the small farms, and the Welsh language—have all been in steady decline. The attitudes of many opinion leaders in the Welsh communities have hardened as the charting and the awareness of the steep decline of the Welsh language increased as official report followed report. It was gradually realized that the origins of the decline of the Welsh culture lay in the changing attitudes and the changing structure of Welsh society, and that it lay in the power of governments to influence society's structural and ideological development. In some quarters, the mood of resignation changed to one of fierce resentment at the parlous state of the native culture, and so to agreement with the nationalist cause. Welsh nationalists in the 1960s imputed to governments enormous power to control the economic and social development of their territories; and they were encouraged in their illusions, very often, by governments themselves. The growing feeling that it is in the power of governments to secure the survival of the Welsh language, for example, has meant that the language, with the aid of the Welsh Language Society, has become a political issue.

There are, however, politicians in Wales and elsewhere who would place most emphasis on factors other than those described above. They argue principally that nationalism is a state of mind, and that the flourishing of political nationalism in Scotland and Wales is but a symptom of a more inward-looking Britain, freed from imperial burdens, yet seeking a role. Now that Britain ceases to exert world power on a grand scale, Scotland and Wales will want to go their own way. This argument by its very nature is unsubstantiatable, for social scientists do not know how to quantify states of mind and relate them to each other. The connection between Britain's loss of empire and

Welsh or Scottish nationalism is always assumed but never demonstrated in this argument. Nor can it be related to other Western European countries which have witnessed a revival of political or linguistic nationalism within their borders. Spain and Belgium have lost their colonies but did not have a role in world politics to lose. South Africa and Canada have lost neither colonies nor world influence, and yet have experienced revivals of nationalism. Separatist and autonomist forces are, however, strongly challenging the omnipotence of the modern state all over the European and transatlantic world. The philosophy of nationalism may have originated and flourished in the eighteenth and nineteenth centuries, but its power over men's minds has been most marked in the present century. Nationalism gave rise to two world wars, and underlay the terms of the Treaty of Versailles. But the nationalist phenomenon evident in Wales, Scotland, Ireland, Brittany, Belgium, Quebec, and the Basque provinces is notable for its concern not with the extension of territory or conquest, but with the defence and protection of minority interests. Such nationalisms challenge the nationalism of larger states, and demonstrate the latter's failure to assimilate fully the nations thay have tried to incorporate. Economic recessions and the gradual accretion of powers to central governments have fanned these minority nationalisms. The rising demand for more autonomy corresponds to the increasing impact on all individuals in modern states of the decisions and activities of centralized governments. In Britain this has been illustrated by the growth of the public sector in relation to the private sector in the economy as a whole, by increased government involvement in economic management and other fields such as the social services, education, and housing. Legislation, especially of the delegated kind, has grown at an accelerating rate. The arms of the administration in Whitehall now stretch firmly to the smallest croft or hill farm in the remotest parts of Scotland and Wales. Governments have, however, generally attempted to meet the problems of all parts of their domain with uniform policies, and in Britain this attitude has been buttressed by a strain of egalitarianism which demands that everybody receives the same kind of treatment and service from public authorities wherever they are situated. The more policies of a uniform kind that governments devise in order to discharge their augmented responsibilities, the greater their unsuitability to meet the situation in every corner of the land. Local interests and localism constantly feed on the discontents thus aroused and demands rise for more powerful local institutions which would be able to represent the local interest adequately against the central government. Yet this argument equates, for example, West-country regionalism with Welsh or Scottish nationalism, and this would be gravely to understate the quality of the latter movements. The distinction between regionalism and nationalism turns on the sense of identity which Welsh and Scots, but not West-countrymen, generally share—national consciousness. Nationalism is a state of mind and a communal emotion which the English have failed conspicuously either to understand or to eradicate in their Celtic dependencies. Welsh nationalism has relied on the Welsh people's sense of identity, one which arises mainly through an awareness of their particular cultural and political tradition, but partly too out of aversion to the English and what they appear to stand for—authority, bureaucracy, and centralized control.[1] For some Welsh people the search for a Welsh identity is the product of their alienation from the cosmopolitan, monochrome, demoralized Anglo-Saxon culture and society that they associate with England. They seek a new society largely based on the old values and look to the Welsh nation with its distinctive cultural traditions to uphold these values. Alienation from England and its way of life is not confined to reactionary idealists among the Welsh. It is often said, by Welshmen as well as by interested outsiders, that the Welsh have an inferiority complex towards England and its people, a feeling that Wales has been outdistanced by England in most fields of human activity. Such feelings of inferiority are not uncommon among Welsh people of all ages and backgrounds, although largely misjudged. It is hardly fair to compare the achievements of the Welsh—whose culture has never yet been shared by more than a million and a half people— with the achievements of the English and their culture which is shared by millions of people in every continent of the world. The natural and human resources of the two countries have always been vastly different, and have largely determined the imbalance in the achievements of the two nations. Yet this feeling of inferiority relative to England is common in Wales, and one of some political significance. It is in itself evidence of Wales's separate identity. Welsh nationalism as a political force in the nineteenth century was largely a struggle for the recognition of Welsh nationhood by the British Government.[2]

---

[1] R. T. Jenkins, 'The Development of Nationalism in Wales', in *Sociological Review*, 1935.

[2] Kenneth O. Morgan, *Wales in British Politics 1868–1922* (Cardiff, 1970, 2nd edn.).

To a lesser extent this remains true of the political manifestations of Welsh national consciousness in the mid twentieth century. The nationalist parties of Scotland and Wales thrived in the political arena in the 1960s mainly because of a sense of greivance about unfair treatment of Scotland and Wales *vis-à-vis* the rest of the United Kingdom. In their appeals for more generous treatment from the London Government the nationalists in both countries showed paradoxically how willing they were to accept the benefits of union with England while berating the disadvantages of this political arrangement.[1] Yet the search for a full identity for Wales continues, since Wales still has relatively few of the institutions which many would equate with recognition of its nationhood. Not even the English can deny the Welsh their nationality, but so far the Welsh have not acquired much autonomy in governmental matters. The nationalist in modern Wales is struggling to preserve the Welsh identity above all else, and he or she does not have to be Welsh-speaking to feel this. For this identity is challenged day by day by the closer integration of culture in Wales and of the Welsh economy with their English counterparts, as well as by the decline of the Welsh language. Geographical situation is the main reason for this: Wales is too near England. It is a sense of crisis, and the sense that remedies must be applied almost immediately to have any success, which has mobilized so many Welsh-speakers, especially those of high educational attainment, behind the nationalist movement. It is the sense of crisis too which has encouraged the intransigence of, for example, the Welsh Language Society and the campaign in 1969 to secure a bilingual motor tax disc. This sense of crisis is specially prevalent among those who hold the survival of the Welsh language and culture to be their main object in engaging in political activity. There is no dispute about the rapid decline in the hold of the language upon the Welsh people: whereas 60 per cent of the population spoke the language in 1891, only 21 per cent claimed to speak it in 1971. The parallel decline in traditionally the strongest bastions of the Welsh tongue, the Welsh chapels and agricultural communities, has reinforced the pessimism of a section of Welsh opinion, and has encouraged its determination to redress the situation and to seek to do so by use of more active, and more political, means. It is hard

---

[1] Wales gains particularly from the inflow of capital from the rest of the United Kingdom, mainly in the public sector. See Gavin McCrone, *Scotland's Future* (Oxford, 1969).

to fault the logic of this development since the initiative on linguistic matters lies, if anywhere, with national and local government.

It is tempting to argue from a different perspective a corresponding theory about the modern development of Welsh nationalism. If it is accepted that an ideology such as nationalism has the power to bind a community together and to create a sense of solidarity, and that ideology serves to organize the role-personalities of individuals, especially the young, then it is possible to argue that individuals who experience the search for identity and the corresponding search for a role will find these searches fulfilled in the ideology of nationalism.[1] If this view is projected on to a different level and it is assumed that nations have personalities akin to those of individuals, then it is possible to argue that Welsh nationalism is the product of a nation's search for its identity *and its role* within the United Kingdom (or within the community of nations), and that the historical search for recognition of Wales from the British Government described earlier is a manifestation of Wales's search for role and identity. This begs at least the question why the chosen ideology of the Welsh should be nationalism as opposed to, say, socialism. It can, however, be argued that for long periods in recent Welsh history these two principal ideologies of modern society have been closely connected, and have ridden the Welsh political scene in tandem. The various social factors which have been seen to be destructive of Welsh society and its solidarity, when combined with those long-term factors manifest throughout Britain which have since 1950 reduced the social control of the Labour Party over large sections of the working classes,[2] have allowed nationalism in Wales to find its political expression again, especially after the fortuitous events surrounding the Carmarthen by-election in July 1966. Nationalism has for some time evoked a strong appeal among young intellectuals in Wales. Circumstances combined in the late 1960s to allow *Plaid Cymru* to broaden its base and its appeal very rapidly. But because the party was unable to develop any means of social control—except in some of the chapels— over its new followers, their support and their commitment was and is likely to prove fragile, particularly in the face of organized competition.

Explanations of this kind offer an extra insight into the pheno-

[1] See discussion in D. H. Apter, 'Ideology and Discontent', in D. E. Apter (ed.), *Ideology and Discontent* (New York, 1964).

[2] The decline of working-class involvement in the Labour Party is discussed in B. Hindess, *The Decline of Working Class Politics* (London, 1971).

menon of Welsh nationalism, but do not put its development into a world perspective. Welsh and Scottish nationalism developed in the 1960s along with Basque, Breton, Quebecois, Tirolese, Flemish, and Walloon nationalism, to name but a few. All the nationalisms mentioned fall into an easily identifiable class: they are nationalisms which have developed in old-established 'European' states, all but one of them having a commonly spoken language which marks out their own nationality.[1] The division of language occurs also in the state of Switzerland where there are four different languages spoken by unequal parts of the population,[2] yet no linguistic nationalism has developed strongly in that country in the years since 1945. It is tempting to suggest that the considerable decentralization of government in the Swiss democracy prevents linguistic grievances from developing very far, and allows a common sense of belonging to the Swiss confederation to grow alongside ancient cantonal particularisms.[3]

There exists even in the British Isles sufficient evidence to suggest that there is no necessary connection between the rise of minority nationalisms and the inferior status of minority languages. In Ireland a linguistic movement centred on the *Gaeltacht* (together with the opposing Language Freedom Movement) developed long after independence was achieved. Indeed, it was Bernard Shaw who remarked that Ireland and England were two nations divided by a common language. Meanwhile the Scottish nationalist revival grew up in the 1960s quite independently of *An Comunn Gaidhealach*, and the bulk of its support came from the lowlands rather than the Gaelic Highlands.[4] Above all, the nationalist electoral following in the Rhondda and Rhymney valleys, for example, could not be accounted for in terms of linguistic demands since Glamorgan is very largely English-speaking.

The problems concerning the status and survival of minority languages may not have been sufficient in themselves to arouse a

---

[1] The exception is Scotland where the distinct Gaelic language is spoken by less than 1 per cent of the population.

[2] The census of 1960 revealed that 69 per cent of the Swiss population was primarily German-speaking, 19 per cent French-speaking, 10 per cent Italian-speaking, and 1 per cent Romansch-speaking.

[3] See Kenneth D. McRae, *Switzerland: Example of Cultural Coexistence* (Toronto, 1964).

[4] See Iain S. McLean, 'Scottish Nationalists', in *New Society*, 9 Jan. 1969; idem, 'The Rise and Fall of the Scottish National Party', in *Political Studies*, Sept. 1970; and idem, 'Scottish Nationalism: Its growth and development, with particular reference to the period since 1961' (Unpublished B.Phil. thesis, University of Oxford, 1969).

minority nationalism, but were raised alongside others where such minorities found their future role in the economies of their countries in some doubt. It is very difficult to disentangle the economic grievances of the small farmers from the linguistic grievances of Wales and Brittany since the economic decline of the farming communities in these areas inevitably has consequences for the language and culture which thrive there. Thus the demands of the linguistic community and those of the farming community become interlinked. This same pattern of interlocking cultural, linguistic, and economic demands can be seen in modern nationalist movements in the Basque country, in Belgium, and in the province of Quebec. Yet it is the economic insecurity of many of these minority areas which is the common factor in all the minority nationalisms reviewed here. Very often forces larger than those of temporary recessions in trade are at work. The very economic basis and structure of such areas seems condemned to permanent obsolescence; the geographical position of these areas may be disadvantageous for trade and industry, and the prospects of attracting new industrial development of a lasting kind appear to be slim. Cases of this economic insecurity leading to local support for nationalist parties include the rise of Flemish nationalism in the thirties, and the appeal of *Plaid Cymru* to the mining valleys of Wales in the 1960s. Declining industry, especially extractive industry such as mining, quarrying, and agriculture, has proved fertile ground for the rise of nationalist movements since 1945. The local population's sense of such decline may even be more apparent than real, as in Flanders in the 1960s. Nevertheless where the local communities begin to feel that the central government has failed over a long period to restore economic prosperity to a minority area, then nationalist feelings seem particularly prone to multiply.[1] The national minority asserts its own nationalism and thereby reveals how far it has failed to be assimilated into the larger state.[2] It is as if the legitimacy of the larger state in which the minority is included, and the authority of its government, become immediately open to challenges of a separatist or autonomist character when the economic demands of their minorities are unsatisfied; nationalism provides the cloak for such demands. However, it would be unwise to conclude the argument at this point, for it assumes that minority nationalisms only

---

[1] The Flemish now form a majority of Belgium's population but still feel they are discriminated against.

[2] See K. W. Deutsch, *Nationalism and Social Communication* (M.I.T. Press, 1966).

pose a serious threat to the state when they are a response to economic grievances, and that somehow nationalist feelings exist inherently in minority populations and await only a catalyst such as failures by central government for them to be raised. The importance of economic distress in underlying nationalist movements since 1945 arises only because economic issues appear to be the most salient issues to citizens and voters in the Western world. This does not exclude the possibility of other issues, such as language, acquiring a greater saliency. In any case, as far as individuals are concerned this is already the position. The members of the Welsh Language Society, for example, usually acquire their interest in the rural economy of Wales by virtue of their interest in the Welsh language, whereas for many other Welsh nationalists the reverse is true. The comparison between the Scottish and the Welsh Nationalist movements this century shows how important a source of strength to political nationalism a linguistic base can be. For while the fortunes and strength of the nationalist movements in Scotland have tended to fluctuate violently, according to the changes of economic and political circumstance, the support for *Plaid Cymru* has been much more steady and uniform. This difference is largely attributable to the constant appeal that *Plaid Cymru* has retained among cultural nationalists, because the position of the Welsh language and culture has been increasingly precarious throughout the last fifty years.

Neither the presence of minority languages nor the economic decline of distinctive regions within a state automatically instils a sense of nationalism in the affected populations. The equation between redress of grievances and a nationalist philosophy has yet to be made before a nationalist movement can develop. This requires some active body of individuals to state the theory in its local or ethnic context. Since the eighteenth century it has fallen to a section of the intelligentsia to provide this catalyst, and the history of nineteenth-century 'national revolutions' in Europe offers many examples.[1] In Wales it was the University which spawned the political Nationalist movement after the First World War, under the aegis of Saunders Lewis. For a long time *Plaid Genedlaethol Cymru* made little headway in Welsh politics beyond a small band of committed cultural-nationalist intellectuals. It was then fairly described as the resort of poets, teachers, and preachers, but its present position reflects a much broader base.

[1] The clearest examples are Fichte and Mazzini.

Nationalist movements have often received considerable political help from Christian churches. Church leaders have frequently become powerful nationalist spokesmen, and the very survival of the churches has sometimes been linked with the good fortunes of the nationalist movement in the political sphere, particularly where a strong linguistic appeal is made. Clear examples since 1945 are afforded by the dominant role of Catholic priests in the Basque provinces of Spain, in Brittany, and in Flanders, the support of the Dutch Reformed Churches in South Africa for Afrikaner nationalism, especially the alliance of the *Nederduits Hervormde Kerk* with 'verkrampte' politics,[1] and by the support of some church leaders in Wales, notably the Independents, for Welsh nationalism. In most cases it does not appear that support for the nationalist and linguistic-nationalist movements among priests and ministers of religion is entirely disinterested. While many have an intellectual commitment to nationalism and a strong interest in the cultural development of society, many too are aware of the general decline of the hegemony of organized Christian sects and see in nationalism a way of preserving or restoring their social control over the populace, especially the young, and thus arresting the decline of church influence. Nationalism does not usually divide countries on class lines as economic issues do, although the example of Northern Ireland suggests that nationalist, economic, and religious cleavages can overlap. Nationalist movements emphasize the unity of the population and therefore attract church support where this would not be controversial. Where church services are normally held in a vernacular and threatened language, church support for linguistic nationalism is perhaps inevitable. The strong support amongst clergy, priests, and ministers for *Plaid Cymru* and Welsh nationalism has already been established,[2] but because Wales is linguistically divided the nationalism of the churches has also antagonized sections of the Christian community.

Thus in Wales economic insecurity and change has become the ally of a linguistic nationalism which is the product of cultural, religious, and economic decline. Increasing public support for state intervention when combined with continued governmental failures in economic policy offered *Plaid Cymru* the opportunity, once Labour

---

[1] It is no coincidence that the brother of the Prime Minister of South Africa, Dr. J. D. Vorster, is Moderator of the *Nederduits Gereformeerde Kerk* which has been described as 'the Nationalist Party at prayer'. See *The Times*, 17 Nov. 1970 and 30 Mar. 1971.

[2] See Chs. 3 and 5.

was in power, to bridge the divisions in Wales and appeal to a common radical discontent. The party was able to do this with considerable electoral success, although its internal balance was not radically altered; the government in London intensified its efforts to bring new industry to Wales, made several concessions to the Welsh language, and set up the Crowther Commission to consider the issue of devolution. The defeat of the Labour Government in 1970 deprived *Plaid Cymru* of important tactical advantages in the political arena, but the economic and cultural crises which had produced its success continued and have proved more significant in the long term for the party's political development.

The Future Outlook

The results of the general election of 1970 ended the suspense that surrounded the degree of progress made by *Plaid Cymru* among the Welsh electorate over the previous four years. Despite the bonus of the reduction of the voting age to eighteen, *Plaid Cymru* gathered only 11·5 per cent of the votes cast in Wales, in a reduced poll. The reduction in the votes cast for Nationalist candidates in 1970 in the three constituencies in which by-elections had been held in the 1966–70 period showed that much of its new electoral support had been transient.[1] Yet the nationalist movement emerged from this general election in a stronger position than it had gained in any previous general election. It had shown that it was able to mount a political fight in every constituency in Wales, and that it was the main electoral challenge to the incumbent party in eight of the thirty-six Welsh constituencies.[2] But the promise of rapid electoral progress had been undermined and, with the return of a Conservative Government at Westminster, *Plaid Cymru* was no longer able to pillory the Labour Party as effectively as when Labour was in power. The Labour Party now became better placed to outflank *Plaid Cymru* in its articulation of Welsh grievances, now that it, too, was in opposition. Indeed, it

[1] The combined results in the three constituencies were as follows:

	1966	1966–8 by-elections	1970
Labour	67,611	42,264	62,470
Plaid Cymru	13,537	40,520	29,845
Liberal	11,988*	9,907*	10,707*
Conservative	12,475	7,696	10,502
Communist	1,853*	1,728*	1,201*

* Some seats were not contested by these parties on this occasion.

[2] See Chs. 7 and 8.

had begun to use its tactical advantage during the 1970 election campaign by claiming to be the only party which had a chance of being returned to power and which would be likely to implement the findings of the Crowther Commission on the Constitution.

The Nationalist advance in the 1970 election was modest in real terms, and poor in relation to their expressed hopes in 1967 and 1968. Above all the *Blaid* was left without a representative in the House of Commons. The Nationalist future in Wales may not conform to the pattern of the period 1966–70. The breadth of its appeal at that time arose very largely because Labour was in power and because the management of the Welsh economy was apparently unsuccessful, though well-intentioned. The *Blaid* concentrated its fire on economic issues, and popular disillusionment paid electoral dividends. In the 1970 Parliament, all such electoral bonuses were likely to accrue to the Labour Party despite the efforts of the *Blaid* to persuade Welsh electors that economic policy failures are the product of inherently faulty constitutional structures. The *Blaid* is unlikely to lose its advantage over Labour when it comes to a policy for the Welsh language, for the Labour Party is too broad a coalition in Wales to remain undivided on linguistic questions, and is thus likely to speak with more than one voice in this area of policy. Yet the very fact that *Plaid Cymru* has championed the cause of the Welsh language and demands the revolutionary programme of full bilingualism for all in Wales by the year 2000 has made the language question difficult for sympathetic elements in the other political parties to pursue. For many years the language issue remained outside party politics and Welsh cultural problems were dealt with, if at all, by the Welsh M.P.s as a body. The Welsh Parliamentary Party achieved little for the language and itself became enfeebled under the numerical dominance of the Labour M.P.s within it. In the 1960s political support for a positive approach to the language was invariably confused with political support for Welsh nationalism. This dampened the initiative of those non-nationalists in politics who were friendly towards the Welsh language, particularly those inside the Labour Party. Concessions to the language took on the appearance of concessions to the Nationalist threat in general and this accelerated the rush of Welsh-speakers into *Plaid Cymru*. The two issues of the language and Wales's future constitutional status were confused, and this inhibited discussions and actions on either question. Welsh-speakers seemed to look only to *Plaid Cymru* for any support for the

Welsh culture, thus contributing to the sense of alienation they felt towards the British political system. Labour politicians were particularly anxious not to lose face on questions affecting the language and devolution by seeming to make concessions while under electoral pressure. Even so, the language issue remains a key issue in Welsh party politics. The Welsh Language Society is determined that this should be so, and it has not failed so far in its objective. The policies of national and local government towards the Welsh language are bound to need reassessment in the light of the parish statistics on the state of the language which are revealed in the 1971 Census. In addition, the Kilbrandon Commission has made recommendations in favour of devolution which will have a bearing on the place of Welsh in society and government. The language issue and its ramifications in the fields of education, broadcasting, and public administration promises to be an ever-deepening political quagmire in Wales.

The question of devolution remains an issue which the political parties in Wales cannot avoid in the short run; the work of the Kilbrandon Commission ensures as much.[1] The Commission was set up in 1968–9 when the fears about the Nationalist advances in Scotland and Wales were most acute. The Conservative Party preferred not to submit evidence to it in order, ostensibly, to leave its hands free when in office. The Welsh Council of Labour put in a plea for an elected council with limited powers over Welsh affairs. Labour leaders in Wales maintained that their party was the only one likely to implement any recommendations of the Commission. The results of the 1970 election did little to quieten the existing demand for devolution in Welsh political and commercial circles, and it is unlikely that the major political parties will be able to ignore the Kilbrandon report for long. The outcome of the 1970 election did give rise to renewed talk of the need for devolutionists in the Labour, Liberal, and Nationalist parties to co-operate.[2] Although such talk has in the past been a sign of weakness rather than a mark of strength for the devolutionist cause, with all three devolutionist parties out of office there was a slight chance of some fruitful outcome. Yet similar

---

[1] The Crowther Commission was set up to consider whether any changes were desirable 'in present constitutional and economic relationships' between 'the various parts of the United Kingdom' (*The Times*, 12 Feb. 1969). On the death of Lord Crowther the chairmanship of the Commission passed to Lord Kilbrandon.

[2] Reports of speeches of Emlyn Hooson and Gwynfor Evans, *Western Mail*, 3 Aug. 1970, and of Gwynfor Evans's address to *Plaid Cymru*'s annual conference, *Guardian* and *Western Mail*, 24 Oct. 1970.

bids to secure a common radical front between Liberals and the
Blaid between 1966 and 1969 came to nothing, and any goodwill
between the parties disappeared behind inter-party competitiveness generated by the imminent general election. The immediate
political threat to Labour posed by *Plaid Cymru* receded after
the 1970 election, since Labour in opposition was once again
able to voice the economic grievances of South Wales. There
is some evidence from opinion polls to suggest that support for
devolution in Scotland and Wales varied according to the economic
discontent of those areas. *Plaid Cymru* certainly acquired a more
working-class political base in industrial parts of Wales under the
Labour Government. *Plaid Cymru* has yet to develop roots in the
trade union movement or local politics, so that its position in industrial Wales is highly vulnerable to Labour initiatives.

The future prospect for Wales and for Welsh nationalism could be
bleak if the cultural and economic orientations of the Welsh people
continue to diverge. It could generate conflict which does not permit
compromise. If the Labour Party does not accommodate the views of
a growing section of the Welsh-speaking community concerning the
future of the language as well as the views of a large section of
informed Welsh opinion over devolution, there must continue to be
turmoil and bitterness in Welsh politics. Such is the Labour Party's
hegemony in Wales that only if it is persuaded of the need for further
action can anything politically significant be achieved in the near
future. It is arguable that if the Labour Party centrally were in the
future to refuse to countenance an elected council for Wales, then much
of the devolutionary wind abroad in Wales would disperse. The same
cannot be said of the language issue. If the Labour Party were to
refuse to agree to further extension of government support for the
language, then the conflict and bitterness surrounding this problem
would become more acute. There already exists in Wales a section
of Welsh nationalist opinion which is on the verge of despair over
the language and its chances of being adequately cared for within
existing parliamentary institutions in Britain. In other parts of the
world such as Quebec or in the Basque provinces, or in Palestine,
nationalists have already resorted to hijacking and kidnapping and
violence in order to draw the attention of the world and of their own
governments to their claims and demands. It is not difficult to see
such a situation developing in Wales in the next few years. There
were many among the intelligentsia in Wales whose hearts beat

sympathetically when so-called 'nationalist-inspired' explosions rocked official buildings in Wales between 1963 and 1969. There are many thousands who support the militancy of the expanding Welsh Language Society in its search for expression and for political action. The political path which the Society has trodden so far does not show it to be a restrained body of people. By any reckoning the Welsh language urgently needs more support, from the people of Wales as much as from its Government, if it is to survive in a living culture; and it is from such a premiss that linguistic nationalists begin to argue for desperate, possibly anti-democratic, action. The language is the touchstone of Welsh nationality, the feature of Wales that most clearly distinguishes that nation from England: it serves as a code in which a counter-culture expresses itself and its hostility to cosmopolitanism, materialism, and the inadequacies and evils of modern industrial society. *Plaid Cymru*, while standing apart from extreme attitudes, channels such feelings into parliamentary activity to the benefit of Welsh democracy as a whole. The party's sympathy for the language and support for bilingualism are vital in giving it coherence as a political organization, and in sustaining it through times of political adversity. Any major efforts to shift the balance of the party's concerns, as between the language and the economy of Wales, would provoke considerable dissension, but the balance of forces could also change autonomously if the new recruits in South Wales slipped away from activity. No such trend was apparent in 1968 or 1969, but it looked a possibility after the 1970 general election. This would merely accelerate the divergence of the forces of cultural separatism and economic integration which characterize Welsh society today. The extremism of some of the Welsh cultural intelligentsia is born of political frustration which will be hard to remove. Tolerance is a rare quality in Welsh politics today, and the cultural divisions of Welsh people are becoming more entrenched. The trend is towards separate development of Welsh-speakers, in the schools, in the *Urdd*, in the Welsh Language Society, or in *Merched y Wawr*—a last bid for self-preservation. There is a real possibility that Welsh will become the 'badge of an in-group'[1] and that linguistic apartheid will become part of the structure of Welsh society. The Archbishop of Wales addressed the governing body of the Church in Wales in 1968 in these terms:

[1] Glanmor Williams, 'Some reflections on the Gittins Report', in *Aspects of Primary Education: The Challenge of Gittins* (London, 1970).

There is a real danger of a Belgian situation here, or even a kind of apartheid based not on race but on language . . . It is intolerable that those who do not speak Welsh should be regarded as second-class citizens, or less genuine lovers of their country than their bilingual compatriots. But it is equally intolerable that in their own country or Church those who speak or think in Welsh should be regarded as eccentric or perverse or expected in matters governmental or official to be provided only with forms in a language in which they are not at home.[1]

Yet it would be unreasonable to make very pessimistic conclusions about the future of Welsh politics. There are imminent dangers, but it still lies within the power of Government to avert them. The linguistic cleavage is potentially explosive, yet the language has made much political progress. The language has become a political issue for the first time, and the precedent of comprehensive legislation was inaugurated in 1967 with the Welsh Language Act. Yet the treatment of this issue within the British political system, even since 1964, has been generally cursory. The Welsh Office issued only one circular on the subject in its first six years of life; the House of Commons discussed the Welsh Language Act briefly in 1967, and the Welsh Grand Committee discussed the language on two occasions between 1960 and 1970. The Pilkington report on broadcasting, in 1962, and the Gittins report on primary education in Wales, in 1968, were both important stimuli for discussion of the wider question of the Welsh language. The problems of the Welsh culture did not generally receive active attention on the part of the authorities even after 1964. Prior to that date they had received much less consideration in Parliament and Whitehall. The House of Commons no more expects to discuss the problems of the Welsh culture than the problems of Fiji. Yet Parliament alone has final power and responsibility for these matters. The many other political problems affecting Wales are also inadequately discussed and surveyed by Parliament in a Welsh context; yet these problems are more thoroughly discussed in a United Kingdom context at Westminster. Unique minority problems, such as the Welsh culture, suffer from the neglect of the British political system until they become impossibly troublesome: an extreme example was the Anguilla crisis in 1969. It is a standing reproach to British democracy that Wales has no institution which debates and decides in a regular way policy which materially affects the position of the Welsh lan-

---

[1] *Western Mail*, 26 Sept. 1968. Professor Glanmor Williams also warned of the possibility of language apartheid in Wales in an address to the Historical Association, *Western Mail*, 3 Apr. 1970.

guage and culture. The language issue in Wales is a political issue, and attempts to make it a non-partisan issue have generally served to conceal the dilemma in which the Welsh culture is placed. Education policy, broadcasting policy, industrial policy, and agricultural policy all have a material effect on the condition of the Welsh culture and the social life that supports it. These are all subjects for political decision, and yet there is no democratic body anywhere in the United Kingdom which systematically surveys these areas of policy, makes decisions with regard to the Welsh language, and which holds civil servants accountable for these policy spheres. Nor does there exist in Wales any conciliatory machinery or any independent body which surveys developments in language policy throughout the country, and which fosters or could foster harmony and reasonable attitudes towards the language and related issues, particularly concerning qualifications for employment. Parliament decided in the 1960s that a Race Relations Board and a Community Relations Commission were both necessary to improve relations between immigrant and indigenous communities in Britain. The Council for Wales and Monmouthshire suggested in 1963 that a body was needed in Wales to survey and report on the development of problems relating to the Welsh language. An independent Community Relations Board, with a wide commission, reporting to the Government and acting on its legislation, could play a most valuable role in Wales today; it could see that government policy on linguistic matters was carried out; it could recommend changes of policy, and investigate complaints and grievances of a communally divisive character. This kind of initiative from the British Government would do much to reduce the friction which is growing between the linguistic communities in Wales, and would help rid the political climate in Wales of its present bitterness and unreason. The report of the Kilbrandon Commission on the Constitution presents the British Government with a suitable opportunity to make such a change of policy. It could equally devise constitutional arrangements which would allow Welsh nationalism a fruitful and constructive role in the political life of Wales. Legislative autonomy cannot solve the problems of any nation but it may give those problems the attention and the understanding they deserve.

APPENDIX A

Plaid Cymru *Voting Analysed by Constituency Characteristics*

TABLE I (*a*) *Welsh-speaking and* Plaid Cymru

Constituency	% of pop. able to speak Welsh*	Average *Plaid* % vote 1964–6	*Plaid* % vote 1970
Caernarfon	87	21½	33½
Carmarthen	79	14	30
Merioneth	76	14	24
Anglesey	76	6½	22
Cardigan	75	9½	20
Llanelli	71	7	17
Gower	59	6½	14
Conway	53	7½	11
Denbigh	50	7	11
Montgomery	32	8	12
Rhondda West	28	9½	14
West Flint	28	3½	7
Neath	27	..	10
Aberdare	26	8	30
Pembroke	24	4	7
Wrexham	24	4½	5
Brecon and Radnor	22	5½	5½
Swansea East	22	7½	10
Rhondda East	21	8	24
Merthyr	20	10½	9½
Aberavon	19	4½	8½
Ogmore	19	5	12
Swansea West	13	..	6
Caerphilly	12	11	28½
East Flint	12	2	4½
Pontypridd	10	..	10
Ebbw Vale	7	..	6
Barry	7	..	7
Cardiff North	6	2	4
Bedwellty	5	..	10
Cardiff West	4	..	10
Cardiff South East	4	..	5
Abertillery	3	6½	6
Pontypool	3	..	5
Monmouth	2	..	2½
Newport	2	..	4

* Source: Census of England and Wales, 1961.

TABLE I (*b*)

% able to speak Welsh, 1961 Census	No. of seats	Plaid Cymru performance 1970		
		Deposits saved	Mean % vote	Change on previous vote*
Over 70	6	6	24·4	+11·4
25–60	8	3	13·6	+7·3
10–25	12	2	10·9	+5·0
Under 10	10	0	6·0	−0·1

Sources: M. Steed, 'An Analysis of the Results', in D. E. Butler and M. Pinto-Duschinsky, *The British General Election of 1970* (London, 1971), p. 402.

* Mean change compared with 1966 election in 20 seats or, in 7 seats uncontested in 1966, with a previous contest in the last fifteen years.

TABLE II. *Employment in Extractive Industries (Mining, Quarrying and Agriculture) and* Plaid Cymru *Voting*

	% of active pop. over 15 employed in extractive industries	Av. *Plaid* % vote 1964–6	*Plaid* % vote 1970
Carmarthen	33	14	30
Montgomery	31	8	12
Abertillery	30	6½	6
Cardigan	27	9½	20
Brecon and Radnor	25	5½	5½
Caerphilly	25	11	28½
Bedwellty	25	..	10
Aberdare	21	8	30
Ogmore	20	5	12
Merioneth	20	14	24
Rhondda West	19	9½	14
Rhondda East	17	8	24
Pembroke	17	4	7
Caernarfon	17	21½	33½
Denbigh	17	7	11
Gower	16	6½	14
Ebbw Vale	14	..	6
Pontypridd	14	..	10½
Wrexham	13	4½	5
Anglesey	12	6½	22
Llanelli	12	7	17
Merthyr	12	10½	9½
Neath	11	..	10
Monmouth	10	..	2½
Pontypool	8	..	5
Aberavon	8	4½	8½
West Flint	8	3½	7
Conway	7	7½	11
East Flint	6	2	4½
Barry	4	..	7
Swansea East	1	7½	10
Swansea West	1	..	6
Cardiff North	1	2	4
Cardiff South East	..	..	5
Cardiff West	..	..	10
Newport	..	..	4

Source: Census of England and Wales, 1966.

APPENDIX B

The Composition of some Plaid Cymru *Branches in the 1960s*

(See p. 344 for Key)

TOWN A (West Glamorgan)

Members 1962–3: 16 men and 13 women. 21 of the members were known to be Welsh-speaking. No new or Youth members.

1 Student (M)	1 Coal merchant and wife
1 Pensioner (M)	4 Steelworkers
1 Pensioner and wife	1 Foreman
2 Shopkeepers	1 Gipsy and wife
1 Shopkeeper's wife	1 Railwayman
1 Typist (F)	1 Stationmaster and wife
3 Housewives	1 Retired man
1 Schoolmaster	2 Women (occupation un-
2 Schoolmistresses	known)

Members 1967–8: 33 men and 24 women. 29 of the members were known to be Welsh-speaking, 29 Youth members, 23 new members.

* † 1 Girl, aged 18	† 1 Schoolgirl, aged 15
* ⎰1 Housewife	* † 1 Schoolgirl, aged 15
⎱1 Housewife's daughter	* 1 Schools organizer
* 1 Schoolmistress	* † 1 Student (M)
* 1 Retired man	† 1 Student (F), aged 16
* †⎰1 Minister	† 1 Student (M)
⎱1 Minister's son, aged 12	⎰1 Doctor
† 1 Boy, aged 16	† ⎱1 Doctor's son, aged 15
1 Secretary (F)	* 1 married woman
1 Single woman	* 1 Forester
† 2 Girls, aged 17	* 2 Single women
† 1 Girl, aged 16	* 1 Schoolboy, aged 14
* 1 Housewife	† 1 Schoolboy, aged 13
* ⎛1 Minister's son, aged 15	* 1 Schoolboy, aged 12
* †⎨1 Minister's daughter, aged 12	* † 1 Schoolboy, aged 12
* †⎝1 Minister's daughter	* 2 Schoolboys, aged 10
* 1 Railway official	* † 1 Schoolboy, aged 7
† 1 Railway fireman	† 1 Schoolboy, aged 12
1 Fitter	2 Schoolgirls
* 1 Tramguard	† 1 Schoolboy
* 2 Engine drivers	† 1 Man
1 Engine Driver's wife	* † 1 Man
† 1 Schoolgirl, aged 13	6 Men (occupation un-
* † 1 Schoolgirl, aged 16	known)

Town B (North Wales)

Members 1962–3: 8 men and 15 women. 22 known to be Welsh-speaking. 10 new members, no Youth members.

1 Post Office engineer (M)	* 1 Fitter
* 1 Retired man	* 1 Fitter's wife
* 1 Minister	* 4 Housewives
* 1 Minister's wife	* 2 Schoolmistresses
* 1 Smith (M)	* 1 B.B.C. worker
* 1 Dairyman	* 1 B.B.C. worker's wife
* 3 Secretaries (F)	* 1 Retired man
* 1 Dentist's receptionist (F)	* 1 Retired man's wife
* 1 Nurse (F)	

Village C (Caernarvonshire)

Members 1962–3: 2 men and 7 women. All Welsh-speakers. 1 Youth member, no new members.

* 1 Vicar	* 1 Shopgirl
* 1 Vicar's wife	* 2 Housewives
* 1 County council worker	* 1 Schoolmistress
* 1 County council worker's wife	* 1 Schoolgirl

Village D (West Wales)

Members 1962–3: 4 men and 4 women. 7 known to speak Welsh. No new or Youth members.

* 1 Minister	* 1 Smallholder (M)
* 1 Minister's wife	* 1 Shopkeeper/postmistress
* 1 Sub-postmaster	* 1 Factory owner
* 1 Sub-postmaster's wife	1 Woman(occupation unknown)

Town E (West Wales)

Members 1962–3: 20 men and 18 women. 35 known to speak Welsh. 1 new member, 1 Youth member.

1 Retired schoolmaster and wife	1 Carpenter
3 Schoolmasters and their wives	1 Ship's mechanic and wife
1 Schoolmaster	1 Café worker
2 Ministers and their wives	2 Pensioners
1 Local government official and wife	1 Pensioner and wife
1 Farmer	2 Men (occupation unknown) and wives
7 Housewives	2 Men (occupation unknown)
1 Commercial traveller	

Town F (West Glamorgan)

Members 1962–3: 21 men and 11 women. 28 known to speak Welsh. 17 new members, 10 Youth members.

2 Schoolmasters
3 Schoolmistresses
4 Students
4 Schoolboys
1 Schoolgirl
2 Ministers
1 Architect
1 Civil Servant
3 Housewives
1 Farmer

2 Steel workers
1 Court official
1 Health visitor
1 Mine undermanager
1 Shoe shopkeeper
1 Electrician
1 Retired electricity board worker
1 Man (occupation unknown) and his wife

Town G (Monmouthshire)

Members 1962–3. 14 men, no women. 2 Welsh-speakers. 4 Youth members, 7 new members.

† 3 Labourers, aged 16
* † 2 Milkmen (father and son)
† 1 Schoolboy, aged 14
1 Labourer
1 Farmer
1 Retired man

† 1 Coal board official
1 Factory worker
1 Ambulance worker and his wife
1 Miner

Town H (North Wales)

Members 1967–8: 120 members, 115 known to be Welsh-speaking. 12 new members, 22 Youth members.

1 Headmaster
5 Schoolmasters
5 Schoolmistresses
1 Schoolmaster's wife
1 Minister
1 School caretaker
9 Schoolchildren
7 Students
3 Farmers
1 Court official
1 Lecturer
1 Doctor
1 Social worker
1 Civil servant
1 Company representative
1 Store manager
1 Local government secretary (M)
1 Hospital official

4 Clerks
1 Garage owner
4 Shopkeepers
2 Local government officials
1 Inland revenue worker
1 Secretary (F)
1 B.B.C. Secretary (F)
1 Nurse
1 Bus owner
1 Librarian
1 Electricity board worker
5 G.P.O. workers
2 Builders
3 Quarrymen
1 Electrical engineer
1 Unemployed man
1 Engine driver
2 Electricians

Town H (*cont.*):

1 Bus driver
30 Housewives
8 Pensioners (M)

3 Retired men
2 Pensioners (F)
1 man (occupation unknown)

Village I (West Glamorgan)

Members 1967–8: 34 men and 12 women. 3 known Welsh-speakers.
37 Youth members, at least 34 new members.

1 Farmer
2 Housewives
1 Warehouse supervisor
5 Students
10 Schoolboys
7 Schoolgirls
2 Boys, aged 17
3 Boys, aged 16
1 Boy, aged 15

6 Boys and 1 girl (all Youth
    members)
1 Steelworker
2 Miners
1 Factory worker
1 Machine operator
1 Unemployed man
1 Unemployed girl

Town J (Monmouthshire)

Members 1967–8: 10 men and 15 women. 1 Welsh-speaker. 20 Youth
members, 20 new members.

1 Student (M), aged 17
1 Student (F), aged 17
2 Students (F), aged 16
2 Students (F), aged 15
2 Schoolboys, aged 16
1 Girl, aged 16
2 Schoolgirls, aged 17
2 Schoolgirls, aged 15
1 Boy, aged 16

1 Schoolboy, aged 13
2 Schoolgirls, aged 13
2 Schoolgirls, aged 12
2 Schoolboys, aged 12
1 Schoolboy
1 Steelworker
1 Electrician
1 Woman (occupation unknown)

Members 1968–9: 50 men and 14 women. 2 Welsh-speakers. 43 new
members, 18 Youth members.

3 Salesmen
1 Art master
1 Schoolmaster
1 College lecturer
1 Nurse
1 Factory inspector
4 Housewives
1 Student (M), aged 19
5 Young boys
2 Young girls
1 Schoolboy, aged 16
1 Schoolgirl, aged 16
3 Schoolboys, aged 15

1 Schoolgirl, aged 12
1 Young man, aged 20
3 Clerks (M)
3 Electricians
1 Electrician's mate, aged 18
1 Steel erector
1 Steel mechanic
1 Steelworker
1 Steelworker's wife
1 Machine operator, aged 18
3 Fitters
1 Welder
1 Tractor driver

Town J (Members 1968–9) (*cont.*):

1 Crane driver
1 Painter
1 N.C.B. labourer
1 Window cleaner

2 Unemployed women
10 Men (occupation unknown)
1 Man and his wife
1 Retired man and his wife

Key: † = Known new member
* = Known Welsh-speaker
M = Male
F = Female

BIBLIOGRAPHY

A. MANUSCRIPT COLLECTIONS

1. *In the National Library of Wales*

(i) *General Manuscripts*

MS. 19,634E: E. S. Millward MSS.
MS. 19,983E: Meic Stephens MSS.
MS. 20,475C: D. Lloyd George MSS.

(ii) *Deposited Collections*

E. T. John Papers
Undeb Cymru Fydd Papers

2. *Privately Owned*

Jenkin Alban Davies Papers. By courtesy of Mrs. Alban Davies.
British General Election Addresses, 1945 to date. By courtesy of the Librarian, The Gladstone Library, National Liberal Club.
Independent Television Authority, Committee for Welsh Papers. By courtesy of Lyn Evans, Wales Regional Officer, I.T.A.
Liberal Party of Wales MSS. By courtesy of Dr. Glyn Tegai Hughes.
Parliament for Wales Campaign, Minutes of Executive Committee. By courtesy of Dr. Glyn Tegai Hughes.
Undeb Cymru Fydd, Minutes of Executive Committee, 1960–4. By courtesy of the late Dr. T. I. Ellis.

B. OFFICIAL PAPERS

1. *British*

Parliamentary Debates (Authorized Edition and Official Reports), Fifth Series.
Census of England and Wales, 1891–1966.
Conference on Devolution (*a letter from Mr. Speaker to the Prime Minister*), Cmnd. 692, H.C. (1920), XVIII, XIX.
Welsh in Education and Life (1927), Board of Education Circulars 1577 and 1585.
Election Expenses, Return to an address of the Honourable The House of Commons, 1945 to date.
Reports on Government Action in Wales, 1946 to date.
Scottish Affairs 1948, Cmnd. 7308.

The Place of Welsh and English in the Schools of Wales (1953), Ministry of Education, Wales Circular 15, 24 February 1953.

Report of the Committee of Inquiry into Welsh Broadcasting 1956, Cmnd. 39 (1956), under the chairmanship of Sir Godfrey Ince.

Government Administration in Wales, Council for Wales and Monmouthshire, Third Memorandum, Cmnd. 53 (1957). Reply of the Prime Minister, Cmnd. 334 (1957).

Council for Wales and Monmouthshire, Fourth Memorandum, Cmnd. 631 (1959).

Language Survey 1961, Report of the Welsh Joint Education Committee.

Report of the Committee on Broadcasting 1960, Cmnd. 1753 (1962), under the chairmanship of Sir Harry Pilkington.

Further Memorandum on the Report of the Committee on Broadcasting, Cmnd. 1893 (1962).

The Welsh Language Today, Report of the Council for Wales and Monmouthshire, Cmnd. 2198 (1963).

Legal Status of the Welsh Language, Report of the committee under the chairmanship of Sir David Hughes-Parry, Cmnd. 2785 (1965).

S.I. 1965, No. 319, Secretary of State for Wales and Ministry of Land and Natural Resources Order (1965).

Wales: The Way Ahead, Cmnd. 3334 (1967).

Local Government in Wales, Cmnd. 3340 (1967).

Schools Council Welsh Committee, *Welsh. A Programme of Research and Development* (1967).

Schools Council Welsh Committee, *Educational Research in Wales* (1968).

Primary Education in Wales, Report of the committee under the chairmanship of Professor C. E. Gittins (1968).

Department of Education and Science, Wales circular 2/69, March 1969.

Welsh Office, Circular 82/69, 1 October 1969.

Commission on the Constitution, *Written Evidence. (1) The Welsh Office*, (1969).

Local Government Re-organisation in Glamorgan and Monmouthshire, Cmnd. 4310 (1970).

Welsh Office, *The Reform of Local Government in Wales*, Consultative Document, February 1971.

2. Other

Final Report of the Commission on the Restoration of the Irish Language (1963), Pr. 7256 (Eire).

The Restoration of the Irish Language (1965), Pr. 8061 (Eire).

Conclusions sur les Travaux de la Commission pour la Réforme des Institutions (1965) (Belgium).

Documents, Annexes aux conclusions des délégations du Parti Social Chrétien et du Parti Socialiste Belge sur les Travaux de la Commission pour la Réforme des Institutions (1965) (Belgium).

Résumé of the First Volume of the Final Report of the Royal Commission on Bilingualism and Biculturalism (1966) (Canada).

C. INTERVIEWS AND PRIVATE SOURCES OF INFORMATION

Formal Private Interviews

Roderic Bowen, Q.C., Lord Brecon, Lord Brooke of Cumnor. Elan Closs Roberts, D. H. Crook.
Cynog Davies, Gwynfor O. Davies.
Owen Dudley Edwards, John Eilian, Dafydd Elis Thomas, The late Dr. T. I. Ellis, The Revd. Dafydd Evans, Gwynfor Evans, Lyn Evans, The late Revd. Sir A. Evans-Jones ('Cynan').
Dr. Garret Fitzgerald, T.D., Professor Idris Foster.
David Gibson-Watt, M.P., James Griffiths, Ian Grist.
Geraint Heulfryn Williams, H. Emlyn Hooson, Q.C., M.P., Deian Hopkin, Gareth Howell, Major W. Howes Roberts, Cledwyn Hughes, M.P., J. Cyril Hughes, Richard Hughes, Peter Hughes Griffiths, Gwilym Humphries.
Basil James, H. Noel Jerman, Gwynoro Jones, M.P., Professor Ieuan Jones, J. Barry Jones, The late J. E. Jones, J. Emrys Jones, J. Idwal Jones, Kathleen Jones, Moses J. Jones, O. G. Jones, The Revd. Principal Dr. R. Tudur Jones, T. Alec Jones, M.P., The late Mrs. K. W. Jones-Roberts, J.P.
Robyn Lewis, Wyndham Lewis, The Revd. Trebor Lloyd Evans, Lord Lloyd of Kilgerran, T. Rowland Lucas.
Ian Macdonald, Peter Madgwick, E. Gwynn Matthews, D. J. Medlicott, Dillwyn Miles, Andrew Moore, Elystan Morgan, Hubert Morgan, Iorwerth C. Morgan, Dr. Prys Morgan, Dr. Gareth Morgan Jones, Ivor Morris, Professor H. Morris Jones.
Stuart Neale.
Lord Ogmore.
B. Parry, Dr. Cyril Parry, Meirion Pennar, M. Pratis, J. A. Price, Caradog Prichard, Mati Wyn Prichard, Gwilym Prys Davies.
E. Chris Rees, Glyn Rees, Haydn Rees, Gwilym Richards, G. S. F. Ritson, Megan Roach, Dafydd Roberts, Elwyn Roberts, Emrys P. Roberts, Margaret Roberts, Professor Richard Rose, Mrs. R. Ross.
Peter Sadler, Graham Saunders, Tom Sherratt, Alan Short, L. Syer.
Aneirin Talfan Davies, Dr. Glyn Tegai Hughes, D. Geraint Thomas, I. Emlyn Thomas, Idris Thomas, Lili Thomas, T. Thompson.
Valerie Walker, E. Walsh, Vaughan Weale, Edward Wheeler, Dafydd Wigley, Ceiriog Williams, Dafydd Williams, The late Dr. D. J. Williams, Professor Glanmor Williams, J. R. Williams, Dr. Phil Williams, Bryan Wilson, L. Wolstenholme, D. Woodward-Smith.

D. PERIODICALS, PAMPHLETS, AND REPORTS

1. *Newspapers*

(*a*) English

Daily Express
Daily Telegraph
Liverpool Daily Post
News Chronicle
Sunday Telegraph
Financial Times
Guardian
Observer
Sun
Sunday Times
The Times

(*b*) Welsh

Aberdare Leader
Baner ac Amserau Cymru

Bridgend Advertiser
Cambrian News
Carmarthen Journal
Carmarthen Times
Denbighshire Free Press
Merthyr Express
Montgomeryshire County Express
North Wales Pioneer
North Wales Weekly News
Rhondda Leader
South Wales Argus
South Wales Echo
South Wales Evening Post
The Western Telegraph
Western Mail
Y Cymro
Y Herald Cymraeg

2. *Other Periodicals*

(*a*) Welsh

Barn
Challenge (1959–60)
Cilmeri
Cofion Cymru
Cymru'r Plant
Efrydiau Athronyddol
Forward
Front
Hamdden
I'r Gad
Llais-y-lli
Llythyr Ceridwen (1960–8)
Mynd
Omnibus
Planet
Progress (1968–9)
Tafod y Ddraig
The Dragon
The Nationalist (1963)
The Welsh Anvil
The Welsh Review

Triban
University of Wales Review
Wales (1911–14, ed. by J. Hugh Edwards)
Wales (1937–9)
Wales (1958–9)
Welsh Dominion
Welsh History Review
Welsh Liberal News (1965)
Welsh Nation
Welsh Nationalist (1932–47)
Welsh Republican (1950–7)
Welsh Unity
Yr Anghor
Yr Athro
Y Ddraig Goch
Yr Rhyd
Y Traethodydd
Y Tyst
Y Wawr (1958–61)
Y Wawr (1968–70)

(*b*) English

Encounter
Liberal Magazine
New Outlook
New Society
New Statesman
Socialist Commentary
The Economist
Time and Tide

(*c*) Other

Celtic News
Courrier Hebdomadaire (Brussels)
L'Express
La Vie Bretonne (Rennes)
Scots Independent

3. Pamphlets

Bowen Rees, Ioan, *The Welsh Political Tradition* (Cardiff, 1963).
Conservative Party, *The Conservative Policy for Wales and Monmouthshire* (Cardiff, 1949).
—— *The Conservative Party and Welsh Affairs* (Cardiff, 1951).
—— *Some Answers and Questions on a Parliament for Wales* (Cardiff, 1954).
—— *Wales with the Conservatives* (Cardiff, 1964).
—— *Action—not Words for Wales* (Cardiff, 1966).
—— *Wales into the '70s* (Cardiff, 1970).
Cymdeithas yr Iaith Cymraeg, *Y Cyfamodwr* (Cardiff, 1966).
—— *The Welsh Language Society: what it's all about* (Cardiff, 1966).
—— *Pam Peintio?* (Aberaeron, 1969).
Daniel, J. E., *Wales. Make or Break* (Caernarfon, 1943).
Davies, D. J., *The Economics of Welsh Self-Government* (Caernarfon, 1931).
—— *Towards an Economic Democracy* (Cardiff, 1949).
—— and Davies, Noelle, *Wales . . . the Land of Our Children?* (Caernarfon, 1944).
Davies, Noelle, *Gruntvig of Denmark* (Caernarfon, 1944).
Edwards, Huw T., *What I want for Wales* (Carmarthen, 1949).
—— *They went to Llandrindod* (Cardiff, 1951).
Ellis, T. I., *Undeb Cymru Fydd* (Aberystwyth, 1943).
Evans, Gwynfor R., *The Labour Party and Welsh Home Rule* (Cardiff, 1954).
—— *The Political Broadcasts Ban in Wales* (Cardiff, ? 1955).
—— *Save Cwm Tryweryn for Wales* (Cardiff, 1956).
—— *We Learn from Tryweryn* (Cardiff, 1957).
—— *Self-Government for Wales and a Common Market for the Nations of Britain* (Cardiff, 1960).
—— *Wales as an Economic Entity* (Cardiff, ? 1960).
—— *Cyfle Olaf Y Gymraeg* (Swansea, 1962).
—— *Welsh Nationalist Aims* (Cardiff, 1967).
—— and Jones, J. E., *TV in Wales* (Cardiff, ? 1958).
Gruffydd, Moses, *Amaethyddiaeth Cymru* (Caernarfon, ? 1937).
Hayward, J. J., *What do You think about the Conservative Policy for Wales and Monmouthshire?* (Cardiff, 1949).

HOOSON, H. Emlyn, *Llythyr at Etholwyr Cymru* (Cardiff, 1970).

—— and JENKINS, G., *The Heartland: a Plan for Mid-Wales* (London, 1965).

HOOSON, Tom, and HOWE, Geoffrey, *Work for Wales* (London, 1959).

JONES, F. M., *Yr Eglwys a'r Blaid* (Llanelli, 1956).

JONES, J. E., *Cychwyn Plaid Cymru 1925–1955* (Cardiff, 1955).

—— *Y Pleidiau Seisnig—a'u Cynffonau—yng Nghymru* (Cardiff, ? 1958).

JONES, J. R., *Christonogaeth a Chenedlaetholdeb* (Swansea, ? 1960s).

JONES, R. E., *Bradychwyd y Ddeiseb* (Caernarfon, 1942).

Labour Party, *Labour is building a new Wales* (Cardiff, 1950).

—— *Labour's Policy for Wales* (Cardiff, 1954).

—— *Britain Belongs to You* (London, 1959).

—— *Signposts to the New Wales* (London, 1963).

—— *Evidence of the Labour Party in Wales to the Commission on the Constitution* (Cardiff, 1970).

LEWIS, J. Robyn, *Iaith a Senedd* (Bangor, 1970).

LEWIS, J. Saunders, *Egwyddorion Cenedlaetholdeb* (Caernarfon, 1926).

—— *The Banned Wireless Talk* (Caernarfon, 1931).

—— *Paham y Llosgasom yr ysgol fomio* (Caernarfon, 1937).

—— *The Party for Wales* (Caernarfon, 1942).

—— *Wales after the War* (Caernarfon, 1944).

—— *Save Wales by Political Action* (Caernarfon, 1945).

—— *Tynged yr Iaith* (London, 1962).

Liberal Party of Wales, *Manifesto. 'To the People of Wales'* (1950).

—— *New Deal for Wales* (Denbigh, 1959).

—— *Liberal Partnership in Wales* (Maesteg, 1964).

LLOYD, D. Myrddin, *Plaid Cymru a'i Neges* (Cardiff, 1949).

LORT-PHILLIPS, Patrick, *The Future of Wales* (Carmarthen, 1961).

'MAB GWALIA', *Wales—the next step* (Cardiff, 1959).

MATTHEWS, E. Gwynn, *This is Plaid Cymru* (Cardiff, 1969).

NEVIN, Edward T., *Wales in the '60s* (London, 1962).

North Wales Liberal Federation, *The Liberal Party and Wales* (? 1953).

Parliament for Wales Campaign, *Campaign for a Parliament for Wales* (Aberystwyth, 1950s).

Plaid Cymru, *Bath and West* (Caernarfon, 1936).

—— *Wales and the Coronation* (? Caernarfon, 1937).

—— *Cymru Rydd: Braslun o Bolisi'r Blaid Genedlaethol* (Caernarfon, 1937).

—— *TVA for Wales* (Caernarfon, ? 1944).

—— *Wedi'r Ddarlith* (Caernarfon, 1945).

—— *TVA points the way* (Caernarfon, ? 1946).

—— *Senedd i Cymru o fewn Pum Mlynedd* (Cardiff, 1949).

—— *Polisi Amaethyddol Plaid Cymru* (Cardiff, 1954).

—— *Why Nationalist?* (Cardiff, ? 1962).

—— *20 Questions and Answers* (Cardiff, 1970).

—— *Action for Wales* (Cardiff, 1970).

PRYS DAVIES, Gwilym, *A Central Council for Wales* (Aberystwyth, 1963).
SIMON, Glyn, *A Citizen of No Mean City* (Llandybie, 1969).
THOMAS, David, *Llafur a Senedd i Gymru* (Bangor, 1954).
THOMAS, S. O., *The Future of the Small Farmer* (Liberal Party of Wales, 1958).
Undeb Amaethwyr Cymru, *Ymunwch nawr i gwtogi eich costau* (1960s).
Undeb Cymru Fydd, *The New Wales Union 1941. . . 1948* (Aberystwyth, 1948).
——— *Undeb Cymru Fydd 1939–1960* (Aberystwyth, 1960).
Urdd Gobaith Cymru, *Yr Urdd. Its Aims, Its Ideals, Its Work* (Llanuwchllyn, 1920s).
——— *The Urdd (The Welsh League of Youth). What it is. What it does. How to help. How to join* (Aberystwyth, 1947).
——— *Urdd Gobaith Cymru. Hanner Canmlwyddiant 1922–1972* (Aberystwyth 1968).
——— *Comisiwn Bywyd a Gwaith Urdd Gobaith Cymru* (unpublished report, 1969).
WILLIAMS, D. J., *Mazzini* (Cardiff, 1954, 2nd edn.).
——— *Codi'r Faner* (Cardiff, 1968).
WILLIAMS-DOO, M., *Spotlight on Wales* (Cardiff, 1955).

4. Reports

(i) *Annual Reports of the following organizations*
British Broadcasting Corporation.
Independent Television Authority.
The Labour Party.
National Liberal Federation.
Plaid Cymru.
Undeb Cymru Fydd.
Urdd Gobaith Cymru.
Wales and Monmouthshire Provincial Area, National Union of Conservative and Unionist Associations.
Welsh (Regional) Council of Labour.

(ii) *Miscellaneous*
Baptist Handbook.
Blwyddiadur y Methodistiaid Calfinaidd.
B.B.C. Handbook.
Congregational Yearbook.
Free Church Directory.
I.T.A. Guide to Independent Television.
Plaid Cymru, Conference Programme, 1967–70.
Plaid Cymru, Cronfa Gwyl Dewi.
Undeb yr Annibynwyr Cymraeg, Rhestr o'r Tanysgrifiadau.
Unitarian and Free Christian Churches Yearbook.

E. WORKS OF REFERENCE

Annual Register.
Arolwg (1967–9).
Board of Trade Journal.
BUTLER, D. E., *The British General Election of 1951* (London, 1952).
—— *The British General Election of 1955* (London, 1955).
—— and ROSE, Richard, *The British General Election of 1959* (London, 1960).
—— and KING, A. S., *The British General Election of 1964* (London, 1965).
—— —— *The British General Election of 1966* (London, 1967).
—— and PINTO-DUSCHINSKY, Michael, *The British General Election of 1970* (London, 1971).
CRAIG, F. W. S., *British Parliamentary Election Results 1918–1949* (Glasgow, 1969).
—— *British General Election Manifestoes 1918–1966* (Chichester, 1970).
Department of Employment and Productivity Gazette.
Dictionary of Welsh Biography (1959).
Digest of Welsh Statistics.
Dod's Parliamentary Companion, 1890 to date.
JENKINS, R. T., and REES, William, *A Bibliography of the History of Wales* (1962, 2nd edn.).
Keesing's Contemporary Archives.
McCALLUM, R. S., and READMAN, A., *The British General Election of 1945* (London, 1947).
Ministry of Labour Gazette.
NICHOLAS, H. G., *The British General Election of 1950* (London, 1951).
Public General Acts and Measures.
Readership Survey of Wales (Thomson Organization, 1961).
Statesman's Year Book.
The Official Index to The Times
The Times Guide to the House of Commons, 1929 to date.
Whitaker's Almanack.

F. OTHER WORKS

ALFORD, R. R., *Party and Society* (London, 1964).
APTER, D. E. (ed.), *Ideology and Discontent* (New York, 1964).
AZKIN, B., *State and Nation* (London, 1964).
BERRINGTON, H. C., 'The General Election of 1964', *Journal of the Royal Statistical Society*, Series A, vol. 128 (1965).
BEVAN, Aneurin, 'The Claim of Wales: a statement', *Wales*, Spring, 1947.
BOWEN, E. G. (ed.), *Wales. A Physical, historical and regional geography* (London, 1957).
BRENNAN, T., COONEY, E. W., and POLLINS, H., *Social Change in South-West Wales* (London, 1954).

BUDGE, Ian, and URWIN, D. W., *Scottish Political Behaviour* (London, 1966).

BUTLER, D. E., and STOKES, Donald, *Political Change in Britain* (London, 1969).

BUTT PHILIP, Alan A. S., 'Plaid Cymru', *New Society*, 9 January 1969.

—— 'Wales After the Investiture', *Socialist Commentary*, October 1969.

—— 'Life and Times', *Planet*, No. 2 (1970).

CAERLEON, Ronan, *Complots pour une république bretonne* (Paris, 1967).

CAMERON, W. B., *Modern Social Movements* (New York, 1966).

CARR, E. H., *Nationalism and After* (London, 1945).

CARSTEN, F. M., *The Rise of Fascism* (London, 1967).

CARTER, H., and THOMAS, J. S., 'Population and Language', in BOWEN, E. G. (ed.), *Wales. A physical, historical, and regional geography* (London, 1957).

—— 'The Referendum on the Sunday Opening of Licensed Premises in Wales as a Criterion of a Culture Region', in *Regional Studies*, vol. 3 (1969).

CARTER, Ian, 'An Analysis of Support for Plaid Cymru as a Test of Class Theories of Voting Behaviour' (Unpublished M.A. thesis, University of Essex, 1968).

Celtic League, *Self-Government for Celtic Countries* (Dublin, 1965).

—— *Celtic Advance in the Atomic Age* (Haverfordwest, 1967).

—— *Maintaining a National Identity* (Dublin, 1968).

—— *The Significance of Freedom* (Dublin, 1969).

—— *The Celt in the Seventies* (Dublin, 1970).

COBBAN, Alfred, *The Nation-State and National Self-Determination* (London, 1969).

COOK, C. P., 'Wales and the General Election of 1923', *Welsh History Review*, vol. 4 (1969).

COOMBES, David, and NORTON-TAYLOR, Richard, 'Renewal in Belgian Politics: The Elections of March 1968', *Parliamentary Affairs*, Autumn 1968.

CORKERY, Daniel, *The Fortunes of the Irish Language* (Cork, 1968).

COUPLAND, Sir Reginald, *Welsh and Scottish Nationalism* (London, 1954).

COX, Kevin R., *Geography, Social Contexts and Welsh Voting Behaviour 1861–1951* (Brussels, 1967).

CRAIK, W. W., *The Central Labour College* (London, 1964).

DAHL, R. A. (ed.), *Political Oppositions in Western Democracies* (New Haven, 1966).

DANIEL, J. E., *Welsh Nationalism: What It Stands For* (London, 1937).

DAVIES, Elwyn, and REES, Alwyn D. (eds.), *Welsh Rural Communities* (Cardiff, 1960).

DAVIES, E. T., *Religion in the Industrial Revolution in South Wales* (Cardiff, 1965).

DAVIES, Gwilym, 'Cymru Gyfan a'r Blaid Genedlaethol', *Y Traethodydd*, July 1942.

DAVIES, W. Pennar, *Saunders Lewis. Ei Feddwl a'i Waith* (Denbigh, 1950).
DELRUELLE, Nichole, *Enquête sur le comportement politique* (Brussels, 1968).
DEUTSCH, K. W., *Nationalism and Social Communication* (New York, 1966).
—— *Nationalism and Its Alternatives* (New York, 1969).
DUVERGER, Maurice, *Political Parties* (London, 1959).
EDWARDS, Huw T., *Hewn From The Rock* (Cardiff, 1967).
EDWARDS, Owen Dudley, *et al.*, *Celtic Nationalism* (London, 1968).
ELLIS, P. Berresford, *Wales: A Nation Again* (London, 1968).
ELTON, G. R., *England Under The Tudors* (London, 1955).
EMMETT, Isabel, *A North Wales Village* (London, 1964).
EVANS, Beriah Gwynfe, 'Cymru Fydd: II', *Wales*, October 1913.
EVANS, Eifion, *The Welsh Revival of 1904* (Port Talbot, 1969).
EVANS, Gwynfor R., 'The Twentieth Century and Plaid Cymru' in WADE-EVANS, A. W., *et al.*, *The Historical Basis of Welsh Nationalism* (Cardiff, 1950).
—— *Rhagom i ryddid* (Bangor, 1964).
—— *Aros Mae* (Swansea, 1971).
EVANS, T. J., *Rhys Hopkin Morris* (Llandysul, 1957).
FARMER, T. J., 'A Study of Redundancy, Re-Deployment and Re-Training of Personnel Resulting from Colliery Closures in South Wales' (Unpublished report to Welsh Office, 1967).
FFOWC ELIS, Islwyn, *Wythnos yng Nghymru Fydd* (Cardiff, 1957).
Fine Gael, *Irish Language Preservation* (Dublin, 1965).
FISHLOCK, Trevor, *Wales and the Welsh* (London, 1972).
FRANKENBERG, Ronald, *Village on the Border* (London, 1957).
—— (ed.), *Communities in Britain* (London, 1966).
GEORGE, William, *Cymru Fydd: Hanes y mudiad cenedlaethol cyntaf* (Liverpool, 1945).
GIBSON, E. L., 'A Study of the Council for Wales and Monmouthshire' (Unpublished M.A. thesis, University of Wales, 1968).
GRANT, W. P., and PREECE, R. J. C., 'Welsh and Scottish Nationalism', *Parliamentary Affairs*, Summer 1968.
GRAZIA, S. de, *The Political Community* (Chicago, 1948).
GREENBERG, William, *The Flags of the Forgotten* (Brighton, 1969).
GRIFFITH, Ll. Wyn, *The Welsh* (Cardiff, 1964).
GRIFFITHS, James, *Pages from Memory* (London, 1969).
GRUFFYDD, W. J., 'Wales in Parliament', *The Welsh Anvil*, April 1949.
GURGAND, Jean-Noël, 'L'exemple breton', *L'Express*, No. 916 (2 February, 1969).
HAEGENDOREN, M. van, 'The Flemish Movement in Belgium' (Unpublished manuscript, 1968).
HANHAM, H. J., *Scottish Nationalism* (London, 1969).
HARGROVE, Ervin C., 'Nationality, Values and Change', *Comparative Politics*, vol. 2, No. 3 (April 1970).

HAYWARD, J. E. S., 'From Functional Regionalism to Functional Representation: The Battle of Brittany', *Political Studies*, vol. XVIII, No. 1 (1969).

HERREMANS, Maurice-Pierre, *The Language Problem in Belgium* (Brussels, 1967).

HERTZ, Frederick, *Nationality in History and Politics* (London, 1945).

HINDESS, Barry, *The Decline of Working Class Politics* (London, 1971).

HOOSON, Tom, 'St. David's Day Speech', *Wales*, No. 7 (1959).

HUDSON DAVIES, Ednyfed, 'Welsh Nationalism', *Political Quarterly*, July–September 1968.

HUGGETT, F. E., *Modern Belgium* (London, 1969).

HUGHES JONES, W., *Wales Drops The Pilots* (London, 1937).

—— *What is happening in Wales?* (London, 1937).

JENKINS, R. T., 'The Development of Nationalism in Wales', *Sociological Review*, 1935.

JONES, Emrys, 'The Changing Distribution of the Celtic Languages in the British Isles', *Transactions of the Honourable Society of Cymmrodorion*, 1967, Part I.

JONES, Glyn, *The Dragon has two tongues* (London, 1968).

JONES, Goronwy J., *Wales and the Quest for Peace* (Cardiff, 1970).

JONES, H. R., 'Rural Migration in Central Wales', *Transactions of the Institute of British Geographers*, No. 37 (December 1965).

JONES, J. E., *Tros Gymru* (Swansea, 1970).

JONES, J. R., *Prydeindod* (Llandybie, 1966).

JONES, R. Brinley (ed.), *The Anatomy of Wales* (Peterston-super-Ely, 1972).

JONES, Thomas, *The Native Never Returns* (Aberystwyth, 1946).

KEDOURIE, Elie, *Nationalism* (London, 1960).

KELLY, G. A., 'Biculturalism and Party Systems in Belgium and Canada', *Public Policy*, xvi (1967).

—— 'Belgium: New Nationalism in an Old World', *Comparative Politics*, vol. 1, No. 3 (April 1969).

KILMUIR, Viscount, *Political Adventure* (London, 1964).

KINNEAR, Michael, *The British Voter* (London, 1968).

LASSWELL, H. D., *World Politics and Personal Insecurity* (New York, 1965).

LE CALVEZ, A., *Un Cas de bilinguisme: Le Pays de Galles* (Lannion, 1970).

LENIN, V. I., *Questions of National Policy and Proletarian Internationalism*.

LEVY, Paul M. G., *La Querelle du recensement* (Brussels, 1960).

LEWIS, J. Robyn J., *Second-Class Citizen* (Llandysul, 1969).

LEWIS, J. Saunders, *Canlyn Arthur* (Aberystwyth, 1938).

—— *Ysgrifau Dydd Mercher* (Llandysul, 1945).

LIPSET, Seymour M., *Political Man* (London, 1960).

—— 'Political Sociology', in SMELSER, Neil J. (ed.), *Sociology: an introduction* (New York, 1967).

LIPSET, Seymour M., and ROKKAN, Stein (eds.), *Party systems and voter alignments: cross-national perspectives* (New York, 1967).

LLOYD, M. G., and THOMASON, G. F., *Welsh Society in Transition* (Cardiff, 1963).

LORWIN, Val R., 'Belgium: Religion, Class, and Language in National Politics' in DAHL, Robert A. (ed.), *Political Oppositions in Western Democracies* (New Haven, 1966).

McCORMICK, Neil (ed.), *The Scottish Debate* (London, 1970).

McCRONE, Gavin, 'Is a separate Scotland viable', *New Outlook*, No. 75 (1968).

—— *Scotland's Future* (Oxford, 1969).

MACKINTOSH, J. P., *The Devolution of Power* (London, 1968).

McLEAN, Iain S., 'Scottish Nationalists', *New Society*, 9 January 1969.

—— 'Scottish Nationalism: its growth and development with particular reference to the period since 1961' (Unpublished B.Phil. thesis, University of Oxford, 1969).

—— 'The Rise and Fall of the Scottish National Party', *Political Studies*, September 1970.

McRAE, Kenneth D., *Switzerland: Example of Cultural Coexistence* (Toronto, 1964).

MANNERS, G. (ed.), *South Wales in the Sixties* (London, 1964).

MASTERMAN, Neville, *The Forerunner* (Swansea, 1972).

MICHELS, Robert, *Political Parties* (New York, 1959 edn.).

MILL, John Stuart, *Considerations on Representative Government* (London, 1861).

MINOGUE, K. R., *Nationalism* (London, 1967).

MORGAN, Gerald, *The Dragon's Tongue* (Cardiff, 1966).

MORGAN, J. Vyrnwy, *The Philosophy of Welsh History* (London, 1914).

MORGAN, Kenneth O., *David Lloyd George, Welsh Radical as World Statesman* (Cardiff, 1963).

—— 'The People's University in Retrospect', *University of Wales Review* (1964).

—— 'Four Constituency Campaigns: Swansea West', in BUTLER, D. E., and KING, A. S., *The British General Election of 1964* (London, 1965).

—— *Freedom or Sacrilege, A history of the campaign for Welsh Disestablishment* (Penarth, 1966).

—— 'The Merthyr of Keir Hardie', in WILLIAMS, Glanmor (ed.), *Merthyr Politics* (Cardiff, 1966).

—— 'Cardiganshire Politics: The Liberal Ascendancy 1885–1923', in *Ceredigion*, vol. V, No. 4 (1967).

—— *Wales in British Politics 1868–1922* (Cardiff, 1970, 2nd edn.).

—— 'Welsh Nationalism: the Historical Background', *Journal of Contemporary History*, January 1971.

NEVIN, Edward T., *et al.*, *The Structure of the Welsh Economy* (Cardiff, 1966).

Ó CUIV, Brian, *A View of the Irish Language* (Dublin, 1969).

OUTERS, Lucien, *Le Divorce belge* (Paris, 1968).

OWEN, T. M., 'Chapel and Community in Glan-Uyn, Merioneth' in DAVIES, Elwyn, and REES, Alwyn D., *Welsh Rural Communities* (Cardiff, 1960).

PARKIN, Frank, *Middle Class Radicalism* (Manchester, 1968).

PARRY, Cyril, *The Radical Tradition in Welsh Politics: A Study of Gwynedd Politics 1900–1920* (Hull, 1970).

PELLING, Henry, *Social Geography of British Elections* (London, 1967).

PHILIPPONEAU, M., *La Gauche et les Régions* (Paris, 1967).

RANDALL, P. J. 'The development of Administrative Decentralisation in Wales from the establishment of the Welsh Department of Education in 1907 to the creation of the post of Secretary of State for Wales in October, 1964' (Unpublished M.Sc.Econ. thesis, University of Wales, 1969).

REES, Alwyn D., *Life in a Welsh Countryside* (Cardiff, 1951).

—— *The Magistrate's Dilemma vis-à-vis the Welsh Language Offender* (Llandybie, 1968).

REES, Sir J. Frederick, 'The Welsh Political Problem', *Nineteenth Century and After*, April 1949.

REES, Thomas D., *Miscellaneous Papers on subjects relating to Wales*. (London, 1867).

REES, W., *Historical Atlas of Wales* (London, 1959).

RENAN, Ernest, *Qu'est-ce qu'une nation?* (Paris, 1882).

REYNOLDS, Reginald (ed.), *British Pamphleteers*, vol. II (London, 1951).

RICHARD, Henry, *Letters on the social and political condition of Wales* (London, 1867).

ROCARD, Michel, *Décoloniser la Province* (Paris, 1966).

ROSE, Richard, 'Class and Party Divisions: Britain as a Test Case', *Sociology*, vol. 2 (1968).

—— 'Social Cohesion, Parties and Regime Strains', *Comparative Political Studies*, vol. 2, No. 1 (1969).

—— 'The United Kingdom as a Multi-National State', Occasional Paper No. 6, Survey Research Centre, University of Strathclyde (1970).

ROSSER, C., and HARRIS, C. C., *The Family and Social Change* (London, 1965).

Royal Institute of International Affairs, *Nationalism* (London, 1939).

RUNCIMAN, W., *Relative Deprivation and Social Injustice* (London, 1966).

'J.A.S.', 'The Welsh Nation and the Conservative Party', in *Souvenir of the Forty-Second Annual Conference 1908* (London, 1908), National Union of Conservative and Unionist Associations.

SIEGFRIED, André, *Tableau politique de la France de l'Ouest sous la Troisième République* (Paris, 1964, 2nd edn.).

STALIN, J. V., *Marxism and the National and Colonial Question* (London, 1942, 2nd edn.).

STEED, Michael, 'An Analysis of the Results', in BUTLER, D. E., and KING, A. S., *The British General Election of 1964* (London, 1965).

358   BIBLIOGRAPHY

SYMMONS-SYMONOLEWICZ, Konstantin, *Modern Nationalism* (New York, 1968).

THAYER, George, *The British Political Fringe* (London, 1965).

THOMAS, Brinley (ed.), *The Welsh Economy* (Cardiff, 1962).

THOMAS, Ned, *The Welsh Extremist: A Culture in Crisis* (London, 1971).

WADE-EVANS, A. W., et al., *The Historical Basis of Welsh Nationalism* (Cardiff, 1950).

'WALES MINOR', 'Unrest in Wales', *Liberal Magazine*, January 1935.

WATKINS, Alan, *The Liberal Dilemma* (London, 1966).

WILLIAMS, C. R., 'The Welsh Religious Revival 1904–5', *British Journal of Sociology*, 1952.

WILLIAMS, David, *A History of Modern Wales* (London, 1950).

WILLIAMS, D. J., *Hen Dy Ffarm* (Aberystwyth, 1953).

WILLIAMS, Glanmor, 'The Idea of Nationality in Wales', *Cambridge Journal*, December 1953.

—— (ed.), *Merthyr Politics: The Making of a Working Class Tradition* (Cardiff, 1966).

—— 'Some reflections on the Gittins Report', in *Aspects of Primary Education: The Challenge of Gittins* (London, 1970).

WILLIAMS, Philip J. S., 'Economic Aims of Welsh Nationalists', *New Outlook*, No. 76 (February 1969).

WILSON, Bryan R., *Religion in Secular Society* (London, 1966).

WOLFE, J. W. (ed.), *Government and Nationalism in Scotland* (Edinburgh, 1969).

INDEX